Theorizing Backlash

Studies in Social, Political, and Legal Philosophy
Series Editor: James P. Sterba, University of Notre Dame

This series analyzes and evaluates critically the major political, social, and legal ideals, institutions, and practices of our time. The analysis may be historical or problem-centered; the evaluation may focus on theoretical underpinnings or practical implications. Among the recent titles in the series are:

Racist Symbols and Reparations: Philosophical Reflections on Vestiges of the American Civil War
by George Schedler, Southern Illinois University

Necessary Goods: Our Responsibilities to Meet Others' Needs
edited by Gillian Brock, University of Auckland

The Business of Consumption: Environmental Ethics and the Global Economy
edited by Laura Westra, University of Windsor, and Patricia H. Werhane, University of Virginia

Child versus Childmaker: Present Duties and Future Persons in Ethics and the Law
by Melinda A. Roberts, College of New Jersey

Gewirth: Critical Essays on Action, Rationality, and Community
edited by Michael Boylan, Marymount University

The Idea of a Political Liberalism: Essays on Rawls
edited by Victoria Davion and Clark Wolf, University of Georgia

Self-Management and the Crisis of Socialism: The Rose in the Fist of the Present
by Michael W. Howard, University of Maine

Ecofeminist Philosophy: A Western Perspective on What It Is and Why It Matters
by Karen J. Warren, Macalester College

Controversies in Feminism
edited by James P. Sterba, University of Notre Dame

Faces of Environmental Racism: Confronting Issues of Global Justice, Second Edition
edited by Laura Westra, University of Windsor, and Bill E. Lawson, Michigan State University

American Heat: Ethical Problems with the United States' Response to Global Warming
by Donald A. Brown, Pennsylvania Department of Environmental Resources

Theorizing Backlash: Philosophical Reflections on the Resistance to Feminism
edited by Anita M. Superson, University of Kentucky, and Ann E. Cudd, University of Kansas

Theorizing Backlash

Philosophical Reflections on the Resistance to Feminism

Edited by
Anita M. Superson
and Ann E. Cudd

ROWMAN & LITTLEFIELD PUBLISHERS, INC.
Lanham • *Boulder* • *New York* • *Oxford*

ROWMAN & LITTLEFIELD PUBLISHERS, INC.

Published in the United States of America
by Rowman & Littlefield Publishers, Inc.
A Member of the Rowman & Littlefield Publishing Group
4720 Boston Way, Lanham, Maryland 20706
www.rowmanlittlefield.com

12 Hid's Copse Road
Cumnor Hill, Oxford OX2 9JJ, England

British Library Cataloguing in Publication Information Available

Library of Congress Cataloging-in-Publication Data Available

Theorizing backlash : philosophical reflections on the resistance to feminism / edited by Anita M. Superson and Ann E. Cudd.
    p. cm. — (Studies in social, political, and legal philosophy)
Includes bibliographical references and index.
    ISBN 0-7425-1373-4 (alk. paper) — ISBN 0-7425-1374-2 (pbk. : alk. paper)
    1. Feminism. 2. Feminist theory. 3. Sexism. I. Superson, Anita M.
II. Cudd, Ann E., 1959– III. Series.
    HQ1154 .T473 2002
    305.42—dc21   2002001815

Printed in the United States of America

♾™ The paper used in this publication meets the minimum requirements of American National Standard for Information Sciences—Permanence of Paper for Printed Library Materials, ANSI/NISO Z39.48-1992.

For Heather and Beth,
and All Women and Men
Who Fight against the Oppression of Women

Contents

Preface

Several years ago at an American Philosophical Association meeting, the editors of this volume were recounting the horrid details of discrimination we each had experienced during our time in the profession since graduate school, events that greatly impacted our professional and personal lives. We recalled that other women, particularly those who were feminists, had similar "war" stories. We noticed that much of the sexism we experienced took place in the context of a perception that women were making progress, or even "taking over." We recognized that the sexism was really part of a backlash against women's progress. This anthology is the product of that discussion.

First and foremost, our goal has been to bring these stories forward not in the form of a "gripe session," but in the form of philosophical reflection on and analysis of various aspects of backlash, motivated by the authors' personal experiences. Making people aware that there is a problem is, of course, the first step to finding a resolution. Sometimes this is difficult because the issues are subtle, due in part to their systematicity. Other times, though, the issues are quite blatant and motivated by persons who are openly hostile to feminism. Often, instances of sexism occur as isolated incidents and when not viewed in a larger context are readily ignored or dismissed. We believe that the essays in this volume, especially when considered jointly, establish conclusively that there is a backlash against feminism. They reveal the variety of often virulent ways in which the backlash has taken hold. With the exception of one essay that addresses the backlash against feminist legal theory, each speaks about the backlash in philosophy, but much of what the essays have to say applies to all of academia, if not the professions more generally.

Although the response to our solicitation for contributions was overwhelmingly positive—people wanted very much to tell their stories—it wasn't so in every case. Some potential contributors were delighted that we were undertaking this project, but did not contribute because they feared repercussion from their departments or from the profession at large. We are highly sensitive to these worries. For this reason, we did not solicit contributions from graduate students. Still, most of our contributors have not yet reached the top of their profession: four are assistant professors, four are associate professors, and only three are full professors. Those not yet at the top are especially vulnerable to retaliation. But the worry about retaliation itself speaks volumes, and demonstrates precisely why there is a need for our stories to be told.

We expect the reactions to this book to be mixed: horror, nonchalance, denial, even anger. Ironically, some of these will indicate a backlash response to our book. But we feel that the privileged position we are in as professionals and as persons philosophically engaging these issues provides us the opportunity to speak out so that changes are made for the better. As professionals, we have autonomy and power, and a chance for our voices to be heard. As philosophical thinkers, we rely on reason, logic, and open-mindedness to lead us to our conclusions. We hope that the reaction to this book is positive. We put it forward with trepidation, but with courage, pride, and confidence, knowing that we are doing the right thing.

Each of us has different people we would like to thank.

Anita Superson: I owe thanks to many people who supported me during the tumultuous time surrounding my tenure case. I thank my parents, Irene and Ted, for teaching me to stand up when wronged. I thank my brother Michael, and sisters Luann and Kristin, whose refreshingly blunt, down-to-earth mannerisms brought humor when it was needed most. I honor the memory of my brother, Tom, who passed away after complications due to a second bone marrow transplant for Hodgkins disease only six months prior to my tenure denial. My fight for justice I am sure was nowhere near as courageous a battle as the one he fought for his life. I also owe many thanks to many of my friends for listening and supporting me, especially Keli and Carolyn, without whose encouragement and genuine concern I never would have made it. Deb DeBruin and Alisa Carse, who contributed to this volume, helped us brainstorm on the title. Kim Dayton put me in touch with a marvelous law firm whose generosity and willingness to take on the kind of case that is most difficult to win leaves me a debt difficult to repay. I hope that this book is the start of some form of compensation. I thank Mike Greenberger, Nancy Stone, and especially Heather Anderson and Beth Robischon for their undaunted efforts, much hard work, patience, unflagging support, and just for "getting it." Finally, for her support, kindness, and deep friendship, I owe a huge debt of gratitude to my co-editor, Ann Cudd, who saw past the rhetoric to what was really going on. I am not sure what I would be doing without her help.

Ann Cudd: I wish to thank my feminist colleagues and mentors in this profession who have befriended and supported me. I wish I could thank two mentors who died far too soon: Jean Hampton and Tamara Horowitz, two sparkling feminist minds, whose lights have pointed the way for me, helping me to succeed in the face of feminist backlash. I will always be grateful to them, and will miss their wise counsel. Marcia Homiak, my former Chair, co-conspirator, and dear friend has guided me through backlash events and supported and joined me in resistance efforts. My former Kansas colleagues Cynthia Willett and Julie Maybee made our time as departmental colleagues seem like genuine feminist progress. Thank you for your fresh ideas and solidarity in projects personal and professional. I also thank Kim Dayton, not only for the suggestion of that great law firm, but for her constant friendship and feminist solidarity. I thank my family, especially my partner, Neal Becker, and our wonderful sons, Thomas and Alex, my mother, Bernice Daniels, and my father, Kermit Cudd. They are my inspiration and my foundation. Most importantly for the present project, I thank Anita Superson, who devoted a sabbatical year to making this project happen. I am grateful to her for taking on more than her share of the work, and for the friendship that has been nurtured by working together.

Introduction

Some people believe that women have "made it" in most circles, that, particularly in academia, we are being hired in record numbers, that we have established ourselves with feminist organizations, professional conferences, courses, books, and journals, and even that we "are taking over the professions." Yet many feminists believe that there still is much work yet to be done, and that in fact, because of the many ways feminism is resisted, we are in the throes of what Susan Faludi has famously described as a backlash. A backlash to a progressive movement such as feminism is characteristically marked by the kind of reaction the movement is met with, one quite different from the reaction to other new or resurrected philosophical orientations such as existentialism, theism, or idealism. The response to feminism is not argument but disdain, not rational disagreement but irrational resentment, not dispassionate debate but sexist attack.

Feminists, both men and women, suffer a wide variety of personal and professional disappointments consequent on this reaction. Some have been denied tenure or forced to leave jobs that they found too hostile to withstand. Some have been harassed by students and faculty. Some have had to struggle to maintain the confidence and self-esteem that is required by a profession in which one must put forward in person and in writing deeply held views. Some have felt pressured by students or colleagues to stifle feminist views or to leave fields in which feminist positions elicit such vicious hostility. Some have felt it necessary to curtail family life or "feminine" attributes in order to pass as one of the boys. Some have curtailed progressive activism to save their careers. Our anthology tells the tales of those who have experienced the backlash against feminism and suffered such personal and professional setbacks. Yet, as the title suggests, the essays in this collection do not constitute a "gripe session," but offer philosophical reflections on the resistance to feminism. One goal of these essays is to bring recognition to the problems inherent in doing feminism, which is a necessary step for ending the backlash. But these essays share the larger goal of eliciting changes in academia that would ensure the same rights, freedoms, privileges, and opportunities for women that men enjoy. It is our hope that our voices will be heard and that the academic community will respond positively so that progressivism is allowed to flourish.

The essays in the middle of the book focus on different aspects of the backlash, including the backlash against feminist theory, the backlash from professional colleagues and institutions, and the backlash from students. All but one of the papers concern the backlash against feminism in philosophy; Martha Chamallas's paper discusses the backlash against feminist thought in the legal profession, which closely parallels that in philosophy. The essays in the last section take up the issue of progress. In the first essay, "Analyzing Backlash to Progressive Social Movements," Ann Cudd analyzes the notion of backlash, which sets the background for the text and fills in a void in contemporary literature on backlash, which to this point has focused mainly on citing examples of backlash. Cudd understands a backlash in the context of social progress and regress. A society progresses when it becomes more good or just, which is measured by its coming to view as equal in dignity and worthy of respect those it once viewed as lesser beings due to some accidental feature(s) they happen to have such as race or gender. One kind of social progress, then, is the reduction of the oppression of social groups, where the individuals in these groups suffer fewer harms, on average, than they previously did.

A society regresses when it denies respect due persons to whole classes of people. When oppression is greater than in a previous period, backlash is evident. Agreeing with Faludi, Cudd notes that backlash is characterized by attitudes of hostility and fear, particularly on the part of members of privileged groups who will be harmed by others' progress, but it can also be the result of unconscious, unorganized, perhaps institutionalized resistance to change.

Cudd distinguishes a full-fledged backlash from a "backlash event," or, an instance of "lashing back," which does not set back a group enough to constitute oppression, but does roll back some progressive gains the group has made. Yet she cautions that backlash events are typically surrounded by other events that lead to characteristic attitudes toward the group that is set back. Finally, she offers a preliminary argument that there is a full-fledged backlash against feminism in philosophy, as evidenced both by hostile comments made about feminism by powerful professionals, and by a resistance from professionals and students in recognizing feminist work and feminists themselves as worthy of respect accorded "mainstream" philosophy and its proponents. Cudd's analysis of backlash and preliminary remarks about the backlash against feminism are supported by the evidence and arguments offered in all of the remaining papers, especially when considered as a whole. The next section on the backlash against feminist theory contains three powerful essays, the theme of which is that feminist scholarship has been unfairly and viciously attacked. This attack constitutes a backlash because it chips away at women's progress by stifling, rendering outlandish, or ignoring feminist ideas with the result that they are not accorded due respect and that students and professionals shy away from them for the sake of their careers. The first essay in the section, Keith Burgess-Jackson's "The Backlash against Feminist Philosophy," exposes philosophical literature that he believes criticizes feminism in a way that is ideologically motivated and bent on destruction, rather than fair, responsible, and charitable. He identifies three forms of backlash against feminist scholarship that even some self-identified feminists have engaged in: lack of charity, applying a double standard, and bullying. The principle of charity enjoins one to be fair to those one criticizes, which means in part representing the arguments of the latter in the best light. Burgess-Jackson cites an article on feminist epistemology which he argues violates the principle of charity because it fails to engage, let alone mention, a large body of work in evolutionary psychology that supports the view that sex differences can be attributed to biology rather than socialization. Burgess-Jackson's concern is not particularly about the truth of evolutionary psychology, though he is sympathetic to it, but about what he perceives to be the author's uncharitable lack of mention of it, which ultimately shapes the conclusions we reach about how to address perceived sex differences in, for instance, the workplace.

A second form of backlash against feminist scholarship takes place when the perpetrator applies a more strenuous standard to feminist work than to nonfeminist work. Burgess-Jackson cites an article in which the author attacks the works of primarily five feminists on grounds of negligence, carelessness, and sloppiness, and attributes these vices particularly to their commitment to feminism. But this is unfair, Burgess-Jackson argues, because the author does not study nonfeminist literature, does not compare feminist to nonfeminist literature on these points, erroneously concludes that all feminist literature is bad, and wrongly attributes such mistakes to the writer's political commitment.

A third form of backlash against feminist scholarship is bullying, or "picking on," feminism. Burgess-Jackson identifies a philosopher whose published work consists largely of criticisms of feminism without either constructively attempting to overcome these criticisms or attacking any other branch of philosophy. In the end, Burgess-Jackson urges feminists not to engage with the "backlashers" because it will only add fuel to their fire.

In "Feminist Epistemology as Whipping-Girl," Mark Owen Webb continues Burgess-Jackson's theme of unfair attacks on feminist scholarship, particularly in feminist epistemology and philosophy of science. Webb suggests that the backlash in these areas is evidenced in feminist claims and challenges to "mainstream" philosophy being met with scorn, dismissal, or alarm, and charges that they are strange, absurd, horrific, a "flight from science and reason," not "real" philosophy, harmful to women's progress, and even that they politicize epistemology. Webb identifies three areas of epistemology that have suffered from such attacks, including feminist empiricism, standpoint theory, and feminist postmodernism, the latter of which has been "the most natural whipping-girl for analytic epistemology" due to its rejection of universal absolutes and its endorsement of the gendered nature of objectivity. All the while, Webb points out, similar radical claims made by nonfeminist philosophers have been taken seriously even if they are rebutted, making the attacks on feminism particularly unfair. Feminist claims and challenges, he argues, ought to be taken seriously at least for the reason that they may provide another path to knowledge.

In "The Backlash against Feminist Legal Theory," the only essay in this volume that speaks specifically about a discipline outside of philosophy, Martha Chamallas argues that there is an organized and growing backlash against feminist legal theory in response to its emergence as a serious academic topic in the 1980s. She discusses three kinds of backlash critiques of feminist views. First is a critique leveled by evolutionary biologists who argue that men and women have different biological propensities or traits that withstand the test of time, and that are responsible for gendered patterns and practices in our society such as the division of labor and the glass ceiling. Their views about marriage, sex, and dating have implications for legal theory. For instance, some evolutionary biologists construe rape as an issue of men's alleged strong, natural sexual desire instead of an issue of power, and believe that the burden falls on women to control men's promiscuity and to screen out potential rapists. They argue that prosecuting date rape might discourage men from dating, thereby reducing heterosexual women's chances of finding the right man. While many feminists deny these links with biology—Chamallas, in contrast with Burgess-Jackson's sympathies, regards them with suspicion—and claim that patterns and practices such as rape are forms of sex discrimination that ought to be legally sanctioned, evolutionary biologists deny that these are forms of sex discrimination and favor repealing many of the hard-won civil rights laws that prohibit sex discrimination.

A second backlash critique of feminist legal theory is typically leveled by younger women writing for a popular audience who ironically attribute women's inequality to the feminist movement. They claim that feminist laws and institutional policies surrounding date rape, pornography, and sexual harassment inaccurately portray women as passive and powerless victims instead of persons who enjoy the freedom and excitement of sexual experimentation and who should take responsibility for their actions. They, too, argue in favor of eliminating many forms of legal regulations of sexual conduct, but on the ground that these are protective and paternalistic. But they fail to notice the social nature of sexual conduct that feminists have drawn attention to, opting instead for individualist responses to sexism.

A third critique comes from social conservatives who believe that women have already achieved equality and that what feminists perceive to be discrimination really is the result of women's choices. Social conservatives believe that feminist rhetoric is in reality a plea for special rights or consideration for women. They advocate inconsistent views on the role of gender in public policy, and even argue that attention to gender is discriminatory. Attacking feminist ideas in the ways Chamallas, Burgess-Jackson, and Webb suggest curtails progress because it means that those fighting for the cause of women's liberation must direct their energy to responding to resistance rather than making headway against oppression.

The next section, personal and political tales about the backlash from the ivory tower, contains three courageous essays whose theme is that both individuals within academia and the structure of academia contribute to the backlash against women's progress by discouraging women's entry into academia, imposing barriers to their advancement once they are in, or dismissing them altogether from it.

In the first essay of the section, "Welcome to the Boys' Club: Male Socialization and the Backlash against Feminism in Tenure Decisions," Anita Superson argues that the number of women in the philosophy profession, especially at the rank of full professor, has not increased much in the last quarter of a century. This is due in part to discriminatory tenure denial caused by strident antifeminists who oppose a particular candidate, those who harbor sexist beliefs about women that inform the standards they employ to judge the merits of a female candidate's case, and/or those who are influenced by these groups but who are unaware that discrimination has become systematically embedded in the tenure process itself. Those who feel threatened by women's presence have reacted to women's perceived increase in power by using their power to deny tenure to women candidates, especially feminists.

Superson discusses the role that three main interrelated features of male socialization—patriarchal masculinity in its emphasis on aggression, separatism, and feelings of solidarity, or, "male bonding"—play in tenure decisions about women. These features are exhibited in an exacerbated form in the socialization of men in some all-male groups, which exemplify a more extreme version of male socialization imposed upon males in society at large. "Masculine" traits, which are viewed as different from and superior to "feminine" traits, confer power to men as individuals as well as to men as a group that is maintained when males stick together and exclude those who are believed to be different from them. Male bonding intensifies group pressure to conform. Superson argues that aggression, male solidarity, and group pressure are among the factors that function jointly to incite behavior that harms women, maintains male separatism, and sustains the backlash against women's progress. Male socialization can result in hatred and contempt for, and aggression against, women. It can explain the link between male despair over loss of power and acts of aggression such as rape and discriminatory tenure denial. Superson discusses several ways in which gender discrimination can enter the tenure process, the most insidious of which she believes occurs when a female candidate is held during her pretenure years to female stereotypes she would otherwise reject, and then is judged partly or entirely on whether she conforms rather than on her credentials. These include stereotypes of sex object, passivity, and subservience to men. She shows how holding women to such stereotypes is both a symptom and a cause of the boys' club mentality, and argues that a tenure process that allows and masks discrimination so well both encourages and perpetuates male bonding and aggressive exclusion of women. Finally, she discusses both individual and group harms women suffer from discriminatory tenure denial that function to maintain the backlash against women.

The next two essays describe a more hidden form that backlash takes, one that is almost strictly institutional rather than merely the product of individuals' attitudes. In "Parenting and Other Human Casualties in the Pursuit of Academic Excellence," Cynthia Willett argues that the backlash specifically targets women who choose to raise children while pursuing academic careers. She identifies three factors that contribute to the backlash. First is the combination of two factors: the recent shift in the meaning of parenting and standards of professional excellence. Meeting new standards of ideal parenting requires that women in particular, since they still bear most of the burden of child rearing, develop special skills, acquire much knowledge, and participate actively in daycare and school activities. This extra burden is exacerbated when coupled with the fact that standards of professional excellence have been inflated since the 1970s, during which time women's numbers in the profession of philosophy have grown. Willett argues that together these factors form the core of the backlash by blocking women's professional advancement or forcing them to adjust their career ambitions accordingly.

The second and third factors contribute to the backlash by stifling women's success in the profession. The second factor is the public/private divide, which makes it difficult for faculty to bring issues of parenting into their professional life without appearing unprofessional. In academia, the family is made irrelevant; pregnancy leaves and other such policies, though beneficial, are still viewed as career liabilities rather than as valuable. Willett reminds us that social activities that originate in the family and other sources of social and civic engagement enhance our research and teaching and help to prevent us from being boring philosophers.

The third factor is philosophy's traditional misconception of reason, which excludes child rearing as a central human activity involving reason. Until philosophy recognizes this, and overcomes the public/private divide, women's success in the profession will be thwarted. Willett offers insightful suggestions for changes the profession ought to make that will benefit all of us, not just women, by making our scholarship and lives richer.

Picking up on the theme of the philosophy profession's attitude toward parenting, Julie Maybee's essay, "Politicizing the Personal and Other Tales from the Front Lines," argues that the backlash has taken a shift away from the racism and sexism in the "old days," which was primarily a function of White people's and men's bad attitudes toward minorities and women, to White people's and men's attempt to maintain power over the institutions and structures that have their points of view and interests built into them. Maybee illustrates her position with the seemingly minor—yet politically charged, to those of us who pay attention to these things—example of a philosophy department's scheduling of evening colloquia, which she argues disadvantaged female faculty with young children, but at the same time advantaged their male counterparts who supported maintaining the timing of these sessions since they posed no burden to them. The females in her example and in other similar kinds of backlash were penalized in terms that are allegedly objective and universal, such as those referring to job dedication and collegiality. Maybee demonstrates that seemingly neutral arguments about why some women fail to meet some professional standards are not socially neutral at all, but in fact express a traditionally White male point of view. Moreover, even though there need be no bad attitudes on the part of these "backlashers," their attacks are really personal ones, since they question the value and success of women in their roles in the institution. And since they are not attitudes, but attempts to preserve a self-advantaging system, they are much more difficult to dismiss.

The next section contains three insightful essays on the disturbing student backlash against feminism. The theme of these essays is that even though progressive movements such as feminism have been added to the college curriculum, some students, many of whom occupy privileged positions, have resisted their message and attacked the messenger. This backlash sets back the movements and disempowers women students and faculty. The stories these essays tell indicate that Cudd's intuition is right, that they constitute a full-fledged backlash, rather than merely backlash events.

In "Marginalized Voices: Challenging Dominant Privilege in Higher Education," Carol Moeller investigates the backlash charge that universities have become indoctrination centers for feminists, racial and sexual minorities, and other marginalized groups. Against this view, she argues that universities are Eurocentric and male-dominated despite talk of "political correctness," as evidenced in demographics, curriculum, pedagogies, and institutional structures, including the fact that Women's Studies and Africana Studies programs have merely been "tagged on," "elective," and seen as "other," instead of being incorporated into the mainstream curriculum.

Moeller investigates why hegemonic culture is so deeply entrenched in students who have refused to recognize any perspective other than the dominant one, rejecting others as "fascist," "undemocratic," and even verbally and sometimes violently attacking them and their proponents. She discusses several forces that are responsible for the cultivation of these views and attitudes in students: the media, the perceived success of marginalized groups on the basis of a few members making it to the top, and the "spectator" observation of inequality in which persons distance themselves from the inequalities surrounding them. For Moeller and many feminists, teaching has become a struggle between hegemonic and counter-hegemonic elements of culture. To begin to overcome narrowmindedness in our students and to counteract the view that the dominant ideology is "objective" and "true," we need to engage in a critical inquiry in which all voices, particularly those that have been previously marginalized, are heard. Such critical thinking found in feminist and antiracist pedagogy is crucial to democracy and the quest for knowledge. Universities are the obvious place for free inquiry, though Moeller urges other informal avenues of education as well.

Debra DeBruin and Alisa Carse, in "Transforming Resistance: Shifting the Burden of Proof in the Feminist Classroom," argue that the narrowmindedness in students that Moeller discusses is a kind of "lashing back," or a response to feminist and other challenges to the dominant ideology. They explain that the feminist pedagogy they employ in their classrooms involves not only critical analysis, but a way of empowering students, transforming them into active participants who can "hold their own" instead of passively absorbing information and who open themselves to others' perspectives. They agree with bell hooks that to teach with these aims "is to challenge domination at its very core." The problem is that students often resist the feminist message, and do so in more or less virulent ways, including being hostile, dismissing others' views as unimportant, and refusing to take matters seriously. They argue that the privileged position that many of these students occupy allows them to react in these backlash ways. They focus on the resistance they call "burden of proof" that occurs when some students rest on their position of privilege which grants them the power to assume that their perspective is normal and neutral, to determine whether other students have equal status, and to determine what counts as proof or challenge to an ongoing assumption. Feminist pedagogy involves revealing this privilege, and DeBruin and Carse offer many useful suggestions as to how we might go about doing this. They share Moeller's goal of having all voices heard.

In "Sexism in the Classroom: The Role of Gender Stereotypes in the Evaluation of Female Faculty," Anita Superson shows how the instances of student "lashing back" against progressive movements discussed by Moeller and DeBruin and Carse can turn against those who are associated with progressivism, namely, female faculty, by concretely impacting in negative ways evaluations of their teaching. Drawing from numerous studies, Superson argues that teaching evaluations are affected in a complex way by students' expectations, which in turn are shaped by gender biases about professor behavior. The ratings of female instructors divide up along the lines of whether these instructors conform to gender stereotypes. But women can be penalized or rewarded for conforming or not conforming to gender stereotypes. Superson argues that negative ratings grounded in sexist reasons contribute to the backlash since they negatively affect decisions about raises, promotion, and tenure of female faculty. Even positive ratings grounded in sexism contribute to the backlash by disciplining gender conformity.

The last section examines the issue of whether progress has been made in the face of the backlash. In "When Sexual Harassment Is Protected Speech: Facing the Forces of Backlash in Academe," Ann Cudd argues that even though the progression of women has been marked significantly by, among other things, the institution of laws about sexual harassment and its inclusion as a form of gender harassment, there has been a backlash against this progress. This backlash is leveled particularly against hostile environment sexual harassment, defined as unwelcome sexual advances and requests for sexual favors that unreasonably interferes with a person's work or education or creates an intimidating, hostile environment. Cudd believes that hostile environment sexual harassment has been wrongly viewed by the courts in a subjective way as dependent on the feelings of the person to whom the conduct is directed, rather than objectively as grounded in harms women as a group suffer.

The main battleground of this form of backlash is the college campus, which traditionally has been conceived to be an arena of completely protected free speech. Like the workplace, previously male-dominated college campuses were places where men could say what they wanted about women. Some now resent women's presence because it impedes their freedom in this regard. Cudd argues that the backlash to progress made in sexual harassment legislation is cloaked precisely by claims about free speech, but at the cost of harm done to women and minorities. She claims that the United States Constitution as it stands cannot be invoked properly to resolve conflicts between freedom of expression and gender discrimination. She motivates her argument with a case she was involved in at Occidental College, where a fraternity that published material that was profoundly offensive to women brought a lawsuit on grounds of freedom of expression against a group that fought this treatment of women. She argues that unlike other cases of political speech that have some value, such as flag-burning and sacrilege, which ought to enjoy First Amendment protection, expression that is profoundly offensive to women ought not to be allowed because it treats women as moral subordinates. In doing so, it cuts off the possibility of political debate, which is the bedrock of free speech. Cudd cites a number of cogent reasons why colleges have a special interest in restricting such kinds of speech and resisting this insidious form of backlash that on its face seems protected by the Constitution.

In the last essay, "Women in Philosophy: A Forty-Year Perspective on Academic Backlash," Linda Bell traces academia's response to women's progress from her graduate school days in the early 1960s to the present. Disappointedly, she does not notice much positive change, and characterizes the negative change as a backlash instead of the mere sexism she experienced early in her career. Indeed, Bell argues that the backlash is more insidious than mere sexism because the former is hidden, making it more difficult to resist, while the latter is clearly evident.

Bell examines three areas of change in the academy. Regarding the first, blatant sexism and racism, Bell notes that the few women in the academy several decades ago were ignored, dismissed, made fun of, and denigrated by some privileged persons who were able to get away with these behaviors because of their privilege. These responses to women still exist today, but they have become more violent, or are hidden in attempts to disguise misogyny in ways that Maybee and others discuss.

Second, although the institution of affirmative action policies marks progress for women and minorities, Bell argues that much of the time the academy merely pays lip service to them, and when it follows them, it does so as a matter of tokenism and window dressing instead of genuine concern for the progress of subordinate groups. Even worse, affirmative action policies are now constantly under fire. The irony is that these reactions are set in the context where others, including sons of alumni, politicians, the rich and famous, and even all of the white men of Bell's and earlier generations, acquired their positions not merely due to ability. Echoing a point made by Moeller and DeBruin and Carse, Bell argues that the privilege these persons enjoy goes unnoticed by them, and is seen as the norm.

Third, Bell argues that the advice women in the profession have been and still are given, to be "good girls" who do not fight back against the injustices of the system and remain reticent in the alleged fairness of the academy, fuels the backlash because it fosters complacency and stands in the way of progress. She reiterates Willett's point that women are warned not to have children and be philosophers, which contributes to the backlash by keeping women out altogether, or by preventing them from making the kinds of positive changes Willett envisions.

Bell ends her essay, and appropriately, this book, by wondering why philosophy, which freed her from "the narrowness, racial bigotry, and sexism of the segregated, Jim Crow South in which [she] grew up," has not been similarly liberating for many of her (our) colleagues, and even has been used in ways that preserve the status quo. We believe that critical analysis, the core of philosophy, will expose inequality and injustice where they exist. But we must engage in it open-mindedly and in an inclusive way that accords equal respect to all. We call upon philosophers and all academics to employ the sharp reasoning skills they have assiduously acquired to lead us to make rather than halt progress.

I

CONCEPTUALIZING BACKLASH

1

Analyzing Backlash to Progressive Social Movements

Ann E. Cudd

INTRODUCTION

In 1991 Susan Faludi published *Backlash: The Undeclared War against American Women*,[1] and the term has become a commonplace of feminist activism and scholarship ever since. Most feminists, and progressives generally, hold that there is currently a backlash to the progress made in the wake of the Civil Rights and Women's movements of the 1960s and 1970s. Although Faludi documents a wealth of examples of the mistreatment of women and the misperception of feminism, her book offers little in the way of conceptual analysis of backlash. Instead it takes the term as clear and goes from there. And little has been done by social theorists to define and clarify the concept of backlash. To say that some event or series of events is an instance of backlash is to make a judgment that is at once both descriptive and normative. For both descriptive and normative purposes, we need to be clear about how to identify backlash and distinguish it from phenomena that are superficially similar. We need to be able to judge whether an event fits into a pattern of growing reaction against some progressive social movement, or whether the event is isolated, anomalous, and not worthy of serious concern by social theorists or activists. Thus, we need a definition of backlash, one that shows how the concept fits into other central concepts of social and political theory, such as equality, oppression, and social progress. This chapter is intended to clarify the concept of backlash in order to ground social theory about progress and backlash.

What counts as a backlash event or period or set of acts and what doesn't count? The case that I think might be taken as paradigmatic for social backlash is the period of increased violence against Blacks in the Jim Crow South following Reconstruction. The case is paradigmatic not only because it was such a strong reversal of progress, but also because the direction of change was clear and unmistakable. Jim Crow was a rapid reversal of rights and freedoms that had previously been secured by Blacks during the period of Reconstruction. The Jim Crow period is sufficiently far back in history now for us to see that it was clearly a systematic change in the laws, institutions, and social climate that reversed the progress of a previous period. A similar period of increased violence against women in the 1980s and 1990s seems to be following on the progress of the Women's movement. This is more clear internationally than in the United States, with the prime example being the Taliban movement in Afghanistan. Also, witness the increased violence against gays and lesbians in the wake of progress in the Gay Rights movement.

Physical violence is the most obvious but not the only sort of reaction to progress. In the academy, where physical violence is rare (but not unheard of), backlash usually comes in the form of institutionally sanctioned, or at least unprevented, abuses of power. At the 1998 Eastern Division American Philosophical Association meeting, a group of feminist philosophers (including the present author) came together to discuss issues of backlash to feminism in the academy. The assembled panel bore witness to a number of problems faced by feminists and women, and discussed how the term "backlash" might apply. First, we noted departments that seemed to be quite eager to hire women, then do a number of uncollegial and unprofessional things to get rid of them—either by harassing them, by disrespecting their work or their other contributions to their departments, by unfairly denying them tenure,[2] or by making their working conditions so difficult that they fail to earn tenure, or give up before trying.[3] Second, we discussed the fact that feminism as a topic and methodology of philosophy has been granted a place at the national meetings, but there remains a reluctance of the philosophers at the top institutions and journals of the first rank to publish feminist pieces. Indeed, in some quarters there is simply outright hostility to feminist philosophy. Two items come to mind here. In his address as chancellor of Boston University and host of the most recent World Congress of Philosophy, philosopher John Silber attacked feminist philosophy as "an assault on reason."[4] In a review of feminist work in various disciplines, the *Times Literary Supplement* asked Colin McGinn for an overview of the significance of feminism in philosophy. He writes, "feminism now has a place in many philosophy departments, for good or ill, but it has not made any impact on the core areas of the subject."[5] Third, we discussed the changing climate for feminism in the classroom. While the students we taught ten or so years ago were either on the Left politically, or at least curious and interested in feminism and generally respectful of me, when I teach feminist perspectives on classical issues in my large intro class now, a small but noticeable number of them walk out. In a recent semester during which I taught an introductory class, I made a point of including works by women and non-Whites. While I had generally good evaluations, one student carved "Cudd is a bitch," "I hate Cudd," and "Fuck Cudd" so deeply into one of the desks of the classroom that it had to be replaced. Again, it is hard to read these events precisely, but taken together they suggest to us an ominous erosion of the progress that many think women and feminism are making in the profession and the academy generally. I would argue that these events are not merely anomalous fluctuations from a norm of civility and progress for women, but that they represent genuine instances of backlash against women and feminism in the academy.

Two kinds of problems threaten the project of identifying a particular period or series of events as backlash. One problem is that an event might not be any kind of a backlash at all, but rather an event that follows another that is difficult to characterize as part of the same narrative of history. Perhaps it is anomalous, perhaps it slightly opposes the previous progress but does not suggest a significant social movement. The other kind of problem is that some periods might indeed oppose the social movements of a previous era, but the previous era was not itself a progressive social movement. For example, let's suppose that the current opposition to affirmative action were overcome and affirmative action programs, perhaps in altered forms, were reinstituted. Then we might imagine those who oppose affirmative action on grounds that it violates the rights of Whites and men would say that there is a backlash occurring in the reinstitution of affirmative action. In another example from a recent article in the *Columbia Law Review*, Mark Roe counts as "backlash" any economic policy that opposes economic efficiency.[6] But such policies would include labor-friendly policies like laws that favor labor unions or impede the ability of businesses to fire employees quickly or buy and dismantle companies, and these are clearly policies that so-called progressives would favor.

In its normative use, "backlash" connotes something to be avoided, something that is excessive in its zeal and reactionary in aim. My aim in this chapter is to outline a theory of backlash that is a normative theory, that carries with it an implicit moral judgment that such a social period is to be avoided, is somehow wrong. To do this we need a theory of backlash to social progress, where progress carries the normative implication that it is good, a period of social change to be encouraged.

PROGRESSIVENESS

In the *Discourse on the Origin of Inequality*, Rousseau argued that civilization has brought increasing inequality and enslavement, and in this sense humans could not be said to be making progress. Indeed, quite the reverse,

Rousseau held that civilization had meant moral decline, and that the decline had worsened as humans strayed further from their origins in the primeval wilderness. Rousseau held that the beginning of the decline came with the origin of private property and the division of labor. It was at this point that humans were able to profit from enslaving one another, by making one person do the work that was required for the survival of two. Increasing technical knowledge in agriculture, manufacture, and social organization thus brought about decreases in freedom and equality. Even if Rousseau has the historical facts wrong, he persuasively argues that increasing civilization can mean political regress, not progress.

If progress does not automatically correspond to growing civilization or technical change, how then are we to define progress?[7] "Progress" is a relational term that implies an end or goal toward which the thing progressing is moving. Rousseau correlates moral decline with the growth of inequality, suggesting that equality itself is progressive. But that view fails to distinguish among different institutional designs that would foster equality. Maoism fostered equality at the total expense of liberty, for example. If we must count that as progress, then the term loses its normative force. There are many possible social goals, but they reduce mainly to two classes of goals: goodness and rightness or justice. A society might pursue some happiness or righteousness, as examples of pursuing goodness, or a society might pursue equality or efficiency in production and trade as a matter of justice. I don't mean to suggest that goodness and rightness are exclusive, though they are likely to compete at times. We might say that a society progresses when it becomes more good or more just, and this in turn is determined by the theory of social goodness or justice which one holds. The good and the right may sometimes conflict, in the sense that making progress toward goodness might require a sacrifice of justice, or vice versa. Since it is unlikely that there is only one way for a society to be either good or just, progress does not require a unique outcome; there are likely to be many ways that a society can make progress.

Now let us look at two paradigm examples of social progress. Perhaps the clearest case of social progress in human history has been the abolition of chattel slavery, insofar as that has happened. Closely behind that in clarity is the institution of universal suffrage, at least in nations where such democracy exists. Both of these changes have clearly marked a change in the way that human beings view other humans (at least other competent adult humans)— as fellow persons of equal dignity and worthy of respect rather than as lesser beings because of some accident of their birth, be it race or class or gender. Now one might argue that there are still blind spots even in the most progressive states: failure to extend the vote to noncitizen residents or the practical enslavement of the underclass in low wage jobs, for example. But that is only to argue that further progress can be made, not that abolishing slavery and extending suffrage are not examples of clear progress. To argue that they are not progressive would require one to show that for every such extension of the concept of personhood to cover adult members of the human species or extension of voting rights, there is a corresponding erosion of humanity or rights somewhere else in the world, or to show that the focus on individuals that democracy and liberalism requires is somehow nonprogressive. While the first of these seems empirically quite implausible, the second is a position that could be argued by a fascist, or by one who holds a religiously based comprehensive moral view, or perhaps by a communitarian, or by a utilitarian under some bizarre conditions of social life. It might be argued by a radical feminist that such individualism is masculinist, and hence nonprogressive. I think all these views are mistaken, but it is beyond the limited space available here to carry out a full defense of the thesis that the human individual is to be held morally primary. I will simply admit that my concept of progress is fashioned assuming this basic liberal bias.

There are also clear cases of regression (again, relative to the basic liberal thesis just stated): genocides and totalitarian regimes of various stripes. What makes these regressive is that they deny the respect due persons to whole classes of people. Take the Jewish Holocaust and the Nazi regime that brought it about. Jews were viewed as "vermin," as something less than human, and (combined with the claim that their existence somehow harmed the German people) their annihilation was thereby alleged to be justified. The Nazi regime was a good example of a fascist totalitarianism, in which the German people were claimed to be personified by a single man, thereby symbolically annihilating the personhood of individual Germans. Dictators like Ferdinand Marcos, who do not even attempt a rhetorical justification for their actions, deny the equal worth of their fellow citizens by ignoring their wishes and needs and plundering their wealth. Religious totalitarians, like Ayatollah Khomeini, claim that God has chosen them to dictate, to overrule the wishes or the needs of the people and demand their ultimate sacrifice when the dictator sees fit to do so. Might someone argue that one or more of these are not cases of regression but are really social progress? One must either deny the equal worth and dignity of individual persons or deny that persons ought to able to have some realm of individual choice and some voice in collective decision making in their society. To persons who would deny either of these tenets, I admit, I have not much to say in this essay.

There are finally some unclear cases of progress or regress that I want to mention to delineate the concept of progress that I am pursuing. Some persons who agree with the tenets of equal worth and dignity and democratic choice, perhaps Rousseau included, would argue that our increasingly technological lifestyle is regressive in that it destroys valuable ways of life. Others would assert that it constitutes social as well as technical progress because the standard of living of the worst off member has been raised (an

argument made by Locke, among others). Some, perhaps Rousseau included, would argue that capitalism is regressive because it reduces a large
class of persons to meaningless automatons, impoverishing some while
making others fabulously wealthy. Others assert it is progressive because the
total social product or average level of wealth is higher than with previous
forms of social production. I don't wish to decide these matters here, but I
do want to offer an account of social progress that explains how reasonable
people, people who agree on the progressiveness of extending human dignity and democratic choice, could disagree on these cases while not on the
clear cases of progress and regress that I identified above.

Generalizing from what I call the clear cases, then, I want to suggest that
increasing social justice is progressive and increasing oppression is regressive. Progress, I propose, is to be defined in terms of the reduction of oppression. Oppression, in my view, is a normative term that names a circum-
stance in which four conditions are satisfied: (1) persons suffer harm
(understood descriptively as a decrease in their overall well-being) within
social institutions or practices; (2) the harm is perpetrated through social institutions or practices on a social group whose identity exists apart from the
harm; (3) there is another social group that benefits from the institutions and
practices that transmit the harm; (4) the social group suffers the harm
through unjustified coercion or force. This account of oppression surely
needs defense, but I am not going to do that in this paper.[8] This view entails
that individuals suffer the harm *of oppression* only as members of groups. If
progress requires reducing oppression, then progress entails that these social groups are harmed less by social institutions, which, in turn, means that
the individuals in them suffer fewer harms, at least on average, than they did
before. Social progress, then, is a reduction in harm that comes about
through the redesign of social institutions. But if progress requires a redesign of social institutions to reduce oppression, and if oppressive social institutions benefit some other social groups, then there will be some social
groups whose interests are opposed to progress. Some social groups will be
deprived of the advantages or privileges that existed under the previous set
of social institutions. For example, the abolition of slavery deprived the slave
owners of property. This harmed the slave owners in the real, material sense
that they owned less after abolition than before. This was an entirely justified
harm, because the ownership of slaves was unjustifiable. However, this fact,
that progress harms some identifiable social group that previously enjoyed
an unjustified advantage, sows the seeds of backlash.

Progress can only be defined in terms of contrast with an earlier period,
and with respect to a particular social group or set of social groups. To say
that time t_2 is progress over time t_1 with respect to social group G is to say
that social group G is less oppressed in t_2 than it was in t_1.[9] It is possible,
then, to say that a progressive period for one group is regressive for another,

if, say, another group suffers from increasing oppression during the same period.[10] I will say that a period of time is progressive *simpliciter* only if that period is progress compared to all previous periods and with respect to all social groups existing at that time.

I am now in a position to explain why the unclear cases of progress (i.e., technology and capitalism) are unclear. First, in each of the cases noted, the social group structure could be seen as changing markedly, so that there is no obvious comparison group with which to make a clear judgment that some social group's oppression has been lessened. In the gross cultural changes from hunting and gathering to agrarian societies, or from agrarian to industrial societies, the social groups (perhaps excepting gender groups) shift so as not to even be comparable. Thus, to say that there is a backlash for a particular group from one of these historical epochs to another is really not possible, since the groups and the causes of their oppression are incomparable. However, not all social change entails such major shifts in the social groupings. Blacks and Whites were still Blacks and Whites before and after the Civil War; Jews were still Jews before and after the Second World War and the founding of Israel; women and men did not change basic identity conditions after the Nineteenth Amendment or the failure of the Equal Rights Amendment. Thus, there can be continuity of social groups across periods, making the comparisons that my analysis requires possible in those and many other cases. The second reason that some cases of progress are unclear is because of competing demands of justice. If justice requires, as has been argued by Rawls and others, both economic efficiency and some degree of equality, then there will be many situations in which these demands conflict.[11] In each of the two unclear cases, technical progress and the advent of capitalism, there is, arguably, an increase in efficiency but a decrease in equality. That is, the whole social product increased but the increases advantage some in greater proportion than others, so the greater share of the increase goes to the better off groups. In these cases those persons who prioritize efficiency could see these changes as progressive while those who prioritize equality could see them as regressive.

BACKLASH

My strategy for defining backlash should now be obvious: it is to be defined in terms of progress or regress, which is defined in terms of oppression. Backlash is clearly in evidence when oppression is greater than in a previous period with respect to some social group and in that previous period the social group suffered less oppression in some still previous period. Note that on this view it is not possible to say that a period of social progress with respect to some social group is at the same time a backlash against the social group whose interests are adversely affected by the increased equality. This is because the group that is adversely affected by increased equality or decreased oppression is not thereby subjected to oppression. While their group interests are damaged, the damage is not unjustified. The damage is justified precisely by the fact that their previous gains were unjustified and unjust. Thus, White men had no justified claim to being oppressed by affirmative action, and would not be justified in using the term backlash to describe any reinstitution of affirmative action after it was temporarily suspended.

It has been suggested to me that "backlash" connotes a mean-spirited, punitive attitude on the part of the backlasher. Faludi suggests this when she introduces the term, defining backlash to feminism as "hostility to female independence," and "fear and loathing of feminism."[12] While I think that backlash can certainly come about through such attitudes, it can also come about as a result of completely unorganized, unconscious, perhaps even institutionalized, resistance to change. Surely the formation and actions of the Ku Klux Klan are examples of organized meanness. But the forces of oppression are often more institutional than personal. For example, a woman is denied tenure on the grounds that her work is not "high quality" or not "philosophical," as judged by the perceived quality and titles of the journals she publishes in. It turns out that journals that her colleagues count as top quality philosophical journals turn down (as insufficiently philosophical), without review by referees, any article that considers gender to be a significant category of philosophical analysis.[13] But the journals that she does publish in are considered "non-mainstream" in the profession (e.g., they have "feminist" in their titles or subtitles). While there *may* be nothing mean-spirited (since this could be a case of *unconscious* sexism) in the editors' decisions, failing to recognize gender as a crucial social category and so worthy of analysis by social philosophers makes their journals unavailable to the woman as a publishing outlet. Likewise her colleagues may not be mean-spirited but simply fail to see newer journals which do accept submissions in this field as good journals and to see that what they consider the good journals are unavailable for the research that the woman does. This case illustrates how institutions and norms can exert an inertial force that resists progress without any individual consciously intending to resist progress.

Although a mean-spirited or punitive attitude is not necessary for a series of events to constitute backlash, it is sufficient when combined with some rolling back of past progressive gains, even if that does not make for greater overall oppression. Consider the example discussed by Faludi of the treatment of the Women's Educational Equity Act program of the Education Department by the Reagan administration. According to Faludi, the WEEA was singled out by the Heritage Foundation's 1981 treatise *Mandate for Leadership*, which was used as a blueprint by the administration to target progressive government programs to cut. The Reagan administration proceeded to harass and demote the director of the program and replace her and her staff with conservative women whose only competence for the job consisted in their conservatism and willingness to do what the administration asked of them. The punitive attitude of the administration is revealed in many of its statements about the program. It was said to espouse "extreme feminist ideology," and the director was described as a "radical feminist," who was a "monarch imperiously guarding her fiefdom."[14] But the projects of the WEEA could hardly be described as radical, as Faludi notes, consisting of "a guide to help teenage handicapped girls; a program to enforce equal education laws in rural school districts; a math-counseling service for older minority women returning to community college."[15] The end result was that the WEEA became a practically worthless name for a minor section in the Education Department. While that surely constituted a rollback of a progressive gain for women, though, it could be argued that women were not more oppressed during the Reagan administration than previously. It could well be argued that women's opportunities have been increasing despite these periodic obstacles. I think that this kind of event is also the kind of lashing back that we want to pick out with the concept of backlash. The punitive attitude indicates an intention on the part of a social group to deny another social group social progress. The fact that it was successful in rolling back some progressive gains, even if not to a great enough degree to clearly constitute greater oppression, in combination with the attitude qualifies it as a backlash event.

Does this imply that a single event can be said to be a backlash event? A completely isolated, unique, anomalous event could not be an instance of backlash in my sense. This is because a single event could not be an event of oppression absent any social structures of constraint. But the existence of a mean-spirited attitude, an intention to deny social progress, means that the event is not really an isolated, anomalous event. For there must be other events, however diffuse and disorganized, that lead to the crystallization of the attitude toward the social group.

This raises a serious epistemological problem of how to tell when we are confronted with a case of backlash or simple rudeness, misfortune, or meanness aimed at an individual. While it is hard not to attribute meanness to all acts that have regressive political effects and so see them all as backlash events, in personal or professional interactions it is more difficult to read backlash. How can we tell if a tenure denial is a part of backlash or a bunch of unconnected forces within an academic institution working against someone? Is it backlash or a mistake that might have happened to a member of a privileged social group or a reasonable, if harsh, judgment of the merits of the case? This is formally like the problem of determining what the overall population looks like from a small sample. At the moment of the event, it may be difficult to tell whether it is an event that constitutes increasing oppression or backlash (although later there will be a pattern of events that makes backlash clear). But it would be naive to suggest that we don't have any basis on which to judge in cases that are similar to past cases. As I argued, because of the fact that there is usually a social group that is harmed by progress, backlashes almost always follow progress. For every feminist movement there has been its antifeminist backlash. Therefore, when the savvy feminist is confronted with misfortune, she wisely bets on the backlash.[16]

TWO OBJECTIONS

Let me briefly respond to two kinds of objections to the theory of backlash that I have sketched here. First, the postmodernist objects that both progress and backlash are modernist notions that presume a grand narrative to history.[17] But the narrative is a fiction of the storyteller. There is no truth of the matter, because there is no fact of history. Hence the whole attempt to define either backlash or progress is mistaken. My response to the postmodernist objection is to deny that historical narratives are pure fictions, and to argue that historical narratives are essential to any meaningful human life. Historical narratives are constrained by the historical facts, even if there is literary license in the precise weaving of the facts. While they may be described in many ways, certain states of affairs did or did not obtain. Either Kennedy died or he did not. Either he was shot by Oswald or he was not. Either there were more gunmen there or there were not. Granted we may not know all the facts, as in this case. But there are facts, and insofar as they are discovered, they limit our possible stories about what happened. While historical fact can allow a set of possible alternative narratives, it rules out many more. The second point against the postmodernist objection is that historical narratives create meaning in our lives and help us to determine who we are; they are necessary to our senses of personal and social identity. Without them we could have no coherent sense of a continuous person or society through time. Yet clearly we do have this sense of ourselves and our societies. The postmodernist denial flies in the face of this commonplace phenomenological fact.

The second objection that I want briefly to address is the methodological individualist objection: there is no movement of history or society, only movements of individuals.[18] The theory of backlash posits a coordination of events and persons that doesn't really exist, but is only an epiphenomenon at best and an illusion at worst.[19] In response I would argue first that contrary to the claim of the strict methodological individualist, there are social facts that arise from cognitive, social, and legal forces acting on individuals that the methodological individualist cannot consistently deny. One cognitive force is stereotyping and other forms of social categorization that cause persons to categorize others and their actions by identifiable and categorizable features of persons (sex, skin color, religious and ethnic traditional appearance or behavior).[20] The social and legal forces include the fact that certain behaviors are prescribed for persons consequent on features that group them, e.g., religious practice, legal prohibitions and requirements. These factors cause social facts through the behavior of individuals who are motivated by these behavioral norms. My theory of backlash concerns these social groups and the social constraints that motivate the behavior of individuals as a result of their social group status. Thus, there need be nothing ontologically spooky about the social facts that the theory of backlash posits.

CONCLUSION

In conclusion I want to argue that there is a backlash now to feminism in philosophy. The argument faces the objection that whatever problems or challenges feminists and women are facing now in academia, there is no backlash because the criterion that we be in a period of regress is not met.[21] Women are represented in greater numbers at all levels in higher education, Women's Studies departments are common and growing, and feminism is reaching into nearly every discipline. I believe that this objection has some merit, but that there is a case to be made for the backlash position in philosophy, at least. While it is true that there are more women at the assistant and associate professor levels, growth at the full professor level has been very modest in most fields, and particularly in philosophy.[22] While there is a feminist journal of philosophy, *Hypatia*, it is still difficult to get one's male colleagues to accept it as equally valuable as, say, *Philosophical Studies*, which has about the same reported acceptance rate.[23] Still, this suggests slower than expected progress, not regress. Yet I think that there is a case to be made that feminism is facing a reactionary response that is closing off opportunities to the top and mainstream of the profession of philosophy. Recall the quotations I cited from Silber and from McGinn. These remarks reveal a hostility and resentment that could only surface after some initial successes by feminists to challenge the discipline. For most liberals and progressives, feminism came initially as a kind of gestalt switch. They believed something like the following syllogism is sound: All men are worthy of equal dignity and respect. Equal dignity and respect requires equal opportunity in the academy. Therefore, all men are worthy of equal dignity and respect. Then, suddenly, it occurred to some (in the face of second wave women's movement): "Oh, yeah, and women too." Making the logical substitution then implied that women deserved equal opportunity in the academy. So far so good. But as it turned out, women's entrance into the profession of philosophy led inevitably (or so I would argue—but that's another essay) to challenges to many traditional issues in philosophy. That meant that either the men in the profession have to carry on the philosophical discussion on new terms, terms set in some cases by women, or dismiss the terms as unworthy. This is a cost, a harm to the privileged position of men in the discipline. Given the economic and status incentives involved, (e.g., maintaining their own positions as arbiters of the mainstream, or securing employment for themselves or their students), there are incentives for those in positions of power in the profession to maintain their position by taking the less honorable position that feminist readings are of less value than the orthodox ones. Surely the motivations behind hostility to feminism in the academy are more complex than this brief analysis reveals, but this is at least a large part of the story. Now, it seems, there has been a hardening of the position that women (or racial minorities) are wanted in the profession, but only if they do not do feminism (or race theory). This amounts to conceptual regress from the initial liberalization of the profession, where there was little or no prejudice against feminism before (since its implications for fundamental change were unclear), or rather, no more than the general prejudice against women that existed then, and, I would argue, still does. Taken together with the slower than expected material progress of women in the profession, this conceptual regress indicates a backlash to feminism, which decent people should resist.

NOTES

This essay was originally published in *The APA Newsletter on Feminism and Philosophy* (Philosophy Documentaion Center, 1999), 42–46. It was first presented to the Society for Analytical Feminism at the 1998 Eastern Division American Philosophical Association (APA) meetings, Washington, D.C., December 28, 1998. I thank the audience and especially my coconspirators on the panel, Julie Maybee and Anita Superson, for helpful comments. I also thank three anonymous reviewers and Cressida Heyes for helpful suggestions.

1. Susan Faludi, *Backlash: The Undeclared War against American Women* (New York: Crown Publishers, 1991).
2. Anita Superson, "Academic Gang Rape: Philosophical Reflections on the Backlash against Women in Tenure Decisions" (paper presented at the 1998 APA Eastern Division Meetings, December 30, 1998). See also ch. 5 of this volume.
3. Julie Maybee, "Politicizing the Personal and Other Tales from the Front Lines" (paper presented at the 1998 APA Eastern Division Meetings, 30 December 1998.) See also chapter 7 of this volume.
4. Scott Allen, "For Philosophers, Criticism and a Call to Service," *Boston Globe* (11 August 1998): 1.
5. "Feminism Revisited: A Symposium," *Times Literary Supplement* (20 March 1998): 13.
6. Mark J. Roe, "Backlash," *Columbia Law Review* 98 (January 1998): 217–41.

7. In this paper "progress" refers to social or moral progress only. I don't mean to deny that there are other kinds of progress, such as economic, technical, or scientific progress.

8. I attempt to mount this defense in *Analyzing Oppression*, unpublished manuscript.

9. An account of how oppression is to be measured and compared is needed at this point, but lies beyond the scope of this paper.

10. I do not mean to say that any group who previously benefited from the oppression of one group then suffers from oppression when their privileges are denied them. I mean only to allow that at the same time one group's oppression may be lessening, another's may be increasing. For example, one might say that while the founding of the United States led to a lessening of religious persecution and so a lessening of oppression for some, it also further entrenched laws enforcing slavery in the Constitution, thereby arguably increasing the oppression of Africans and their descendants in North America.

11. This point might also be put in terms of the competing goods of positive and negative liberty. That is, in order to increase positive liberty, the ability of persons to choose autonomously, it is necessary to curb some negative liberty, defined as the absence of interference in individuals' actions. I prefer the equality/efficiency way of putting the point because I see them as having a tighter connection to justice than does liberty.

12. Susan Faludi, *Backlash: The Undeclared War*, xix. She also acknowledges, however, that backlash is not a conspiracy, and that some of the agents of backlash are not even aware that they are opposing feminism.

13. That there are such journals I know from personal experience. Quoting from a letter I received rejecting without review a paper of mine, an editor of *Economics and Philosophy* writes, "Economic gender inequality is an important social issue and the explanation model you use may well be helpful and illuminating. But the paper does not seem to us to be 'philosophical' enough. We do publish essays both on social philosophy and the conceptual foundations of game theory but your contribution does not belong to these categories."

14. Quoting from Susan Faludi, *Backlash: The Undeclared War*, 259–61.

15. Susan Faludi, *Backlash: The Undeclared War*, 260.

16. One of the savviest is bell hooks, see "All Quiet on the Feminist Front," *Artforum* 35 (December 1996): 39–41.

17. Elayne Rapping, "Gender and Media Theory: A Critique of the 'Backlash Model'" *Journal of Social Philosophy* 25 (1994): 7–21.

18. Jon Elster, *Making Sense of Marx* (New York: Cambridge University Press, 1985).

19. This objection is closely related to the conspiracy theory objection. See Brian Keeley, "Of Conspiracy Theories," *Journal of Philosophy* 96 (March 1999):109–26.

20. I make an argument for the claim that stereotyping creates social groups, one type of social fact, in "Psychological Explanations of Oppression," in *Introduction to Multiculturalism*, ed. Cynthia J. Willett, 187–215 (New York: Blackwell, 1998).

21. Virginia Valian raised this objection to me, citing her own book *Why So Slow?* (Cambridge, Mass.: MIT Press, 1998) for evidence that women are making progress, slowly, in academia.

22. See Virginia Valian, *Why So Slow?* (Cambridge, Mass.: MIT Press, 1998).

23. Eric Hoffman, ed., *Guidebook for Publishing Philosophy*, 88 and 133 (Bowling Green, Ohio: Philosophy Documentation Center, 1997). The rates are 16 percent and 15 percent, respectively.

BIBLIOGRAPHY

Allen, Scott. "For Philosophers, Criticism and a Call to Service." *Boston Globe* (11 August 1998): 1.
Cudd, Ann E. *Analyzing Oppression.* Unpublished manuscript.
———. "Psychological Explanations of Oppression." In *Introduction to Multiculturalism*, ed. Cynthia J. Willett, 187–215. New York: Blackwell, 1998.
Elster, Jon. *Making Sense of Marx.* (New York: Cambridge University Press, 1985).
Faludi, Susan. *Backlash: The Undeclared War against American Women.* New York: Crown, 1991.
"Feminism Revisited: A Symposium." *Times Literary Supplement* (20 March 1998): 13.
Hoffman, Eric, ed. *Guidebook for Publishing Philosophy.* Bowling Green, Ohio: Philosophy Documentation Center, 1997.
hooks, bell. "All Quiet on the Feminist Front." *Artforum* 35 (December 1996): 39–41.
Keeley, Brian. "Of Conspiracy Theories." *Journal of Philosophy* 96, no. 3 (March 1999): 109–26.
Maybee, Julie. "Politicizing the Personal and Other Tales from the Front Lines." Paper presented at the 1998 APA Eastern Division Meetings, December 30, 1998.
Rapping, Elayne. "Gender and Media Theory: A Critique of the 'Backlash Model.'" *Journal of Social Philosophy* 25, no. 1 (1994): 7–21.
Superson, Anita. "Academic Gang Rape: Philosophical Reflections on the Backlash against Women in Tenure Decisions." Paper presented at the 1998 APA Eastern Division Meetings, December 30, 1998.
Valian, Virginia. *Why So Slow?* Cambridge, Mass.: MIT Press, 1998.

II

BACKLASH AGAINST FEMINIST THEORY

2

The Backlash against Feminist Philosophy

Keith Burgess-Jackson

back-lash: The jarring reaction or striking back of a wheel or set of connected wheels in a piece of mechanism, when the motion is not uniform or when sudden pressure is applied.[1]
backlash 1a: a sudden violent backward movement or reaction b: the play between adjacent movable parts (as in a series of gears); *also:* the jar caused by this when the parts are put into action 2: a snarl in that part of a fishing line wound on the reel 3: a strong adverse reaction (as to a recent political or social development)[2]

INTRODUCTION

Until beginning work on this essay, I misunderstood both the origin and the meaning of the word "backlash." This misconception created the wrong image in my mind. I had what might be considered the layperson's understanding of the term. To lash, literally, is "to strike with a whip, to beat or strike violently."[3] The term is used nonliterally in sentences such as "the lizard lashed its tail." Anything that can move like a whip can lash like a whip. If this is what lashing is, then a *back*lash (I thought) must consist in lashing *back* at someone or something. This made sense, since whenever I encountered the term, it was in a context in which one person or group, such as men, was trying to keep some other person or group, such as women, from advancing or drawing near.

But the term "backlash," as the definitions show, has to do (or *had* to do, since we might say that its meaning has changed) with mechanical devices, not whips. A backlash occurs when sudden pressure is applied to a smooth-running mechanism, such as a series of gears or wheels. The pressure disrupts

19

the mechanism, which responds by lurching, jarring, or striking back. Not to anthropomorphize, but the machine is "striving" to retain its equilibrium. Anyone in the vicinity of the mechanism at the time of the lurch may be injured or killed, especially if there is a protruding handle or crank on one of the wheels, so prudence dictates that one not apply sudden pressure (or that one get away from the apparatus as soon as one does).

On reflection, this is an appropriate metaphor for the kind of backlash that is the focus of this anthology.[4] The mechanism in question is the social "machine" that works to the advantage of certain individuals and to the disadvantage of others. Left to its own devices, the machine, consisting of various "gears," "pulleys," and "wheels" (i.e., institutions, norms, practices, roles, and all the other elements of society) runs fine. It is in stasis or equilibrium. But if some disaffected individual or group applies pressure, the machine lurches, jars, or strikes back, creating the aforementioned risks of harm.

The difference between these images (whip and machine) is this. Lashing is a conscious, intentional act. One does not ordinarily (although I suppose one *could*) set up a whip so that it lashes out at random. Moreover, lashing is the act of a concrete individual, as opposed to an abstract whole or a mere collection of individuals. One imagines a whip-wielder on the back of a horse-drawn wagon, keeping would-be wagon-riders away by lashing out at those who get close. But machines can be set up to run on their own, over a long period of time, and they can produce effects that benefit many people, even those who are unaware of the machine's operation. When feminists discuss the so-called backlash against feminism, they are not thereby committing themselves to the view that it is *individuals* who are (consciously and intentionally) keeping women at bay. Feminists should allow for the possibility that what keeps women at bay is a large-scale, smooth-running social machine, a kind of mindless but effective mechanism, one that privileges men qua men while disadvantaging women qua women. In short, the mechanistic image is not just true(r) to the origin of the word "backlash," but more accurate as well.[5]

The backlash against feminism—with feminism being understood simply as a social movement designed to promote equality between the sexes—takes many forms. It can be personal, as where an avowed or suspected feminist is ridiculed, despised, or mistreated, or professional, wherein a particular feminist's work (scholarly or otherwise) is marginalized, discredited, or repudiated by colleagues. The profession of philosophy, despite its pretensions to objectivity, open-mindedness, and fairness, has not been receptive to feminism and has not taken kindly to feminists. Indeed, it has been antagonistic toward feminist critics of the discipline. I do not think it an exaggeration to say that some philosophers have reacted quite badly (morally as well as psychologically) to the feminists in their midst.[6]

My aim in this essay is to identify, document, and criticize *some* of the backlash that has taken place against feminist philosophy—and to explain why it is a backlash. (I am sure that similar essays could be written about feminist legal theory, feminist economics, feminist psychology, feminist biology, feminist anthropology, feminist theology, and so forth.) In the process, I will develop a rudimentary typology of backlashing. One theoretical problem that I and other feminists confront as we investigate the concept of backlash is how to distinguish fair, responsible, charitable criticism, which is not just desirable but essential to the discipline of philosophy, from politically or ideologically motivated bashing.[7] In practice, it can be difficult to distinguish the two. One of my aims in this essay is to make the task less difficult.

To make the essay concrete, as well as to exemplify the categories of backlashing that I identify, I examine the critical work of three credentialed philosophers: Harriet E. Baber, Alan G. Soble, and Iddo Landau.[8] Each has, in different ways, contributed to the backlash against feminist philosophy (and hence to feminism in general). As the list shows, not all backlashers are men.[9] Perhaps more surprisingly, not all backlashers are non- or antifeminists. At least two of those whose work I discuss (Baber and Landau) consider themselves feminists! One irony that emerges from my essay is that some of those who condemn feminist philosophy for being ideologically motivated are themselves in the grip of an unarticulated (and often unacknowledged) ideology.

UNCHARITABLENESS

An open-minded writer does not fabricate facts or play up evidence as if it establishes more than it actually does, so avoid the unrestrained language that suggests you might do this. An open-minded writer does not treat other views unfairly, so avoid undisciplined expressions that suggest that you are not above such contrivance.[10]

The first form in which backlash occurs is lack of charity (or fairness). Simon Blackburn, author of *The Oxford Dictionary of Philosophy*, defines "principle of charity" as follows: "Principle especially highlighted by [Donald] Davidson as governing the interpretation of others. In various versions it constrains the interpreter to maximize the truth or rationality in the subject's sayings."[11] The normative basis of this principle is nothing less (or more) than the Golden Rule: If you would like critics to be fair to you, then you should be fair to those you criticize. In particular, if you would like your arguments or theories to be charitably and sympathetically construed, then you should charitably and sympathetically construe the arguments and theories that you (go on to) criticize.

The idea is this. Before I criticize an argument or theory, I should make it the best it can be. If there are two plausible readings of a premise, for example, I should prefer the reading that is most plausible or that has the most evidence in its favor. If there are two forms in which an argument might be cast, one valid and the other invalid, I should prefer the valid form. If there are two or more plausible interpretations of a text, thesis, or theory, I should prefer the interpretation that is most defensible, all things considered. Robert George illustrates the use of this principle in his criticism of Patrick Devlin's "disintegration thesis":

> My interpretation [of Devlin] is preferable [to that of H. L. A. Hart] not because it better accords with what Devlin said but because it renders Devlin's case more compelling (without ignoring or in any way distorting what he said). I appeal to the following canon of interpretation: select among equally plausible interpretations of a text that interpretation under which the position taken or argument made in the text is more plausible.[12]

I take it that the insistence on charity is a ground-norm of philosophy (although not of other disciplines, professions, and occupations, such as law and politics). To be a philosopher, I submit, *just is* to be charitable in these ways.[13]

Here is an example of uncharitableness in which the target, or victim, is feminist philosophy. In her 1994 essay, "The Market for Feminist Epistemology," Harriet Baber[14] criticizes what has come to be known as "feminist epistemology." Although she does not explicitly define "feminism," it is clear from her discussion that it concerns "benefits" and "harms" to women. The assumption seems to be that the goal of feminism is to benefit women (or, at a minimum, to keep them from being harmed).[15] Baber's conclusion is that feminist epistemology harms women. It is therefore, by her definition, not properly feminist. Why, then, do feminists propound such a theory? Because, Baber says, it benefits *them* (at the expense of women generally). As Baber explains it, "women in business and in the sciences stood to gain by promoting the idea that there were uniquely feminine talents and 'management styles' since these were an entrée into management and the professions that they would not otherwise have had. . . . Rhetorically, it was effective to promote the idea that hiring women was 'good business.'"[16]

The problem, according to Baber, is that what benefits some women in the short run can, and in this case does, harm all women—even the short-run beneficiaries—in the long run. Feminist epistemology postulates psychological (including cognitive, affective, and conative) differences between the sexes. These differences, Baber says, are not real; they are "myths," "dogmas," "superstitions," and "stereotypes." Women who "buy into" these "falsehoods" unwittingly perpetuate them, to the detriment of women who fail to conform. A woman who wishes to climb the corporate ladder alongside her male colleagues may find herself disadvantaged by assumptions made by her superiors. She will be assumed to be nurturing, uncompetitive, or risk-averse, for example, when she is none of these. The cumulative effect of such stereotyping is to devalue women's capacities. "Academic women in particular lose insofar as the growing industry of 'feminist scholarship' facilitates the construction of academic pink-collar ghettoes" (419).

The most insidious effect of feminist epistemology (or feminist philosophy generally) is what it does to the women who deviate from the stereotype. Baber explains:

> [T]he visibility of "feminist philosophy," including "feminist epistemology," makes it difficult for women in the profession to avoid guilt by association unless they actively distance themselves from this enterprise by ignoring issues that concern women, remaining aloof from women's organizations in the profession and even by denying that they are feminists. These seem to me to be some of the worst consequences of the rise of "feminist philosophy." . . . Worst of all, "feminist philosophy" has provided grist for the mill of conservatives in the profession—including some who claim to be feminists—who lampoon it in order to exploit anti-feminist backlash. (420–21)

The conclusion Baber draws from this is that anyone who cares about women—anyone who wishes to prevent harm to women, anyone who wishes to promote women's interests—should oppose feminist philosophy. It is "motivated by unsubstantiated assumptions about psychological differences between men and women," assumptions that are "detrimental to women's interests."

This is an interesting argument. What makes it fascinating as well as interesting is that Baber considers herself a feminist. How could a feminist have such disparaging things to say about feminist philosophy and feminist epistemology? The answer, of course, is that feminism is no monolith. Baber is a liberal feminist. Those she criticizes are, for lack of a better term, radical feminists. Liberals and radicals have different theories or understandings of human nature.[17] In fact, this goes to the root of Baber's lack of charitableness. Baber denies the radical thesis that there are innate (i.e., nonsocial) differences between the sexes. She devotes a large portion of her essay to supporting this denial. For example, she says that "Such theories [of innate sex difference] are highly speculative and do not appear to be confirmed by empirical data which suggest that those psychological and behavioral differences which do exist are explained not by early development and relation with one's primary care-taker so much as by one's current situation in life— and that, far from being deeply entrenched and virtually ineradicable, they are subject to modification" (408).[18]

One of Baber's targets is Carol Gilligan. "Gilligan's research methods," she says, "were flawed and her results were disconfirmed by subsequent research" (406). Gilligan, as is well known, heard distinct moral "voices" as she conducted her research on moral development, and reported that, while not all male subjects speak in the "justice" voice and not all female subjects speak in the "care" voice, that is nonetheless the pattern or tendency. Boys and men are oriented to, and think in terms of, rights, rules, and respect, while girls and women are oriented to, and think in terms of, responsibilities, relationships, and roles. Baber quotes Carol Tavris to the effect that, "In study after study, researchers report no average differences in the kind of moral reasoning that men and women apply" (406). She concludes from this not that men and women have a common (human) nature (although she believes that they do), but that the thesis of a *different* nature lacks empirical support. "At the very least," Baber writes, "the theses about psychological differences between men and women which [Alison] Jaggar and others believe to have been 'demonstrated' and which have become commonplaces in pop psychology and self-help literature, have not been established" (407).

Where is the uncharitableness in this picture? Where, to be precise, has Baber substituted an implausible for a plausible premise or rendered an argument invalid rather than valid? Recall the structure of Baber's critical argument. She says that feminist epistemology *falsely* postulates sex-based psychological (including epistemic) differences. These "differences," when institutionalized in the form of dogmas, myths, or stereotypes, may benefit some women, or even many women in the short run, but they work to the disadvantage of all women in the long run. Unfortunately, the only version of the feminist difference thesis that Baber considers is that of Gilligan—as if anyone who believes that men and women have different psychologies must rest such a belief on Gilligan's research. The problem is that Gilligan offered no theoretical *explanation* of her findings. Specifically, she did not assert either that the differences are biological in origin or that they are social in origin (or some combination of the two). What Baber overlooks is a large and rapidly expanding body of scientific work that not only identifies and describes sex-based differences but purports to explain them. I refer to evolutionary psychology.

Before examining the data of this field, let me make a conceptual point. Philosophers, as such, have neither theoretical nor factual expertise. This does not mean that a philosopher cannot appeal to the facts (i.e., to how things are) in support of a conclusion. It means that the philosopher is in the same situation as everyone else, namely, beholden to experts (or to common sense). If I, a philosopher, make an empirical claim in, say, biology, I must support it by citing appropriate biological authorities.[19] Baber, as we saw, rejects the factual claim that men and women differ psychologically. Any evidence for sex-based differences, such as women's over-representation in nurturing professions, or men's over-representation in mathematical or scientific fields, is also evidence, in her view, for differential socialization. The implication is that no evidence supports sex-based differences. Is this correct? Or rather, is it *obviously* correct, such that any feminist who believes otherwise is laboring under a stereotype (or perpetuating a myth, or disseminating a dogma)?

It is not obviously correct. There is by now, and was at the time Baber's essay was written, a large body of empirical work on the topic of sex-based psychological (including cognitive and epistemic) differences. Kingsley Browne, a law professor with biological training, summarizes the research:

> One of the leading insights of the recent scholarship is confirmation of the popular view that there are substantial psychological differences between men and women. But the public-policy literature, whilst conceding a difference in reproductive biology, largely ignores sex differences that extend to temperament and behavior. The prevailing view in the social sciences is that any behavioral sex differences that exist are products of differences in child-rearing practices and cultural influences. Yet the anthropological literature alone demonstrates a remarkable cross-cultural consistency in the sex differences under consideration, and the biological and psychological literatures are bulging with data revealing robust differences between the sexes. This literature suggests that we may have been confusing cause and effect; our patriarchal social structure—to the extent we have one—may be more an effect of sex differences than their cause.[20]

Among the differences to be accounted for, and of which there is at present ample documentation, are the following. Statistically speaking, men are more aggressive and competitive than women; they devote far more resources (time, energy, and attention) to status-seeking; and they engage in more kinds and a greater degree of risk-taking activity. Women, by contrast, are more nurturing, more empathetic, and less single-minded than men in the pursuit of their aims.[21] "In sum," Browne writes, "males and females have grossly different temperamental styles. Men tend to be competitive, while women tend to be more co-operative. Men want to be at the top of a dominance hierarchy, while women seek to cement less-stratified social relations."[22]

There should be little question, by this time, that men and women differ psychologically. The only questions are why and what, normatively, follows from it (if anything). Evolutionary psychologists say that the differences are largely (although not exclusively) genetic. Just as body shape, size, and function are the products of natural selection, so are behavior and thought (by which I mean cognition [i.e., belief], conation [desire], and sentiment or affect [feeling]). The mind, we might say, has adapted to its environment.[23] Ultimately, men's and women's differential psychology is a function (or result) of differential sex strategies. What a man feels, how he thinks, what motivates him, what attracts and repulses him, are precisely those things that enhanced his reproductive success in the ancestral environment. The same is true of women. The behavioral and psychological differences that we observe are precisely those that evolutionary psychology predicts.[24] This branch of biology may be in its infancy, but it has already given us a rich and suggestive explanation of what we find.

The striking thing about Baber's essay, from a philosophical point of view, is her failure to engage, or even to mention, this body of literature. Therein lies the uncharitableness of which I spoke. Had she engaged the literature and sought to challenge it on its own grounds (by marshaling her own authorities), or drawn congenial conclusions from it, the scent of unfairness that surrounds her essay would dissipate. Let us pursue this suggestion. What effect would acceptance of the findings and explanations of evolutionary psychology have on Baber's critical argument? What difference, if any, would it make if we not only accepted that men and women differ, psychologically, but agreed that these differences have a genetic or biological basis (perhaps reinforced or augmented by social structures)? Would it be a net harm to women?

The answer depends on which aspects of our social world we take to be "up for grabs." If we accept the workplace as it is, namely, as a competitive, hierarchical environment, then women, who, by hypothesis, are less competitive than men, will fare poorly (or not as well) in it. But why should feminists accept the workplace as it is? If the workplace works to the advantage of men and to the disadvantage of women, given their natures, then equality would seem to require that the workplace be transformed. This brings us back to the distinction between liberal and radical feminism. Baber is a liberal feminist if she is a feminist at all. Since, qua liberal, she believes that men and women have a common (human) nature, and not separate male and female natures, she sees no problem with the workplace as it is. Women, in her view, are able to function in that environment as well as men do, *provided* they are not socialized, as they usually are, to be uncompetitive. Baber's conception of equality is formal. Treating individuals equally, in her view, consists in treating them in accordance with their respective natures. But men and women have a common (human) nature, so they must be treated the same.

The radical feminist conceives of equality differently. Equality, to the radical, is substantive, not formal.[25] First we decide what we want to equalize (and why); then we adopt policies that are calculated to achieve it. Suppose we want men and women to have an equal opportunity for both a challenging, remunerative career and a fulfilling family life. We do not, in pursuing this objective, ignore their different natures. Rather, we see to it that their different natures do not *make a difference* in their employment prospects. We ensure, for example, that women who choose to bear and rear children are not thereby disadvantaged vis-à-vis their male colleagues. For consider: If a man doesn't have to choose between, or make trade-offs concerning, career

and family, why should a woman? What forces the choice on women, as
things stand, is the way the workplace is configured. But this configuration
is not inevitable; it is contingent and changeable. The radical, in short, questions what the liberal takes for granted. The radical (as the name implies)
wishes to destroy inequality at its *root*. The liberal leaves the root intact while
trimming—repeatedly—the undesirable stems, leaves, and fruit.

Baber's mistake is a common one. Peter Singer could have been talking
about her when he wrote the following words more than a quarter of a century ago:

> The appropriate response to those who claim to have found evidence of
> genetically-based differences in ability between the races or sexes is not to
> stick to the belief that the genetic explanation must be wrong, whatever evi-
> dence to the contrary may turn up: instead we should make it quite clear that
> the claim to equality does not depend on intelligence, moral capacity, physical
> strength, or similar matters of fact. Equality is a moral ideal, not a simple asser-
> tion of fact. There is no logically compelling reason for assuming that a factual
> difference in ability between two people justifies any difference in the amount
> of consideration we give to satisfying their needs and interests. The principle
> of the equality of human beings is not a description of an alleged actual equal-
> ity among humans: it is a prescription of how we should treat humans.[26]

Singer's immediate concern was the argument that because there are factual
differences (such as intelligence) between humans and animals, the principle of equality cannot be extended to animals. But the logic of his response
applies to any sort of factual difference, whether genetic or environmental
(or a combination of the two). Morally speaking, it doesn't *matter* whether
men and women are the same or different, environmentally *or* genetically.
Baber and other liberal feminists would do well to heed Singer's advice, to
wit: "It would be folly for the opponent of racism [or sexism] to stake his [or
her] whole case on a dogmatic commitment to one particular outcome of a
difficult scientific issue which is still a long way from being settled."[27]

I said earlier that I do not wish to engage Baber on the merits, and it may
seem that I have done so. So let me be clear: My aim is not to refute her (although it should be clear that we disagree), but to show that she is unfair to
those she criticizes. She is unfair because there is an interpretation of feminist epistemology that is superior to that which she provides and criticizes.
She has attacked a straw person. I have shown that feminist epistemologists
need not rest their belief in sex-based psychological differences on socialization. As Browne says, socialization, which is a real phenomenon, may itself reflect and reinforce underlying biological processes. It may be (to use
philosophical jargon) an epiphenomenon or emergent property.

Had Baber engaged the biological literature, and specifically the burgeoning literature of evolutionary psychology,[28] and had she not been in the grip

of a liberal ideology that refuses to see equality in anything but a formal way, she would have realized that the issue is not factual but normative. The issue is not *whether* men and women differ,[29] or even *why*, but what should be *done* about the differences, given a commitment to (and a proper understanding of) equality. It is as if Baber begins with the proposition (curiously unquestioned) that the workplace is fair and just, conjoins it with the premise that women fare badly in that environment when they are viewed as being different from men, and concludes that women should *not* be viewed as different from men. Since feminist epistemology asserts that women *are* different from men, she concludes that feminist epistemology must be rejected. This, with all due respect, is tortured (and tortuous) reasoning.[30]

Let us turn Baber's argument on its head. Baber says that those who postulate sex-based differences harm women (albeit unwittingly). Some women may gain, or gain in the short run, but all women lose in the long run. What if Baber's factual premise is false? That is to say, what if evolutionary psychology is correct in its assertion that there are, as well as in its explanation of why there are, sex-based differences?[31] Then applying a single (male) standard to all women works to the disadvantage of most of them! By expecting women to conform to the norms of the male workplace, Baber ensures, perversely, that many or most of them will fail.[32] Those who do not fail may be miserable or frustrated in their success, since they have had to become something, or pretend to be something, that they are not. To be sure, some women may succeed in this environment, but these will be the exceptional (male-identified, male-biographied) women. Baber, whether she realizes it or not, valorizes the masculine. Perhaps she and other women can thrive in a male world, but it hardly follows that all women can do so, much less that they should have to try.[33]

To summarize this section: I am not asserting the truth of evolutionary psychology. But neither am I denying it. In fact, I accept it as the best account of the facts. I also believe that it is compatible with feminism (although not liberal feminism). My argument is therefore conditional in nature. Given the truth of evolutionary psychology, Baber's argument collapses. Of course, if evolutionary psychology were obviously false, this would not be a problem. But it is not obviously false. It is a plausible, viable, and attractive theory, scientifically speaking. Thus, there are two interpretations of feminist epistemology, one plausible (that which is rooted in evolutionary psychology) and one implausible (that which is rooted in Gilligan's work). Baber's uncharitableness—the thesis of this section—consists in ignoring the plausible interpretation.[34]

THE DOUBLE STANDARD

Judge not, that you be not judged. For with that judgment you judge, you will be judged; and with the *same* measure you use, it will be measured back to you.[35]

So much for lack of charity. If there is a distinctively philosophical vice, this is it. A second form in which the backlash against feminist philosophy occurs is the application of a double standard.[36] The perpetrator in this case applies one standard (a strenuous one) to feminist work and another (a lenient or less-strenuous one) to nonfeminist work. The exemplary piece here is a 1999 essay by Alan Soble,[37] "Bad Apples: Feminist Politics and Feminist Scholarship."[38] Soble's aim in this essay is to propound—and to go some way toward confirming—what he calls a "hypothesis," viz., "that political commitment undermines scholarship" (356). His specific target, as the subtitle suggests, is "feminist scholarship." While admitting that feminist scholars have "exposed sexist bias in the humanities and sciences" (356), and while noting that "there is, of course, good feminist scholarship" (377), he nonetheless concludes that some (much? most?) of it is bad. The bad feminist scholars are, presumably, the "bad apples" of his title.

Soble devotes 21 pages of his essay—84 percent of the text—to an examination of the work of five scholars: Ruth Bleier, Ruth Hubbard, Susan Bordo, Sandra Harding, and Rae Langton. Other scholars (such as Catharine MacKinnon and Martha Nussbaum) come in for criticism in passing, but these five are his focus. Bleier and Hubbard are taken to task for misquoting the sociologist David Barash. Bordo is chastised for failing to document certain empirical claims and for "misdescribing" (365) a case on which she relied. Harding is condemned for failing to "provide accurate citations" (367) to work she discussed. Langton's academic sin consisted of "relying uncritically on popular feminist literature, which detracts from the quality of her scholarly work" (370). The published writings of these scholars (and, by implication, others) exemplify what Soble calls "negligence" (375), "sloppiness" (376), and "carelessness" (366, 376) (even "dramatic carelessness" [356]), although sometimes he suggests something more sinister, namely, recklessness and purposiveness. In each case, Soble writes, the best explanation for the lack of care is "political commitment" (363). In their zeal to promote feminism, these writers have compromised their scholarly integrity and principles. He concludes by calling upon social scientists to investigate the matter—"not to condemn feminist scholarship but to ferret out some causes of bad research, knowledge of which could improve scholarship in all areas" (356).

The first thing to observe is that, by Soble's own admission, he has not examined a representative sample of feminist scholars or scholarship. He says that he came across the aforementioned "examples of carelessness in feminist scholarship by accident, guided by [his] natural scholarly curiosity" (377).[39] Then, sheepishly, he admits: "I have not carried out a controlled investigation of the relative incidence of carelessness in the academic work of feminists" (377). So it would be fallacious of Soble (or anyone else) to infer from the fact (if it is a fact) that Bleier et al. are careless scholars that feminists *in general* (the superset of which these are a subset) are careless scholars. One bad apple, after all, doesn't spoil the whole bunch.

But let us suppose, for the sake of argument, that feminist scholarship is bad. Let us suppose, that is, that feminist scholars *in general,* and not just the five observed, exhibit the intellectual vices of negligence, carelessness, and sloppiness. (These may be one vice with three names rather than three vices, but since Soble uses all three terms, so do I.) What would that show? The answer is "Nothing." For nonfeminist scholarship may be no better, or even worse, than we are supposing feminist scholarship to be.[40] This raises the question: Has Soble examined any other body of scholarship? If so, he has not published the results of it; nor does he make any comparisons between or among bodies of scholarship in the essay under consideration. For all we know, Christian scholars, Marxist scholars, libertarian scholars, even liberal scholars such as Soble and Baber may misquote, fail to document, mis-cite, and rely uncritically on popular authors, and for the same hypothesized reason, namely, that they are in the grip of ideology (what Soble calls "political commitment").

I call this an example of the double standard because, whether he is conscious of it or not, Soble is applying one standard to feminist scholarship and another to nonfeminist scholarship. By not offering comparisons, he implies that feminist scholarship is *worse* than other types; but all he has shown (again, assuming this for the sake of argument) is that feminist scholarship is *bad*. How bad? That depends. Anything short of perfection can be viewed as bad, but since no body of scholarship is perfect, every type of scholarship is on a par with every other. The point is: Unless and until comparisons are made, it is premature and unfair to evaluate feminist scholarship—either adversely *or* favorably. To apply a standard of perfection to feminist scholarship but not to other types of scholarship is to let those others off the critical hook.

Another problem with Soble's reasoning is his unanalyzed notion of "feminism." Suppose he is correct that the five observed scholars are negligent, and suppose also, as he does, that all five are feminists. What entitles him to assume that it is the scholars' *feminism* (or feminist political commitment) that accounts for their negligence? Each scholar, after all, is many things besides a feminist. Each is a woman, for example. Is Soble calling for a social-scientific investigation of the effect of one's *sex* on one's propensity to make errors? The worst instance of this fallacy (for that is what it is) is Soble's backhanded (underhanded?) criticism of Martha Nussbaum. In the final section of his essay, he points out that "Other scholars [besides him] have found similar curiosities [read: errors] in feminist writings" (377). The note to this passage reads as follows: "See Sommers (1996); Carol Iannone (1989); Alan Dershowitz (1994, 33–37); Kenneth Lasson (1992); and, on Martha Nussbaum's white-out escapade, Daniel Mendelsohn (1996)" (383 n. 50).

Soble is referring to an exchange between Nussbaum and John Finnis. His note suggests that Nussbaum's *feminism,* rather than some other aspect of her identity, is responsible for "the white-out escapade." But why should this be? The exchange (I have read it carefully) had nothing to do with feminism. It was about the interpretation of ancient Greek texts dealing with homosexuality (and ultimately about norms of scholarship).[41] Besides being a feminist, Nussbaum is an Aristotelian (she often uses the expression "neo-Aristotelian" to mark the fact that she departs from Aristotle in certain important respects), a classicist, an internationalist, and a liberal.[42] Why does her "abuse of scholarship" (to use Finnis's term, and to assume its accuracy) stem from, and therefore count against, her *feminism?* Isn't it just as plausible to infer that her Aristotelianism or her liberalism got the better of her? Soble, I am afraid, is doing precisely what he accuses Bleier et al. of doing, namely, seeing "what [he] want[s] to see and . . . not look[ing] for what [he doesn't] want to find" (377).[43]

This, with all due respect to Soble, is hypocrisy, which, as the quoted verses from Matthew imply, is the application of a double standard when one of the parties is oneself. Matthew is often interpreted (by my students, for example) to mean that one should not judge. What it says, however, is that *when* one judges (contemplating that this will—and may—occur), one should be prepared to be judged by that very standard. A hypocrite is a person who does not practice what he or she preaches, someone who says one thing but does another, someone who is two-faced. Not to be flippant, but if Nussbaum cheated on her income tax, betrayed a friend, or accepted a bribe from a student, would it be because of her feminism? By the same token, is Soble's condemnation of feminist scholarship caused by a "political commitment" to patriarchy, sexism, conservatism, or antifeminism? This inference is not just distasteful; it is illogical.[44]

BULLYISM

bully: A blustering 'gallant'; a bravo, hector, or 'swash-buckler'; now, *esp.* a tyrannical coward who makes himself a terror to the weak.[45]

A third form of backlash, related to but subtly different from the second, consists in "picking on" or "bullying" feminism.[46] The exemplar of this class (there are, unfortunately, many) is Iddo Landau.[47] According to *The Philosopher's Index,* Landau has published fifteen philosophical essays.[48] Seven of these essays—almost half of his scholarly output—are about feminism, and all seven are critical of it.[49] For example, he has challenged the idea of feminist epistemology,[50] denied the "androcentricity" (male-centeredness) of Western philosophy,[51] argued that much feminist research is biased,[52] defended Francis Bacon from the charge that his metaphors are sexist,[53] repudiated a feminist definition of "sexual harassment,"[54] and, most recently, alleged that feminist research on sexual harassment is biased.[55]

No self-respecting feminist scholar, whether liberal, radical, or otherwise, wishes to avoid criticism. It is the lifeblood of academia. But scholarly criticism goes hand in hand with—or *should* go hand in hand with—constructive work. I agree, therefore, with Richard Posner that "It is easier to find the holes in other people's work than to build a durable structure of one's own. But a merely critical approach lacks staying power; and even devastating criticisms fail to devastate when the critic has nothing to offer in the place of the ruins that he wishes to make."[56] I think it is fair to say that Landau has done nothing (or next to nothing) to advance the feminist cause. He has done much, regrettably, to retard it. Had he published at least one essay in which he defends a feminist ideal, clarifies a feminist concept, or responds to a critic of feminism, his credentials as a feminist might be plausible. As it is, they are suspect. (He says, at one point, "I nowhere object to feminism; I consider myself a liberal feminist."[57])

Note what I am not doing. I am not questioning the soundness of Landau's arguments against feminism. (I am not endorsing their soundness, either.) Nor am I claiming (as in the case of Soble) that Landau applies a double standard, evaluating feminist scholarship by a different (i.e., more stringent) standard than other scholarship. (Indeed, I have not read his other work; some of it is on Jacques Derrida, whose writing, frankly, I find incomprehensible.)[58] I am questioning his single-minded zeal in challenging feminist research, methods, definitions, and claims. Even if his criticisms were sound, and even if he would apply the same critical standards to other sorts of work, the fact is that he has not. He seems obsessed with feminism, eager to pick it apart, uninterested in making it better than it is. He is, in short, a bully. Unless and until he publishes essays that are favorable to feminism, or that defend it from its critics, his credentials as a feminist must be questioned. Worse, he must be viewed as an agent of the backlash against feminist philosophy.[59]

Let me propose a sincerity test. Those who criticize feminist work can show their good faith in either of two ways: first, by doing constructive feminist work; second, by criticizing other bodies of work besides feminism—while using the same standards. Ideally, one should do both. Landau does neither. He has, to my knowledge, published no constructive feminist work; nor has he done any other criticizing. It is as if he reserves his criticism for feminism. I should add that while neither Baber nor Soble has done constructive feminist work, each has deployed his or her critical skills in other areas. Soble, for example, has challenged certain Marxist accounts of pornography, while Baber has criticized Kierkegaard and condemned dwarf-tossing.[60]

What can (and should) be done about the likes of Landau? I believe that feminists should ignore him. At least one feminist, Susan Mendus, has engaged him in print. This will only encourage him in his bullying ways. I realize that the tendency of scholars is to join issue with, or debate, their critics, and usually this is salutary, but when one shows no willingness to engage in constructive work, or even constructive criticism, a dire solution is appropriate. Please note that I am not advocating censorship. Landau has every legal and moral right to publish his bullying work (provided he does not defame anyone). But, by the same token, feminists have every legal and moral right, and maybe a moral duty, to ignore it. A scholar without an audience is . . . a diarist. Landau may find that in order to secure uptake for his biased and mean-spirited proclamations, he must (1) cease his bullying tactics and (2) demonstrate that he is genuinely committed to, and therefore concerned to promote, the feminist cause. He should make good his claim to being a feminist.

I would like to make a final comment about Landau's (and Baber's) "feminism." This may be blasphemous, but what is *feminist* about liberal feminism? Let me put my criticism in the form of a dilemma. Either there are psychological (and corresponding behavioral) differences between men and women or there are not. If there are such differences, as our best theories (viz., evolutionary biology and psychology) suggest, then applying a single "neutral" standard to them, as liberals advocate, thwarts, rather than promotes, sexual equality (especially when, as is usually the case, the standard conforms to and reflects male biography). Catharine MacKinnon makes the point well:

> On my reading, sex discrimination—this law under which we are offered a chance to assert equality with men—offers women two routes to sex equality. The primary avenue views women as if we were men. It measures our similarity with men to see if we are or can be men's equals. This standard is called the equality rule. It is considered gender-neutral, abstract, neutral, principled, essentially procedural and objective. I will argue that it substantively embraces masculinity, the male standard for men, and applies it to women. The second approach available under sex discrimination doctrine views women as men view women: in need of special protection, help, or indulgence. To make out a case, complainants have to meet the male standard for women: femininity.[61]

The second route to sexual "equality"—paternalism—is clearly unacceptable, so I will say no more about it. But the first is also problematic, as MacKinnon goes on to explain:

> Women who wish to step out of women's traditional relations with men and become abstract persons, to be exceptional to women's condition rather than to receive the protections of it, are treated as if we are seeking to be like men, without any realization that that concedes the gender of the standard. Women who seek to meet this standard under sex discrimination doctrine are served equality with a vengeance. To win sex discrimination cases under the equality rubric, athletes, academic women, professional women, blue-collar women, and military

women, for instance, have to meet the male standard: the standard that men are trained and prepared for socially as men. [One might add: "and that is rooted in biology."] They tell us no, it's not a male standard, it is just *the* standard. If you protest that, they say measure up or get out.[62]

Fortunately, these are not the only two routes to sexual equality. A third route, which MacKinnon endorses, is substantive equality without condescension, an application of what might be called the anti-subordination principle. The objective is to ensure that differences between men and women, such as they are (and whether they be social or biological [or both] in origin), do not work to the disadvantage of women. Its aim is to destroy existing sex-based hierarchies and to keep new hierarchies from forming.[63]

That is the first horn of the aforementioned dilemma. Suppose now that there are *not* psychological (and corresponding behavioral) differences between men and women (i.e., that men and women are psychologically indistinguishable). Then applying a single "neutral" standard to them does indeed promote sexual equality. But why is this *feminism?* It is more accurately called "humanism," since the traits in question are common to all humans regardless of sex. In neither case, therefore, is the label "feminism" appropriate. Liberal feminism, pace Nussbaum, Baber, and Landau, is simply liberalism applied to the issue of sexual difference. Accordingly, these individuals should refer to themselves as liberals (simpliciter) or as humanists, not as liberal feminists, even if their arguments have the effect of improving the lot of women. Their scholarly work, as I have shown, does nothing to advance the cause of women *as women,* which, I should think, is the sine qua non of feminism.[64]

CONCLUSION

I have described and illustrated three ways in which feminist philosophy is victimized by backlash. The three ways are uncharitableness, application of a double standard, and (for lack of a better word) bullyism.[65] These are by no means the only ways in which the movement to promote equality between the sexes is retarded or arrested. I leave to other philosophers, and to scholars generally, the task of completing and refining the typology. The pessimist in me says, however, that the typology will never be complete (in the sense of jointly exhaustive). As long as even one person has an interest in thwarting sexual equality, which is to say as long as *anyone* has a stake in the sexist status quo, there will be attempts to undermine and defeat feminism—to throw a wrench, as it were, into the feminist works. This may be discouraging, but it is also, strangely, empowering, for to be forewarned is to be forearmed.

NOTES

This essay is dedicated to my beloved canine companion, Ginger, who died unexpectedly—at a mere seven years of age—on Thanksgiving Day, 2000. She was indomitable, but her little body succumbed to a malignant lung tumor. Nobody who has not lived with, played with, cared for, learned from, laughed at, and loved a dog, especially a beautiful, sensitive, and intelligent dog such as Ginger, can understand the depth of my grief. My philosophical colleagues must not be insulted when I say that I learned more about virtue, character, and integrity from Ginger than from all of their abstruse reasonings. I love you, Ginger.

1. *Oxford English Dictionary*, 2nd ed., s.v. "back-lash." The word was first used (without the hyphen) in 1815. It appears to have acquired a figurative (i.e., nonmechanical) meaning in 1929.

2. *Merriam-Webster's Collegiate Dictionary*, 10th ed., s.v. "backlash" (italics in original).

3. *Oxford American Dictionary*, s.v. "lash."

4. It is not unusual for a term to be exported from one context to another, or, more specifically, from a technical to a nontechnical context. The term "stereotype," for example, was coined by printers (typesetters) in the late 1700s. *Oxford English Dictionary*, s.v. "stereotype" (giving 1798 as the date of first use). "Stereo" means solid, so a stereotype is a solid type/plate/mold, as opposed to one containing individual characters. Metaphorically speaking, a stereotype (of, say, homosexuals) is "an idea or character etc. that is standardized in a conventional form without individuality." *Oxford American Dictionary*, s.v. "stereotype." For a discussion of the nature and function of stereotypes, see Richard D. Mohr, *Gays/Justice: A Study of Ethics, Society, and Law* (New York: Columbia University Press, 1988), 22–27.

5. I am not suggesting that individual men cannot, or do not, consciously and intentionally oppress women. Clearly, they can, and some, unfortunately, do. I am saying that the backlash against women does not consist in, or is not exhausted by, these acts. The machine metaphor brings out the mindlessness and "everydayness" of oppression. See Ann E. Cudd, "Analyzing Backlash to Progressive Social Movements," *The American Philosophical Association Newsletter on Feminism and Philosophy* 99 (fall 1999): 42–46, at 45. [Chapter 1]

6. One example. In the preface of his 1993 book, *Essays on Bioethics* (Oxford: Clarendon Press), the eminent moral philosopher R. M. Hare writes: "Many of the papers [constituting the volume] were written before 'non-sexist' language (so called) became 'politically correct.' I have not altered them in this respect, although more recently I have found a way of conforming which is stylistically just tolerable. The contortions which would have been necessary to make the older papers conform illustrate very well what the feminists are doing to our style" (vi). Hare is notorious for insisting that morality, as such, is overriding. Thus, if a moral principle conflicts with an aesthetic principle or with a principle of etiquette, the moral principle prevails. See, e.g., R. M. Hare, *Freedom and Reason* (Oxford: Oxford University Press, 1963), sec. 9.3; R. M. Hare, *Moral Thinking: Its Levels, Method, and Point* (Oxford: Clarendon Press, 1981), sec. 3.6. But stylistic considerations are aesthetic in nature, so Hare must either (1) not believe that writing *can* be sexist, (2) not believe that *his* writing *is* sexist, or (3) not believe that sexism is wrong.

7. Bashing is related to, but different from, backlashing. Unfortunately, I cannot explore the similarities or differences here. For an interesting essay on bashing, see Susan H. Williams and David C. Williams, "A Feminist Theory of Malebashing," *Michigan Journal of Gender and Law* 4 (1996): 35–127.

8. By "credentialed," I mean having formal training and advanced degrees in the field. All three individuals are members of the American Philosophical Association. Baber and Soble are regular members and Landau an international associate (i.e., nonvoting) member. See *Proceedings and Addresses of the American Philosophical Association* 74 (November 2000): 229, 327, 402.

9. Cressida Heyes implies that only men can be backlashers when she writes that "The agents of backlash are sometimes individuals—male philosophers threatened by political theories that portray them in an unflattering light, for example." Cressida J. Heyes, "The Backlash against Feminist Scholars and Scholarship: Introduction," *The American Philosophical Association Newsletter on Feminism and Philosophy* 99 (fall 1999): 36–40, at 36. Heyes also implies that only women can be feminists (37). Both propositions are false. The second, besides being false, is regrettable, since it is likely to antagonize and alienate feminist men.

10. Zachary Seech, *Writing Philosophy Papers,* 3rd ed. (Belmont, Calif.: Wadsworth/Thomson Learning, 2000), 16. For a review of this and two similar works, see Keith Burgess-Jackson, review of *Philosophical Writing: An Introduction,* 2nd ed., by A. P. Martinich; *Writing Philosophy Papers,* 2nd ed., by Zachary Seech; and *Thinking and Writing about Philosophy,* by Hugo Bedau, *Teaching Philosophy* 20 (December 1997): 430–37.

11. Simon Blackburn, *The Oxford Dictionary of Philosophy* (Oxford: Oxford University Press, 1994), 62. See my review of this book in *Teaching Philosophy* 21 (March 1998): 75–80.

12. Robert P. George, *Making Men Moral: Civil Liberties and Public Morality* (Oxford: Clarendon Press, 1993), 65. George not only applies this principle; he criticizes others for violating it. He says, for example, that Ronald Dworkin "is frequently guilty of presenting and rebutting not the better, more finely nuanced cases for moral paternalism, but crude or caricatured cases" (105). Richard Posner invokes a similar principle when he writes: "The broader principle, which applies to the Constitution as much as to a spoken utterance, is that if one possible interpretation of an ambiguous statement would entail absurd or terrible results, that is a good reason to reject it." Richard A. Posner, *Overcoming Law* (Cambridge, Mass., and London: Harvard University Press, 1995), 234.

13. The so-called straw-man fallacy, which every introductory philosophy student learns, institutionalizes this norm. According to one account, "The straw man fallacy is committed when an arguer distorts an opponent's argument for the purpose of more easily attacking it, demolishes the distorted argument, and then concludes that the opponent's real argument has been demolished." Patrick J. Hurley, *A Concise Introduction to Logic,* 7th ed. (Belmont, Calif.: Wadsworth/Thomson Learning, 2000), 129 (bold type omitted); see also Irving M. Copi and Keith Burgess-Jackson, *Informal Logic,* 3rd ed. (Upper Saddle River, N.J.: Prentice Hall, 1996), 106–7 (discussing "straw-person" fallacy).

14. Baber was awarded the Ph.D. degree in philosophy in 1980 by The Johns Hopkins University. Her dissertation was entitled "Person-Stages." She is now a tenured

professor of philosophy at The University of San Diego. (I have two sources for this information. The first is *Dissertation Abstracts Online;* the second is Baber's Internet homepage, which is accessible by means of any Internet search engine.)

15. For a discussion of the various senses of "benefit," one of which (the broad sense) includes forbearance from and prevention of harm, see Joel Feinberg, "Harm to Others," in *The Moral Limits of the Criminal Law*, vol. 1 (New York: Oxford University Press, 1984), 130–50, esp. 139.

16. Harriet Baber, "The Market for Feminist Epistemology," *The Monist* 77 (October 1994): 403–23, at 415. Subsequent references to this essay are in the text, parenthesized.

17. See, e.g., Alison M. Jaggar, *Feminist Politics and Human Nature* (Totowa, N.J.: Rowman & Littlefield, 1983), chaps. 3 and 5. I realize that the terms "liberal" and "radical" are used in different ways. I use them in Jaggar's sense.

18. Baber's main "source" for this information is Carol Tavris, *The Mismeasure of Woman* (New York: Touchstone, 1992).

19. This is, or should be, elementary. See Hugo Bedau, *Thinking and Writing about Philosophy* (Boston: Bedford Books, 1996), 62 ("When confronted by *empirical* assertions in particular disciplines—geography, sociology, chemistry, astronomy, and so on—philosophers, like everyone else, must turn to experts and other resources in those disciplines to determine whether the assertions are true" [italics in original]).

20. Kingsley Browne, *Divided Labours: An Evolutionary View of Women at Work* (New Haven, Conn., and London: Yale University Press, 1999 [1998]), 1–2. Browne documents these claims in his "Suggestions for Further Reading." See, for example, Eleanor E. Maccoby and Carolyn N. Jacklin, *The Psychology of Sex Differences* (Stanford, Calif.: Stanford University Press, 1974); Diane Halpern, *Sex Differences in Cognitive Abilities,* 2nd ed. (Hillsdale, N.J.: Lawrence Erlbaum, 1992); Katharine B. Hoyenga and Kermit T. Hoyenga, *Gender-Related Differences: Origins and Outcomes* (Boston: Allyn and Bacon, 1993). Browne's scholarly work includes the following essays (in chronological order): "Biology, Equality, and the Law: The Legal Significance of Biological Sex Differences," *Southwestern Law Journal* 38 (June 1984): 617–702; "Sex and Temperament in Modern Society: A Darwinian View of the Glass Ceiling and the Gender Gap," *Arizona Law Review* 37 (winter 1995): 971–1106; and "An Evolutionary Perspective on Sexual Harassment: Seeking Roots in Biology Rather than Ideology," *The Journal of Contemporary Legal Issues* 8 (spring 1997): 5–77.

21. I cannot emphasize enough the importance of the qualifying expression "statistically speaking." No biologist claims that all men and no women have any particular characteristic (aside, perhaps, from chromosomes or genitalia). Therefore, it is no objection to what biologists tell us that (1) some women have some of the traits attributed to men or (2) some men have some of the traits attributed to women. Nor is the language of "counterexamples" appropriate here, since we are dealing with generalizations. *There are no counterexamples to generalizations.* Moreover, generalizations can be true. Even *sex-based* generalizations can be true. It is a true generalization—one that no feminist, even Baber, can reasonably deny—that men are taller than women. This means that the average man is taller than the average woman. It does *not* mean that every man is taller than any woman. What biologists are saying

is that it is a true generalization that men are more aggressive and competitive than women. That some women are more aggressive and competitive than some men goes no way toward undermining this generalization, any more than the fact that some women are taller than some men goes any way toward undermining the (true) generalization that men are taller than women. I am indebted to the editors, Ann Cudd and Anita Superson, for encouraging me to elaborate this point. They should not be assumed to agree with it.

22. Browne, *Divided Labours*, 26. Robin West, who, like Browne, is a law professor, has made similar generalizations about men and women, although her generalizations are (1) not explicitly grounded in empirical research and (2) not given a theoretical explanation. See Robin West, "Jurisprudence and Gender," *The University of Chicago Law Review* 55 (winter 1988): 1–72. I should point out that West cannot be dismissed, as Browne might be, as a male or as a nonfeminist.

23. See the essays in Jerome H. Barkow, Leda Cosmides, and John Tooby, eds., *The Adapted Mind: Evolutionary Psychology and the Generation of Culture* (New York: Oxford University Press, 1992).

24. See, e.g., David M. Buss, "Psychological Sex Differences: Origins through Sexual Selection," *American Psychologist* 50 (March 1995): 164–68; John Marshall Townsend, *What Women Want—What Men Want: Why the Sexes Still See Love and Commitment So Differently* (Oxford: Oxford University Press, 1998).

25. See, e.g., Catharine A. MacKinnon, *Feminism Unmodified: Discourses on Life and Law* (Cambridge, Mass., and London: Harvard University Press, 1987), passim.

26. Peter Singer, "All Animals Are Equal," in *The Right Thing to Do: Basic Readings in Moral Philosophy*, 2nd ed., ed. James Rachels, 207–17, at 212 (Boston: McGraw-Hill College, 1999). This essay was originally published in 1974. For Singer's latest thinking on this topic, see *A Darwinian Left: Politics, Evolution, and Cooperation* (New Haven, Conn., and London: Yale University Press, 2000 [1999]).

27. Singer, "All Animals Are Equal," 211.

28. The best way into this literature is Robert Wright, *The Moral Animal: Evolutionary Psychology and Everyday Life* (New York: Vintage, 1995) (first published as *The Moral Animal: The New Science of Evolutionary Psychology* in 1994).

29. "[T]he question of whether sex differences exist has evolved into the more demanding question of why the sexes sometimes differ considerably and at other times differ moderately or minimally or do not differ at all." Alice H. Eagly, "The Science and Politics of Comparing Women and Men," *American Psychologist* 50 (March 1995): 145–58, at 148; cf. Janet Shibley Hyde and Elizabeth Ashby Plant, "Magnitude of Psychological Gender Differences: Another Side to the Story," *American Psychologist* 50 (March 1995): 159–61 (pointing out that "there is great variability in the magnitude of gender differences across different behaviors" [160], but arguing that "there are more close-to-zero effect sizes for gender differences than for effects in other areas of psychology" [159]).

As these quotations show, Baber is behind the times, scientifically. Eagly, a psychologist, writes: "Despite the meta-analytic evidence (and other types of evidence) showing many consequential sex differences, many feminist empiricists have worked energetically to preserve the 1970s scientific consensus that sex-related differences are null or small. Such a reaction is routine in science: Mere research findings rarely displace an entrenched consensus." Eagly, "The Science and Politics of Comparing

Women and Men," 150. Robert Wright is blunt: "There is not a single well-known feminist who has learned enough about modern Darwinism to pass judgment on it." Robert Wright, "Feminists, Meet Mr. Darwin," *The New Republic* 211 (28 November 1994): 34–46, at 36–37.

30. For a brilliant exposition of the relation between evolutionary psychology and the various types of feminism, see Wright, "Feminists, Meet Mr. Darwin." Here is Wright on liberal feminism: "Some consider the liberal equity feminists the most sober of the major schools of feminism, and [Katha] Pollitt in particular has become known as the voice of calm reason. Yet she and the other mainstream liberals may have the most warped vision in all of feminism. Quite unlike the difference feminists, and more than the radical feminists, they are committed to ignoring basic features of reality. Imagine a social observer as acute as Pollitt [or, one might add, Baber] not sensing how deeply—well, for lack of a better term—*maternal* women are compared with men. That must take a lot of perceptual restraint." Wright, "Feminists, Meet Mr. Darwin, 46 (italics in original). Baber might reply to Wright that women are, indeed, more maternal than men, but insist that the difference is social (i.e., the result of differential socialization) rather than biological. If she took this tack, however, she would have to explain why the difference is universal. Women have been significantly more maternal than men in every known human society.

31. I hope that no reader of this essay believes that evolutionary psychology is incompatible with, much less hostile to, feminism. It might be incompatible with *liberal* feminism, which insists that men and women have a common (human) nature (see, e.g., Jaggar, *Feminist Politics and Human Nature*, 32, 37), but it is not incompatible with *radical* feminism. Indeed, evolutionary psychology is not only consistent with radical feminism (in the bare logical sense); it coheres with it (in the epistemological sense). Law professor Katharine Baker, whose feminist credentials are impeccable, has recently argued as much:

> My argument is that biology's findings can support feminist visions, not that biology necessarily proves that feminist solutions are the correct ones normatively. Biology's claims are descriptive, not normative. If biology proves anything, it is with regard to facts. However, those facts (if proven) are deeply disturbing. Indeed, they are facts that most people, feminist or not, biologist or not, normatively evaluate as inequitable and harsh. It is the law's job to channel that normative evaluation into cultural norms and rules that curb the inequity and harshness. Thus, biology's facts support feminist visions because biology's facts make us keenly aware of how imperative normative visions are.

Katharine K. Baker, "Biology for Feminists," *Chicago-Kent Law Review* 75 (2000): 805–35, at 824 (citations omitted). See also Wright, "Feminists, Meet Mr. Darwin." For a different take on the matter, see R. C. Lewontin, "Women versus the Biologists," *The New York Review of Books* 41 (7 April 1994): 31–35.

To be clear: I am not saying that radical feminists should endorse evolutionary psychology because it serves their purposes. That is to commit Baber's mistake in the other direction. They should endorse it because it's true, or rather, because it's the best account—the best theoretical explanation—of how things are. That it serves radical-feminist purposes by confirming their view of how things are is incidental (but nonetheless welcome). To the extent that liberal feminism and evolutionary psychology conflict, so much the worse for liberal feminism. I might add in passing that just as Thomas Aquinas sought to reconcile his Christian faith with the best science of his day, feminists should try to reconcile their "faith" (i.e., their commitment to sex-based equality) with the best science of their day. The best science of our day is, without question, evolutionary biology (and psychology). Until feminism comes to grips with this body of work, it will lack credibility. As a feminist, I am greatly disturbed by feminist antagonism to evolutionary biology. Has science been used against women? Yes. Must it be? No.

32. According to MacKinnon, "the abstract equality of liberalism permits most women little more than does the substantive inequality of conservatism." Catharine A. MacKinnon, *Feminism Unmodified*, 16. In a later work, MacKinnon noted that "The women that gender neutrality benefits, and there are some, . . . are mostly women who have achieved a biography that somewhat approximates the male norm, at least on paper. They are the qualified, the least of sex discrimination's victims. When they are denied a man's chance, it looks the most like sex bias." Catharine A. MacKinnon, *Toward a Feminist Theory of the State* (Cambridge, Mass.: Harvard University Press, 1989), 225. Note how this fits with what I said earlier about generalizations. A given policy can benefit those women who deviate from a norm even as it harms those who comply with it. MacKinnon's thought is perfectly consistent with evolutionary biology—which is not to say that she has embraced it.

33. Baber, qua liberal, will not like my saying this, but her work on feminist epistemology exemplifies political correctness. Here is Richard Posner: "Another game of faith today is 'political correctness.' If you show a player in that game a sheaf of scientific reports purporting to show that the races or the sexes differ in their potential for doing mathematics, the player will refuse to read them; the empirical investigation of racial and sexual differences is rejected in that game, just as the empirical investigation of planetary motion was rejected by [Cardinal] Bellarmine [who refused to look through Galileo's telescope at the moons of Jupiter]." Posner, *Overcoming Law*, 7. In the same vein is this passage by the philosopher (and, significantly, the feminist) Louise Antony: "The question whether there is anything like human nature is, at least in large part, an empirical issue and is not one that can be settled either by a priori reasoning or by legislation. Failure to acknowledge this opens us [feminists] to the charge of Lysenkoism and plays into pernicious stereotypes of feminists as dangerous loonies, zealots advocating 'politically correct' views at the expense of science and common sense." Louise M. Antony, "Natures and Norms," *Ethics* 111 (October 2000): 8–36, at 9.

The reason Baber will not like my saying this is that liberals tend to think of themselves as neutral, impartial, and "above the fray." They are as critical of "political correctness" as conservatives tend to be. But liberalism, we must not forget, is an ideology (a normative system). Baber, no less than radical feminists, has ideological commitments. The difference may be that radical feminists, but not (certain) liberal feminists, are *aware* of their commitments. It is interesting to note that both Posner and Antony are self-described liberals. Each, however, recognizes a need to come to grips with, and not distort or evade, science.

34. Sometimes, in reading or listening to my fellow feminists, I come across the following (often implicit) line of reasoning: "Even if evolutionary biology (including psychology) is true, it is too dangerous to accept. It not only has been used against women; it probably always will be so used. Therefore, a feminist—someone who

cares for women—should dismiss it (for example, on grounds that it reflects male bias)." I understand the sentiment behind this reasoning. But it must be resisted. I am convinced that in the long run, feminism will fail, and miserably so, if it does not engage and absorb science. What feminists must do is show that how things are (the determination of which falls to science) is a separate question from how they should be (which is the province of morality and law). Even if we assume, for the sake of argument, that biological differences have normative significance, it does not follow that the law may take account of those differences, for, as we have seen, the differences are merely statistical. It is unfair—a violation of the principle of respect for individuals—to prevent women from doing X simply because most women cannot or do not want to do X (or, conversely, to allow men to do X simply because most men can or want to do X). I believe that ordinary people (i.e., nonphilosophers) can grasp these distinctions and arguments. But they need instruction and guidance, especially given what appears to be a natural propensity to commit the naturalistic fallacy (viz., "X is the case; therefore, X ought to be the case"). If feminists devoted half as much energy and creativity to domesticating science as they do to disparaging it, the world would be a better place for women. Again, I am indebted to Ann Cudd and Anita Superson for persuading me that this point needs clarification. This should not, of course, be taken as signaling their agreement with what I say.

35. Matthew 7:1–2 (italics in original).

36. For an illuminating historical treatment of the topic, see Keith Thomas, "The Double Standard," *Journal of the History of Ideas* 20 (April 1959): 195–216.

37. Soble was awarded the Ph.D. degree in philosophy in 1976 by The State University of New York at Buffalo. His dissertation was entitled "Legal Paternalism." He is now a tenured professor of philosophy (and University Research Professor) at The University of New Orleans. (My sources for this information are *Dissertation Abstracts Online* and Soble's Internet homepage.)

38. Alan Soble, "Bad Apples: Feminist Politics and Feminist Scholarship," *Philosophy of the Social Sciences* 29 (September 1999): 354–88. Subsequent references to this essay are in the text (or in the notes), parenthesized.

39. One wonders whether Soble's (and other feminist critics') noticing only certain errors is "a psychological effect of political commitment" (377).

40. Soble suggests as much when he writes: "Feminist treatises, *along with the rest,* are full of extravagant, equivocal propositions; reasoning and evidence are weak; and conventions for quoting and citing sources are abandoned" (355 [emphasis added]). On the following page, he says: "All these social influences have undermined the quality of feminist scholarship, as they have undermined the quality of *all scholarship*" (356 [emphasis added]). Unless I misread these passages, Soble is making a blanket condemnation of contemporary scholarship. Why then has he chosen to criticize only one segment of it? Has he written, or does he plan to write, similar critical essays on other bodies of scholarship, or on scholarship generally? He faces a dilemma: Either feminist scholarship is worse than other types of scholarship or it is not. If it is, then he contradicts what he says in these passages. If it is not, then why the selective treatment?

41. The exchange is intrinsically interesting, so let me direct the curious reader to the literature. The essays, in chronological order, are as follows: John M. Finnis, "Law, Morality, and 'Sexual Orientation,'" *Notre Dame Law Review* 69 (1994): 1049–76; John

Finnis, "'Shameless Acts' in Colorado: Abuse of Scholarship in Constitutional Cases," *Academic Questions* 7 (fall 1994): 10–41; Martha C. Nussbaum, "Platonic Love and Colorado Law: The Relevance of Ancient Greek Norms to Modern Sexual Controversies," *Virginia Law Review* 80 (October 1994): 1515–651; Robert P. George, "'Shameless Acts' Revisited: Some Questions for Martha Nussbaum," *Academic Questions* 9 (winter 1995–96): 24–42; and Daniel Mendelsohn, "The Stand: Expert Witnesses and Ancient Mysteries in a Colorado Courtroom," *Lingua Franca* (September/October 1996): 34–46.

42. See her most recent essays: Martha C. Nussbaum, "Aristotle, Politics, and Human Capabilities: A Response to Antony, Arneson, Charlesworth, and Mulgan," *Ethics* 111 (October 2000): 102–40; and Martha C. Nussbaum, "The Future of Feminist Liberalism," *Proceedings and Addresses of the American Philosophical Association* 74 (November 2000): 47–79.

43. Soble commits the same fallacy with respect to Langton, whom he describes as "smart, well educated, and well read" (377). He points out that, in addition to her feminist-inspired writings, Langton has "written on Kant" (370) and many other subjects. Before attributing Langton's "negligence" to her feminism, shouldn't Soble do a comparative study of *all* of Langton's work, including that on nonfeminist subjects such as Kantian humility, to see whether she commits more errors in her feminist work than in her nonfeminist work? For all we know, Langton's "negligence" crops up everywhere, in all of her work, even when she has no feminist "ax to grind" (as a critic might put it). She may be a careless *person*. But then, this would disconfirm Soble's hypothesis about the "sloppiness" of feminist scholarship, and maybe he does not want disconfirmation.

44. I should point out, for the record, that I read Soble's essay in draft and provided him with written comments. This is why he says, in the final note, that he is indebted to me. In my comments to him, I made most of the points that I make herein. Unfortunately, he took few of them to heart.

45. *Oxford English Dictionary*, s.v. "bully."

46. A bully (noun use) is "a person who uses his strength or power [one might add "status"] to hurt or frighten others." To bully (verb use) is "to behave as a bully toward, to intimidate." *Oxford American Dictionary*, s.v. "bully."

47. Landau was awarded the Ph.D. degree in philosophy in 1991 by McGill University. His dissertation was entitled "The Role of Reflexivity in Philosophical Systems." He is now a senior lecturer in philosophy at The University of Haifa. (My sources for this information are *Dissertation Abstracts Online* and Landau's Internet homepage.)

48. The search was conducted by the author on December 21, 2000, using the online version. I should point out that Landau has published at least one essay in a legal periodical.

49. The percentage of essays devoted to feminism (whether critical or constructive) is much lower for Baber and for Soble than it is for Landau, although I don't have precise figures. Soble has written on a variety of topics, not all of which fall within the broad field of social philosophy. (Some, for example, are in epistemology or the philosophy of science.) Baber, for her part, has written on topics unrelated to feminism. See, e.g., H. E. Baber, "The Ethics of Dwarf-Tossing," *International Journal of Applied Philosophy* 4 (fall 1989): 1–5. This fact, as I go on to show, is relevant to the "bullying" charge, for bullies tend to be obsessed with (i.e., to want to "pick

on") their victims. Baber and Soble appear to be interested in other topics besides feminism.

50. Iddo Landau, "Should There Be Separatist Feminist Epistemologies?" *The Monist* 77 (October 1994): 462–71. Subsequent references to this essay are in the text, parenthesized. Many of the criticisms I made of Baber's essay apply with equal force to this essay by Landau. Both individuals seem oblivious to the scientific findings (and explanations) of sexual difference.

51. Iddo Landau, "How Androcentric Is Western Philosophy?" *The Philosophical Quarterly* 46 (January 1996): 48–59; Iddo Landau, "Mendus on Philosophy and Pervasiveness," *The Philosophical Quarterly* 47 (January 1997): 89–93. The second of these essays is a rejoinder to Susan Mendus, "How Androcentric Is Western Philosophy? A Reply," *The Philosophical Quarterly* 46 (January 1996): 60–66.

52. Iddo Landau, "Good Women and Bad Men: A Bias in Feminist Research," *Journal of Social Philosophy* 28 (spring 1997): 141–50.

53. Iddo Landau, "Feminist Criticisms of Metaphors in Bacon's Philosophy of Science," *Philosophy* 73 (January 1998): 47–61. Interestingly, Soble published an essay on the same topic just two and a half years earlier. See Alan Soble, "In Defense of Bacon," *Philosophy of the Social Sciences* 25 (June 1995): 192–215.

54. Iddo Landau, "On the Definition of Sexual Harassment," *Australasian Journal of Philosophy* 77 (June 1999): 216–23.

55. Iddo Landau, "Is Sexual Harassment Research Biased?" *Public Affairs Quarterly* 13 (July 1999): 241–54.

56. Posner, *Overcoming Law*, viii.

57. Landau, "Mendus on Philosophy and Pervasiveness," 93. Landau seems hurt by Mendus's suggestion that he is non- or antifeminist.

58. For a critique of the unnecessary obscurity of Continental prose, see Keith Burgess-Jackson, review of *The Columbia History of Western Philosophy*, edited by Richard H. Popkin, *Teaching Philosophy* 23 (March 2000): 63–71, at 69–71.

59. Utilitarians provide a good example of constructive critical engagement. When a rule-utilitarian such as Richard B. Brandt criticizes the work of an act-utilitarian such as J. J. C. Smart, or conversely, the aim is ultimately to work out a better version of the theory (or theory-type) to which each is committed. Their squabble is intramural. Another example is the ongoing engagement of liberal and radical feminists. (See, e.g., Rosemarie Tong, *Feminist Thought: A Comprehensive Introduction* [Boulder, Colo.: Westview Press, 1989].) Each attacks the other (i.e., criticizes the other's arguments) while simultaneously defending oneself from the other's attack. (I apologize for the military metaphor. I use it because it is familiar and because it makes the point.) But Landau, despite his arrogation of the label "liberal feminist," has done nothing to work out a plausible liberal feminism, or even to begin such a project. He has built no fort, as it were; hence, he has nothing to defend from attack. Instead, he roams the countryside searching for targets or victims.

60. Kenneth Lasson, a law professor, is an example of someone who has done no constructive feminist work but who has issued sharp critiques—using the same standards—of many disciplines, occupations, and movements. This, whatever his demerits, is to his credit. See his "Scholarship Amok: Excesses in the Pursuit of Truth and Tenure," *Harvard Law Review* 103 (February 1990): 926–50; "Feminism Awry: Excesses in the Pursuit of Rights and Trifles," *Journal of Legal Education* 42 (March

1992): 1–29; "Lawyering Askew: Excesses in the Pursuit of Fees and Justice," *Boston University Law Review* 74 (November 1994): 723–75; "Political Correctness Askew: Excesses in the Pursuit of Minds and Manners," *Tennessee Law Review* 63 (spring 1996): 689–733. It would be nice—and would show his good faith—if Lasson were to publish an essay on the good that feminism has wrought, but at least he is not a bully, like Landau.

61. MacKinnon, *Feminism Unmodified*, 71.

62. MacKinnon, *Feminism Unmodified*, 72 (italics in original).

63. The best statement of this view is in Catharine A. MacKinnon, "Reflections on Sex Equality under Law," *The Yale Law Journal* 100 (March 1991): 1281–328.

64. I do not deny that liberal feminism has improved the lot of women—or rather, as MacKinnon claims, *some* women. What I deny is that it has improved the lot of women *as women*. It cannot do this, since it does not view women as having a distinct nature. It views women as persons or as humans rather than as women. Radical feminism of the sort espoused by MacKinnon (despite her reluctance to use the "modifier") seeks to promote the cause of women *as women*. Why, MacKinnon asks, should women have to be other than women, or categorized as other than women, in order to be equal to (or be seen as equal to) men? I thank Ann Cudd and Anita Superson for stimulating me to expand on this point. I am sure that they reject some or all of what I say.

Incidentally, I believe that feminism would benefit from frank and open discussion not only of what distinguishes the various types of feminism, but of whether each is properly a type of feminism. That, of course, requires a normative theory of feminism (a theory of what feminism should be). My view, which I cannot defend here, is that liberal feminism is not, properly speaking, feminism, even if it has as a by-product the improvement of (some?) women's condition or status. For a discussion of the differences between so-called liberal feminism and radical feminism in the context of a radical-feminist reclamation project, see Keith Burgess-Jackson, "John Stuart Mill, Radical Feminist," *Social Theory and Practice* 21 (fall 1995): 369–96. See also Keith Burgess-Jackson, "A Crime against Women: Calhoun on the Wrongness of Rape," *Journal of Social Philosophy* 31 (fall 2000): 286–93.

65. Yes, this is a word. See the *Oxford English Dictionary*.

BIBLIOGRAPHY

Antony, Louise M. "Natures and Norms." *Ethics* 111 (October 2000): 8–36.

Baber, H. E. "The Ethics of Dwarf-Tossing." *International Journal of Applied Philosophy* 4 (fall 1989): 1–5.

———. "The Market for Feminist Epistemology." *The Monist* 77 (October 1994): 403–23.

Baker, Katharine K. "Biology for Feminists." *Chicago-Kent Law Review* 75 (2000): 805–35.

Barkow, Jerome H., Leda Cosmides, and John Tooby, eds. *The Adapted Mind: Evolutionary Psychology and the Generation of Culture*. New York: Oxford University Press, 1992.

Bedau, Hugo. *Thinking and Writing about Philosophy*. Boston: Bedford Books, 1996.

Blackburn, Simon. *The Oxford Dictionary of Philosophy.* Oxford: Oxford University Press, 1994.

Browne, Kingsley R. "Biology, Equality, and the Law: The Legal Significance of Biological Sex Differences." *Southwestern Law Journal* 38 (June 1984): 617–702.

———. "Sex and Temperament in Modern Society: A Darwinian View of the Glass Ceiling and the Gender Gap." *Arizona Law Review* 37 (winter 1995): 971–1106.

———. "An Evolutionary Perspective on Sexual Harassment: Seeking Roots in Biology Rather than Ideology." *The Journal of Contemporary Legal Issues* 8 (spring 1997): 5–77.

———. *Divided Labours: An Evolutionary View of Women at Work.* New Haven, Conn., and London: Yale University Press, 1999 (first published in 1998).

———. "Women at War: An Evolutionary Perspective." *Buffalo Law Review* 49 (winter 2001): 51–247.

Burgess-Jackson, Keith. "John Stuart Mill, Radical Feminist." *Social Theory and Practice* 21 (fall 1995): 369–96.

———. Review of *Philosophical Writing: An Introduction,* 2nd ed., by A. P. Martinich; *Writing Philosophy Papers,* 2nd ed., by Zachary Seech; and *Thinking and Writing about Philosophy,* by Hugo Bedau. *Teaching Philosophy* 20 (December 1997): 430–37.

———. Review of *The Oxford Dictionary of Philosophy,* by Simon Blackburn. *Teaching Philosophy* 21 (March 1998): 75–80.

———. Review of *The Columbia History of Western Philosophy,* ed. Richard H. Popkin. *Teaching Philosophy* 23 (March 2000): 63–71.

———. "A Crime against Women: Calhoun on the Wrongness of Rape." *Journal of Social Philosophy* 31 (fall 2000): 286–93.

Buss, David M. "Psychological Sex Differences: Origins through Sexual Selection." *American Psychologist* 50 (March 1995): 164–68.

Copi, Irving M., and Keith Burgess-Jackson. *Informal Logic.* 3rd ed. Upper Saddle River, N.J.: Prentice Hall, 1996.

Cudd, Ann E. "Analyzing Backlash to Progressive Social Movements." *The American Philosophical Association Newsletter on Feminism and Philosophy* 99 (fall 1999): 42–46.

Eagly, Alice H. "The Science and Politics of Comparing Women and Men." *American Psychologist* 50 (March 1995): 145–58.

Feinberg, Joel. *Harm to Others.* Vol. 1 of *The Moral Limits of the Criminal Law.* New York: Oxford University Press, 1984.

Finnis, John M. "Law, Morality, and 'Sexual Orientation.'" *Notre Dame Law Review* 69 (1994): 1049–76.

———. "'Shameless Acts' in Colorado: Abuse of Scholarship in Constitutional Cases." *Academic Questions* 7 (fall 1994): 10–41.

George, Robert P. *Making Men Moral: Civil Liberties and Public Morality.* Oxford: Clarendon Press, 1993.

———. "'Shameless Acts' Revisited: Some Questions for Martha Nussbaum." *Academic Questions* 9 (winter 1995–96): 24–42.

Halpern, Diane. *Sex Differences in Cognitive Abilities.* 2nd ed. Hillsdale, N.J.: Lawrence Erlbaum, 1992.

Hare, R. M. *Freedom and Reason.* Oxford: Oxford University Press, 1963.

———. *Moral Thinking: Its Levels, Method, and Point.* Oxford: Clarendon Press, 1981.

———. *Essays on Bioethics.* Oxford: Clarendon Press, 1993.

Heyes, Cressida J. "The Backlash against Feminist Scholars and Scholarship: Introduction." *The American Philosophical Association Newsletter on Feminism and Philosophy* 99 (fall 1999): 36–40.

Hoyenga, Katharine B., and Kermit T. Hoyenga. *Gender-Related Differences: Origins and Outcomes.* Boston: Allyn and Bacon, 1993.

Hurley, Patrick J. *A Concise Introduction to Logic.* 7th ed. Belmont, Calif.: Wadsworth/Thomson Learning, 2000.

Hyde, Janet Shibley, and Elizabeth Ashby Plant. "Magnitude of Psychological Gender Differences: Another Side to the Story." *American Psychologist* 50 (March 1995): 159–61.

Jaggar, Alison M. *Feminist Politics and Human Nature.* Totowa, N.J.: Rowman & Littlefield, 1983.

Landau, Iddo. "Should There Be Separatist Feminist Epistemologies?" *The Monist* 77 (October 1994): 462–71.

———. "How Androcentric Is Western Philosophy?" *The Philosophical Quarterly* 46 (January 1996): 48–59.

———. "Mendus on Philosophy and Pervasiveness." *The Philosophical Quarterly* 47 (January 1997): 89–93.

———. "Good Women and Bad Men: A Bias in Feminist Research." *Journal of Social Philosophy* 28 (spring 1997): 141–50.

———. "Feminist Criticisms of Metaphors in Bacon's Philosophy of Science." *Philosophy* 73 (January 1998): 47–61.

———. "On the Definition of Sexual Harassment." *Australasian Journal of Philosophy* 77 (June 1999): 216–23.

———. "Is Sexual Harassment Research Biased?" *Public Affairs Quarterly* 13 (July 1999): 241–54.

Lasson, Kenneth. "Scholarship Amok: Excesses in the Pursuit of Truth and Tenure." *Harvard Law Review* 103 (February 1990): 926–50.

———. "Feminism Awry: Excesses in the Pursuit of Rights and Trifles." *Journal of Legal Education* 42 (March 1992): 1–29.

———. "Lawyering Askew: Excesses in the Pursuit of Fees and Justice." *Boston University Law Review* 74 (November 1994): 723–75.

———. "Political Correctness Askew: Excesses in the Pursuit of Minds and Manners." *Tennessee Law Review* 63 (spring 1996): 689–733.

Lewontin, R. C. "Women versus the Biologists." *The New York Review of Books* 41 (7 April 1994): 31–35.

Maccoby, Eleanor E., and Carolyn N. Jacklin. *The Psychology of Sex Differences.* Stanford, Calif.: Stanford University Press, 1974.

MacKinnon, Catharine A. *Feminism Unmodified: Discourses on Life and Law.* Cambridge, Mass., and London: Harvard University Press, 1987.

———. *Toward a Feminist Theory of the State.* Cambridge, Mass.: Harvard University Press, 1989.

———. "Reflections on Sex Equality under Law." *The Yale Law Journal* 100 (March 1991): 1281–328.

Mendelsohn, Daniel. "The Stand: Expert Witnesses and Ancient Mysteries in a Colorado Courtroom." *Lingua Franca* (September/October 1996): 34–46.

Mendus, Susan. "How Androcentric Is Western Philosophy? A Reply." *The Philosophical Quarterly* 46 (January 1996): 60–66.

Mohr, Richard D. *Gays/Justice: A Study of Ethics, Society, and Law.* New York: Columbia University Press, 1988.

Nussbaum, Martha C. "Platonic Love and Colorado Law: The Relevance of Ancient Greek Norms to Modern Sexual Controversies." *Virginia Law Review* 80 (October 1994): 1515–651.

———. "Aristotle, Politics, and Human Capabilities: A Response to Antony, Arneson, Charlesworth, and Mulgan." *Ethics* 111 (October 2000): 102–40.

———. "The Future of Feminist Liberalism." *Proceedings and Addresses of the American Philosophical Association* 74 (November 2000): 47–79.

Posner, Richard A. *Overcoming Law.* Cambridge, Mass., and London: Harvard University Press, 1995.

Seech, Zachary. *Writing Philosophy Papers.* 3rd ed. Belmont, Calif.: Wadsworth/Thomson Learning, 2000.

Singer, Peter. "All Animals Are Equal." In *The Right Thing to Do: Basic Readings in Moral Philosophy,* 2nd ed., ed. James Rachels, 207–17. Boston: McGraw-Hill College, 1999. First published in *Philosophical Exchange* 1 (summer 1974): 103–16.

———. *A Darwinian Left: Politics, Evolution, and Cooperation.* New Haven, Conn., and London: Yale University Press, 2000 (first published in 1999).

Soble, Alan. "In Defense of Bacon." *Philosophy of the Social Sciences* 25 (June 1995): 192–215.

———. "Bad Apples: Feminist Politics and Feminist Scholarship." *Philosophy of the Social Sciences* 29 (September 1999): 354–88.

Tavris, Carol. *The Mismeasure of Woman.* New York: Touchstone Books, 1992.

Thomas, Keith. "The Double Standard." *Journal of the History of Ideas* 20 (April 1959): 195–216.

Tong, Rosemarie. *Feminist Thought: A Comprehensive Introduction.* Boulder, Colo.: Westview, 1989.

Townsend, John Marshall. *What Women Want—What Men Want: Why the Sexes Still See Love and Commitment So Differently.* Oxford: Oxford University Press, 1998.

West, Robin. "Jurisprudence and Gender." *The University of Chicago Law Review* 55 (winter 1988): 1–72.

Williams, Susan H., and David C. Williams. "A Feminist Theory of Malebashing." *Michigan Journal of Gender and Law* 4 (1996): 35–127.

Wright, Robert. "Feminists, Meet Mr. Darwin." *The New Republic* 211 (28 November 1994): 34–46.

———. *The Moral Animal: Evolutionary Psychology and Everyday Life.* New York: Vintage Books, 1995 (first published in 1994).

3

Feminist Epistemology as Whipping-Girl

Mark Owen Webb

That there has been an academic backlash against feminism is apparent to all. While feminist theorists hold positions of respect in various academic departments around the country, you only have to notice how much attention and respect is given to figures like Camille Paglia, Christina Hoff-Sommers, and Katie Roiphe to realize that, in the academy in general, feminism is tolerated rather than celebrated. Women's Studies departments and programs are given lip service, but little or no resources. Even when they do get resources, faculty who teach Women's Studies courses frequently find that when tenure and/or promotion is at issue, their teaching, thesis supervision, and the like count toward service, but not toward teaching and research, which almost always carry more weight in tenure and promotion decisions. Feminist ethics and political theory have made their case that there are inequities in American society that can be attributed only to sexism, but they, too, are still subject to backlash. For example, figures like Catharine MacKinnon and Andrea Dworkin still come in for a good deal of ridicule and not very much serious rebuttal; also, ethics texts frequently do not include readings on feminist ethics, or only include them in a kind of afterthought ghetto, after all the serious theorizing is over.

But my topic is how the backlash has affected feminist epistemology and philosophy of science. In general, claims made in the name of feminist epistemology and philosophy of science are treated with scorn and dismissal, rather than with serious rebuttal. Conferences are held and anthologies published on the subject of the "flight from science and reason," and careers are made sounding the alarm that feminism will lead us into a new dark age, or a new Stalinism, by "politicizing science." Feminist epistemology has become one of the whipping-girls of choice for overtly and covertly sexist elements in philosophy.

49

When I began in philosophy in 1979, feminism was, to me, a political movement which raised philosophical issues in politics, law, and ethics, but that was all. It never occurred to me that there might be feminist insights relevant to the areas of philosophy I took to be harder, more objective, and more fundamental. I was myself pretty uninterested in feminism, even as a movement. It is thanks to one of my fellow M.A. students at Texas Tech University, Abby Wilkerson (who later received her Ph.D. from the University of Illinois at Chicago), that I came to see that I, too, ought to be committed to feminism. In 1985, I began my work toward the Ph.D. at Syracuse University, and found out firsthand how reactionary and antifeminist philosophers can be. It should be said, however, that the faculty there were all friendly to feminism, though there was a range of views, and even the most radical were somewhat less radical than I was on that score. No, it was the graduate students who stunned me with their closed-minded, if not Neanderthal, attitudes. It struck me that in the only two philosophical communities with which I had any experience, there is an unwritten list of topics that are considered respectable philosophical questions, and people who show concern for others are considered to be wasting their time. This list is different in each community, and disagreements about what belongs on the list can be a source of tension in a community. This is, of course, no deep insight; philosophy departments have fragmented over precisely this problem. Nevertheless, as obvious as the insight may seem to others, it was only in this situation (being a newly arrived graduate student), with respect to only this issue (feminism), that I was finally able to have this obvious insight. As part of my acculturation to Syracuse, I had to learn to sneer and snicker at the right things. Feminist epistemology and philosophy of science were two of those things.

Two events, in rapid succession, began to shake things up. First, a brand-new post-doctoral fellowship was established at Syracuse, and Mark Lance (now of Georgetown University) became the first to hold it. He came with a freshly minted Ph.D. from Pittsburgh, where he had worked with Robert Brandom, and he brought a whole new set of approaches with him. Since he was quasi-faculty, his interest in a question was sufficient to give the subject respectability; as a post-doc, and therefore quasi-graduate-student, he spent a lot of time with the graduate students, and by his presence, could make them see that a sneer and a snicker did not constitute philosophical argument. He taught seminars based on his dissertation, which made extensive use of social theories of both language and epistemology, and thereby made room in logical space for feminist theories.

Not long after that, Syracuse hired three more junior faculty, one of whom was to be a Continentalist with some expertise in epistemology. Linda Alcoff gave a paper for her campus interview that showed how some insights from Continental philosophy could be used to address traditional analytic questions in epistemology, and handled the vigorous questioning from the Syracuse faculty as well as I have ever seen anyone do, of any rank, experience, or area of expertise. She accepted the position, and began to teach both feminism and Continental philosophy in a department where most of the graduate students were hostile to both.

But with her presence as an obviously well-trained and talented philosopher, in addition to the presence of Mark Lance, the rhetorical strategies of dismissal had to change. Her admission to the faculty, while sometimes dismissed as a mere token, constituted endorsement of her areas of research as "real philosophy," so most people realized that a sneer and a snicker were not enough. Initially, graduate students would move to the slightly less shallow strategy of merely reciting her philosophical positions, followed by "Can you believe that?" And this in a department in which Peter van Inwagen notoriously believed that tables and chairs didn't exist. Of course, some incredulity was aimed at him, too, but always with the understanding that he had strong reasons for his views. His incredible views were idiosyncratic and brave, while Alcoff's were merely cranky, foolish, and possibly insane.

As time went on, and Alcoff began to attract students of her own, the population of the graduate students changed, and even "can you believe that?" was seen to be an inadequate response to her views (except in small groups of like-minded students). What accounts for this change? It is important to see that the presence of Linda Alcoff, an extremely talented and energetic philosopher, was not enough. Though no one could doubt her credentials, there was still a feeling on the part of sexist elements that at least part of the reason she got the job was that she was a woman. It seemed to me at the time that Mark Lance's presence was the decisive factor, because (since he was a man with feminist commitments) his espousal of feminist views and defense of Alcoff's work could not be dismissed as merely partisan, and his solid work in a male-approved area (philosophy of language and logic) made it impossible to doubt his intelligence. When the graduate students saw Mark standing in solidarity with Alcoff, they were forced to reexamine their prejudices. It is a sad truth that even someone as brilliant as Alcoff could not be recognized on her own merits. Some may say that it is Alcoff's commitment to Continental texts and styles of reasoning that exposed her to this kind of treatment. While it is true that Continental philosophers do meet with the same kind of resistance, especially in departments that are analytically oriented, it is also true that feminism meets with additional resistance of a special kind. Even feminist work that is analytically oriented meets with this kind of disapproval. My own work in feminist epistemology, although certainly analytic in style, has met with puzzlement; I have been asked, "When are you going to get back to real epistemology?" and even "You're just doing that to get a job, aren't you?"

In the fifteen years since the publication of *The Science Question in Feminism,* even my own admittedly contingent and idiosyncratic experiences have exposed me to a range of rhetorical strategies of dismissal. The strategies that developed over that period were the same ones that have been employed all over the profession. It is important to note that there is a large and objective difference between dismissal and criticism, and that it is not wholly a matter of tone. I take it that feminist epistemology has to stand up to critical scrutiny in the same way that any philosophical view has to; its being feminist should give it no special immunity. However, critics have a responsibility to take the view seriously and fairly. Seriousness and fairness are precisely what is lacking in what I call "dismissal." Some features of these strategies (the ones that will figure in the examples I will consider) are: lumping different views together, and criticizing all for the weaknesses of one; judging arguments on the basis of whether the conclusion is congenial; and denying that a project is interesting or important. Good philosophical criticism distinguishes different varieties of an argument or view, and takes the argument on its own merits. To place those strategies in context, let me first give a brief account of what feminist epistemology is.

WHAT FEMINIST EPISTEMOLOGY PURPORTS TO BE

Many critics of feminist epistemology begin by asking what feminist epistemology could be. The implication is that the label itself is so strange that the burden is on those who use it to give it a sense. This is, in some ways, a bizarre question. No one asks a similar question about feminist ethics, or feminist political philosophy, or even feminist aesthetics. (Though there was a time when these areas faced similar questions; after all, isn't ethics universal? How can gender have anything to do with it?) The short answer is that feminist epistemology is the project of bringing feminist insights to bear on questions in epistemology. What is so strange about that? Still, many feminist thinkers (generously) admit that the label is a little strange, and proceed to take up the burden of justifying its use. If there is anything strange about feminist epistemology, it must be because epistemology is different in some relevant way from ethics, political philosophy, and aesthetics. Certainly many have thought that it is. So it is worthwhile to try to offer a more nuanced answer to the content question.

First of all, we should note that feminist epistemology doesn't involve the idea that women, by virtue of their hormones or reproductive organs, have some magical insight into the nature of things. One very good answer to the question is given by Alcoff and Potter, in their anthology *Feminist Epistemologies*.[1] They claim that contemporary epistemology has an excessively narrow conception of epistemology—one which, by the way, is narrower than the traditional conception. A broader and more traditional understanding of epistemology makes room for feminist projects. They say,

Our title, *Feminist Epistemologies*, is meant to indicate that the term does not have a single referent and, for reasons that we will explore later, it may never. Feminist theorists have used the term variously to refer to women's "ways of knowing," "women's experience," or simply "women's knowledge," all of which are alien to professional philosophers and to epistemology "proper"— that is, alien to a theory of knowledge in general. But this latter conception of proper epistemology leaves unchallenged the premise that a general account of knowledge, one that uncovers justificatory standards a priori, is *possible*. This is precisely the premise that feminist epistemologists have called into question.[2]

In other words, there are questions, like the one of the possibility of a general theory of knowledge, that are more basic than, or at least as basic as, the questions pursued by contemporary analytic epistemology, and that can reasonably be seen as being raised by feminist insights.

Alcoff and Potter also give "women's ways of knowing" as one way of characterizing such insights. This phrase has raised hackles in many quarters.[3] Many feminist opponents to feminist epistemology and philosophy of science take such a conception to play into the hands of misogynist and androcentric elements by agreeing with them that women think differently from men. In particular, it reinforces the sexist stereotype that women are not good at objective, logical thinking. Such an objection is misguided for two reasons. First of all, a claim can be true and still be used in sexist arguments. The fact that women are biologically different from men has also been used in sexist arguments, but that should not keep us from accepting it as a fact (though it is an open question how many of the differences are really biological and anatomical, and how many are socialized). Secondly, it is obvious that there are many different kinds of knowledge, and many different paths to knowledge. If some of those have been discounted as less important, and at the same time encouraged in women but not in men (after all, we need not be essentialist about whatever differences we find), recovering the respectability of those kinds of knowledge and "ways of knowing" would be a victory for humanity generally. How could one object to recovering real avenues to knowledge?

Part of the problem is that the phrase "women's ways of knowing" has been read in an essentialist way, even though it need not. Essentialists believe that whatever differences there are between men and women are essential differences, not socialized differences. While this is a position that some feminists have held, it is not necessary that a feminist be an essentialist. Many feminists—in fact, probably most—think that where there are gender differences, those differences are socially constructed. In other words, there may well be avenues to knowledge that come more readily to those socialized as women, or that make use of abilities most often found in women because of socialization, without those differences being biologically essential. Understood in a non-essentialist way, then, "women's ways of knowing" may have no more implications than that gender-socialization encourages different cognitive styles in the different genders.

Perhaps the least controversial of all the projects in feminist epistemology and philosophy of science is the examination of actual knowledge-producing practices for sexist bias. Alcoff and Potter speak of the presupposition behind contemporary epistemology that it is possible to produce a general and universal theory of knowledge. This presupposition is certainly worth questioning, but there can be presuppositions that underlie particular knowledge practices that are not so basic and theoretical, the exposing of which would still be substantive epistemology. Some, for example, have argued that the very notions of rationality and objectivity used by contemporary epistemology are notions designed to exclude women's experience.[4] Rationality and objectivity, according to this view, require an impossible universal standpoint, a "God's-eye view." In practice, the theorizings of women are seen as partial, both in the sense of being incomplete, and in the sense of being biased. Since these failings are failings of universality, the resulting theories are not sufficiently universal, and so are not either rational or objective. Many feminists believe that a total and perspectiveless theory of the world is impossible; all knowledge should be recognized to be partial, in both senses. Since this is so, to stigmatize women's knowledge claims as inadequate for those reasons is unfair. Harding has famously tried to replace the standard notion of objectivity with another, more feminist one, which will still do the realist job that science needs it to do.[5] Helen Longino has argued that the list of theoretical virtues used in theory choice excludes respectable alternatives that could be expected to be used by feminist scientists.[6] At a more practical level, several thinkers have examined particular scientific practices, both historical and contemporary, to look for ways in which sexist thinking has affected theory choice and data interpretation.[7] These are all, of course, controversial claims, and should be subjected to close scrutiny and vigorous debate. What they should not receive, though, is the combination of curt dismissal and moral outrage that they have received. They are real projects in what can reasonably be called "feminist epistemology"; they are clearly epistemological projects, and are informed by feminist concerns. So, as strange as it may seem, there is such a field as feminist epistemology.

HARDING'S TAXONOMY

My consciousness of feminist epistemology began with Sandra Harding's 1986 book, *The Science Question in Feminism*.[8] Although work in feminist epistemology had certainly been done before that[9]—though perhaps not under the rubric "feminist epistemology"—her seminal book on the relation of feminist thought to science was certainly a landmark. For one thing, it laid out the territory in a systematic way, identifying different strands, different research projects, in the wider field. It also issued a challenge, turning traditionally unquestioned orders of explanation on their heads. She asks why feminism has had to justify itself to science, when we could also reasonably ask how science can justify itself to feminism. In many ways, it set the agenda for feminist epistemology and philosophy of science from that time on.

Harding divides feminist epistemological theories into three categories: feminist empiricism, standpoint theory, and feminist postmodernism. While this threefold division is probably not exhaustive, it certainly covers a wide range of orientations. Feminist empiricism is the least radical view, and therefore the one that sits most comfortably with mainstream contemporary epistemology. Feminist empiricists claim that there is nothing wrong with contemporary epistemology or science, as ideally and abstractly conceived; the problems that sexism causes in actual knowledge practices can be corrected "by stricter adherence to the existing methodological norms of scientific inquiry."[10] The view is that, while there is nothing wrong with scientific methods, their actual execution has in the past incorporated and reinforced sexist biases. The remedy proposed by feminist empiricists is to use feminist insights, including political insights, to uncover areas where bias creeps in undetected, and to increase the objectivity of scientific endeavors by eliminating those biases. Any criticism leveled by a feminist empiricist will therefore be the kind of criticism that any scientist should take seriously, as it is an application of the canons of scientific method. Lynn Hankinson Nelson, in her first major epistemological work,[11] identifies herself as a feminist empiricist. This brand of feminist epistemology is surely the least controversial, since it reaffirms all the analytic shibboleths about science, objectivity, rationality, and truth. But, as we will see in the next section, it does not thereby avoid contemptuous dismissal. Part of the reason some are suspicious of even this eminently reasonable view is that some have thought that science is essentially self-correcting, and so there need be no special, politically motivated effort to save science from bias.

Feminist standpoint theory has its origin in Marxist thought. The idea, according to Marx, is that by being a member of the ruling class, for whom the social system works, one gives up the ability to see how the system works. Only the working class actually understands how the system works. For this reason, the working class is epistemically privileged, by virtue of having a special standpoint. The analogous theory in feminism is that women, by virtue of their oppression, have an epistemically privileged standpoint, too. Harding says that, according to this view, "men's dominating position in social life results in partial and perverse understandings, whereas women's subjugated position provides the possibility of more complete and less perverse understandings."[12] Nancy Hartsock, a feminist standpoint theorist, says it this way:

> Women's work in every society differs systematically from men's. I intend to pursue the suggestion that this division of labor is the first and in some societies the only division of labor, and moreover, that it is central to the organization of social labor more generally. On the basis of an account of the sexual division of labor, one should be able to begin to explore the oppositions and differences between women's and men's activity and their consequences for epistemology.[13]

The workings of the system are made invisible to those for whom it works, and are only visible to those who make it work. To see why this is true, at least in some cases, we need only consider the Ozzie and Harriet version of the traditional family. Papa dresses for work in the morning, eats breakfast, gets in his car, and goes to work. Chances are he has never given a thought to how clean shirts appear in his closet, or how breakfast appears on the table, or how his car works (unless he has cooking or car repair as a "hobby"). His house works like a well-oiled machine, designed to produce his effortless comfort. As long as it works well, he doesn't have to think about it, and so he doesn't. Since he doesn't think about it, he has no idea the kind of work Mama does, or the political implications of their relationship. On the other hand, Mama understands her role all too well. She knows the world from his point of view, because it is the view she sees described in the news and popular culture. She also knows the infrastructure that keeps that world going, because she takes part in it. As a result, her understanding is more complete and less perverse than his. The argument of the standpoint theorists is the most convincing when confined to sociopolitical matters, but many standpoint theorists have argued that women's standpoint gives them epistemic privilege more generally, even to the point of claiming that women will make better scientists. Like feminist empiricism, standpoint theory accepts—and, in fact, depends on—the presuppositions that there is a mind-independent reality and that it is possible to have a better or worse view of it. Also like feminist empiricism, this concordance with mainstream epistemology has not immunized it from dismissal.

Feminist postmodernism[14] is the most natural whipping-girl for analytic epistemology. Like postmodernism in other areas, it thrives on fractures, ruptures, and subversions. While there is no doctrine common to all postmodernists, they share a general skepticism about universal absolutes. It is in these that we find claims that reality is constructed, objectivity is a gendered notion, logic is androcentric, there is no human nature, there is no unitary self, there is no "one true story of the world," and the like. While some of these views are treated with respect when they are uttered by Dummett, Feyerabend, or Rorty, they become ridiculous or alarming when uttered by feminists.

STRATEGIES OF DISMISSAL

While there is a wide variety of feminist epistemologies, the strategies of dismissal are amazingly simple. It amounts to a disjunction: for whatever thinker we are considering, either what she says isn't epistemology, or it isn't feminist. The strategy usually begins with some narrow conception of the role of epistemology. For example, Radcliffe Richards[15] argues that since feminist epistemology calls for the rejection of traditional epistemology, one cannot have epistemological reasons for adopting it. She imagines a committed feminist who is also a traditional epistemologist trying to decide whether to adopt feminist epistemology. In a section entitled "Epistemology Proper," she tries various arguments, and rejects them all, saying,

> Because the root of the matter is a logical one it makes no difference how many variations of detail are tried. The point is essentially the one made at the beginning of this piece, about the foundations of feminism, that criteria by which proper treatment and assessment can be recognized need to be in place before it can be said that the present state of things is falling short of them. The claim that some set of epistemological and scientific standards results in inappropriate treatment of women cannot be used as an argument against those standards, because, necessarily, to accept those standards *is* to accept that women should be treated according to them.[16]

The idea is that one can have only epistemological reasons for rejecting epistemological standards, and epistemological reasons can't be feminist reasons; they must be general and universal. Later, at the end of the same section, she says,

> Feminism, in other words, can never escape its beginnings as an applied field. Conclusions about what should be done by feminists for women—irrespective of whether they want what is just or right for women, or merely what is good for them—are at all stages essentially derivative, and dependent on more fundamental ideas. No beliefs about matters of fact, and no theories of epistemology or science, can be required by feminism, because feminist conclusions depend on them. This means that to attach the label "feminist" to particular theories of epistemology or anything else is completely arbitrary. In no sense that is not seriously misleading can there be any such thing as feminist epistemology.[17]

In other words, either it isn't epistemology (because it is political), or it isn't feminist (because the addition of "feminist" is arbitrary and misleading). This argument is particularly puzzling given the role of intuition and counterexample in epistemology. Edmund Gettier's famous article[18] did not argue for the conclusion that justified-true-belief theories failed because they failed to meet some fundamental epistemic principle; the idea was that cases could be constructed that these views would count as knowledge, and yet are not really knowledge. Many other epistemologists have argued similarly. View A has the consequence that such-and-such counts as knowledge, but it isn't knowledge, so view A is wrong. The feminist epistemologists Radcliffe Richards is arguing against are doing nothing different, except that the counterexamples they argue from are instances of women's knowledge.

Susan Haack gives the most sympathetic treatment of feminist epistemology and philosophy of science, but even her treatment comes to the same dismissive disjunction; either it isn't epistemology "proper," or it isn't feminist. The following passage comes from her "Epistemological Reflections of an Old Feminist":[19]

> Still, you may ask, given that I have not denied that some themes presented under the rubric "feminist epistemology" are true, and that I grant that some feminist criticisms of sexist science seem well-founded and have a bona fide epistemological role, why do I make all this fuss about the label? Well, since the idea that there is an epistemology properly called "feminist" rests on false presuppositions, the label is at best sloppy. But there is more at stake than dislike of sloppiness; more than offense at the implication that those of us who don't think it appropriate to describe our epistemological work as "feminist" don't care about justice for women; more than unease at sweeping generalizations about women and embarrassment at the suggestion that women have special epistemological insight. What is most troubling is that the label is designed to convey the idea that *inquiry should be politicized*. And *that* is not only mistaken, but dangerously so.[20]

Inasmuch as Haack grants a great deal of the content that goes under the name of feminist epistemology—so much that all but the postmodernists are all right in her book—feminist epistemologists should probably count her among their friends. Still, the scattershot nature of her concerns in this paragraph, together with her balking at a label, are signs that the backlash is at work here, too. She claims offense at something I have never heard or seen claimed by *any* feminist epistemologist—that epistemologists who don't call themselves feminist epistemologists don't care about justice for women— and embarrassment by a claim that may, if the standpoint analysis of things is right, be simply true. And it is worth remembering (on many views, at least) that "special epistemic insight" does not come from any ovarian magic, but by social positioning. Haack surely grants that not everyone is equally well placed epistemically; there's nothing to be embarrassed about there. Her most serious charge is that feminist epistemology is committed to the view that inquiry should be politicized (assuming in the background that it is not *already* politicized, a claim that much of feminist epistemology challenges). This characterization is meant to alarm. If it means that inquirers should tailor their inquiries to get only politically preapproved results, then she has a legitimate complaint. However, if it means that inquirers should be careful not to build political biases into their inquiries, or that they should be suspicious when their inquiries lead them to certain results, then it is a lot less alarming, and pretty clearly legitimate. It is also salutary to remember that it is the label "feminist epistemology" that is so alarming to her. She is most alarmed by postmodernism, and only embarrassed by standpoint theory. As for feminist empiricism, in a footnote to the same paper she says, "I would say that the 'feminist' in 'feminist empiricism' is redundant. In this sense, Stephen Jay Gould, or myself, qualify as 'feminist empiricists,' even though we both deny that a specifically feminist epistemology is required."[21] But to say that the word "feminist" is redundant is to say that empiricism is already, by definition, feminist. Surely, since many empiricists would deny such a thing, there is some point for empiricists who want to claim that empiricism is by nature supportive of feminist aims to call themselves by a name that calls attention to that fact. Stephen Jay Gould and Susan Haack *are* feminist empiricists, and perhaps they should accept that they are. Here is nervousness about the F word (or the F phrase, "feminist epistemology"), not opposition to the theory itself.

Another strain of dismissal is to be found in writers who, like Haack, are self-identified feminists. According to this view, feminist epistemology is actually antifeminist because it is harmful to women's interests. (You might wonder why this matters, since inquiry shouldn't be politicized.) For example, in her essay "The Market for Feminist Epistemology,"[22] Harriet Baber begins by asking "Is Feminist Epistemology Feminist?" Her answer is "no" (as you probably guessed), because "the identification of these theories as 'feminist' motivated by unsubstantiated assumptions about the psychological differences between men and women, is detrimental to women's interests."[23] How has it harmed women? She cites two ways. First, it taints other women in the profession with "guilt by association";[24] second, it provides "grist for the mill of conservatives in the profession."[25] As substantiation for her claims, she tells a story of wearing a "Repeal Leibniz's Law" button as a joke about her work on relative identity, and its being taken as some sort of feminist comment on logic by one man. Leibniz's law is a purported law of logic that says that if *a* and *b* are identical, then anything that is true of *a* is true of the *b*, and vice versa. Relative identity theorists claim at minimum that there is a sense of identity in which *a* and *b* might be identical under one description, but not under another; they may be the same *F*, but not the same *G*. If relative identity is viable, Leibniz's law doesn't hold in those cases, and so isn't a real law of logic. Since some feminist thinkers (Andrea Nye,[26] for example) have held that Western logic has an androcentric bias, the interlocutor in this story wondered if Baber was one of those thinkers. I really don't know what to make of worries like these. People make unwarranted inferences on the basis of silly generalizations. Must a whole field of philosophical endeavor go underground to protect those who don't want to be associated with it by strangers? Baber shows the same horror of the F phrase that Haack shows.

The saddest part of this kind of dismissal by feminists is that it mimics a strategy used by antifeminists: the horror story inviting a hasty generalization. This is the whole strategy of Christina Hoff-Sommers in her epistemology chapter of *Who Stole Feminism?*[27] She cites standpoint theory, then asks, "What do mainstream philosophers make of 'standpoint theories'?" She then quotes extensively from Susan Haack. We are left with the impression that Haack speaks for "mainstream philosophy," a claim Haack herself would never make. There follows a litany of horror stories. Yolanda Moses, then president of City University of New York, is quoted as saying that Western society, because of a masculine bias, values achievement and objectivity over cooperation, connectedness, and subjectivity. Hoff-Sommers then adds, "In President Moses's view, the masculine emphasis on achievement and objectivity is an obstacle to progress!"[28] Thus her "anti-intellectual bias" is exposed. A Catholic conference in Albuquerque in 1993 is held up to ridicule. All she tells us about the conference is that "many goddesses were honored," and that the women were asked to bring and play on drums. The content of the conference receives no attention at all. A 1993 conference in Parsippany, New Jersey, on transforming the curriculum is treated similarly. The New Jersey chancellor of higher education, who was present at this conference, called its subject "a vindication of the simple and honest concept that scholarship should reflect contributions of all." But Hoff-Sommers has a different take. She says,

> Apparently he did not see that beneath the charges of sexism and gender unfairness is an illiberal, irrational, and anti-intellectual program that is a threat to everything he probably believes in: American democracy, liberal education, academic freedom, and the kind of mainstream feminism that has gained women near-equality in American society.[29]

The upshot, we are invited to infer, is that feminist epistemologists generally are anti-intellectual, antiscientific, and cognitively irresponsible.

Paul Gross and Norman Levitt use the same strategy in their *Higher Superstition*.[30] It should be noted that, unlike Hoff-Sommers, Gross and Levitt actually address some of the central figures in the literature of feminist epistemology and philosophy of science. They quote from Garry and Pearsall's introduction to *Women, Knowledge, and Reality*,[31] and they have an extended treatment of Longino's *Science as Social Knowledge*.[32] While I think their criticisms of these two works are inadequate, at least they sometimes rise to the level of engagement with the material. Still, they also use the horror-story strategy. Their example of horror committed in the name of feminist epistemology is Campbell and Campbell's "Toward a Feminist Algebra." Perhaps this paper is badly argued; I don't know. I do know, however, that it is not typical of the wide range of feminist epistemology. Yet Gross and Levitt say (after holding up sentence after sentence to ridicule),

All this reveals a mind-set we shall encounter again and again in feminist science criticism. Metaphorical language is scrutinized microscopically for evidence that the science in which it occurs is tainted by sexist ideology. . . . Metaphor mongering is the principal strategy of much feminist criticism of science. It is invoked to accomplish what analysis of actual ideas will not.[33]

They then take on the Biology and Gender Study Group and their article, "The Importance of Feminist Critique for Contemporary Cell Biology,"[34] in the same terms. After choosing a few sentences here and there, they conclude, "So far this critique is nothing but the all-too-familiar metaphor mongering, likely to convince no one who is not already excited by the idea that Francis Bacon and Isaac Newton were advocates of rape."[35] They conclude the chapter with the following *cri de coeur:*

Hélas! What begins as an epistemological inquiry into science ends as familiar anti-science tricked out in the ambient clichés of the business—science "harnessed to the making of money and the waging of war"—the old moral one-up*woman*ship, and the call to political action. It ends with the universal complaint of religious zealots, utopians, and totalizers generally. Science as-it-is is untrustworthy. We can't bend it to our will because, as a powerful institution of the present, compromised world, it is protected. It will not be bent until the enemy is weakened and the world is redeemed. (But then, once the world has been remade in the image of our ideals—then, we shall see.) We have heard this from ideologues, politicians, and thought police in various uniforms since Galileo's time. How sad it is that it should now emanate from the scholarly halls of universities and reverberate there among intellectuals who inherit the Enlightenment.[36]

Again, the alarm is sounded. Watch out for those feminist epistemologists; they're just like Hitler and Stalin.

CONCLUSIONS

I have taken no stand here on whether I think any of the many approaches to feminist epistemology are right (anyone who cares what I think can look me up in *Philosopher's Index*). I do think many feminist epistemologists are wrong. What has concerned me here is the tone of dismissal that has pervaded much of the criticism of feminist epistemology. Many, perhaps all, feminist approaches to epistemology and philosophy of science are wrong; they are not crazy, they are not stupid, and they are not the thin end of a totalitarian wedge. That they are treated as crazy, stupid totalitarians only serves to underline the fact that feminism in general is still not safe in the world. The backlash continues, and when the academy needs a whipping-girl, feminism is pressed into the job.

NOTES

I am grateful to Anita Superson for comments that substantially improved this essay.

1. Linda Alcoff and Elizabeth Potter, *Feminist Epistemologies* (New York: Routledge, 1993).

2. Alcoff and Potter, *Feminist Epistemologies*, 1.

3. See especially the discussion of Susan Haack later in this essay.

4. See, for example, Elizabeth Anderson, "Knowledge, Human Interests, and Objectivity in Feminist Epistemology," *Philosophical Topics* 23 (1995): 27–58; Margaret Atherton, "Cartesian Reason and Gendered Reason," in *A Mind of One's Own: Feminist Essays on Reason and Objectivity*, ed. Louise M. Antony and Charlotte Witt, 19–34 (Boulder, Colo.: Westview, 1993); Elizabeth Grosz, "Bodies and Knowledges: Feminism and the Crisis of Reason," in *Feminist Epistemologies*, ed. Linda Alcoff and Elizabeth Potter, 187–215 (New York: Routledge, 1993); Sally Haslanger "On Being Objective and Being Objectified," in *Feminist Epistemologies*, ed. Linda Alcoff and Elizabeth Potter, 85–126 (New York: Routledge, 1993); Genevieve Lloyd, "Maleness, Metaphor, and the 'Crisis' of Reason," in *A Mind of One's Own*, ed. Louise M. Antony and Charlotte Witt, 69–83 (Boulder, Colo.: Westview Press, 1993), and *The Man of Reason: "Male" and "Female" in Western Philosophy*, (Minneapolis: University of Minnesota Press, 1994); Phyllis Rooney "Gendered Reason: Sex, Metaphor, and Conceptions of Reason," *Hypatia* 6 (1991), 77–103.

5. *Feminist Epistemologies*, ed. Linda Alcoff and Elizabeth Potter, 49–82 (New York: Routledge, 1993); and "Strong Objectivity and Socially Situated Knowledge," in "Whose Science? Whose Knowledge?" ed. Sandra Harding, 138–64 (Ithaca, N.Y.: Cornell University Press, 1991).

6. See her *Science as Social Knowledge* (Princeton, N.J.: Princeton University Press, 1990).

7. A few examples in this burgeoning literature: Nancy Tuana, "The Weaker Seed: The Sexist Bias of Reproductive Theory;" and the Biology and Gender Study Group, "The Importance of Feminist Critique for Contemporary Cell Biology," both in *Feminism and Science*, ed. Nancy Tuana (Indianapolis: Indiana University Press, 1989); and Desley Deacon, "Political Arithmetic: The Nineteenth-Century Australian Census and the Construction of the Dependent Woman"; Daphne de Marneffe, "Looking and Listening: The Construction of Clinical Knowledge in Charcot and Freud"; and Emily Martin, "The Egg and the Sperm: How Science Has Constructed a Romance Based on Stereotypical Male-Female Roles," all in *Gender and Scientific Authority*, ed. Barbara Laslett et al. (Chicago: University of Chicago Press, 1996).

8. Sandra Harding, *The Science Question in Feminism* (Ithaca, N.Y.: Cornell University Press, 1986).

9. See, for example, Sandra Harding and Merrill B. Hintikka, eds., *Discovering Reality: Feminist Perspectives on Epistemology, Metaphysics, and Philosophy of Science* (London: D. Reidel Publishing Company, 1983).

10. Harding, *The Science Question*, 24.

11. Lynn Hankinson Nelson, *Who Knows? From Quine to a Feminist Empiricism* (Philadelphia: Temple University Press, 1990).

12. Harding, *The Science Question*, 26. Terri Eliott gives the view a brief and compelling defense using Heideggerian categories in "Making Strange What Had Appeared Familiar," *Monist* (1994): 424–33.

13. Nancy Hartsock, "The Feminist Standpoint," in *Discovering Reality: Feminist Perspectives on Epistemology, Metaphysics, and Philosophy of Science*, ed. Sandra Harding and Merrill B. Hintikka, 289 (London: D. Reidel Publishing Company, 1983).

14. Donna Haraway is one of the most prolific figures in this group of thinkers. I would place Jane Duran in this group, too.

15. Radcliffe Richards, "Why Feminist Epistemology Isn't," in *The Flight from Science and Reason*, ed. Paul Gross, Norman Levitt, and Martin W. Lewis, 385–412 (Baltimore: Johns Hopkins University Press, 1996).

16. Richards, "Why Feminist Epistemology Isn't," 398.

17. Richards, "Why Feminist Epistemology Isn't," 399.

18. Edmund L. Gettier, "Is Justified True Belief Knowledge?" *Analysis* 23 (1963): 121–23.

19. Susan Haack, "Epistemological Reflections of an Old Feminist," *Reason Papers* 18 (1993): 31–43.

20. Haack, "Epistemological Reflections," 37.

21. Haack, "Epistemological Reflections," 41.

22. Harriet Baber, "The Market for Feminist Epistemology," *Monist* 77 (1994): 403–23.

23. Baber, "Market," 421.

24. Baber, "Market," 421.

25. Baber, "Market," 421.

26. Andrea Nye, *Words of Power: A Feminist Reading in the History of Logic* (New York: Routledge, 1990).

27. Christina Hoff-Sommers, *Who Stole Feminism?* (New York: Simon & Schuster, 1994), chapter 4.

28. Hoff-Sommers, *Who Stole Feminism*, 76.

29. Hoff-Sommers, *Who Stole Feminism*, 82–83.

30. Paul R. Gross and Norman Levitt, *Higher Superstition* (Baltimore: Johns Hopkins University Press, 1994), chapter 5.

31. Ann Garry and Marilyn Pearsall, eds., *Women, Knowledge, and Reality: Explorations in Feminist Philosophy* (Winchester, Mass.: Unwin Hyman, 1989).

32. Helen E. Longino, *Science as Social Knowledge* (Princeton, N.J.: Princeton University Press, 1990).

33. Gross and Levitt, *Higher Superstition*, 116.

34. Reprinted in Nancy Tuana, ed., *Feminism and Science* (Indianapolis: Indiana University Press, 1989), 172–87.

35. Gross and Levitt, *Higher Superstition*, 119.

36. Gross and Levitt, *Higher Superstition* 148.

BIBLIOGRAPHY

Alcoff, Linda, and Elizabeth Potter, eds. *Feminist Epistemologies*. New York: Routledge, 1993.

Anderson, Elizabeth. "Knowledge, Human Interests, and Objectivity in Feminist Epistemology." *Philosophical Topics* 23 (1995): 27–58.

Atherton, Margaret. "Cartesian Reason and Gendered Reason." In *A Mind of One's Own*, ed. Antony and Witt, 19–34. Boulder, Colo.: Westview, 1993.

Baber, Harriet. "The Market for Feminist Epistemology." *Monist* 77 (1994): 403–23.

Biology and Gender Study Group. "The Importance of Feminist Critique for Contemporary Cell Biology." In *Feminism and Science*, ed. Nancy Tuana. Indianapolis: Indiana University Press, 1989.

de Marneff, Daphne. "Looking and Listening: The Construction of Clinical Knowledge in Charcot and Freud." In *Gender and Scientific Authority*, ed. Barbara Laslett et al. Chicago: University of Chicago Press, 1996.

Deacon, Desley. "Political Arithmetic: The Nineteenth-Century Australian Census and the Construction of the Dependent Woman." In *Gender and Scientific Authority*, ed. Barbara Laslett et al. Chicago: University of Chicago Press, 1996.

Eliott, Terri. "Making Strange What Had Appeared Familiar." *Monist* (1994): 424–33.

Garry, Ann, and Marilyn Pearsall, eds. *Women, Knowledge, and Reality: Explorations in Feminist Philosophy*. Winchester, Mass.: Unwin Hyman, 1989.

Gettier, Edmund L. "Is Justified True Belief Knowledge?" *Analysis* 23 (1963): 121–23.

Gross, Paul R., and Norman Levitt. *Higher Superstition*. Baltimore: Johns Hopkins University Press, 1994.

Grosz, Elizabeth. "Bodies and Knowledges: Feminism and the Crisis of Reason." In *Feminist Epistemologies*, ed. Linda Alcoff and Elizabeth Potter, 187–215. New York: Routledge, 1993.

Haack, Susan. "Epistemological Reflections of an Old Feminist." *Reason Papers* 18 (1993): 31–43.

Harding, Sandra. "Rethinking Standpoint Epistemology: What Is 'Strong Objectivity'?" In *Feminist Epistemologies*, ed. Linda Alcoff and Elizabeth Potter, 49–82. New York: Routledge, 1993.

———. *The Science Question in Feminism*. Ithaca, N.Y.: Cornell University Press, 1986.

———. "Strong Objectivity and Socially Situated Knowledge." In *Whose Science? Whose Knowledge?* ed. Sandra Harding, 138–64. Ithaca, N.Y.: Cornell University Press, 1991.

Harding, Sandra, and Merrill B. Hintikka, eds. *Discovering Reality: Feminist Perspectives on Epistemology, Metaphysics, and Philosophy of Science*. London: D. Reidel, 1983.

Hartsock, Nancy. "The Feminist Standpoint." In *Discovering Reality: Feminist Perspectives on Epistemology, Metaphysics, and Philosophy of Science*, ed. Sandra Harding and Merrill B. Hintikka. London: D. Reidel, 1983.

Haslanger, Sally, "On Being Objective and Being Objectified." In *A Mind of One's Own*, edited by Louise M. Antony and Charlotte Witt, 85–126. Boulder, Colo.: Westview, 1993.

Hoff-Sommers, Christina. *Who Stole Feminism?* New York: Simon & Schuster, 1994.

Lloyd, Genevieve. "Maleness, Metaphor, and the 'Crisis' of Reason." In *A Mind of One's Own*, edited by Louise M. Antony and Charlotte Witt, 69–83. Boulder, Colo.: Westview, 1993.

———. *The Man of Reason: "Male" and "Female" in Western Philosophy*. Minneapolis: University of Minnesota Press, 1994.

Longino, Helen. *Science as Social Knowledge*. Princeton, N.J.: Princeton University Press, 1990.

Martin, Emily. "The Egg and the Sperm: How Science Has Constructed a Romance Based on Stereotypical Male-Female Roles." In *Gender and Scientific Authority*, ed. Barbara Laslett et al. Chicago: University of Chicago Press, 1996.

Nelson, Lynn Hankinson. *Who Knows? From Quine to a Feminist Empiricism*. Philadelphia: Temple University Press, 1990.

Nye, Andrea. *Words of Power: A Feminist Reading in the History of Logic*. New York: Routledge, 1990.

Richards, Radcliffe. "Why Feminist Epistemology Isn't." In *The Flight from Science and Reason*, ed. Paul Gross, Norman Levitt, and Martin W. Lewis, 385–412. Baltimore: Johns Hopkins University Press, 1996.

Rooney, Phyllis. "Gendered Reason: Sex, Metaphor and Conceptions of Reason." *Hypatia* 6 (1991): 77–103.

Tuana, Nancy, ed. *Feminism and Science*. Indianapolis: Indiana University Press, 1989.

———. "The Weaker Seed: The Sexist Bias of Reproductive Theory." In *Feminism and Science*, ed. Nancy Tuana. Indianapolis: Indiana University Press, 1989.

4

The Backlash against Feminist Legal Theory

Martha Chamallas

The developments in feminist legal theory in both the 1980s and 1990s have taken place in a social context freighted with complexity and contradiction. In the crosscurrents of the 1980s, feminist legal theory emerged as a serious academic topic, despite the resurgence of conservative politics in the larger society. The parallel in the 1990s is that while feminist legal theory has become established in the legal academy, critics of legal feminism have also proliferated, becoming more visible and more organized. Much of the criticism is constructive and directed toward finding genuine points of agreement and disagreement. Some of it, however, displays an unmistakable contempt for feminist scholars and their projects. This decade has thus been characterized both by a growing respect for feminist legal theory in some quarters and by a persistent backlash that continues to mark the field as controversial and risky for many students and writers.

Perhaps the most telling evidence of the rise of feminist legal theory has been the growth in the number and diversity of casebooks in the field. In law schools, the casebook has an unusual place in the curriculum because it is often the only text assigned for a course. Typically, as fields in the law begin to emerge, professors will assemble unpublished packets of materials for new courses or seminars before they attempt to define the area through means of a published casebook. The appearance of a casebook often signals that the subject has "arrived," in the sense that publishers have confidence that there will be a market for the book in the upcoming years. The first two casebooks on the law of sex discrimination were published in the mid-1970s,[1] with a heavy emphasis on case analysis of constitutional law, family law, and employment discrimination law. By the late 1990s, there were six casebooks in the field, with titles such as *Gender and Law, Feminist*

Jurisprudence, and *Law and Violence against Women*.[2] One of the most prominent features of the new and revised casebooks is that each contains extensive treatment of feminist legal theory, although several retain an emphasis on case analysis and historical context.

The burgeoning interest in feminist legal theory is also in evidence among law students, the group responsible for editing and running most law reviews and law journals. By the end of the decade, there were sixteen legal journals specifically devoted to gender issues and several more concentrating on the intersection of race, sexuality, and gender.[3] Among the "mainstream" law journals, moreover, citation counters noticed that feminist articles and articles written from a critical race perspective were increasingly making it onto the "most cited" lists, indicating an interest in, if not wholehearted acceptance of, these new scholarly movements.[4]

The creation of these new outlets for feminist-oriented articles and books had a material impact beyond the circulation of feminist ideas and theories to a wider audience. Some feminist law teachers—the vast majority of whom are women—found it possible to secure tenure, promotions, and even chaired professorships on the basis of "outsider" scholarship that might not have qualified as "legal" scholarship a decade ago. Law students with feminist inclinations discovered that there was at least a corner of the curriculum receptive to their interests and that they did not necessarily have to abandon their interest in feminist topics when they made law review.

Perhaps because of the rapidity of some of these feminist incursions into legal education and legal scholarship, it is easy to overstate the degree of change that has taken place. Neither the presence of women in the profession nor the existence of feminist legal theory has gone unchallenged. Several studies of the experience of women law students in the late 1980s and early 1990s indicate that large numbers of women continue to regard the law school environment as hostile, male-dominated, and alienating. The most publicized study,[5] which Lani Guinier and others conducted at the University of Pennsylvania Law School, found that, despite equal entry-level credentials, male law students were three times more likely than women to end up in the top 10 percent of the class and were disproportionately represented in prestigious positions and extracurricular activities. The researchers hypothesized that a hostile learning environment existed at Penn, which, to a significant degree, accounted for women's disparate performance.[6] The qualitative portion of the study indicated that women were often silenced in class by the taunts and ridicule of their classmates or intimidated by belittling comments from professors.[7] Over the course of three years, women reported lower levels of class participation than their male peers and a disaffection with the Socratic method, which many perceived as humiliating, overly aggressive, and intolerant of different perspectives.[8] Although studies from other schools did not always replicate the Penn findings on disparate performance between men and women, they did tend to confirm that equality remained elusive for large numbers of women law students, despite the fact that nationally women make up 43 percent of the law school enrollment.

Moreover, as feminism has become established in the legal academic world, a vigorous critique has emerged along with it, focusing on some of feminism's basic premises and accompanied by a resistance to what some perceive to be the feminization of legal studies, whether represented by increasing numbers of women students and women faculty or the influence of feminist thought. One particularly caustic op-ed essay in the *National Law Journal*,[9] for example, complained that the feminization of law schools had produced lawyers who were ill suited to the practice of law and lambasted progressive law faculty for embracing ideals of "feel-goodism and empathy." In terms that echoed nineteenth-century tracts against the higher education of women, the author warned that enrolling yet more women in law school would not ease the problems of the profession because "a lawyer's success depends on skill, not ideology."

As was characteristic of many backlashes in the past, this latest backlash against feminist legal theory has occurred well before the establishment of gender equality in law schools or in the legal profession. The point made by Susan Faludi in her popular book *Backlash* seems appropriate to describe a quality of the response to feminist legal thought in the 1990s. As Faludi sees it, "the antifeminist backlash has been set off not by women's achievement of full equality but by the increased possibility that they might win it. It is a preemptive strike that stops women long before they reach the finish line."[10]

It has probably always been the case that the critics of legal feminism have been as plentiful and diverse as the field of feminist legal theory itself. In the 1970s and 1980s, the most prevalent negative response to feminist legal theory was simply to ignore it and proceed to analyze an area of law as if feminist approaches to the subject were nonexistent or unimportant. Such marginalization of the field persists, as evidenced by the fact that feminist legal scholars still tend to be classified separately from their colleagues in the mainstream of legal philosophy and jurisprudence. However, as feminist legal theory has become more established in the 1990s, the critiques have also become more explicit and elaborate. There is now a fairly large number of articles and books devoted principally to attacking feminist legal theories, tracking a growing criticism of women's studies and feminism more generally.

The criticism has come from so many quarters that it is impossible to capture it fully in a short summary such as this one. Some of the critics would not hesitate to label themselves antifeminists. Others, however, regard themselves as feminists, even though they disagree with much of what conventionally comes under the heading of feminist legal thought. To give you a flavor of the types of arguments directed against feminist legal theory, I mention here three distinct genres of criticism that have proliferated in the

1990s. This by no means exhausts the varieties of critiques leveled at feminist legal theory, but is meant to suggest some of the different attitudes, tones, and intellectual stances of the critics.

The first genre of criticism employs the perspective of evolutionary biology (sometimes referred to as sociobiology) to explain and justify women's unequal status. Evolutionary biology is an active field of study outside the law that has begun to attract law professors to its ranks. Some in this group of predominately male scholars have challenged feminist assertions that phenomena such as the wage gap, occupational segregation, the glass ceiling, and the prevalence of sexual harassment should be regarded as systemic forms of sex discrimination and made subject to legal sanctions. In a modern version of "biology is destiny," they argue that different biological predispositions of men and women are responsible for the gendered patterns and practices in our society and propose repeal of many of the civil rights laws prohibiting sex discrimination.

The second genre has focused its attack largely on what it regards as feminism's excessive focus on the victimization of women. Many in this group are younger women who write primarily for a popular audience. Their particular targets have been laws and institutional policies related to date rape, pornography, and sexual harassment which they believe have inaccurately portrayed women as passive and powerlessness. Critics in this second group are more likely to identify themselves as feminists, although their work is largely directed toward exposing the flaws of feminist theory and activism, and proceeds from a premise that a primary cause of women's inequality is the feminist movement itself.

The third genre, represented most recently by the Independent Women's Forum, is a familiar brand of social conservatism that espouses traditional family values and promotes sex segregation in education and military training. Critics in this group believe that women have already achieved equality, embracing a contemporary version of "separate but equal." They have set as their goal the defeat of the "feminist establishment," particularly through initiation of law-related battles in the media, legislatures, and courts.

EVOLUTIONARY BIOLOGY

Criticism based on the perspective of evolutionary biology resonates strongly with familiar narratives of gender difference in the popular culture. Within academia, scholarship emphasizing the socially constructed nature of gender difference is on the rise in a variety of disciplines, particularly in feminist and postmodern writings. Outside the ivory tower, however, gender difference is most often discussed as if it were largely a "given," with its source in biological or natural differences between men and women and boys and girls. The discomfort popular writers often display when addressing racial differences has no parallel in discussions of sex differences. Resort to code words to signal race, such as "inner city" or "gang," is often unnecessary in media discussions about gender because it remains acceptable journalism to draw sharp contrasts between men and women and to assume that women and men have fundamentally different human natures.

Academic versions of the biological approach to gender differences generally pay more attention to the origin of such differences than their popular counterparts. For Kingsley Browne, for example, the key to the evolutionary approach is accepting the notion of "reproductive success" in the development of human psychology.[11] He starts from the premise that there is a biological imperative for each sex to maximize the chances that they will produce offspring who will survive and, the more offspring, the better. Evolutionary theorists propose that the strategy for reproductive success differs greatly for males and females. As Richard Posner asserts, supposedly females have to "make every pregnancy count"[12] and to this end they are "choosier" when selecting a mate. Browne posits that females have little interest in casual sex that is unlikely to result in another successful pregnancy.[13] The successful strategy for males, on the other hand, is said to entail far less "parental investment"—the theory is that males are better off pursuing many females and thereby multiplying the chances that some of their conquests will result in biological offspring. Part of this evolutionary story is also that males put considerable energy into competing with other males for the most "desirable" (i.e., young, beautiful, sexy) females.

Evolutionary theorists do not contend that, under current social arrangements, reproductive success is the most important value for men and women to pursue. Indeed, in an age where many persons choose not to have children, decide to abort fetuses, or decide to have only one child, it seems strange to insist that what matters most is having genetic offspring, particularly in cases where parents have no day-to-day relationship with their children. Instead, what often distinguishes contemporary evolutionary theorists from many popular commentators is the theorists' understanding that the biological predisposition may not be functional under modern conditions. Rather, the contention is that men and women are the way they are in part because such biological predispositions somehow become "embedded in the brain"[14] or "hard-wired" into human beings, persisting long past the time of their usefulness.

The gender differences most often highlighted by legal scholars from the evolutionary camp echo familiar scripts about "male" and "female" traits. They are often synonymous with masculine and feminine behaviors commonly regarded as stereotypes. Thus, evolutionary scholars claim that men are risk-takers, more driven to competition than women, and more focused on acquiring resources—that is, more interested in money. Women are said

to be nurturers, interested in children, and oriented towards others. With respect to sexuality, these authors assert that men are most interested in the
physical aspects of sex, while women are more concerned with love and intimacy. Finally, evolutionary scholars contend that men are better at spatial
relationships, while women tend to excel in language skills.[15]

The interesting twist that evolutionary writers give the old repertoire of
gendered traits, however, is their insistence that they are predispositions inherited from an ancient time which live on into the present. For many of
these scholars, the fact that many individuals do not follow the gendered
script does not undercut their hypotheses. In this genre of legal scholarship,
the method is to link perceived patterns of behavior to general predispositions, most often followed by a defense of the status quo.

Writers from an evolutionary perspective have focused on two topics of
particular interest to feminists: motherhood and sexuality. In an early example of the sociobiological approach, for example, Richard Epstein attempted
to explain and justify the gender division of labor in the workforce by linking it to gender differences in spatial perception and women's distinctive capacity to breast-feed. After listing the benefits to be gained from specialization, Epstein hypothesized that women were naturally suited to child-raising,
while men were predisposed to do everything else.

> The mere fact that the mother carries with her a supply of milk makes it clear that
> she is the better candidate for staying with the child, consequently leaving the
> male of the species to engage in a broad class of explorative activities. The nur-
> turing instincts usually attributable to women are a set of attitudinal adaptations
> that reduce the cost of doing activities that help promote the survival of both her
> and her offspring. Although modern women operate in settings far different from
> those of their ancient mothers, the initial tendency remains: If nurturing brings
> greater pleasure to or requires lower cost for women than for men, then we
> should expect to see women devote a greater percentage of their resources to it
> than men. This specialization will endure in the aggregate and should be accepted
> for what it is: a healthy adaptation that works for the benefit of all concerned.[16]

As could be expected, feminists have disputed Epstein's sociobiological
account of the gender division of labor at the various critical points of his
analysis. In particular, Kathryn Abrams has sought to advance feminist theory by engaging some of its fiercest critics. In response to Epstein, Abrams
first sought to "interrogate the assertion of biological influence"[17] on
women's supposed preference for nurturing. She noted that there was no
convincing scientific evidence locating a predisposition to nurture in a particular portion of the brain. Without totally rejecting the possibility of biological influence, Abrams offered a cultural account of women's propensity
to nurture. Rather than being inherited, Abrams argued that the special capacity to nurture could just as easily be viewed as an adaptation to specific

situations, as behavior learned by "women watching and mothering each other."[18] Abrams also doubted the rationality of singling out breast-feeding as the gender difference that produced the gender division of labor, particularly given that for quite some time there have been adequate substitutes for nourishing infants. Rather than accept women's "instinct" to nurture as biologically driven, Abrams deconstructed women's "choice" to nurture by spelling out the powerful cultural reinforcements behind such choices, including husbands' disapproval of their wives working outside the home, the social labeling of child care as "women's work," and the entire history of exclusion, discrimination, and lack of accommodation of women in the workplace, particularly with regard to pregnant employees and new mothers.

Perhaps the most well-known book embracing an evolutionary perspective on the law is Richard Posner's *Sex and Reason*. In it, Posner develops an economic or rational-choice theory of sex. His approach is also informed by evolutionary biology, which he regards as "a parallel mode of inquiry to economic analysis."[19] His analysis of rape, sexual harassment, and a host of other sexually oriented topics proceeds from the assumption that "men and women have pursued different sexual strategies, that these are related to the different reproductive capacities of the two sexes, and that sexual attractiveness is related to reproductive fitness."[20] Similar to Epstein's analysis, Posner's theory incorporates a belief that men strive to have intercourse with as many women as possible, while women are interested in stable relationships with a man who can provide for their children.[21]

Despite the use of some economic vocabulary, the narrative of men's and women's different sexual strategies in *Sex and Reason* is reminiscent of conventional 1950s attitudes towards marriage, sex, and dating. This feature is perhaps most pronounced in the chapter on coercive sex. In marked contrast to feminist accounts such as Catharine MacKinnon's, for example, Posner's analysis of rape downplays power and accentuates sexual desire. He regards rape as "primarily a substitute for consensual sexual intercourse rather than a manifestation of male hostility toward women or a method of establishing or maintaining male domination."[22] In his sexual version of rape, it is because men's sex drive is stronger than women's that women are given the assignment of controlling natural male "promiscuity" and must do their best to "screen out potential rapists."[23] Rape is described as if it were a market transaction in which women try to protect their sexual goods from men bent on stealing them, if they cannot arrive at a satisfactory price. For Posner, date rape inevitably occurs when men who are single-mindedly searching for sex find it hard to distinguish among "coy women" who pretend to resist (but "no" really means "yes"), from women who mean it when they say no.[24] The downside to prosecuting date rape in Posner's view is that it might discourage some men from dating, which he worries might harm heterosexual women who use dating as a means of finding the right man.[25]

Throughout his analysis, Posner treats injury to women's reproductive autonomy as the central injury of rape, in line with the evolutionary emphasis on reproductive fitness. He notes that marital rape is of concern because it can cause an unwanted pregnancy,[26] suggesting that the injury might be less if there were no chance that the woman would become pregnant. By linking sexual autonomy so closely to reproductive choice, Posner's commodified view of sex eclipses women's interest in personal autonomy apart from concerns about pregnancy.

Carol Sanger's feminist review of Posner's book took issue with two of its underlying assumptions: that the male need to have sex should be treated as a "given" or a "prior preference,"[27] and that sex is an undifferentiated commodity, equally encompassing consensual intercourse and rape. In "He's Gotta Have It," Sanger charged that Posner's evolutionary/economic perspective was fundamentally male-oriented, reflecting "sex and reason from a boy's point of view."[28] For Sanger, Posner's very concept of "sex" reflected male experience: She protested that by the book's definition, "sex begins, and to a large extent quickly ends, with male ejaculation."[29] She pointed out that with this singular focus on intercourse, many relational and emotional aspects of sexuality are likely to be lost, with the result that women's experiences of sex were largely unrepresented in the book. Echoing a dominant theme in radical feminist accounts of rape,[30] Sanger disputed the view that rape was primarily about sex. She insisted that "rape is not a sex substitute,"[31] citing empirical studies of men who are sexually active with consenting wives and partners at the time they rape other women. In Sanger's world, many men as well as women "simply define sexual intercourse to exclude rape."[32] In a Gilliganesque approach to moral reasoning, Sanger argued that it was not irrational for an individual to act out of respect or sympathy towards another and yet to regard such action as within one's *self*-interest. Her scathing review of *Sex and Reason* demonstrates how some of the basic premises of the evolutionary approach conflict with feminist theories, from both radical and cultural feminist viewpoints.

Up to this point, the legal writers espousing an evolutionary perspective have tended to be antifeminist, or at least not sympathetic with the desire for thoroughgoing social change that characterizes most feminist writings. One reviewer has suggested that evolutionary psychology may be fundamentally aligned with social conservatism because the evolutionary approach "identifies the main obstacles to radical social change as lying within the individual rather than outside of him."[33] Particularly when it comes to analyzing women's choices with respect to work and family, evolutionary writers often seem happy to have a crisp answer ("it's in the genes") to explain why women would voluntarily choose paths that produce poverty, expose them to violence, and accord them low social status and esteem.[34]

However, as several scholars have pointed out, acceptance of an evolutionary perspective need not necessarily be antifeminist. Few assert these days that biologically influenced preferences can never be altered. Indeed, some cultural conventions may be more resistant to change than biological conditions. Thus, the nature/nurture debate over origins should not be confused with the very different question of whether patterns can be changed, and whether it is worthwhile to do so.[35] Nevertheless, perhaps because of the long history of subordinating women in the name of nature, the rhetoric and reasoning of the work inspired by evolutionary biology most often reads like an apology for sex discrimination and an attack on feminism. For this reason, it is difficult to envision this genre of criticism taking a feminist turn.

VICTIM FEMINISM

The portrait of women most often projected by evolutionary theorists is maternal and oddly reminiscent of Victorian stereotypes: The woman maximizes her chances for reproductive success by being modest, uninterested in casual sex, and nurturing toward children. Critics from the evolutionary school such as Epstein chastise feminists for denying gender differences and for embracing an equality of "equal outcomes" that seeks elimination of gender disparities in wealth, occupations, and material aspects of life. In the evolutionary critique, feminism is often equated with a wooden type of liberal feminism and the most immediate targets of these critics are antidiscrimination laws characteristic of the 1970s equality stage of feminist activism.

The next group of critics—those decrying what they call "victim feminism"—have little quarrel with liberal feminism. Like feminists of the late 1960s and 1970s (their mothers' generation), they employ a rhetoric that deplores protectionism and cherishes freedom and equality. This younger group of writers is most troubled by what they perceive as the wrong turn feminism took in the 1980s, when scholars such as MacKinnon began to focus on issues of coercive sexuality, particularly rape, sexual harassment, and pornography. Interestingly, the image of women that this second group of critics finds so objectionable is also a Victorian portrait of femininity—namely, the image of the innocent, fragile, vulnerable, sexless woman. What is most striking about their critique, however, is that they connect this image to dominance feminism and largely hold feminists, rather than more traditional groups, responsible for constricting young women's freedom and opportunities.

One widely read book that captures the flavor of the victim feminism critique is Katie Roiphe's *The Morning After: Sex, Fear, and Feminism* (1993). The title evokes a prominent theme in the book questioning the crisis surrounding date rape. As a Harvard undergrad in the late 1980s and Princeton graduate student in the early 1990s, Roiphe encountered a feminism that she felt was obsessed with sexual danger and that robbed her and her classmates of the excitement and freedom that comes with sexual experimentation. She describes how organized efforts on college campuses from Take Back the Night marches to safe-sex workshops, managed to instill a fear of AIDS and rape in young women, but did little to help women deal with the ambiguity and complexity of real sexual relationships. She claims that although there is no longer talk about affronts to women's honor or virtue, the contemporary discussion about "posttraumatic stress syndrome" and "trauma" continues to construct women as passive victims of male sexual aggression. According to Roiphe, feminists are now in the strange position of warning women against the dangerous ways of men and in the process, they treat women as if they lacked the intelligence and courage to take care of themselves.

> The image that emerges from feminist preoccupations with rape and sexual harassment is that of women as victims, offended by a professor's dirty joke, verbally pressured into sex with peers. This image of the delicate woman bears a striking resemblance to that fifties ideal my mother and the other women of her generation fought so hard to get away from. . . . But here she is again, with her pure intentions and her wide eyes. Only this time it is the feminists themselves who are breathing new life into her."[36]

Roiphe equates feminism with a rigid and caricatured version of dominance feminism (which she calls "rape-crisis feminism") that revels in tales of women's victimization and has the effect of duping college-age women into believing that they have been sexually exploited by men, sometimes after the fact—as the title puts it, the morning after. She is skeptical of accounts of professed rape victims at public rallies because, for Roiphe, their stories all sound the same and their credibility is undermined by a self-congratulatory rhetoric that belies genuine trauma. Rather than being transgressive or unconventional, Roiphe regards feminism as the new orthodoxy, with pages taken from the recovery movement (such as the Twelve-Step Program) and social conservatism. Her critique trades on the backlash against "political correctness" by claiming that it is the feminists themselves who are most adept at silencing dissent, as they "vie for the position of being silenced."[37]

Roiphe's critique of feminism blends in with more traditionalist views about dating and sex when she approaches the topic of individual responsibility. She has little patience for women who complain that they were induced by men to drink too much at a party, remember little about the circumstances under which they had intercourse, and wake up to find themselves alone in a strange room. In such circumstances, Roiphe would hold the woman responsible for "[her] choice to drink or take drugs,"[38] even if her judgment was impaired at the time she had sex. For Roiphe, to do otherwise would be to assume that women are "helpless and naive" and to buy into Victorian stereotypes of women as devoid of passion and sexual desire. There is a strong strain of individualism in critiques such as Roiphe's. Rather than enforce rules against sexual harassment, Roiphe commends the "sticks and stones" approach to verbal harassment, urging women to "put offenders in their place" by sharp retorts or even physical retaliation. She recounts with approval one incident in which a college woman was playing pinball at the local lunch place when a teenage boy came up and grabbed her breast. Roiphe was impressed by the way the woman responded: "She calmly went to the counter and ordered a glass of milk and then walked over and poured it over his head."[39] More recently, another critic has made a similar plea for "female Rambo-ism" in an essay about Paula Jones's lawsuit against former President Clinton. Her view was that even though Jones justifiably might have been offended by Clinton's alleged exposure of his penis, she should not have resorted to the courts. She felt that Jones should have responded by "suitable speech (the phrase 'Put that shrivelly stump back in your pants' comes to mind), or by ignoring the conduct, or by storming out of the room."[40] For such critics of victim feminism, these individualistic responses have the advantage of showing women to be strong and capable of "taking it" because "[a] woman who disses the phallus, whether by disrespect or disregard, denies its power."[41] The disadvantage, of course, is that few people, men *or* women, have the presence of mind to respond at the moment with style or confidence. Particularly for women, many attempts at retaliation simply come off as being silly, or overreactions, or incoherent.

In its more extreme form, individualism translates into libertarianism and an argument for deregulation. For example, journalist Cathy Young[42] takes the victim feminism critique so far as to regard advocacy of the "reasonable woman" standard in sexual harassment litigation as "protective feminism" and virtually indistinguishable from social conservatives' call for decency and a return to traditional sex roles. Young believes that legal regulation of sexual conduct in the workplace is invariably a form of legal paternalism and is even wary of equality feminists such as Justice Ruth Bader Ginsburg who support using the law to eliminate all forms of disparate treatment of men and women.[43] Like Roiphe, Young seems to believe that women as individuals possess a preexisting power that can liberate them from second-class citizenship, if only feminists, institutions, and the state will get out of the way.

As part of her more extensive analysis of the relationship between victimization and agency,[44] Kathryn Abrams has responded to the victim feminism critics by articulating the ways in which their critique misunderstands the arguments of MacKinnon and other dominance theorists. In a review of Roiphe's book, Abrams argues that Roiphe confuses advocacy of legal intervention with a concession that women are inherently too weak to protect themselves. Abrams's position is that establishing a legal cause of action against sexual harassment or acquaintance rape says nothing specific about the actions or the character of the victims, drawing the analogy that "[l]aws that make theft or assault a crime make no statement about the capacity of victims, and require nothing more than that the victims give evidence."[45] Abrams denies that affording women a legal right to sue for sexually offensive conduct necessarily discourages women from developing assertive individual responses to harassment or somehow implies that such individual responses are inappropriate. In defense of dominance feminism, Abrams underscores the difference between spelling out how women have been victimized, that is, exposing mechanisms of subordination, and claiming that women are the "walking wounded" who have been personally immobilized by male aggression.

The most important question for Abrams is how feminist accounts of victimization can so easily be misread and taken as "insults," even by writers such as Roiphe who identify themselves as feminists. Abrams theorizes that critics such as Roiphe have thoroughly embraced the liberal view of the individual as autonomous and self-directing. For them to acknowledge that women are constrained in their choices by a sexist society becomes tantamount to saying that women "suffer a kind of compromised personhood"[46] or are less than full-fledged individuals. Abrams thus has a response to Roiphe's complaint that contemporary feminism has catapulted women back into the 1950s, forgetting the lessons of liberal feminism. As I read Abrams, she is claiming that it is Roiphe who missed out on the teachings of the 1980s difference theorists, particularly their powerful critique of liberalism. While presumably both writers would agree that feminism, of whatever variety, has not yet succeeded in freeing women, Abrams does not take feminism's lack of success to mean that it is a principal cause of women's subordination. Instead, she seeks to understand women simultaneously as agents and victims, placing feminism also on the side of agency.

THE NEW RIGHT-WING ATTACK

The charge of victim feminism is just one of many charges leveled at legal feminism by right-wing critics such as the leadership of the Independent Women's Forum, who exemplify a third genre of criticism. Unlike evolutionary theorists or liberal individualists like Roiphe, critics in this third group do not endorse a theoretically unified set of beliefs about gender, sexuality, or equality. Their positions are more reactive, taking aim at what they regard as the priorities in the agenda of the feminist "establishment." Thus, they sometimes advocate formal equality and sex blindness, as in their campaigns against affirmative action and the Violence against Women Act.[47] With respect to other controversies, however, they defend sex segregation and the use of explicit classifications based on gender. The politics of this third group of critics are very close to that of older, ultra-conservative groups such as Phyllis Schlafly's Eagle Forum, which was most famous for its opposition to equality feminism, particularly the proposed Equal Rights Amendment. The new rhetoric associated with the Independent Women's Forum, however, eschews labels like liberal or conservative, claiming instead to be "the voice of reasonable women," who make arguments from "common sense" and "logic" rather than "divisive ideology."

What is most striking about the publicity of the Independent Women's Forum, however, is their intemperate tone with respect to people and ideas allied with feminism. The executive director of the group, lawyer Anita Blair, regards feminism as on a par with racism, and has stated that "a feminist is a person who irrationally puts women ahead of men and, frequently, ahead of children," which echoes her definition of a racist as "somebody who irrationally puts his own race ahead of others."[48] In her view, feminism is a cynical enterprise that elitist women use to gain advantages over less elite women.[49] In this critique, feminists have no genuine interest in solving real problems facing women, such as domestic violence, but want only to assure that there is "a constant stream of victims"[50] to justify their requests for government funding. The Independent Women's Forum has tried to position itself as the voice of reason, offering "an intelligent refutation of the leading feminist nonsense that is swallowed so uncritically by the mainstream press."[51]

As the preceding paragraph suggests, this third genre of criticism is full of ironies and internal contradictions. In my view, Anita Blair embraces an upside-down worldview that distorts and lumps together the varieties of feminist approaches in a pugnacious style not likely to produce thoughtful responses and rejoinders. By labeling feminist positions as irrational and nonsensical, her call to "reason" and "common sense," for example, has the opposite effect of cutting off debate before the merits of a position are addressed. Feminist concerns about diversity and feminist opposition to hierarchy are dismissed out of hand as disingenuous, simply by claiming that it is feminists, not antifeminists, who are the elitists. Perhaps most importantly, feminists' struggle for equality for women is recast as a plea for special rights, playing into the stereotype of feminists as man-haters and abortion supporters who have little regard for children.

The Independent Women's Forum's critique of feminism resembles what Carolyn Heilbrun has called "The Smear." In Heilbrun's analysis, the right-wing backlash against feminism and multiculturalism in the 1980s and 1990s has often taken the form of name-calling and accusations, and employs a political version of projection: accusing your opponent of what you yourself are doing.[52] One response to Blair's critique, for example, would be to point out how the campaign of the Independent Women's Forum relies heavily on divisive ideology and is often short on reasoned analysis. For this reason, it is difficult to summarize this genre of criticism by teasing out recurrent themes or positions. The following three lines of opposition to feminism, however, can be seen in recent publicity from the group.

First, particularly with respect to issues relating to segregation, critics in this group believe that it is inappropriate to analogize sex and race discrimination. In marked contrast to many feminist writers who see racism and sexism as interrelated forms of oppression, many of today's conservative critics argue for different legal treatment of explicit race and sex classifications. Thus, in a brief in support of Virginia Military Institute's policy of excluding women, the Independent Women's Forum argued that while "racial differences are purely superficial," differences between men and women are "real and substantial."[53] Implicit in their argument is the belief that gender differences are biologically based and that segregating the sexes is an appropriate way of marking and responding to such differences. The group has also opposed gender integration during basic training in the military on the basis that integration reduces standards and compromises the military's effectiveness. Unlike some feminists who support women-only institutions as a way of helping women overcome sexism in society, the concern of critics such as the Independent Women's Forum is with protecting male institutions from women and their values.

A second, somewhat contradictory theme of this genre of criticism is antipathy to gender-consciousness and the corresponding belief that gender has no proper place in the framing of public policy. This theme has been most evident in the group's opposition to the work of the task force on gender and race bias in the D.C. Circuit.[54] In a statement criticizing the task force's report, Blair took the position that it was objectionable for the task force even to count the number of women and minorities judges in the D.C. Circuit, claiming that any evaluation of the demographics of the judiciary infringed on the president's right to nominate judges and the Senate's right to confirm judicial nominations.[55] Such extreme hostility to gender and race consciousness echoes conservative complaints against affirmative action, which proceed from the assumption that any use of race or gender is discriminatory, even when the objective is to eliminate or prevent race or gender discrimination. From this perspective, merely searching for possible bias undermines judges' impartiality and threatens to erode public confidence in the courts. This position also makes changing the status quo nearly impossible. Judith Resnik sees such opposition to the usually uncontroversial work of the gender and race bias task forces as part of a larger right-wing backlash that generally disputes the existence of systemic discrimination in legal institutions and regards feminism as the evil to be guarded against.

Task forces, the critics claim, violate "our" traditions by creating "faction in civil society." Under this plot, we (that is literally all of us) are equal before the law. Courts are blind to distinctions based on race, color, gender, and/or ethnicity. Objectors accuse task forces that mark differences of *making* differences by seeking special favor and undermining the impartiality of law [and contend] that naming differences between women and men creates differences, that affirmative action creates prejudice rather than responds to it."[56]

The third and perhaps most prominent theme in this genre of criticism is that women have already achieved equality. The critics part company with feminists most sharply in their denial of systematic bias against women in society. For example, representatives of the Independent Women's Forum claim that there is no widespread gender discrimination in compensation, despite acknowledging the fact that full-time women workers in 1992 earned only 72 percent of wages of men working full-time. In support of their claim that there is no inequity, they rely on a study finding that among people age 27 to 33 who have never had a child, women earn almost 98 percent of men's wages.[57] The selection of that statistic is revealing because it suggests that the gender disparity in compensation is correlated to motherhood, given that it does not affect the relatively small number of younger women workers in this cohort with no children. It also underscores an important point of disagreement in the interpretation of workplace statistics between feminists and conservative critics. Feminists tend to infer discrimination from data showing that males on average earn more than females, controlling for type of work and number of hours of work. In contrast, conservative critics more often assume that mothers earn less than similarly situated fathers because they have voluntarily chosen to subordinate their work to family concerns. What feminists regard as discrimination, conservative critics ascribe to women's choice. Underneath the conservative contention that gender equality already exists lies a conception of motherhood as fundamentally different from fatherhood and a belief that women who also care for children cannot expect to achieve parity in the workplace. The "equality" heralded by the Independent Women's Forum is a vastly different concept of equality than is embraced by legal feminists, and, to my mind, marks the boundary between feminism and the backlash against feminism.

Much of the criticism of feminism and feminist legal theory described above assumes that feminism has become the dominant ideology and positions its critics as dissenters who wage an uphill battle against the establishment. Feminists find this claim amusing because, from their vantage point, the forces undermining feminism have always been strong and have only gained considerable strength during the "culture wars" of the 1990s. There is fundamental disagreement about what constitutes the "mainstream." The degree of recognition recently accorded to feminist legal theory hardly seems enough to transport the field from the margin to the center of legal discourse.

Instead, as a teacher of feminist law courses, I find that the backlash has had a concrete and cumulative effect. Each year, students shy away from courses with "feminism" in their title because they sense that their careers might suffer if they are linked to the feminist movement, however tangentially. They admit that they worry about having the "f" word appear on their transcript of courses or on their résumé, in case a prospective employer might get the wrong impression. The day has not yet arrived when students can satisfy their curiosity and interest, sign up for courses in feminism, and not give it a moment's thought. Until the stigma of feminism has been erased, it seems premature to speak of the "feminist establishment" or to locate feminist legal theory within the mainstream of legal thought.

NOTES

This essay was reprinted from *Introduction to Feminist Legal Theory, First Edition, 1999,* with the permission of Aspen Law & Business.

1. Barbara Allen Babcock, Ann E. Freedman, Eleanor Holmes Norton, and Susan D. Ross, *Sex Discrimination and the Law* (Boston: Little, Brown, 1975); Kenneth M. Davidson, Ruth Bader Ginsburg, Herma Hill Kay, *Sex-Based Discrimination* (St. Paul, Minn.: West Publishing, 1974).

2. The seven casebooks are Herma Hill Kay and Martha S. West, *Sex-Based Discrimination*, 4th ed. (St. Paul, Minn.: West Publishing, 1996); Barbara Allen Babcock, Ann E. Freedman, Susan Deller Ross, Wendy Webster Williams, Rhonda Copelon, Deborah L. Rhode, and Nadine Taub, *Sex Discrimination and the Law*, 2nd ed. (Boston: Little, Brown, 1996); Mary Becker, Cynthia Grant Bowman, and Morrison Torrey, *Feminist Jurisprudence* (St. Paul, Minn.: West Publishing, 1994); Katharine T. Bartlett and Angela P. Harris, *Gender and Law*, 2nd ed., (New York: Aspen Law & Business, 1998); Mary Jo Frug, *Women and the Law* (New York: Foundation Press, 1992); Beverly Balos and Mary Louise Fellows, *Law and Violence against Women* (Durham, N.C.: Carolina Academic Press, 1994). Catharine MacKinnon's casebook, *Sex Equality* (New York: Foundation Press, 2001), was published in 2001.

3. Anderson's *1997 Directory of Law Reviews and Scholarly Legal Periodicals* (Cincinnati, Ohio: Anderson Publishing, 1997), 27–28, 24–25.

4. Fred R. Shapiro, "The Most-Cited Law Review Articles Revisited," *Chicago-Kent Law Review* 71 (1996): 751.

5. *See* Lani Guinier, Michelle Fine, and Jane Balin, "Becoming Gentlemen: Women's Experiences at One Ivy League Law School," *University of Pennsylvania Law Review* 143 (1994): 1.

6. Guinier, Fine, Balin, "Becoming Gentlemen," 59.

7. Guinier, Fine, Balin, "Becoming Gentlemen," 43, 51–52.

8. Guinier, Fine, Balin, "Becoming Gentlemen," 46–47.

9. Arthur Austin, "Womanly Approach Harms Future Lawyers," *National Law Journal* 18 May 1998.

10. Susan Faludi, *Backlash: The Undeclared War against American Women* (New York: Crown, 1991), xx.

11. Kingsley R. Browne, "An Evolutionary Perspective on Sexual Harassment: Seeking Roots in Biology Rather than Ideology," *Journal of Contemporary Legal Issues* 8 (1997): 5.

12. Richard A. Posner, *Sex and Reason* (Cambridge, Mass.: Harvard University Press, 1992): 91.

13. Browne, "Evolutionary Perspective," 17.

14. Richard A. Epstein, "Gender Is for Nouns," *DePaul Law Review* 41 (1992): 981, 990.

15. See Kingsley R. Browne, "Sex and Temperament in Modern Society: A Darwinian View of the Glass Ceiling and the Gender Gap," *Arizona Law Review* 37 (1995): 971.

16. Richard A. Epstein, "Gender," 990.

17. Kathyrn Abrams, "Social Construction, Roving Biologism, and Reasonable Women: A Response to Professor Epstein," *DePaul Law Review* 41 (1992): 1021, 1023.

18. Abrams, "Social Construction," 1026.

19. Posner, *Sex and Reason* (1992): 108.

20. Posner, *Sex and Reason* (1992): 108.

21. Posner, *Sex and Reason* (1992): 90–94.

22. Posner, *Sex and Reason* (1992): 384.

23. Posner, *Sex and Reason* (1992): 391.

24. Posner, *Sex and Reason* (1992): 391.

25. Posner, *Sex and Reason* (1992): 395.

26. Posner, *Sex and Reason* (1992): 390.

27. Carol Sanger, "He's Gotta Have It," *Southern California Law Review* 66 (1993): 1221, 1224–25 (review of Richard Posner, *Sex and Reason*).

28. Sanger, "He's Gotta Have It," 1223.

29. Sanger, "He's Gotta Have It," 1223.

30. See, e.g., Catharine A. MacKinnon, *Towards a Feminist Theory of the State* (Cambridge, Mass.: Harvard University Press, 1989): 173.

31. MacKinnon, *Towards a Feminist Theory of the State* (1989): 1232.

32. MacKinnon, *Towards a Feminist Theory of the State* (1989): 1231.

33. Amy L. Wax, "Against Nature—On Robert Wright's *The Moral Animal*," *University of Chicago Law Review* 63 (1996): 307, 336.

34. See especially Kingsley Browne, "Sex and Temperament," 1083–92.

35. For elaboration on this point, see David A. Strauss, "Biology, Difference, and Gender Discrimination," *DePaul Law Review* 41 (1992): 1007.

36. Katie Roiphe, *The Morning After: Sex, Fear, and Feminism* (Boston: Little, Brown, 1993): 6.

37. Roiphe, *The Morning After: Sex, Fear, and Feminism*, 34.

38. Roiphe, *The Morning After: Sex, Fear, and Feminism*, 53–54.

39. Roiphe, *The Morning After: Sex, Fear, and Feminism*, 101.

40. Terry Diggs, "Reach Out and Slap Someone: The Real Reason Why Working Women Have Snubbed Paula Jones," *Legal Times* (13 April 1998): 24.

41. Diggs, "Reach Out and Slap Someone," 24.

42. Cathy Young, "The New Madonna/Whore Syndrome: Feminism, Sexuality, and Sexual Harassment," *New York Law School Law Review* 38 (1993): 257.

43. Young, "The New Madonna," 268–69.

44. See Kathryn Abrams, "Complex Claimants and Reductive Moral Judgments: New Patterns in the Search for Equality," *University of Pittsburgh Law Review* 57 (1996): 337, 348; Kathryn Abrams, "Sex Wars Redux: Agency and Coercion in Feminist Legal Theory," *Columbia Law Review* 95 (1995): 304, 352.

45. Kathyrn Abrams, "Songs of Innocence and Experience: Dominance Feminism in the University," *Yale Law Journal* 103 (1994): 1533, 1553.

46. Abrams, "Songs of Innocence," 1554.

47. See Testimony of Anita Blair on Behalf of the Independent Women's Forum before the House Appropriations Committee, Subcommittee on Commerce, Justice, State and Judiciary and Related Agencies, 11 May 1995 (urging Congress not to fund Violence against Women Act).

48. Stephen Goode, "Armed with Common Sense, Anita Blair Attacks Feminism," *Insight on the News* (24 November 1997): 31.

49. Goode, "Armed with Common Sense," 31.

50. Goode, "Armed with Common Sense," 31.

51. Web page: <http://www.iwf.org/about.cfm>.

52. Carolyn G. Heilbrun, "The Thomas Confirmation Hearings or How Being a Humanist Prepares You for Right-Wing Politics," *Southern California Law Review* 65 (1992): 1569, 1571.

53. *Supreme Court* vs. *VMI* Amicus Brief by IWF, <http://www. iwf. org/newsitem .cfm> (11 May 1998).

54. For discussion of the work of the "bias in the courts'" task forces, see Judith Resnik, "Asking about Gender in Courts," *Signs: Journal of Women in Culture and Society* 21 (1996): 952.

55. Anita Blair, "Proceedings of the 55th Judicial Conference of the District of Columbia Circuit," F.R.D. 160 (1994): 169, 194.

56. Judith Resnik, "Changing the Topic," *Cardozo: Studies in Law and Literature* 8 (1996): 339, 347.

57. See <http://www.iwf.org/about.cfm>.

BIBLIOGRAPHY

Abrams, Kathryn. "Complex Claimants and Reductive Moral Judgments: New Patterns in the Search for Equality." *University of Pittsburgh Law Review* 57 (1996): 337, 348.

———. "Sex Wars Redux: Agency and Coercion in Feminist Legal Theory." *Columbia Law Review* 95 (1995): 304, 352.

———. "Songs of Innocence and Experience: Dominance Feminism in the University." *Yale Law Journal* 103 (1994): 1533, 1553.

———. "Social Construction, Roving Biologism, and Reasonable Women: A Response to Professor Epstein." *DePaul Law Review* 41 (1992): 1021.

Anderson's *1997 Directory of Law Reviews and Scholarly Legal Periodicals.* Cincinnati, Oh.: Anderson Publishing Co., 1997: 27–28, 24–25.

Austin, Arthur. "Womanly Approach Harms Future Lawyers." *National Law Journal* (May 1998): 18.

Babcock, Barbara Allen, Ann E. Freedman, Susan Deller Ross, Wendy Webster Williams, Rhonda Copelon, Deborah L. Rhode, and Nadine Taub. *Sex Discrimination and the Law.* 2nd ed. Boston: Little, Brown, 1996.

Babcock, Barbara Allen, Ann E. Freedman, Eleanor Holmes Norton, and Susan D. Ross. *Sex Discrimination and the Law.* Boston: Little, Brown, 1975.

Balos Beverly, and Mary Louise Fellows. *Law and Violence against Women.* Durham, N.C.: Carolina Academic Press, 1994.

Bartlett, Katharine T., and Angela P. Harris. *Gender and Law.* 2nd ed. New York: Aspen Law & Business, 1998.

Becker, Mary, Cynthia Grant Bowman, and Morrison Torrey. *Feminist Jurisprudence.* St. Paul, Minn.: West Publishing, 1994.

Blair, Anita. "Proceedings of the 55th Judicial Conference of the District of Columbia Circuit." F.R.D. 160 (1994): 169, 194.

Browne, Kingsley R. "An Evolutionary Perspective on Sexual Harassment: Seeking Roots in Biology Rather than Ideology." *Journal of Contemporary Legal Issues* 8 (1997): 5.

———. "Sex and Temperament in Modern Society: A Darwinian View of the Glass Ceiling and the Gender Gap." *Arizona Law Review* 37 (1995): 971.

Chamallas, Martha. *Introduction to Feminist Legal Theory.* New York: Aspen Law & Business, 1999.

Davidson, Kenneth M., Ruth Bader Ginsburg, and Herma Hill Kay. *Sex-Based Discrimination.* St. Paul, Minn.: West Publishing, 1974.

Diggs, Terry. "Reach Out and Slap Someone: The Real Reason Why Working Women Have Snubbed Paula Jones." *Legal Times* 13 (April 1998): 24.

Epstein, Richard A. "Gender Is for Nouns." *DePaul Law Review* 41 (1992): 981.

Faludi, Susan. *Backlash: The Undeclared War against American Women.* New York: Crown, 1991.

Frug, Mary Jo. *Women and the Law.* New York: Foundation Press, 1992.

Goode, Stephen. "Armed with Common Sense, Anita Blair Attacks Feminism." *Insight on the News* 24 (November 1997): 31.

Guinier, Lani, Michelle Fine, and Jane Balin. "Becoming Gentlemen: Women's Experiences at One Ivy League Law School." *University of Pennsylvania Law Review* (1994): 143.

Heilbrun, Carolyn G. "The Thomas Confirmation Hearings or How Being a Humanist Prepares You for Right-Wing Politics." *Southern California Law Review* 65 (1992): 1569, 1571.

Kay, Herma Hill, and Martha S. West. *Sex-Based Discrimination.* 4th ed. St. Paul, Minn.: West Publishing, 1996.

MacKinnon, Catharine A. *Towards a Feminist Theory of the State.* Cambridge, Mass.: Harvard University Press, 1989.

———. *Sex Equality.* New York: Foundation Press, 2001.

Posner, Richard A. *Sex and Reason.* Cambridge, Mass.: Harvard University Press, 1992.

Resnik, Judith. "Asking about Gender in Courts." *Signs: Journal of Women in Culture and Society* 21 (1996): 952.

———. "Changing the Topic." *Cardozo: Studies in Law and Literature* 8 (1996): 339, 347.

Roiphe, Katie. *The Morning After: Sex, Fear, and Feminism.* Boston: Little, Brown, 1993.

Sanger, Carol. "He's Gotta Have It." 66 *Southern California Law Review* 66 (1993): 1221, 1224-25.

Shapiro, Fred R. "The Most-Cited Law Review Articles Revisited." *Chicago-Kent Law Review* 71 (1996): 751.

Strauss, David A. "Biology, Difference, and Gender Discrimination." *DePaul Law Review* 41 (1992): 1007.

Wax, Amy L. "Against Nature—On Robert Wright's *The Moral Animal*." *University of Chicago Law Review* 63 (1996): 307, 336.

Young, Cathy. "The New Madonna/Whore Syndrome: Feminism, Sexuality, and Sexual Harassment." *New York Law School Law Review* 38 (1993): 257.

III

BACKLASH FROM THE IVORY TOWER: PERSONAL AND POLITICAL

5

Welcome to the Boys' Club: Male Socialization and the Backlash against Feminism in Tenure Decisions

Anita M. Superson

On my office door hangs a humorous list of top ten reasons why God was denied tenure, to which I have added another, sober one: God was a "She." In this chapter I offer a philosophical analysis of denial of tenure to women which is motivated by gender discrimination (hereafter, discriminatory tenure denial).[1] I want to explicate how social and systematic forces, particularly those supporting an ideology of male separatism, function in tenure decisions to instigate a backlash against feminism and maintain male domination in philosophy.

INTRODUCTION: THE BACKLASH

In her Pulitzer Prize-winning book, *Backlash: The Undeclared War against American Women,*[2] Susan Faludi describes a backlash against feminism as a response to the perception that women are enjoying many economic, political, and social advancements. A backlash is not mere sexism; it occurs when hostility to female independence, and fear and loathing of feminism, is in an acute stage. According to Faludi, a backlash is

> caused not simply by a bedrock of misogyny but by the specific efforts of contemporary women to improve their status, efforts that have been interpreted time and again by men—especially men grappling with real threats to their economic and social well-being on other fronts—as spelling their own masculine doom.

Although the more virulent, outspoken antifeminists commonly harbor hatred toward both women's advancement and women themselves whom they perceive to advance on the wings of feminism, and instigate a backlash in response, backlash participants need not be conscious of the political nature of their actions—some even consider themselves feminists—and anyone, even women who endorse patriarchal assumptions, can participate. Faludi notes,

> The backlash is not a conspiracy, with a council dispatching agents from some central control room, nor are the people who serve its ends often aware of their role; some even consider themselves feminists. For the most part, its workings are encoded and internalized, diffuse and chameleonic.

The workings—as opposed to the outspoken advocates—of the backlash against feminism in philosophy, I want to argue, are embedded in and can be attributed at least partly to the tenure process itself. The actions that occur during a backlash, whether or not their agents intend them, jointly aim to push women back into their "acceptable" roles. And although feminism is the direct target of a backlash, women are its victims, for it is their progress that is halted. I compare a backlash to a wave in the ocean, with each roll toward the beach representing an advancement women have made toward equality, and each pull back toward the sea representing a setback women have suffered to their advancements. Women never seem to make it completely in a man's world, just as the water from the wave never seems to stay on the shore. Even women themselves begin to internalize the message of the backlash—Faludi says that a backlash is "most powerful when it goes private"—with the effect that they set back themselves in the same way the ocean water pulls back the wave into itself.

Backlash participants, Faludi says, blame feminism for the unhappiness women are said to suffer.[3] Feminism makes women veer away from traditional roles, and dupes them into believing that they can make it in a man's world. If women would just learn to conform to traditional roles, tenure denial, for instance, would not be an issue, and women would be happy. But this line of reasoning is erroneous for, as I shall argue, discriminatory tenure denial has a lot more to do with male power than female competence, and feminism should not be blamed for men's insecurity.

One piece of evidence of the backlash in academia is women's not making it through the ranks as quickly or as measurably as we would expect, even though, according to one report, "the influx of women into the [philosophy] profession commenced well over 20 years ago," and the number of women and men receiving doctorates has been equalizing over the years.[4] Indeed, the percentage of women receiving doctorates in philosophy rose steadily from 18 percent between 1970 and 1979, to 29 percent between 1980 and 1989, to 36 percent between 1990 and 1995, to 41 percent in 1996, then tapered off slightly to 37 percent in 1997.[5]

We would expect to see a concomitant increase in the number of women in the profession, reflected most accurately at the rank of full professor. Yet women's numbers in philosophy have gone up measurably only in recent years, though not by much. The number of women in philosophy rose from 13 percent between 1970 and 1975, to only 17 percent in 1989.[6] In 1989 women constituted only 9 percent of full professors and 11.8 percent of tenured faculty. According to a 1995 study which was based on data culled from the *Directory of Philosophy,* thirty-three departments of philosophy in Ivy League institutions and major graduate programs ("top ten" departments), women constituted only 11 percent of total faculty, but only 6 percent of full professors and 7 percent of tenured professors. In sixteen of thirty-three of the same departments, there were no women full professors at all, indicating that women are leaving the profession perhaps because they are not being promoted. According to data I tallied up in the same fashion from the 1998–1999 *Directory,* in the same thirty-three universities, sixteen had an increase since 1995 in the *percentage* of female full professors, six had a decrease, and eleven showed no change.[7] However, only eleven departments had an increase in the actual *number* of female professors, and in each case the number of women increased only by one. Since the 1995 study, then, the number of women full professors has jumped from 6 percent to only 9 percent. Only two of the thirty-three departments had three female full professors; the remainder had none (ten), one (seventeen), or two (four).

A broader, 1994 study conducted by the Committee on the Status of the Future of the Profession of the APA reported that there are no tenured women in two-thirds of private institutions, two-thirds of undergraduate departments, and 20 percent of graduate departments.[8] Fifty-eight percent of graduate departments have only one or two, and only 21 percent have more than two. Things are not likely to change because, according to the report, in 58 percent of public institutions, and 68 percent of private ones, there are no tenure-track women.

We can safely conclude from these statistics that women are not advancing through the profession to the extent that we would expect. The explanation for the continual underrepresentation of women in philosophy, which I defend in this chapter, is that those who consciously or not feel threatened by women's presence and/or their feminist ideology are not letting them progress through the ranks.

Who are the backlashers, and who are their targets? The backlashers, it seems, are mostly men—though not all men are backlashers—since men dominate the field of philosophy, and thus decide women's tenure. Faludi is right that women can participate in a backlash, not because they feel threatened by women's presence in the profession, but because they oppose feminism, are unaware of the political nature of their actions, or succumb to group pressure. The targets of the backlashers are mostly women, particularly, though not exclusively, feminists. Backlashers often do not distinguish between being a woman and being a feminist. Since women's entry into the workforce *en masse* is at least partly due to feminism, and since the back-lashers oppose feminism, they oppose having women in the workforce where women threaten men's job security and control over highly esteemed professions. I suspect, though, that backlashers also aim to get rid of feminist men since they support or promote an ideology that backlashers believe harms all men. The statistics available on the retention of either men or women in philosophy do not reveal ideology. I will focus on male back-lashers who target women.

Blatant antifeminists are in the throes of a backlash, the cause of which is not the reality of women's numbers in the profession, but the *perception* that women are "taking over" the profession, which undoubtedly is based on the mark that women—particularly feminists—have made on the profession. Feminists have critiqued the history, and have carved out a niche in almost every area, of philosophy. A rash of journal articles, anthologies, and mono-graphs influenced by feminist thought has been published in recent years. Feminist courses in philosophy have been officially added to the books in many institutions and are now taught on a regular basis. At least two major feminist philosophical organizations have formed, each of which enjoys a rel-atively large membership and hosts annual conferences and/or sessions at the American Philosophical Association meetings. Many backlashers believe that women are unfairly advantaged compared to men in the philosophy job market.[9] Yet even if women have made a significant mark on the profession, discriminating against them is morally unjustified. And in reality, feminism is marginalized in the profession. Publishing in feminism, especially in "top tier" journals, is still difficult; teaching feminism is almost always met with hostil-ity;[10] colleagues strongly resist accepting or even taking seriously feminist ideas; and men are hired for full-time, tenure-track positions at dispropor-tionately higher rates than women. Still, even snippets of progress indicate to the backlashers a takeover that must be halted, especially when it is felt on the home front. The obvious solution is to get rid of women—especially feminists—in the profession, by not hiring them, hiring them but then mak-ing their lives so miserable that they leave, or denying them tenure.

To have tenure is to have power. Tenure grants an academic a lifelong po-sition and academic freedom. Backlashers do not want to grant this power to those whose presence makes them uncomfortable or threatens them. They want to maintain the status quo by controlling the profession, determining women's future in the academy, and promoting their own conservative ideas.

THE SOCIALIZATION OF MEN: THE BOYS' CLUB

In the typical tenure case at major research universities and many teaching colleges in the United States, a candidate puts together a file which defends her qualifications in the areas of research, teaching, and service. The research is sent out to external reviewers deemed experts in the candidate's area(s) of specialization who write letters about its quality. To promote fairness, the department usually selects external reviewers from names suggested by both the candidate and its own members. The tenured members of the department ("internal reviewers") meet to discuss the merits of the candidate's case, and either vote on her tenure, or write individual advisory letters to the chairperson who then decides whether to support tenure. The file then goes through various advisory committees outside the department who assist the relevant administrators in making their decision, up the chain of command to the head of the institution. Even though the individuals involved appear to operate in isolation from the others at various levels, they in fact jointly decide whether the candidate should be tenured, since everyone has a say in the matter, and the views of those at the earlier stages form the basis of the decisions made by those at the top.

As a point of clarification, I construe the "tenure decision" more narrowly to refer to the tenure procedure itself, including anything from the initial stage of selecting external reviewers to the final decision made by the relevant administrator in the institution. This procedure typically lasts a good portion of an academic year. I construe the "tenure process" more broadly to refer to the entire time under which a candidate is under review (arguably beginning with her job hire), prior to and through the tenure decision. The tenure process typically lasts six or seven years.

I have described the tenure decision as one based on merit and free from sexism. But I want to show in this section *why* discrimination may enter the tenure process, and in the next section *how* it enters in sometimes subtle, seemingly neutral, and/or invisible ways. Discriminatory tenure denial, then, is markedly different from a standard case of tenure denial in which the candidate straightforwardly lacks the merit. Discriminatory tenure denial is tainted by discrimination caused by strident antifeminists who oppose this particular candidate, those who harbor sexist beliefs about women which inform the sexist standards they employ to judge the merits of a female candidate's case, and/or those who are influenced by these groups but who are unaware that discrimination has become systematically embedded in the tenure process itself.

"Masculinity," Separatism, and Solidarity

To understand best the discriminatory nature of the tenure decision, which is typically carried out mostly or solely by men in many academic disciplines, we need to appreciate the dynamics of patriarchal male socialization. Three main interrelated features of male socialization are relevant to discriminatory tenure denial: patriarchal masculinity, separatism, and feelings of solidarity ("male bonding"). I argue that these features, which are central to patriarchal socialization of males but not females, provide a reasonable explanation for why discriminatory tenure denial takes place.

Larry May, who has written extensively on male socialization, argues that both official and unofficial all-male groups including (formerly) the Citadel and all-male sports teams support the value of separatism and perpetuate a form of masculinity which is the model of patriarchal man.[11] May cites the Virginia Military Institute, whose model of education includes inducing physical rigor, mental stress, minute regulation of behavior, and punishment such as beatings to underclassmen, all of which are designed to promote leadership and strong character. Aside from dominance and strength, I would add that patriarchy's version of masculinity includes independence, intelligence, rationality, and aggression. Male socialization eschews the development of "feminine" traits in males, including weakness, dependency, passivity, subservience, being "bodily" or "closer to nature," intellectually inferior, and helpless. May argues further that men in official all-male groups who succeed in their rigorous training feel a sense of bonding with fellow sufferers. Since such groups have traditionally excluded females, male bonding "is made easier because there is an 'Other' that males can bond against."[12] This "Other" is identified with "feminine" traits. "Traditional" males separate themselves from females and males who lack "masculine" traits.

The kind of socialization offered by official all-male groups, according to May, can result in a "learned hatred and contempt for women"[13] against whom men might play out their aggression. Members of the Citadel greeted Shannon Faulkner, the first woman to enroll, by painting her home with graffiti, throwing firecrackers on her lawn, and handing out bumper stickers throughout the state referring to her as a "bitch" or a "bovine."[14] May deems the Citadel a classic example of an institution that claims to channel young male aggression into socially acceptable forms, but, he argues, fails to do so. Like athletes, soldiers have trouble containing their aggression to combat situations, partly because when aggression is deemed acceptable, it "sometimes makes it more likely that a man will display more and stronger aggressiveness than would otherwise be true."[15] I would add to May's account that when these men use aggressive tactics to exclude women from their ranks, they reinforce feelings of solidarity among themselves, which in turn serve to intensify separatism.

May's account of a particular sector of male socialization is instructive because it exemplifies a more extreme version of male socialization that I believe is imposed upon males in society at large. The same interrelated features of male socialization are relevant here: the cultivation of "masculine" traits, male separatism, and feelings of solidarity.

The inculcation of "masculine" traits in males is carried out by a variety of social forces. At all levels of education, teachers pay more attention to boys' answers in class than to girls',[16] which fosters the view that boys are smarter than girls and that their views are more worthy; boys are reared to be leaders of families and organizations, which encourages dominance instead of passivity; and GI Joe dolls, one of the best-selling toys for boys on the market, have increased their "muscle mass" considerably over the past few decades, which sends boys the message that they need to be physically strong—in the words of one young man, "It's all about intimidation. If I go into a room looking big, no one will mess with me."[17] Aggression—even violence—is the "masculine" trait that factors most significantly in May's views about separatism in all-male groups such as the Citadel and in what I have to say about discriminatory tenure denial. Boys are encouraged to play with toys that mimic real weapons of destruction such as guns, slingshots, and bows and arrows, as well as toys that are not necessarily destructive but have been made to be so by their manufacturers, such as bicycles and trucks bearing the inscriptions "Terminator" or "Dominator." Boys are encouraged to watch and participate in violent sports such as football, hockey, boxing, and wrestling. Boys learn to settle their disputes physically by fighting with each other. When they get older they are taught that they should "score" with as many women as possible, that force in sex with females is permissible, and that the harm of rape is outweighed by the satisfaction of their own needs and the desire to prove their own masculinity. Fifty percent of teenage boys said they would commit rape if they thought they could get away with it.[18] Gang activity in many cities is on the rise, and the majority of gang members are boys who join at increasingly younger ages. Aggression in males can take other than physical forms, including relentlessly challenging authority, complaining loudly about service in a restaurant or shop, engaging in road rage, and vociferously attacking others' arguments. Society sanctions, encourages, and then normalizes aggression in males—"Boys will be boys."

"Masculine" traits are viewed under patriarchy as being different from and superior to "feminine" traits. The lessons of male superiority are learned at a young age, through everything from the games boys play to the fairy tales they read, which portray men as strong, clever rescuers of weak, helpless damsels in distress. Boys learn that if they are smarter than girls, they will be believed more often than girls, and their views will count for more; if they are stronger than girls, they can do more, do it better, and get others to do what they want; if they are independent, they can choose to be but do not need to be with a female; if they are aggressive, they will get what they want, whatever it is. Boys learn both that they are better than girls if they are these ways, and that it is in their interest to develop "masculine" traits since having and acting on such traits confers power both to individual males as well as to men as a group.

This power is maintained when males stick together with those who are like themselves and exclude those who are believed to be different from them.

Organized all-male groups help to ensure that males develop "masculine" traits that serve to maintain male power. They promote camaraderie by having their members suffer through a rigorous training period with each other. Even non-organized males promote camaraderie among those who meet the conditions of "manhood": boys at play often fiercely compete with each other for mental and physical superiority, dare each other to engage in risky behavior, and encourage each other to "take it like a man" and become "real men." The winners feel a sense of bonding and superiority over those who do not make it.

Feelings of camaraderie are reinforced when males exclude those who are not like themselves. When the Citadel excludes women from its ranks, the men feel different from, and superior to, those from whom they set themselves off. When boys in general exclude girls, they feel superior to them: they see girls as different and inferior rather than equal playmates. They poke fun of girls' "prissiness," alleged incompetence at "masculine" tasks, and general purported stupidity. They know that the harm they cause girls will often go unpunished or even unnoticed and that girls will be deemed "crybabies" if they complain, which only intensifies the gender division. The discipline boys receive for their unfair treatment of girls is often carried out tongue-in-cheek or with an air of excusability: "Be nice to your sister; she's only a girl." Boys come away from such discipline believing that they still hold power over girls and may come to resent girls for snitching on them and trying to take away some of their power. Boys also resent other boys who fail to conform to stereotypical male behavior—"sissies"—since the nonconformists threaten the security and power of the group. Separatist behavior extends to adulthood when heterosexual men not only ostracize but fear and hate homosexual men, and sometimes even resort to violent acts of gay bashing. Separatism reinforces male bonding in the conformists, and group security reinforces their power.

Separatism grounded in a "difference in traits" theory serves to subordinate other oppressed groups such as the Jews in Nazi death camps. In order to deny their common humanity, the Nazi guards made the Jews appear inferior or as "Other" by dehumanizing them through starvation and degradation.[19] This separatism, too, led to harmful treatment of the subordinates. My analyses of the treatment of subordinates are supported by Zimbardo's 1970 experiment in which a group of "morally normal" college-aged men who initially saw themselves as "likes" were assigned to roles of Nazi-like guards and prisoners that they played out in their dress and behavior. Zimbardo had to stop the experiment early because the guards became excessively abusive and degrading, demonstrating that even "morally normal" persons who initially see others as likes come to treat them inhumanely when they come to see them as different. More generally, I would add, oppression of subordinate groups is sustained by divisions based on characteristics deemed inferior that support separatism.

In addition to the features of male socialization that I have been discussing is group pressure to conform, which is intensified by male bonding. Psychologists believe that banishment from a group is one of the worst tragedies that might befall an individual, and fear of it accords great power to individual members of a group.[20] They deem group pressure to be "enormously effective" in influencing task selection, individual beliefs, attitudes, and perceptions of reality.[21] They conclude from experiments that an individual's need for acceptance in a group can be so strong that it extends even to strangers, and that conformity is so natural that people often are unaware that they are practicing it.[22] Group pressure is not sex dependent, and is one reason some women side with male colleagues in tenure decisions, but it can cause males in particular, whose sense of solidarity with other males is strong, to endorse beliefs and engage in behavior, including sexist ones, that they would otherwise not.

Finally, note that female socialization in our society is unlike male socialization in that it does not enjoin separatism, aggression, or solidarity. Separatism is reserved as a privilege enjoyed by those believed to be superior but not by females, who are told they are inferior and can elevate themselves only by attaching to a man. Aggression is discouraged in girls, who are taught to play with toys such as dolls that foster feelings of care for others, steered away from violent sports into "ladylike" activities such as homemaking tasks, and made to settle disputes verbally and not hurt others' feelings. Females do not experience solidarity in formal and informal groups the way men do. May notes that women historically have organized into official groups, especially ones with the power structure and admission and retention tests, much less frequently than men. Women's lack of solidarity can be attributed, I believe, to lack of time due to their having to shoulder the burden of work, their lack of power and resources, the belief that other women are competitors rather than supporters,[23] and an ideology that blames and isolates victims. Subordinate groups tend to form social groups whose identity lies with their victimhood, e.g., "Take Back the Night" rallies and the "Million Man March," but such groups typically empower their members in a relatively narrow way by giving them a sense of unity or providing a forum for freedom from their oppressors, and so are unlike all-male groups that are formed in the context, and for the sustenance, of privilege and power. My point is not that if academia were dominated by women, men would not be excluded for the reasons I argue they exclude women. I am suggesting instead that male but not female socialization provides a reasonable explanation for discriminatory tenure denial.

Male Socialization and Harm to Women

Aggression, male solidarity, and group pressure are among the factors that function jointly to incite behavior that harms women, maintains male separatism, and sustains the backlash against women's advancement particularly in academia. Like the kind of socialization offered by the Citadel, male socialization in society at large can result in a "learned hatred and contempt for women," and lead to aggression against females. The number of victims of sexual harassment (up to 88 percent of women[24]), woman battering (six million women a year in the United States [25]), and rape (one every five minutes[26]) exemplify the virulent forms male aggression takes.

Interestingly, Faludi interprets the recent huge increase in the number of reported rapes, which is not attributable merely to an increase in *reports* of rape, to be a strong indicator of the current backlash against women's making it into traditionally all-male circles.[27] She reports that when women were making measurable progress in historically male domains in the 1980s, rape rates rose disproportionately to the rate of violent crime overall. Between 1983 and 1987, rape arrests of boys under the age of 18 increased 15 percent; between 1987 and 1989, in New York City, rape arrests of boys under the age of 13 increased 200 percent; and during the 1980s, in Alaska, rapes and sexual abuses from young men increased ninefold.

Faludi takes rape to be evidence of the backlash against feminism because of its link to male despair over loss of power. Many men believe that they have suffered due to women's gaining power, and fear that they will lose out because of their own inadequacy. They render women the "Other," and some engage in aggressive or violent behavior as a way of taking back women's power and excluding them from the group. Faludi cites the Yankelovich Monitor survey, a nationwide poll that over the past 20 years has asked subjects to define masculinity and has repeatedly come up with the response: being a "good provider for [my] family."[28] She believes that women's striving for economic equality is the most direct threat to the American male. During the 1980s, the decade in which the number of reported rapes rose dramatically, American men suffered financially. In households where White men were the sole provider, men's income fell 22 percent; many blue-collar men lost their jobs because of plant closings; and the "average man under 30 was earning 25 to 30 percent less than his counterpart in the early 1970s," but if he had only a high school education he made only 50 percent of his counterpart in the early 1970s. The group of men referred to in the study as the "Contenders" had a median age of 30, were mostly single, and, Faludi says, "were slipping down the income ladder—and furious about it." They blamed feminism for their loss of power. Faludi believes that men who had more economic, social, and political power also contributed to the backlash at this time but, she notes, poorer or less-educated men "have picked up and played back the backlash at distortingly high volume."

I would not dismiss Faludi's claims as "pie in the sky" sociology; in fact, I would strengthen them by adding that more powerful, antifeminist men pit economically deprived men against women because they create in them the belief that women are taking away their jobs. This effectually has poorer men do the "dirty work" for those at the top by acting—and taking the blame for acting—in ways that sustain hatred for women and violence against them, and maintains male separatism. A similar phenomenon is revealed in the Nazi war criminals trials, according to which as part of German propaganda the Nazis made people in underprivileged groups such as poor, non-Jews side against the Jews by making them feel superior in comparison.[29]

One noteworthy example of a man who felt threatened by his apparent loss of power vis-à-vis women is Yusef Salaam, who was one of six men charged with raping and crushing the skull of a professional woman jogger in Central Park. According to Faludi, Salaam apparently told the court that he felt "like a midget, a mouse, something less than a man." For men like Salaam, rape disempowers women and simultaneously empowers men by bolstering feelings of masculinity and solidarity with other men. Apparently a common theme, feelings of weakness, inadequacy, or "less-than-maleness" were cited as reasons why men engage in group rape in psychologist W. H. Blanchard's 1959 study of two groups of men who engaged in gang rape of a woman. One of the perpetrators described his feelings as follows: "I was scared when it began to happen. I wanted to leave but I didn't want to say it to the other guys—you know—that I was scared. . . . Yes, I was always the big man. I didn't want to look little so I would go ahead and do it—getting in fights—you're chicken if you don't do it, so I would do it."[30]

Gang rape aptly demonstrates the bonding and group pressure that men like the "Contenders" feel when their fear of diminishing group power incites them to act jointly in ways that aggressively exclude women from male circles.[31] The courage of each member of the group is fortified by the mere presence of the others; men are more likely to engage in rape when they are in groups.[32] Members of the group who feel particularly vulnerable to suffering a loss of power are likely candidates for assuming the role of leadership in spurring the others into participating in the group action. Blanchard reports that in his study of gang rapists, the leader of the group was "a crucial figure in crystallizing and mobilizing the intent of the group," and that in the cases he studied, the rape would not have taken place without the presence of the leader.[33] Group pressure yields conformity; no individual wants to opt out because doing so would threaten his masculinity, his security in the group, and ultimately his own and the group's power.

Rape, particularly gang rape, reveals how men use violence in an extreme way to exclude women from their group and to maintain male dominance in ways harmful to all women, including instilling fear in all women, diminishing women's freedom, creating in women passivity and dependence on men, perpetuating the myth that women are weak, helpless victims in need of protection, and disadvantaging women economically.[34] I want to argue next that discriminatory tenure denial, although not a physically violent act, nevertheless also demonstrates how male bonding, group pressure, and aggression function jointly to exclude women from the group men and to maintain male dominance.

I focus on the "Contenders" of academia—men who feel threatened by women's advancement and who respond by instigating a backlash against it. These men have gone through both male socialization and the rigorous training of the discipline which they believe entitles them to membership in an exclusive club that bears the right to decide on its future membership. Their graduate school and pre-tenure training is in major ways different from the training that all-male groups such as the Citadel offers, yet it is rigorous and teaches intellectual aggression especially in philosophers who are encouraged to engage in vicious attacks on their opponents' arguments. Academics spend many years working toward their doctorates, undoubtedly making personal and financial sacrifices, yet are generally very poorly paid relative to other professionals whose training is comparably intense and demanding. They feel a sense of bonding with the others—who are mostly men—who have made it through the system. This "boys' club" sentiment became evident when a male colleague "complimented" me after I was awarded tenure by declaring that I "was one of the boys," as if I had survived some initiation rite about toughness, when another praised me for not being a "prima donna" but for "fighting back" as a man would even though my "aggression" conflicted with the female stereotypes I was held to, and when a friend who complained publicly about her department's discriminatory practices was chastised for being "a traitor."

Unlike careers in the armed forces, academic positions are not stereotypical "macho" jobs, yet some male professors may feel threatened by women's presence as colleagues precisely because they have rejected traditionally masculine careers and already feel more "feminized" than other men. Indeed, the fact that academia is not stereotypically masculine might intensify their desire to keep women out so as to make the profession *seem* more masculine. Moreover, like the Contenders in Faludi's study, and in a more direct way than rapists who feel demasculinized, these individuals, consciously or not, believe that women threaten their masculinity because they threaten their means of livelihood. This is particularly true for those whose credentials are weaker than those of the woman they judge. One wonders whether it is merely a coincidence that tenure standards have recently increased dramatically since women's inception into academia? Feelings of inadequacy contribute to bonding with colleagues in a similar position, and to rendering women who threaten them the "Other." After all, women are supposed to be inferior to men.

The Contenders who want to retain the male "pureness" of the profession hire and retain only likes, and sometimes resort to aggressive tactics such as discriminatory tenure denial to get their way. Some believe that women are incompetent; others feel hostility toward a particular woman candidate. A negative voter(s) harboring such beliefs can take on the role of leader and turn enough others against the candidate, especially without being forthright in admitting discriminatory attitudes. Succumbing to group pressure, individuals who were supportive of or neutral about a candidate might come to see things from the others' perspective and believe that her work is not that good after all. They muster the courage they would otherwise lack to voice negative views until, as with gang rape, there is a snowballing effect where almost everyone disputes the candidate's credentials in aggressive and unjust ways, desiring to join in and harm the victim. Even when politicking takes place in a one-on-one setting behind closed doors, the lifelong bond colleagues often form with each other renders the decision a group one which few would buck. The "mob mentality,"[35] of a department is likely to go up the chain of command since deans and other higher officials are reluctant to go against a department's negative decision, especially when they are friendly with the well-established faculty. They typically operate under the principle that it is better for all not to send a candidate back into a department that has rejected her. Their decision is facilitated by the unspoken rule that any negative comment in a file is sufficient to damn the candidate. This alone is telling, for it almost guarantees that any individual will never have to buck the group. And it puts solidarity before merit.

The very nature of group acts makes them different from, and in some instances, more insidious than singular acts. First, individuals acting as members of groups engage in riskier behavior that is more harmful to their victim than the behavior they would engage in on their own. Second, in some collective actions, group members are concerned first and foremost with pleasing themselves and *each other*, while rendering their victim's interests subservient to their own, or worse, ignoring them entirely. Blanchard remarks that the sexual experience in gang rape of the groups he studied "was largely a relationship between the boys rather than between any of the boys and the girl involved."[36] In the case of discriminatory tenure denial, a chairperson's desire to please "some people I really respect" means more than removing a deserving candidate from a job, if not the profession. Colleagues who engage a dismissive attitude toward the woman and try to "comfort" her with the alleged fact that "women who have been denied tenure have a great track record on the market," or with the advice that she return to her hometown and do something else, completely overlook her desire and subsequent efforts to succeed in the profession. Third, violent and aggressive acts performed by members of a group are mitigated and sanctioned by the presence of the other members; no single member has to take responsibility for his actions, none has to face guilt alone, and they can wallow in self-denial of any wrongdoing. Fourth, the act's being carried out by a group facilitates blaming the victim and exonerating the group for the group's own immoral behavior. In the case of rape, the woman was in the wrong place at the wrong time, dressed too provocatively, or really wanted sex with more than one man; in the case of discriminatory tenure denial, the candidate did not do enough work, it was of insufficient quality, or she was not collegial. It will be their collective word against hers; so many of them could not possibly be wrong. But if their act is not wrong, their behavior is not deemed immoral, but normal. Sex with good old boys is not rape; discriminatory tenure denial is just another way of criticizing a philosopher's work. All in all, when men put their interests ahead of the victim's, do not take responsibility for their actions, and are not appropriately sanctioned, they strengthen the bond between themselves, and continue to view women as different and exclude them in sometimes virulent ways, thereby sustaining the backlash against women's progress.

THE TENURE SYSTEM, FORCED CONFORMITY TO STEREOTYPES, AND PERSONAL ANECDOTES

Male socialization functions jointly with various systems, customs, and practices, including the tenure system as it is designed in most major universities in the United States, to incite harmful acts against women and to sustain the backlash. Indeed, the systems and such permit men to use aggressive tactics to exclude women, endorse separatism, and thereby promote male solidarity. Gender discrimination often enters the tenure process in subtle ways; it is masked by seemingly neutral practices and language about a candidate's qualifications, rendering it invisible; it is leveled against a candidate who has little or no recourse to fight back; it is carried out by those in power and without repercussion; it is typically not prevented by checks in the system; and it can take the form of isolated incidents that are not directly connected to the tenure decision but which nonetheless indicate a pattern of discrimination that reveals negative attitudes about women's place in academia. Systematic discrimination best illustrates how others besides the outspoken antifeminists can discriminate without intent. I will rely on personal experience to illustrate the ways in which gender discrimination can enter both the tenure decision itself and the entire tenure process.

Discrimination in the Tenure Decision

Let me begin by highlighting the main ways that gender discrimination can taint the tenure decision. First, despite written rules about avoiding bias, departments might select external reviewers who are hostile to the candidate or who have even publicly expressed their opposition to feminism in works that are antifeminist in nature. Departments might act out of malice or ignorance. Since universities do not solicit a candidate about a reviewer's bias, when such bias colors the review it is likely to go unnoticed by internal reviewers unfamiliar with the area. Care will undoubtedly be taken to prevent this bias when a department is favorably disposed toward a candidate, but even when it creeps in, internal reviewers reserve the right to discount it for what it is. They will do so for candidates they want to keep in the "club," which did not happen in my case when an antifeminist reviewer who wrote negative comments was added to "my" list of suggested reviewers because "the department would find it remiss" if I did not include his name. During times when universities are loathe to grant tenure, a letter from a negatively biased reviewer is sufficient to damn unfairly a deserving candidate. When such "breaks" are given mostly to men, the result is that the high tenure standards of today in reality apply unilaterally to women.

Second, internal reviewers might discount the expertise of women reviewers by ignoring it and/or directly or indirectly asserting their own alleged expertise in the contentious area. Feminism is particularly prone to such arrogance as it is deemed to be an "easy" area of study that anyone allegedly can master by reading an article or two. The negative comments of internal reviewers who fail to acknowledge the expertise of feminists will detract reviewers up the line from recognizing this subtle yet insidious form of discrimination. Discounting the expertise of feminist reviewers reveals that women who make it into the "club" are still not granted full membership and subsequently lack the power men have to bring in and retain members who are like themselves.

Third, reviewers might not fully appreciate the value of feminist scholarship. Publishing feminist work in the very best journals is still quite difficult due to the rather conservative nature of these journals and the marginalization of feminism in the profession. Those who work in feminism often are not credited or even docked for not publishing in such journals even if their critics have not done so. Even when their work is published in "top tier" journals, reprinted in anthologies, and meets other standards of professional excellence as my own work did, a biased department can discredit it.

Fourth, not much if anything is recorded in print about the tenure decision, rendering legal action difficult and personal responsibility moot. Typically the department chairperson's letter is based on his or her colleagues' views, but it does not say who said what or why he or she said it, and it may exaggerate negative points, contain outright lies, and be grounded in ignorance of the candidate's work. Department members are never called upon to defend their views and thus reveal biases, and their own letters, if required, sometimes reveal that irrelevant—and illegal—factors formed the basis of their decision. Since ordinarily the candidate is not allowed to respond to or even review her file, biases are likely to infect the decisions made by those up the line. Counteracting negative comments, when permitted, is difficult.

Fifth, internal reviewers can easily cloak their discriminatory attitudes in neutral language about the candidate's work, e.g., "I heard some negative things about her teaching." Even when discriminators are not so savvy and their language reveals their attitudes, their comments may come across merely as negative points about the candidate which inevitably ensure tenure denial. There is simply no check on whether the comments are based in fact. Using neutral language to mask discrimination effectually blames the victim for the discriminator's own immoral action; she deserves her fate. For the "Contenders," the blame extends to feminism in general: feminists aren't good philosophers, and if women would just stay away from it—and stay home—they would not get into such trouble.

Sixth, the abnegation of individual responsibility is facilitated by the fact that department members know full well that they have a system on their side that affords them a great deal of freedom and protection to do what they want in tenure cases. They know that few candidates are in the lucky position of being able to sue, and few tenure cases have been won through internal university appeals or in the courts. If a candidate were to sue, the suit would be brought not against a particular individual or group but against the university, which would provide its own legal defense.

Another, more subtle kind of discrimination related to solidarity is that men often favorably assist only their male colleagues in establishing a clear and easy tenure case. Being female or a minority puts one at an immediate disadvantage in the collegial, clublike context that is characteristic of the White male professions, especially in their top echelons.[37] Men may be reluctant to adopt female protégés because they believe that women are "financially less dependent upon a job," or because they fear others' suspicion of a sexual liaison when they work so closely together. I would add that many men simply do not think about rallying for their female protégés because women are invisible to them; people unconsciously favor likes. The result is that a male tenure candidate's professional success is due partly to his connections with his mentors, which puts him ahead of his female counterparts from the start. A related point is that professional "standards of excellence" are not universally defined, but are subject to interpretation.[38] In particular, one's acceptance into the informal circle of the "club" informs the judgments made about one's credentials. But one female philosopher remarked that women cannot really join the "club" because they cannot engage in activities such as rooming with the men at conventions where a lot of friendships become solidified.[39] Yet all of these factors inform a candidate's success in her profession. Colleagues *should* help each other, but if benefits are routinely conferred only upon some, the others are disadvantaged. And it looks as if nothing bad, but only something good, has been done.

Discrimination in the Tenure Process

The above forms of discrimination clearly violate standards of equal treatment. But I believe that the most insidious kind of aggression against women, the eighth way discrimination taints the tenure process, occurs when a female candidate is judged on the basis of whether she has conformed to female stereotypes during her pretenure years. This is degrading and in this respect is unlike forcing untenured males to do things they would rather not. The threat to comply is more subtle and diffuse than physical force; there is often no direct connection made between holding a woman to the stereotype and her tenure case, and the threat ordinarily is carried out in seemingly isolated incidents by various members of the department. Thus it is easy for the individual who engages in such behavior, let alone his colleagues, to miss their political significance. These "background" behaviors maintain a climate of exclusion since a woman who is subjected to them will have a much harder time being collegial than her male counterparts who are welcomed and treated with respect. Note that this form of discrimination can operate independently of the others, but in any form discrimination has pernicious effects.

First is the stereotype of sex object which I illustrate with a personal example. During my interview and for several months after I was on the job, a male colleague very crudely ogled my body. When several of us gathered for drinks after I presented my interview paper to the department, he remarked that I looked like a famous, attractive actress. Later he turned a five-minute drive from the restaurant to an evening session into one lasting over half an hour, pretending to be lost. When we finally arrived, several male colleagues teased him, egging him on and showing their approval that I would be a "nice hire" for him. This experience was completely degrading, since I had realized that all the philosophy I had done with this group for three days prior did not really matter—I was being screened as a potential mate or sex object for this man. Complaining would jeopardize my chance of getting the job and foreclose the opportunity to form collegial relations. Acquiescing, though, perpetuates the view that women are sex objects and not competitive workers.

Discriminators might use the threat of tenure denial to force women to be passive, reserving aggression for, and praising it in, men. Four personal examples illustrate this point. First, several male faculty members advised me, but not the male junior faculty members, not to speak up at department meetings, which affronted my professionalism and diminished my authority. Second, another male colleague chastised me for my "willful attitude," and denied my tenure partly for this reason, when I requested on a couple of occasions that an exam committee meet during the semester so that I could leave town promptly thereafter during a family crisis. Third, when I set aright an older male undergraduate student after he unfoundedly insisted that he knew more about an area I had been researching for ten years and rudely interrupted me throughout the semester, he complained to several male colleagues who were his friends and they saw fit to deny my tenure as justified punishment for brazenly standing up to a man who was a lot like them. Fourth, another male colleague told me on several occasions that I "would never be a Southern belle," and once, foreseeing a problem with my tenure case in the upcoming years, advised me that the only thing I needed to change to get a positive department vote was my "aggression." I realized quickly from such incidents that I could not confront each individual because to do so would be to buck the entire group, which, surely to their minds, would only have proven their point.

A third sexist standard that women are forced to comply with, generated, I believe, by the belief that women are less worthy of respect and deference than men, is that of subservience to men. Unlike respect which acknowledges the equal humanity of persons, subservience involves subsuming one's interests to the interests of those regarded arbitrarily as superior to oneself. I—but no untenured male—was forced to be subservient when a senior male colleague expected me to "chat" with him in his office at his behest, sometimes several times a week up to four hours each time, for a couple of years. Although some of the discussions about my work and professional issues were interesting, they quickly became increasingly fruitless and even hostile. After I reduced the time I spent at the office for professional and personal reasons, on several occasions he threatened that I needed to be "collegial," and voted against my tenure because I failed in this regard.

The expectation of subservience extended even to my relations with male students. When, as chair of the speaker's committee, I tried to invite an up-and-coming young star, I was rebuffed for inviting one of my "friends" and told to solicit the opinion of a male graduate student who entered the program the prior week. When a male undergraduate student, whom I had not previously met but who in a brief conversation examined my body in suggestive and offensive ways, complained that I did not treat him warmly, I was chastised for being "rude" to a student who was "a friend of many people in the department." My own complaint about the student's behavior was readily dismissed, and I was pulled aside and told that I seemed "distant" and "unhappy," itself a sexist redescription of the truth. The cumulative effect of such behaviors was the creation of a situation in which I was forced to be subservient to some of the powerful men in the department and to anyone they deemed a friend or "member of the club."

Holding women to sexist stereotypes is both a symptom and a cause of the boys' club mentality. Note its presence in the various behaviors I have discussed: the woman is a sex object for *our* friend, she should not speak up and disrupt *our* power, she is too aggressive for *us*, she stood up to a student who is *like us*, she should give up her time for *one of us*, and she was rude to *our* friend. These descriptions reflect men's awareness of their group membership and subsequent power and their view of women as different and disruptive of men's solidarity. Their female colleague will not, indeed, *cannot*, fit in. At tenure time, they chalk up her failure to fit in to genuine academic reasons; a political issue becomes an objective issue of competence. Note that women are in a Catch-22: if they do not conform to sexist standards, sexist people will exclude them; but if they do conform, the same people will exclude them because they are not enough like men, who are (allowed to be) autonomous, independent, and aggressive.

A tenure process that masks discrimination so well both encourages and perpetuates male bonding and aggressive exclusion of women. When men get away with pre-tenure discriminatory acts because women are reticent to complain for fear of losing their jobs, they are signaled to go on to riskier, more aggressive acts such as tenure denial. When they construct sexist attitudes neutrally to make it appear that the woman alone must be at fault for her failure, there is no reason for them to change their behavior. And when they can easily fire a woman for hidden discriminatory reasons, they strengthen feelings of solidarity, endorse separatism, and ultimately maintain their own position of power.

INDIVIDUAL AND GROUP HARMS AND THE BACKLASH

Discriminatory tenure denial harms both its direct victims and all members of the group women, and in so doing contributes to the backlash against women's progress. I turn first to its direct harms.

Susan Brison, who has written intriguingly on rape, describes a traumatic event as:

> one in which a person feels utterly helpless in the face of a force that is perceived to be life-threatening. The immediate psychological responses to such trauma include terror, loss of control, and intense fear of annihilation. Long-term effects include the physiological responses of hypervigilance, heightened startle response, sleep disorders, and the more psychological yet still involuntary responses of depression, inability to concentrate, lack of interest in activities that used to give life meaning, and a sense of a foreshortened future. . . . When the trauma is of human origin and is intentionally inflicted . . . it not only shatters one's fundamental assumptions about the world and one's safety in it but also severs the sustaining connection between the self and the rest of humanity. Victims of human-inflicted trauma are reduced to mere objects by their tormenters. Their subjectivity is rendered useless and viewed as worthless.[40]

I do not want to belittle what I believe to be the unique evil of rape by analogizing every aspect of it to discriminatory tenure denial. But there are some similarities between these assaultive, devastating acts. Rape is life threatening, but discriminatory tenure denial threatens some of the victim's most deeply held values and beliefs, which constitute a fundamental aspect of her being. Professional philosophers tend to be identified with their own work, as it is often inspired by events in their lives or reflects a lifelong quest for answers to questions that interest them. When one's work comes under an onslaught of unfair criticisms, especially ones that amount to a gender-based attack, one feels as if one's very self, in addition to one's livelihood and well-being, is threatened. This is a kind of annihilation, albeit not physical in nature and certainly not confrontational in the way a physical assault is.

I can draw out the analogy to rape just a bit further. Some of the reactions I met with on my tenure case and my responses to them bear similarity to those for rape victims. I felt helpless against the system ("There's nothing you can do; everyone is entitled to his view"), was blamed for my predicament ("Maybe you brought some of this on yourself"), and made to believe that I should have done more to ward off the attack ("The standards are really high"). Since these comments came from my supporters, I could only believe that they, like well-intended supporters of rape victims, were heavily influenced by the surrounding culture and failed to see things as they really were. It took having an attorney confirm that I had been a victim of something more than simple tenure denial for me to believe it.

I am not aware of any studies about the harms victims of discrimination in tenure suffer, but the experiences of professional colleagues with whom I am acquainted indicate that some of them are strikingly similar to those Brison describes, including feelings of isolation, loss of self-confidence, self-esteem, and self-worth, loss of trust, inability to concentrate, anger, depression, and intense stress and anxiety, which can take the form of frequent panic attacks, trembling hands, heart palpitations, chest pains, and sleeping and eating disorders. The panic attacks I suffered during almost every lecture I gave, which I assiduously managed to hide from the students, lasted well past a year after my tenure denial. Richard Delgado confirms similar effects of discrimination in minorities, who experience feelings of humiliation, isolation, self-hatred, self-doubt, lack of self-respect, impaired capacity to form close interracial relationships, antisocial behavior, hypersensitivity, mental illness and psychosomatic disease, high blood pressure and associated cardiac ailments due to inhibited, constrained, or restricted anger, and poor job performance.[41] Interestingly, Delgado notes that "the incidence of severe psychological impairment caused by the environmental stress of prejudice and discrimination is not lower among minority group members of high socioeconomic status."[42] The commonality between various kinds of discrimination and the traumatic events Brison refers to is that the tormentor reduces the victim to a useless, worthless object. Stereotyping, a form of discrimination, fails to regard its victims as rational, autonomous beings possessing dignity and deserving of respect.

Obviously if a person experiences daily panic attacks, perpetual anxiety, deep depression, and a loss of self-confidence because of unfair criticism, her teaching and research are likely to suffer. The physical and psychological effects and subsequent loss of productivity will inevitably have a cumulative negative effect on her salary, putting her at a financial disadvantage vis-à-vis men. Additionally, they will decrease her chances of getting another position, especially one in a job market in philosophy that is arguably now at its worst. Victims who successfully appeal a negative tenure decision and remain in the same department face the challenge of gaining respect from their colleagues and the university at large, and must overcome the stigma and any gossip spread by those who wanted to defame them. Their opportunities for advancement both in their institution and in the profession at large are diminished since the likelihood of being nominated for and winning prestigious in-house awards, outside fellowships, or the best jobs, has decreased. These setbacks effectually maintain men's power in the academy and society at large.

Discriminatory tenure denial harms women as a group, too, which also maintains the backlash against women's progress and perpetuates male separatism by setting off men as superior to women. Marilyn Friedman and Larry May set out three conditions that mark group harm.[43] First, some identifiable members of the group suffer direct harms which are compensable. Second, the members of the group to which the direct victim belongs are interdependent and interrelated in such a way as to transmit to other group members the harm suffered by the direct victim. Third, there is evidence of a culturally pervasive negative stereotype of the members of the group such that when a member of the group acts in ways contrary to the stereotypes assigned to the group, she will be denigrated, ostracized, or excluded by those outside the group to which she belongs. Thus women as a group are harmed by the practice of rape because all women, not just direct victims, lack freedom to live the way most men are free to live, fear all men as potential rapists, and are degraded because they "are seen as in need of protection, as weak and passive, and available to all men."[44] I want to argue that the group women is similarly harmed by discriminatory tenure denial, though this is more difficult to explain because not all women are faced with the threat of tenure denial per se. Any firing of a woman from a highly esteemed profession for discriminatory reasons reverberates to all women who work or will work in the paid labor force, in these positions or others. Women learn about and pass along warnings about job discrimination suffered by women in highly esteemed positions including Frances Conley, a distinguished neurophysician at Stanford,[45] Anita Hill, Shannon Faulkner, and countless others whose stories have been made famous by the media. Women learn that if it happens to these women, it can easily happen to them and there is little, if anything, they can do to prevent it. In philosophy, women on the job market are warned by senior women that they will get interviews only because they are women, but are unlikely ever to be hired. Discriminatory job termination in traditionally male fields creates anxiety in all women, which effectively curtails women's striving for the top, makes them settle for less prestigious—and less powerful—positions in the workforce, or keeps them out of the paid workforce altogether. Yet if women heed these warnings, they will not gain the economic, social, and political power that being in these professions yields and that is necessary for overcoming subordination. Moreover, all women learn that they are not free to act in the ways men are on the job, including speaking out against sexism and rejecting sexist standards, since men who hold power over them can use their behavior against them by arbitrarily firing them. The fear of being fired for arbitrary, sexist reasons silences all women in the workforce just as rape silences women in the presence of men since both threaten women's livelihood and well-being.

Finally, discriminatory tenure denial degrades women as a group since the practice contributes to the stereotype of women as weak, vulnerable, intellectually inferior beings. When women reach esteemed positions they are in the relevant ways just like men, yet when they are routinely subject to discriminatory job termination, they are seen as the targets of men, as vulnerable beings, who, despite their accomplishments, are weak and in need of protection. As in the case of rape, women are advised how to act on the job in order to avoid this treatment, while men are allowed to be free in this respect. Discriminatory tenure denial also perpetuates the stereotype that women are intellectually inferior to men in that they are seen as not smart enough to handle or ward off their discriminators, or as not smart enough to establish a clear, indisputable job record so that this kind of discrimination would never succeed against them. Attributing women's underrepresentation in the profession of philosophy to their not being able to "cut it" is, unfortunately, a common sentiment. As women are routinely blamed for rape, they will be blamed for discriminatory tenure denial. Women are seen as lesser beings, as merely sexual beings in the case of rape, and as intellectually inferior beings in the case of discriminatory tenure denial. Further, by inferiorizing women, men put themselves in a superior position by bolstering their sense of self-importance and their status among their peers. The Central Park rapist uses rape to erase his feelings of being a midget, less than a man; the academic "Contender" feigns expertise about the woman's work and attempts to make her look incompetent, which makes him look better. Both individual and group harm support the backlash, male separatism, and male bonding.

As I have suggested, the arguments in this essay are applicable in a much wider arena than tenure denial per se since women in many professions have run up against the glass ceiling and have been made to conform to sexist stereotypes. But the backlash against women's progress in academia is particularly disturbing because in it women have the power not only to serve as role models, but to educate many people about women's oppression and influence the behavior of future generations. This backlash almost guarantees that the waves will never stay on the shore.

FINAL THOUGHTS

My conclusion is not that universities should abolish the tenure system, but that they need to make good on their commitment to being equal opportunity employers by taking steps to eliminate the ways in which discrimination enters the tenure process. They need to acknowledge that many men, both younger and older, after years of feminist influence still view women in stereotypical ways, and that this bias is likely to infect tenure decisions. Although there is no quick and easy way of eradicating discrimination, a few suggestions are in order. Universities need to instill a sound system for women to voice their complaints about discrimination prior to the tenure decision. Currently the onus is on the woman to come forward with a complaint addressed to the affirmative action officer, typically the university's attorney. Under a better system, the behavior might stop and women accorded due respect, or at the least, a paper trail will provide evidence to which a woman can point if things go against her unfairly in the tenure decision. Isolated, seemingly petty incidents of sexism should not be ignored or written off since each "little" act is indicative of a sexist persona and part of a pattern that is predictive of future behavior. Universities need to appoint to tenure committees faculty who have a proven record of being sensitive to issues of discrimination. They should hire administrators and appoint department chairpersons who are aware of how deeply sexism still runs and do not dismiss women's complaints as ones not grievous enough to warrant action. Administrators need to change their predisposition not to put a woman back into a department that has voted her out, in favor of taking an attitude suspicious of discrimination. All universities should adopt an open records policy enabling candidates to have access to their tenure files, which can prove to be helpful in filing a discrimination appeal. And they should take strong steps to ensure that all faculty involved in tenure decisions are held accountable for their views by providing detailed, solid evidence for them, and provide an in-house forum for response from the candidate.

Finally, I urge all women who feel that they are victims of discrimination in tenure decisions to take action. This is undoubtedly difficult; filing an appeal is time-consuming and overwhelming, and simply unaffordable in the typical case if done through legal channels. Yet any kind of action that makes the philosophical community and academia at large aware of the current backlash against feminism is a step in the right direction. It is simply unfair that deserving men are awarded the golden opportunity of embarking on the next stage of their careers, but that deserving women sometimes have to fight for it. Women need to send their own message: The tide is coming.

NOTES

I thank the audiences at the 1998 Eastern and 1999 Central Division American Philosophical Association meetings, my copresenters Ann Cudd and Julie Maybee, and Ed Tverdek, for useful comments on an earlier version of this essay.

1. Aside from gender, discriminatory tenure denial may be rooted in race, sexual orientation, age, religion, or the intersection of two or more of these features. Since this essay is a reflection on my personal experiences, I focus exclusively on gender.

2. Susan Faludi, *Backlash: The Undeclared War against American Women* (New York: Crown, 1991), xviii–xix and xxi–xxii.

3. Faludi points out that the media, the medical profession, and academia have portrayed women as suffering from mental and physical ills and general unhappiness, and even as having less stable families and committing more crimes as a result of their freedom. (Faludi, *Backlash,* in introduction.) But if women do suffer in these ways, their suffering, Faludi correctly states, is more appropriately attributed to discrimination than to feminism.

4. "Special Report of the APA Committee on the Status of Women," *Proceedings and Addresses of the American Philosophical Association* 68, no. 5 (May 1995): 151–54, quote from 153.

5. *Survey of Earned Doctorates*, National Science Foundation, National Institutes of Health, National Endowment for the Humanities, United States Department of Education, United States Department of Agriculture, 29 February 1996, 14, 16, 22, 25, and 67.

6. Leonard Harris, "'Believe It or Not' or the Ku Klux Klan and American Philosophy Exposed," *Proceedings and Addresses of the American Philosophical Association* 68, no. 5 (May 1995): 113–37, esp. 134. Statistics about women in academia in general are similarly depressing. According to one report, 70 percent of all college professors are men, but they constitute 86 percent of all full professors. See Susan A. Basow, "Student Evaluations of College Professors: When Gender Matters," *Journal of Educational Psychology* 87, no. 4 (1995): 1–10, esp. 1, citing *Academe* (1993). The *Boston Globe* reports that in 1975, 18 percent of tenured faculty nationwide were women, but in 1999 the number had increased to only 26 percent, despite the fact that in 1995, according to the American Association of University Professors, 43 percent of faculty in tenure-track positions nationwide were women. See Kate Zernike, "MIT Women Win a Fight against Bias: In Rare Move, School Admits Discrimination," *Boston Globe*, 21 March 1999.

7. My study was not carried out scientifically. The data is based exclusively on the information available in Archie J. Bahm, ed., *Directory of American Philosophers 1998–1999*, 19th ed. (Bowling Green, Ohio: Philosophy Documentation Center, 1998). I am aware of some erroneous information that would modify these statistics in ways indicating that the situation for women is even worse than reflected here. Additionally, my count does not reflect the fact that a department may have held steady

or even increased its number of women faculty not because women have made it through the ranks, but because it has hired additional women and/or replaced women who left with other women.

8. "Special Report of the Committee on the Status and Future of the Profession," *Proceedings and Addresses of the American Philosophical Association* 70, no. 2 (November 1996): 131–53, esp. 136–37. The report notes that approximately 500 survey forms were at least partially completed, yielding the most complete report the APA has ever had, but that there was no way of knowing which departments did not respond since the survey was conducted anonymously.

9. The 1995 APA report stated that it "heard complaints that white males are disadvantaged in the current market, due to concerns for increasing diversity." See "Issues in the Profession," *Proceedings and Addresses of the American Philosophical Association* 69, no. 2 (1995): 134. One philosopher argued vigorously that White males are being treated unfairly because women and minorities have a better chance of getting a job in philosophy than they do. See A. D. Irvine, "Jack and Jill and Employment Equity," *Dialogue: Canadian Philosophical Review* 35 (1996): 255–91.

10. See my "Sexism in the Classroom: The Role of Gender Stereotypes in the Evaluation of Female Faculty," *American Philosophical Association Newsletter on Feminism and Philosophy* 99, no. 1 (fall 1999): 46–51. [Chapter 10]

11. Larry May, "Socialization and Separatism," in *Masculinity & Morality*, ed. Larry May (Ithaca, N.Y.: Cornell University Press, 1998), 116–34, esp.117–18. In 1995, the Citadel was forced by court order to admit women. On May 8, 1999, Nancy Mace became the first woman to graduate from this institution. The Citadel now has 41 women in its ranks. West Point has admitted women since 1976. See Sophronia Scott Gregory and Don Sider, "Point Woman: Unshakable Nancy Mace Excels as the Citadel's First Female Graduate," in *People Weekly*, 24 May 1999, 79–80.

12. Larry May and Robert Strikwerda, "Rape and Collective Responsibility," in *Masculinity & Morality*, ed. Larry May, 79–97, esp. 93 (Ithaca, N.Y.: Cornell University Press, 1998).

13. May, "Socialization and Separatism," 132.

14. May, "Socialization and Separatism," in notes on 171, footnote 26.

15. May, "Socialization and Separatism,"132.

16. "How Schools Shortchange Girls," *Better Homes and Gardens* 71, no. 4 (April 1993): 40–41. The data comes from the American Association of University Women's 1992 report.

17. *ABC Nightly News*, 16 November 1999 (interview).

18. May and Strikwerda, "Rape and Collective Responsibility," 93.

19. John Sabini and Maury Silver, "On Destroying the Innocent with a Clear Conscience: A Sociopsychology of the Holocaust," in *Moralities of Everyday Life*, ed. John Sabini and Maury Silver, 55–87, 74–78 (New York: Oxford University Press, 1982).

20. S. Berent, "Group Pressure," *Encyclopedia of Psychology*, vol. 2, ed. Raymond J. Corsini, 92–93, esp. 92 (New York: Wiley, 1994).

21. Berent, "Group Pressure," 93.

22. Entry on "Conformity" in *The Gale Encyclopedia of Psychology*, ed. Susan Gall, 85 (Detroit: Gale Research, 1996). The author reports on the first classic experiment on conformity which was carried out by Muzafer Sherif in the 1930s.

Sherif found that when several subjects were placed together in a room with a stationary light and each was asked to describe its movement out loud, their answers became increasingly similar as they unconsciously sought to establish a group norm. The power of social norms was demonstrated even more strikingly when the subjects continued to adhere to the norm later when they were retested individually.

Sherif's experiment demonstrates one of the important conditions that produces conformity: ambiguity. There was no clear-cut answer to the question asked of different lengths on two cards, where one answer was obviously the right one. However, each subject was tested in a room full of "planted" peers who deliberately gave the wrong answer in some cases. About three-fourths of the subjects tested knowingly gave an incorrect answer at least once in order to conform to the group.

23. See Naomi Wolf, *The Beauty Myth: How Images of Beauty Are Used against Women* (New York: Anchor Books, Doubleday, 1991), 75.

24. Rosemarie Tong, "Sexual Harassment," in *Women and Values*, ed. Marilyn Pearsall, 148–66 (Belmont, Calif.: Wadsworth, 1986). The statistic comes from a study conducted by *Redbook*—which certainly is not a feminist periodical—based on 9,000 readers (149).

25. See Wanda Teays, "Standards of Perfection and Battered Women's Self-Defense," in *Violence against Women: Philosophical Perspectives*, ed. Stanley G. French, Wanda Teays, and Laura M. Purdy, 57–76 (Ithaca, N.Y.: Cornell University Press, 1998); and Kathleen Waits, "The Criminal Justice System's Response to Battering: Understanding the Problem, Forging the Solutions," in *Feminist Jurisprudence*, ed. Patricia Smith, 188–209 (New York: Oxford University Press, 1993). This figure is likely to be much higher since wife abuse is the most unreported crime in the country.

26. This statistic comes from a news report I heard in 1998. Susan J. Brison reports that one rape is committed in the United States every six minutes, but that the FBI is "notorious for underestimating the frequency of sex crimes." See "Surviving Sexual Violence: A Philosophical Perspective," in French, Teays, and Purdy, *Violence against Women*, 11–26, esp. 13.

27. Faludi, *Backlash*, 465, footnote xvii.

28. Faludi, *Backlash*, 65. The ensuing discussion can be found on 65–67.

29. See Herman Goring, *Trial of the Major War Criminals before the International Military Tribunal, Nuremberg* (Nuremberg, Germany, 1947–1949), 24–25.

30. W. H. Blanchard, "The Group Process in Gang Rape," *The Journal of Social Psychology* 49, no. 2 (May 1959): 259–66, passage on 261–62.

31. I am arguing that male socialization is merely one factor that contributes to the prevalence of rape. Other factors contribute to a "rape culture," and so perhaps to the prevalence of rape, including a "blaming the victim" mentality in the American legal system, a male-biased view of force and consent, and sexual mores and dating customs in North America that blur the line between consensual sex and rape. See Susan Estrich, "Rape," in Smith, *Feminist Jurisprudence*, 158–87; and Lois Pineau, "Date Rape: A Feminist Analysis," in *Law and Philosophy* 8 (1989): 217–43.

32. May and Strikwerda, "Rape and Collective Responsibility," 93.

33. Blanchard, "Group Process," 260.

34. For insightful discussions of the harms rape causes to women as a group, see the following sources: Susan Griffin, "Rape: The All-American Crime," in *Feminism and Philosophy*, ed. Mary Vetterling-Braggin, Frederick A. Elliston, and Jane English,

313–32, esp. 323, 325, 329, and 331 (Totowa, N.J.: Littlefield, Adams, 1981); Tim Beneke, "Men on Rape," in *Gender Basics: Feminist Perspectives on Women and Men*, ed. Anne Minas, 352–58, esp. 353 and 354 (Belmont, Calif.: Wadsworth, 1993); Ann Cudd, "Enforced Pregnancy, Rape, and the Image of Woman," *Philosophical Studies* 60 (1990): 47–59, esp. 51.

35. Interestingly, the groups I describe fit the description of a mob. This is a stronger claim than the one that members of such groups merely succumb to group pressure. Psychologists attribute the following features to mobs: "(1) like-mindedness or 'mental homogeneity,' (2) emotionality, and (3) irrationality." See M. S. Greenberg, "Mob Psychology," in *Encyclopedia of Psychology*, vol. 2, ed. Raymond J. Corsini, 421 (New York: Wiley, 1994). Members of a mob feel a loss of responsibility because of their anonymity, and the group itself gives an impression of universality. In the discriminatory tenure denial case, the negative voters hide behind the "expert" testimony of external reviewers to capture the idea of universality. Members of mobs believe that their actions cannot be wrong. I would add that mobs, especially what psychologists refer to as "aggressive mobs," (e.g., lynch mobs), who display aggression toward a person, necessarily engage in immoral behavior. Insofar as tenure deniers display aggression or hostility toward their victim and are moved by these emotions instead of fairness, they constitute an aggressive mob.

36. Greenberg, "Mob Psychology," 263.

37. Debra Renee Kaufman, "Professional Women: How Real Are the Recent Gains?" in *Feminist Philosophies*, 2nd ed., ed. Janet A. Kournay, James P. Sterba, and Rosemarie Tong, 189–202, esp. 200 (Upper Saddle River, N.J.: Prentice Hall, 1999).

38. Kaufman, "Professional Women," 200.

39. The remark was made by an audience member at a presentation of an early version of this paper to the American Philosophical Association, Eastern Division, the Society for Analytical Feminism, at a Panel Session entitled "Analyzing the Backlash to Feminism," Washington, D.C., December 1998.

40. Susan Brison, "Outliving Oneself: Trauma, Memory, and Personal Identity," in *Feminists Rethink the Self*, ed. Diana Tietjens Meyers, 12–39, quote on 13–14 (Boulder, Colo.: Westview, 1997).

41. Richard Delgado, "Words That Wound: A Tort Action for Racial Insults, Epithets, and Name Calling," in *Words That Wound: Critical Race Theory, Assaultive Speech, and the First Amendment*, ed. Mari J. Matsuda, Charles R. Lawrence III, Richard Delgado, and Kimberle Williams Crenshaw, 89–110 (Boulder, Colo.: Westview, 1993). The discussion of the harms of racism takes place on 90–93.

42. Delgado, "Words That Wound," 91. A study conducted by Harvard University confirms a link between discrimination and high stress levels (radio report, January 1997). Researchers found very high stress levels in African Americans living in big cities in the northeast who had regularly experienced job discrimination. Responding to objections that the stress was really the result of living in poor economic conditions, Harvard conducted a second study on African Americans living in poor economic conditions in more rural areas in the south, but who either were unemployed or did not experience job discrimination. The study showed that the stress levels of the latter group were nowhere near as high as those in the former group. Finally, there is a strong link between stress and more serious, long-term ills such as cancer and heart disease.

43. Marilyn A. Friedman and Larry May, "Harming Women as a Group," *Social Theory and Practice* 11, no. 2 (summer 1985): 207–34. The discussion about this issue can be found on 220–21.

44. See Cudd, "Enforced Pregnancy," 51.

45. Some of her male colleagues used *Playboy* spreads during lectures, routinely called her "hon," invited her to bed, and fondled her legs under the operating table. *Chicago Tribune*, 9 June 1991, Section 1, 22.

BIBLIOGRAPHY

Bahm, Archie J., ed. *Directory of American Philosophers 1998–1999*. 19th ed. Bowling Green, Ohio: Philosophy Documentation Center, 1998.

Basow, Susan A. "Student Evaluations of College Professors: When Gender Matters." *Journal of Educational Psychology* 87, no. 4 (1995): 1–10.

Beneke, Tim. "Men on Rape." In *Gender Basics: Feminist Perspectives on Women and Men*, ed. Anne Minas, 352–58. Belmont, Calif.: Wadsworth, 1993.

Berent, S. "Group Pressure." In *Encyclopedia of Psychology*, vol. 2, ed. Raymond J. Corsini, 92–93. New York: Wiley, 1994.

Blanchard, W. H. "The Group Process in Gang Rape." *The Journal of Social Psychology* 49, no. 2 (May 1959): 259–66.

Brison, Susan. "Outliving Oneself: Trauma, Memory, and Personal Identity." In *Feminists Rethink the Self*, ed. Diana Tietjens Meyers, 12–39. Boulder, Colo.: Westview, 1997.

———. "Surviving Sexual Violence: A Philosophical Perspective." In *Violence against Women: Philosophical Perspectives*, ed. Stanley G. French, Wanda Teays, and Laura M. Purdy, 11–26. Ithaca, N.Y.: Cornell University Press, 1998.

Chicago Tribune, 9 June 1991.

"Conformity." In *The Gale Encyclopedia of Psychology*, ed. Susan Gall, 85. Detroit: Gale Research, 1996.

Cudd, Ann E. "Enforced Pregnancy, Rape, and the Image of Woman." *Philosophical Studies* 60 (1990): 47–59.

Delgado, Richard. "Words That Wound: A Tort Action for Racial Insults, Epithets, and Name Calling." In *Words That Wound: Critical Race Theory, Assaultive Speech, and the First Amendment*, ed. Mari J. Matsuda, Charles R. Lawrence III, Richard Delgado, and Kimberle Williams, 89–110. Boulder, Colo.: Westview, 1993.

Estrich, Susan. "Rape." In *Feminist Jurisprudence*, ed. Patricia Smith, 158–87. New York: Oxford University Press, 1993.

Faludi, Susan. *Backlash: The Undeclared War against American Women*. New York: Crown, 1991.

Friedman, Marilyn A., and Larry May. "Harming Women as a Group." *Social Theory and Practice* 11, no. 2 (summer 1985): 207–34.

Goring, Hermann. *Trial of the Major War Criminals before the International Military Tribunal, Nuremberg*. (Nuremberg, Germany, 1947–1949).

Greenberg, M. S. "Mob Psychology." In *Encyclopedia of Psychology*, vol. 2, ed. Raymond J. Corsini, 421. New York: Wiley, 1994.

Griffin, Susan. "Rape: The All-American Crime." In *Feminism and Philosophy*, ed. Mary Vetterling-Braggin, Frederick A. Elliston, and Jane English, 313–32. Totowa, N.J.: Littlefield, Adams, 1981.

Harris, Leonard. "'Believe It or Not' or the Ku Klux Klan and American Philosophy Exposed." *Proceedings and Addresses of the American Philosophical Association* 68, no. 5 (May 1995): 113–37.

"How Schools Shortchange Girls." *Better Homes and Gardens* 71, no. 4 (April 1993): 40–41.

Irvine, A. D. "Jack and Jill and Employment Equity." *Dialogue: Canadian Philosophical Review* 35 (1996): 255–91.

"Issues in the Profession." *Proceedings and Address of the American Philosophical Association* 69, no. 2 (1995): 134.

Kaufman, Debra Renee. "Professional Women: How Real Are the Recent Gains?" In *Feminist Philosophies*, 2nd ed., ed. Janet A. Kournay, James P. Sterba, and Rosemarie Tong, 189–202. Upper Saddle River, N.J.: Prentice Hall, 1999.

May, Larry. "Socialization and Separatism." In *Masculinity & Morality*, ed. Larry May, 116–34. Ithaca, N.Y.: Cornell University Press, 1998.

May, Larry, and Robert Strikwerda. "Rape and Collective Responsibility." In *Masculinity & Morality*, ed. Larry May, 79–97. Ithaca, N.Y.: Cornell University Press, 1998.

Pineau, Lois. "Date Rape: A Feminist Analysis." *Law and Philosophy* 8 (1989): 217–43.

Sabini, John, and Maury Silver. "On Destroying the Innocent with a Clear Conscience: A Sociopsychology of the Holocaust." In *Moralities of Everyday Life*, ed. John Sabini and Maury Silver, 55–87. New York: Oxford University Press, 1982.

Scott Gregory, Sophronia, and Don Sider. "Point Woman: Unshakable Nancy Mace Excels as the Citadel's First Female Graduate." *People Weekly*, 24 May 1999: 79–80.

"Special Report of the APA Committee on the Status of Women." *Proceedings and Addresses of the American Philosophical Association* 68, no. 5 (May 1995): 151–54.

"Special Report of the Committee on the Status and Future of the Profession." *Proceedings and Addresses of the American Philosophical Association* 70, no. 2 (November 1996): 131–53.

Superson, Anita M. "Sexism in the Classroom: The Role of Gender Stereotypes in the Evaluation of Female Faculty." *American Philosophical Association Newsletter on Feminism and Philosophy* 99, no. 1 (fall 1999): 46–51.

Survey of Earned Doctorates. National Science Foundation, National Institutes of Health, National Endowment for the Humanities, U.S. Department of Education, U.S. Department of Agriculture, 29 February 1996.

Teays, Wanda. "Standards of Perfection and Battered Women's Self-Defense." In *Violence against Women: Philosophical Perspectives*, ed. Stanley G. French, Wanda Teays, and Laura M. Purdy, 57–76. Ithaca, N.Y.: Cornell University Press, 1998.

Tong, Rosemarie. "Sexual Harassment." In *Women and Values*, ed. Marilyn Pearsall, 148–66. Belmont, Calif.: Wadsworth, 1986.

Waits, Kathleen. "The Criminal Justice System's Response to Battering: Understanding the Problem, Forging the Solutions." In *Feminist Jurisprudence*, ed. Patricia Smith, 188–209. New York: Oxford University Press, 1993.

Wolf, Naomi. *The Beauty Myth: How Images of Beauty Are Used against Women.* New York: Anchor Books, Doubleday, 1991.

Zernike, Kate. "MIT Women Win a Fight against Bias: In Rare Move, School Admits Discrimination." *Boston Globe*, 21 March 1999.

6

Parenting and Other Human Casualties in the Pursuit of Academic Excellence

Cynthia Willett

There is a type of backlash against women's progress in academia that may be fostered by coworkers or institutional practices otherwise supportive of the advancement of women. This type of backlash targets those women who choose to raise children while pursuing their academic careers. Over the past couple of decades, as women have increasingly entered academia, the standards for evaluation and promotion have risen sharply. Not only have academic institutions failed to alter standards of productivity originally designed for the traditional man with a stay-at-home wife, these institutions have inflated these standards at the very time that women have entered the academia in large numbers. These inflated standards hit hardest on women who combine a career with parenting, although these standards affect all workers who have to assume caregiving responsibilities traditionally consigned to a stay-at-home wife. These standards hit particularly hard on women who decide to have children because of limits imposed by the biological time clock and because women continue to perform more of the work of parenting than do men. The disparate impact of higher standards partly explains the glass ceiling that blocks the advancement of women who are otherwise encouraged into the profession. It also accounts for the diminishing ambition among younger women, who often describe themselves as postfeminist. These young women, among whom are our students and children, witness the stress of the double shift on their mothers or teachers, and lower their family or career ambitions accordingly. But inflated standards in the quantity of publications do not only adversely affect women who choose to parent. These standards also adversely affect the quality of academic and intellectual life for those of us who are not parents. We need academic policies that reflect the fact that many of the newest and most vulnerable members of the changing work force may also be the primary caregivers in their family. But the more progressive policy changes would also address the dearth of artistic, intellectual, and political life fostered by the inflationary policies of current academic life.

I discovered the backlash against the advance of women who are mothers in 1993, during my first pregnancy. The chairperson of a philosophy department who does in fact support the advancement of women told me that I could not be both a philosopher and a mother. He did not have the same view of men and parenting. In part, his judgment against mothers as philosophers reflects the cultural expectation that when push comes to shove, women will continue to do what they have done for eons: shoulder most of the burden for raising children. In my experience, this disparity in burden continues today among academic families. The causes for the disparity are unclear and probably overdetermined. The intimacy that mothers experience with pregnancy and lactation may make it more likely that they develop stronger social bonds with their children. Fathers diminish in the eyes of their predominantly male peers if they show the inordinate investment in child rearing that is expected of mothers. Women who parent risk losing status and visibility as workers, but gain social standing as mothers, if they are White and supported by a man who works for good pay. Whatever the reasons, social expectations and individual choices continue to yield disproportionate numbers of men who focus on careers and women attempting to balance careers with primary responsibility for parenting. Observing this disparity (and citing a title from a Beckett play that many of us do not have the time to read), the legal scholar Susan Estrich draws the conclusion that "waiting for the connection between gender and parenting to be broken is waiting for Godot."[1] There are men who take equal or even primary responsibility for children, but these men are, as Estrich remarks, "extraordinary." The burdens of child rearing are not going to be resolved by waiting for men to bear half the burden, at least not in any time in the immediate future.

Meanwhile, the meaning of parenting in the middle class has shifted significantly since the 1950s images of quiet suburban life. Parenting is no longer viewed, and I doubt ever was experienced by the engaged caregiver, as the passive nurturing of a dependent. Increasingly over the past couple of decades, parenting has transformed into what one sociologist terms "intensive labor." The "good enough mother," praised by Winnicott and other child experts in the 1950s, has given way to a new ideal of parenting. Parenting now involves the cultivation of the requisite social, cognitive, and cultural skills in children so that they may succeed in an increasingly competitive labor market. The proliferation of courses on parenting, beginning with pregnancy, labor, and breast-feeding, render it clear that it does not suffice for the parent to love, cherish, or otherwise "care" for a child. The parent must learn special skills and a great deal of knowledge about the availability of medical and educative resources in order to assure that the child develops properly. As parents we are not only expected to become involved in day care, PTA, and a whole host of other weekly school activities, but we also spend a great deal of time working one-on-one with our children at home. This labor includes helping children with sharply escalating amounts of homework geared towards achievement on standardized tests, interacting with doctors, music teachers, soccer coaches, gymnastic teachers, and more. Partly as a consequence of the ideological shift from "passive carework" towards intensive parenting, and partly from the hardcore realities of child care, mothers experience personal and social pressures to treat their professional career as a form of moonlighting. In fact, academic parents with flexible schedules may literally achieve much of their work while their children are asleep. This extra time is not free. It leaves these parents deprived of sleep, under much stress, and frequently impaired by illness or exhaustion.

Women of all races have achieved an unprecedented level of acceptance in academic circles, but progress for these women has slowed to a standstill. After examining a recent study of apparently "unconscious" discriminatory practices at MIT, Estrich concludes that "there seems to be something almost magical about the figure of 8 percent; it appears over and over again in tenured faculties, firm partnerships, and management jobs" (44). There are multiple explanations for the glass ceiling on women's progress in academia and the professions. Three factors strike me as especially important for mothers in academia. First of all, the more intensive practices of parenting accompany inflated standards for excellence in professions, rendering it increasingly difficult to raise children on the side. Second, the public/private divide makes it difficult to bring issues of parenting into professional life without appearing unprofessional. Third, the problem of discussing issues of parenting is exasperated in my own discipline of philosophy, which persistently defines the intellectual or professional elite in terms of the capacity for emotional and interpersonal detachment. Each of these three factors has impoverished our intellectual, social, *and* family life, and all in the name of professional excellence. The second and third factors reflect traditional biases against women and so-called feminine values in professional life, and now operate to effect a backlash against the growing success of women in the professions. The first factor constitutes a direct reaction to the entry of women (not to mention oppressed racial groups) into academia, and therefore functions as the core of the backlash against women.

First: Career advancement, promotions, and raises often demand that the academic spend an overly extended workweek (perhaps closer to 70 or 80 hours than 40 hours) on one's professional duties. When I ask my colleagues *without* children how many hours a week they work, they usually reply, "When am I ever not working?" An increasing amount of this work involves overnight and weekend travel. Over the past couple of decades, expectations for productivity have grown exorbitantly high. For example, at the University of Kansas, where I held a tenure-track position while I was pregnant with two children, expectations for tenure had jumped from three articles and a half-dozen conference presentations in the 1970s to six articles and many more conference presentations. (Requirements for conference presentations were less well defined, but expectations seemed to increase from one a year in the 1970s to three a year in the 1990s). Curiously, this doubling in demands for productivity accompanies the movement of women (and racial minorities) into the workplace. This rise in productivity did not accompany the entrance into the academy of GIs from World War II, which suggests that women and minorities have been targeted unfairly. At the same time, standards for excellence in child rearing (from the continual pressure on our children to perform well on standardized tests in the school system to the proliferation of extracurricular activities) are also rising. The double demand for excellence in the profession and in parenting render it increasingly difficult for the professional also to be a parent at the same time that women are encouraged to do both.

While all caregivers, including those extraordinary men who take on primary caregiving responsibilities, and those of us (again mostly women) who take care of an aging or sick relative, experience hardships in the attempt to balance career and unpaid carework, mothers in academia experience an extra hardship. This is because pretenure years typically coincide with the "ideal time" for childbearing given that many women postpone pregnancy until after the dreaded graduate school and job market days are over. Those women who attempt to postpone having children until after tenure risk lower fertility rates and medical complications that increase with the age of the mother.

The escalating demands in the work world threaten more than just the practice of parenting. These demands also threaten the intellectual and social life of the academic, who in earlier days had thought of himself less as a career man and more as a scholar, intellectual, and/or civic individual. Some of my friends in academia have expressed their disappointment over the lack of free time for pursuing pure research, intellectual community, or even solitary reflection. These higher concerns that brought them into their professions have been pushed aside by the excessive demands for productivity and visibility (or status) that define professional life. I share some of their nostalgia, but also have some concerns of my own. The image of academic life as a place of detachment from market forces and corporate values has been threatened for good and bad reasons. Traditionally, the leisure to pursue the pure virtues of research and reflection depends upon the stay-at-home mother who maintained the household and raised the children. The family wage that once-upon-a-time supported these women rendered them economically dependent on the absent patriarch, but also allowed both women and men in these families to enjoy the leisure to participate in civic activities (including political, religious, and civic organizations as well as sports or music and other hobbies). The corporatizaton of the university, with its increasing demands for productivity, puts enormous pressure on the working parent, making it difficult to find quality time for socializing activities within the family. It also erodes the basis for intellectual and civic community, undermines the leisure to develop friendships and personal relationships, and threatens to reduce the hyper-productive individual to a more contemporary version of what in the 1950s and 1960s social critic Herbert Marcuse diagnosed as "one-dimensional man." The demands for academic excellence (measured by corporate standards of productivity) wreak havoc on our social life both within the family and in our intellectual, political, and other civic communities. If we do not challenge these demands for what our institutions call "excellence," we all lose.

Arguably, this diminished social life is a concern not only for philosophers, intellectuals, and middle-class professionals, but also for the working class. In an essay calling for "free time for a free people" written for *The Nation*, Arthur Waskow explains that the "overwork/overstress reality runs across class lines."[2] Blue-collar workers are "shanghaied into compulsory overtime, working as much as a seventy-hour week," and have lost both the family wage and the eight-hour workday that these workers won as the result of hard-fought labor struggles beginning in the 1880s. In general, U.S. citizens work 160 hours more per year than they did 20 years ago. Gains in productivity are offset by symptoms of depression and stress in the work environment as well as in interpersonal relationships. Waskow urges labor unions, religious communities, and women's organizations to respond to these changes by demanding public policies that "free more time for spiritual search, family and community" (24). I will return to some of his suggestions when I examine proposed remedies to the problem.

A second factor that contributes to the glass ceiling experienced by women in academia turns on the division between the public and private domain in our culture. While discussions of the erosion of intellectual life or community frequently take place in the public domain of the universities and colleges, the frustrations of parenting do not. This is in part because the public/private divide makes it difficult to bring so-called personal issues concerning the raising of our children into the public domain of professional life without appearing unprofessional. I have heard the articulation of these concerns described as mere "whining." Over the past half-dozen years, this problem has grown despite partial successes that parents have achieved in parental leave polices. Both the successes and the failures accord with the growing corporatization of universities. While demands for productivity, networking, and visibility increase, academia (including academic research) is ever more disconnected from the values of civic, social, or intellectual community. The family, which should be treated as part of and not as apart from the larger socioeconomic sphere, sinks into greater irrelevance in relation to the productivity demands of the corporate university.

Many universities and colleges are trying to address some of the concerns of families, as mentioned, through parental leave and other progressive policies. These institutions recognize that pregnancy is not a medical disability, but a normal condition for some women, and are beginning to offer such policies as maternity leaves, stopping the tenure clock, and better day care services. My own university, Emory, made these changes this year. While these policies are enormously helpful to women, they are not enough. These policies continue to render pregnancy and child care as akin to a disability or illness inasmuch as child rearing is viewed as a career liability rather than as a positive socioeconomic value. While it is true that many women may themselves view child rearing as a career liability, this view fails to reflect the deeper meaning of work that should inform our larger social and economic system.

First of all, as a society we fail to respect child rearing as a mode of work that makes significant, indeed irreplaceable, contributions to society, and thus as a vital *career* in its own right. The failure to respect child rearing as a socially significant form of work, however, is not a simple oversight. This failure conspires with a larger failure to reflect upon how we as a society define and value work. I think Aristotle is right when he argues that the highest dimension of human existence, and the essential determinate of human excellence, grows out of our nature as social creatures. The value of work should reflect its contribution to sustaining the social fabric of our lives, and not our need to produce for the sake of producing. Since the industrial revolution, our social lives have diminished as we measure our status (or excellence, to use the language of Aristotle) ever more exclusively in terms of the values of corporate culture. We have allowed ourselves to measure excellence in terms of increasing standards in the quantity of production. While preindustrial societies recognized the household as part of our economic, political, and social lives, capitalism increasingly reduces our social life to the family, and severs the family from the socioeconomic sphere. Excluded from the focus of our productive lives are the meaningful social activities that begin in families or other sources of social and civic engagement, and that should animate our research and our teaching. The failure to recognize the social nerve of academic life threatens to render our proliferating research ever more sterile (or "academic" in the pejorative sense), and our narrowed lives ever more busy. Child rearing is not a handicap to our so-called real career. Child rearing is a source of connection with the larger society, and as such it is a basic source of meaning and value for all of our work, including our work as teachers and scholars. Some of the most exciting and original philosophical prose comes from scholars who root their research in matters of deepest personal, social, or political concern. Scholarship that is not so rooted is dead and dull, and it does nothing for our shared human lives.

The sad irony is that instead of bringing the emotional, social, and reflective selves that are immersed in parenting or other sources of social life to the workplace, parents carry standards of excellence from the workplace to the family. For as parents, we now engage in what has come to be called competitive parenting. Just as professionals aim to advance in the workplace, so we push our children to score ever higher on those ubiquitous standardized tests that are used to measure their individual achievement as well as the success of our educational institutions. It is wrong to use these tests as the primary measure of academic achievement for our children. It is equally wrong to rely upon quantitative measures of productivity for ourselves as teachers and scholars.

The rising standards of parenting may be fueled by the fact that stay-at-home mothers feel that they have to do more than did previous generations of mothers in order to justify not earning a paycheck. If so, then the competition for claims to social recognition between stay-at-home mothers and mothers who work the double shift makes life more difficult for both groups of women. Middle-class women who in some ways have more choices than did previous generations are made to pay for this freedom through the greater difficulty of their work inside and outside the home. We as a society may not consciously intend to punish women for their greater freedom of choice, but punishment is the effect of our changing standards of excellence. As such, these standards function as part of a backlash against women who now know motherhood as a choice rather than as a duty, but only at a price.

Third, philosophical reflection has been defined in the dominant traditions of the West as an endeavor among the elite, and in particular those who are detached from the emotional investments and primary obligations of child rearing. At the very core of a long history of philosophical analysis of excellence in character, moral responsibility, and the highest form of reason lies an ancient and originally patriarchal view of social life. This view excludes or subordinates child rearing as of secondary importance, utter irrelevance, or as a major interference with the predominantly stoic virtues of the intellectual life. I am not convinced that stoicism should be a virtue. Aristotle and Hegel, perhaps more than any other traditional philosophers, theorize the social basis of human nature. But even these philosophers subordinate love, friendship, and especially family life to the higher demands of civic duty and, finally, a stoic intellect. At the same time, these two philosophers perpetuate the standard misconceptions of childhood. According to these misconceptions, children are passive, illogical, or egocentric. Aristotle portrays children as presocial creatures motivated passively by appetites and lacking practical reason in his *Nichomachean Ethics*. In the *Phenomenology of Spirit*, Hegel traces the emergence of self-consciousness from a primordial experience of consciousness (presumably in early childhood) as narcissism. Engaged parents and the new experts on child care agree that very young children are both cognitively and socially active. Infants actively seek out the scents of those who care for them, toddlers can take the perspective of others, and cognitive development melds with emotional development. An intellect that is stoic cannot be the natural telos of our social origins.

A corrected understanding of childhood challenges the basic presumptions of Western philosophers from Aristotle and Hegel through Rawls, Habermas, and Levinas. The systematic work of each and every one of these thinkers is flawed by the fact that they make assumptions about human nature, about our origins in childhood in particular, that fail to reflect the experience of the engaged caregiver. I am arguing that the intellectual's unwillingness to be engaged in the realm of parenting and child care perpetuates systematic blind spots, and sometimes, strange distortions, in our prevailing views of moral character and rationality. Aristotle's standard for true friendship valorizes perfect creatures who view each other as a narcissistic extension of the self (*Nichomachean Ethics*, 1155a30). Friendships based on personal growth, as those that happen in the family, are relegated to an inferior type, presumably based on utility or pleasure and not virtue. For Hegel, the mythic origins of consciousness in primordial narcissism predisposes the dialectic to seek for its telos the kind of unity that is celebrated in the excesses of nationalism.

The discipline's ignorance of social sources of development in children has blocked philosophers and other theorists from comprehending diverse cultural and emotional dimensions of human interaction, not only in children, but also in so-called rational adults. As I have argued extensively elsewhere, such philosophers as Charles Taylor and Jurgen Habermas perpetuate the idea that rational adults who happen to come from Western elites can judge the objective merit of claims made by subordinated groups of people.[3] These groups are already judged by these philosophers to suffer from cultural, moral, or cognitive deficits. Elite philosophers, including Taylor and Habermas, fail to acknowledge the social, cultural, and emotional forces that constitute elements of so-called rational judgment. Among the inevitable forces shaping perceptions and evaluations are associations that we have absorbed from our diverse cultures about race and sex. If cognition cannot function apart from emotive influences, then it is unlikely that objective evaluations of academic performance or intellectual merit can ever be separated from the subjective impact of cultural and personal prejudices. New studies in cognition and emotion should fully destroy the illusion that the academy or any other institution could operate on the basis of a pure meritocracy, if by meritocracy we mean a system of reward that is not colored by cultural associations regarding the value of ethnically, racially, or sexually diverse people as coworkers.

The hidden prejudices that guide our so-called objective judgments of merit contribute to the invisible ceiling that blocks the progress and recognition of the achievements of White women. White women associated with motherhood are perceived as less focused on their tasks. They should be recognized as capable of focusing on multiple tasks. For Black women, hidden prejudices create, not a glass ceiling, but a "concrete barrier."[4] Regardless of whether Black women are mothers, they are viewed through our social prejudices as more likely to get pregnant, and are therefore less likely to be hired at any job level. Moreover, while middle-class White women are socially rewarded and highly regarded for becoming mothers, Black women have to deal with presumptions that they are not adequately trained for careers and that they are undeserving mothers. While White women experience only mild resistance and sometimes tolerance of the occasional need to bring their children to the office or classroom, African American women whom I have known have experienced outright hostility from their predominantly White institutions.

The academy needs to set up policies that curb the hostility towards Black women who may or may not be mothers, and that acknowledge and valorize the work of parenting regardless of race or gender. At the same time, the academy needs policies that acknowledge and valorize civic, artistic, or intellectual commitments outside of narrow measures of productivity in the profession. These commitments are stifled by corporate values and academic bureaucracies, and yet they can enrich our teaching and research as well as our individual lives. The unbridled demand for greater productivity leads to more but not better research. Research and teaching that grow out of community work or other social service would offer a much needed alternative to the jargon-ridden, hyper-technical, or inconsequential research that is the hallmark of the academic style of the modern, bureaucratic university. The academic indifference to family life is just one aspect of what Sylvia Hewlett and Cornel West diagnose in their study of our society's "war against parents."[5] And as Hewlett and West point out, the social life nourished in the family lays the basis for our larger social infrastructure eroded by the neoliberal policies of corporate America.

Hewlett and West argue that the best remedy for the erosion of our social lives is a state-sponsored bill of rights for parents. This bill of rights would guarantee tax subsidies for parents by taxing corporate profits. It is not clear, however, that public legislators will ever heed the call for a parents' bill of rights. In this era of weak governments and strong corporations, a more effective strategy might be to make demands for change directly on our universities, colleges, and businesses. From my own position as an academic in philosophy, three sorts of changes come to mind.

First, clear limits need to be set on requirements for tenure, promotion, and so-called merit raises. In order to establish these limits, we might take as our model the 35–36-hour workweek won by unionized laborers in France and Germany. The European model recognizes the importance of leisure, not only for the relaxation, but also for raising families and participating in the civic life of the state. The current U.S. model of the 70-hour plus work-week contributes towards the political, civic, and cultural apathy that characterizes American culture, and it puts a special burden on parents. The U.S. model is structured for workers with no child care (or other care) responsibilities, and as such it is inherently discriminatory. It is ironic that in this country where we pride ourselves on family, we define ourselves rather one-sidedly in terms of what Marcuse termed the performance principle. The proposal for the European model of the shorter workweek is focused around the demand for greater leisure, but it takes some of the unfair burden off of working parents. This proposal fails to recognize parenting as a form of work that, as I would argue, merits pay. However, this proposal has the advantage of not overburdening workers without families. Workers without family responsibilities express resentment when they have to take up the slack in the workplace for absent coworkers who are attending to family matters. While parental leave and other policies are especially crucial at the early stages of child rearing, a shortened workweek aims to redress the fact that family or other equally valid forms of civic engagement normally continue over the course of one's life. The idea of a shortened workweek reflects the concern that individuals not be defined by economic interests alone, but by social, cultural, and political engagement as well.

In the essay referred to earlier, Waskow calls for his readers to support a statement called "Free Time/Free People." This statement, already endorsed by numerous spiritual and intellectual leaders, including Cornel West, calls for reducing the workweek in order to "encourage the use of more free time in the service of family, community and spiritual growth" (Waskow, 24). Rather than demanding major new governmental policies, the petition seeks ways that the government or other organizations might offer incentives to businesses that grant workers paid family and community leave on a regular basis. In order for the "Free Time/Free People" proposal to better support working families, as well as the spiritual and intellectual life that seem to be the primary focus of concern for the statement's original signers, I would recommend that the workweek directly correspond to the 35–36 hours a week that we might expect children to be in school. Here I assume that proposals for a longer school day (as currently under consideration by several state legislatures, including Georgia) succeed. Otherwise, the workweek might reflect the 30 hours that children are now in school. Longer school days, however, make it more likely that children from disadvantaged social groups receive the extra hours of tutoring and the extracurricular activities easily attained by privileged social groups. For this reason, I prefer expanding the school week while shortening the workweek to 35–36 hours. But, as

Waskow argues, shortening of the workweek cannot entail the reduction of salary and wages, or else family life will not prosper. It will suffer.

In academia and other professions that are not on a fixed timetable, we might demand that institutions return to 1970s standards of excellence. Philosophy departments, like Kansas University's, that have doubled the number of publications expected for tenure could return to these earlier standards without sacrificing quality. If faculty preparing for tenure at research institutions were asked to select their three best articles for external review, these faculty would lose some incentive for publishing a larger quantity of articles, but they would gain incentive to work more carefully on the articles that they do publish. An emphasis on quality rather than quantity would discourage excessive publishing, perhaps cutting down on the number of articles and books that are published, but then also on the excessive demands for reading and reviewing made on informed scholars.

It is a curious fact that as soon as affirmative action policies opened doors for oppressed groups in our major institutions, demands for productivity and measures of achievement were raised. If we were to return to 1970s standards of productivity, while strengthening our commitment to affirmation action policies, we might begin to crack through the glass ceiling, and break down the concrete wall, that women continue to experience in academia.

Second: The divide between professional and domestic life needs to be altered in order to allow for movement back and forth between these two spheres of life. The structure of the work world was not designed to accommodate a woman's biological clock. Women who choose to work part-time while they focus their attention on child rearing suffer irrecoupable damages on their careers (Estrich, 104). In my experience, I have observed that women who apply to graduate school after having taken off some years to raise children are less likely to gain admittance than similarly qualified candidates who have taken off several years for military service. Those who wait and have their children later find that it is difficult to advance from part-time lectureships or adjunct teaching positions to tenure-track positions if a considerable amount of time has passed since one has earned a doctoral degree. But lectureships and adjunct positions are especially attractive to women who are trying to combine careers with parenting. Part of the social stigma that hinders mothers in the workplace is the assumption that raising children, unlike "real work," does not contribute towards the development of important professional skills. As Estrich points out, child-rearing experience should be viewed as no less valuable than military service. We need to recognize that those who spend several years raising children have more than likely acquired skills in handling interpersonal conflict. For mothers who are Black, these skills combine with skills in recognizing sources of conflict that Whites often enough cannot see.

It is also important to note that the sharp divide between professional and family life in modern America has not characterized previous societies. The historian Phillip Aries describes the social life of European societies immediately preceding the Enlightenment and the Industrial Revolution as lacking clear boundaries between public and private domains. During the ancient régime, important business deals might be reached at the dinner table with the active presence of young children. Contemporary disabilities theorists favor reconceptualizing public space in such a way as to minimalize the impairments of those who are "differently abled," and their success suggests that parents who are also architects and social theorists might offer similar proposals for opening up the public domain to families with children. The public space of professional life from the design of buildings to the organization of events at conferences needs to be altered for accessibility to families. Campuses might build social centers where faculty can exchange ideas with other faculty from their own as well as other departments, but these centers should also have play structures and recreational or cultural facilities that allow faculty to bring their families. Faculty might more readily attend conferences if professional activities included time and occasion for family-oriented events, including hikes along mountain or forest trails.

Third: Philosophers need to make an effort to change the basic methods and paradigms of philosophy in order to open deeper, more socially and emotionally rooted, conceptions of personal identity and broader contexts of what we call "thinking." I envision a move in philosophy parallel to ongoing changes in the disciplines of literature and history. In these latter disciplines, discourse domains have been expanded to include oral poetry or history. Philosophy might reengage the styles of thinking and forms of discourse that are rooted in the lives we share with our families, neighbors, and civic organizations. This means expanding the canon beyond our usual focus on written texts and abstract arguments for the sake of socially engaged modes of communication and thought. Contributions towards service should be recognized as a vital part of faculty governance within the academy, and what counts as service should expand to include extra-academic pursuits including participation in the PTA and civic organizations. Participation in these organizations establishes either directly or indirectly greater ties between academic institutions and communities. This participation is good for us all.

In the name of excellence, the corporate university rewards productivity. But this type of university does not nourish our soul. If higher learning is to foster the deeper sources of human excellence, intellectual wisdom, and social justice, then the university should not impose demands that entail weakening our ties with our families and our communities. The current structure of career advancement in academia, and in corporations, discriminates against women with children and fuels the backlash against feminism. This structure also reduces the productive scholar to a species of one-dimensional man. We need to make our universities and corporations reflect the multiple dimensions of the civic and social individual. This begins with recognizing and valorizing the work of mothers.

NOTES

I am very grateful to Anita Superson, Ann Cudd, Randy McBee, and Michael Sullivan for their excellent comments on an earlier version of this essay. I am also grateful to Emory University's School of Law for providing an occasion for discussing the ideas in this essay.

1. Susan Estrich, *Sex and Power* (New York: Riverhead Books, 2000), 96.
2. Arthur Waskow, "Free Time for a Free People," *The Nation* (1 January 2001): 23.
3. See Prologue in Cynthia Willett, *The Soul of Justice* (Ithaca, N.Y.: Cornell University Press, 2001), 1–27.
4. "Women of Color Report a 'Concrete Ceiling' Barring Their Advancement in Corporate America," *Catalyst* (13 July 1999): 17–19.
5. Sylvia Ann Hewlett and Cornel West, *The War against Parents* (Boston: Houghton Mifflin, 1998), 96.

BIBLIOGRAPHY

Estrich, Susan. *Sex and Power.* New York: Riverhead Books, 2000.
Hewlett, Sylvia Ann, and Cornel West. *The War against Parents.* Boston: Houghton Mifflin, 1998.
Waskow, Arthur. "Free Time for a Free People." *The Nation* (1 January 2001): 23–24.
Willett, Cynthia. *The Soul of Justice.* Ithaca, N.Y.: Cornell University Press, 2001.
"Women of Color Report a 'Concrete Ceiling' Barring Their Advancement in Corporate America." *Catalyst* (13 July 1999): 2–3.

7

Politicizing the Personal and Other Tales from the Front Lines

Julie E. Maybee

We are, in my view, experiencing a backlash against feminism, even in the profession of philosophy. I provide examples that help to demonstrate that this claim is true, but this demonstration is not my main aim here. To say that we are in a "backlash" is to say that things are getting worse for women and feminists than they were before. The idea of a backlash suggests that there is an attempt to re-entrench, so to speak, to shore up the defenses, against the perceived gains of women and feminists in the profession. But what is this re-entrenchment preserving? As I see it, the re-entrenchment is largely an attempt to preserve power and control over social institutions; there is a sense that women are changing the professions and there is a desire to prevent the change. In this chapter, I would like to take a look at what I take to be the nature of that re-entrenchment, and at some of the positive directions in which the nature of the backlash points us.[1]

I have titled the essay "Politicizing the Personal" in an attempt to echo the earlier rallying cry of feminists: "The personal is political." But I want to point us toward a particular interpretation of that slogan that I think needs to be reinvigorated in light of the backlash. As I understand it, that earlier rallying cry was sometimes understood to mean that we should integrate our feminist political convictions into our personal lives—by demanding, as women, more control over the how money is spent in our families, for example. It urged women to look at their personal frustrations as a function of external, social oppression, and to get men to share the burdens and responsibilities of household work. In its more general sense, I think the slogan was sometimes understood to mean that we should apply the considerations of justice that were traditionally restricted to the public sphere to the private sphere.[2] The slogan also sometimes meant that we should personally address sexism

133

when we come across it by, for example, addressing the sexism of one of our colleagues. As important as these strategies were, and without suggesting that I am endorsing a sharp distinction between the public and the private spheres of life (which, of course, the slogan itself was supposed to call into question), I want to argue that the nature of the backlash actually points us in one particular direction today that the slogan also suggested. Whereas some interpretations of the slogan pointed us toward addressing the political on a personal level, and hence focusing on the personal as our battleground, the backlash points us toward making the personal political, and focusing on the political realm as our battleground. I will argue that refocusing on the political in our strategy is required today because the backlash involves a *shift in ground tactics*, and the shift in the nature of sexist oppression under the backlash will require a shift in the nature of our response.

In characterizing the backlash against feminism, I have been particularly influenced by critical race theorists. The comparison between sexism and racism is particularly apt in my experience because the story that I tell is both my story and "our" story, since I could not have come to see the story the way I do without two particular White sisters and one African American brother who shared my experiences with the profession. Although there are important differences between racism and sexism, I believe that the current backlashes against antiracism (which we are witnessing in the attack on race-based affirmative action programs, for example) and against feminism (which also appears, of course, in the attack on gender-based affirmative action) have a similar character, a character that critical race theorists have been particularly good at describing. In particular, although the backlash against feminism is addressed to the personal, as I will argue, it has as its main aim the political. Hence, I will suggest, we need to refocus on politicizing the personal—we need to address the personal as primarily political, rather than address the political as primarily personal.

Let me explain. In the old days, we thought of racism as a function of White people's bad attitudes toward Blacks or other non-Whites, and sexism as a function of men's bad attitudes toward women. Given that account, the interpretations of the slogan that turned our attention toward the personal as our battleground made sense. Since attitudes are held by individuals, it would make sense to address bad attitudes on a personal and individual level. If our husbands have bad attitudes and refuse to allow us to have a fair share of control over the money in our families, then we should resist those bad attitudes and insist on such control. And if we come across men with bad attitudes at the office, it would be strategically important to address those attitudes on a personal level as well. Again, if sexism is in bad attitudes, then we can fight it by changing people's bad attitudes on an individual and personal level; our strategy should be to make the political personal, as I have suggested the slogan "the personal is political" sometimes expresses.

However, as critical race theorists point out, and as our own experiences in the profession of philosophy have confirmed, things have changed today, and today is not the "good old days." In particular, the backlash we are currently experiencing does not seem to be primarily a function of people's bad attitudes toward women or minorities. Indeed, you will have a hard time finding anyone nowadays who is willing to express a bad attitude toward Blacks or women. In fact, I want to suggest, what is particularly scary about the backlash is that it is currently supported by many young men who genuinely think of themselves as feminists (and as antiracist). As one critical race theorist has observed, Martin Luther King Jr. may have been correct when he wrote in his "Letter from a Birmingham Jail" that the people who are most dangerous to the cause of Black freedom are moderate Whites, and, I would add, the people who are most dangerous to the cause of feminism today are moderate men.[3] But if sexism and racism are no longer in bad attitudes, where are they? And if people who genuinely think they are feminist can be sexist, then what is going on? Understanding just how all this is possible will take us in the direction of the positive suggestions I want to make. I will focus my discussion on the experiences of the backlash in the profession of philosophy, but I believe these experiences may be generalized to some other disciplines as well.

STRUCTURES OF DISADVANTAGE

In this section, I define the backlash not as attitudinal or personal but as a structural phenomenon, with political consequences in the profession. I am not, of course, original in pointing out the structural or institutional nature of sexism (or racism). Many feminists and some critical race theorists have been advising us to see sexism and racism as structural or institutional for some time.[4] Black feminist bell hooks has even already suggested that we should turn our attention toward the political, rather than the personal.[5] What I would like to do in this essay, then, is to explore these observations within the particular context of the profession of philosophy, and to draw out some implications for our future thinking and strategies.

To say that a system of oppression is structural or institutional is to say, in part, that the structures and systems of our society are sexist (and racist) at such a deep level that they carry on the oppression of women (and non-Whites), even if no one has any explicit, negative attitudes toward women or non-Whites. The oppression may be embedded in economic structures, social traditions, or social realities. Let me give some examples of how these structures may work.

One of the best arguments that shows how an economic reality may be oppressive can be found in an important article by Ann E. Cudd, called

"Oppression by Choice."[6] In the article, Cudd argues that the wage gap between men and women sets up a vicious cycle which leads to the oppression of women, even though no one involved expresses any bad attitudes toward women. What oppresses women, Cudd argues, is the economic reality that women—no matter what their education—earn approximately 64 cents for every dollar that a man with the same level of education earns. Suppose a married couple consisting of two people of equal education, talent, and abilities, and with no prejudices about men's and women's work, decide to have children, and suppose that both of them agree that children receive the best care, given the current social conditions, if there is one parent who specializes in their care, while one parent works. Because of the wage gap, Cudd argues, it would be rational for them to decide that Lisa, as Cudd calls her, should drop out of the workforce to care for the children, while her husband, Larry, as Cudd calls him, continues in the workforce. It is rational for Lisa and Larry to make this particular decision in light of the fact that Larry will be able to earn more for the family over the long run—given the wage gap—than Lisa will. Since they are both concerned about the family's overall income, they correctly decide that the family would be better overall if Lisa specialized in child care while Larry continued working.

Cudd argues convincingly, I think, that this decision will lead to the oppression of Lisa, whose economic vulnerability and dependence increases as she loses ground in the wage market. Moreover, Cudd argues, because it is rational for the Lisas and Larrys of the United States to make this choice, employers perceive women as less reliable employees in the long run, which leads them to expend fewer resources on women, thus creating the very wage gap which makes it rational for women like Lisa to drop out of the job market and be less reliable employees over the long run. In other words, the wage gap leads to the unreliability that sets up the wage gap; the wage gap is its own cause and effect.

There are other important elements of Cudd's argument, but the conclusion I want to draw our attention to is that, as Cudd argues, Lisa and Larry make a rational decision which leads to the oppression of Lisa (and benefits the Larrys of the world, who no longer have to compete with the Lisas for jobs), even though neither of them has any bad attitudes about women. Indeed, we can imagine Larry to be the most wonderful husband in the world—we can imagine that, aside from child care, he does a fair share of the household duties (although Cudd argues convincingly as well that the imbalance in their power outside the relationship will more likely lead to an imbalance of power inside the relationship as well, wherein the Larrys will use their economic power to get more of their desires satisfied and so, likely, do less housework). But the fact is that no matter what he does around the house, nothing he does there can change her overall economic dependence on him and hence her economic vulnerability. She is oppressed, as Cudd argues, not in relation to Larry's bad attitudes, but in relation to an economic structure, a structure which makes it rational for her and for Larry—no matter how well meaning—to make decisions which decrease her economic and social power in relation to men, including in relation to her own husband.

Moreover, Cudd argues, Lisa agrees to the decision which oppresses her not because she wants to be oppressed, but because her other choices are even worse. Here are her choices: she can refuse to marry, refuse to have children, care for her children in a way she does not approve of (given current social conditions), or agree to oppress herself by being willing to stay home and care for the children. Although she chooses what seems to her to be the best of a poor set of options, the system coerced her into choosing the option which leads to her oppression. We would not say that Sophie, in *Sophie's Choice*, "freely" chose to send one of her children to the gas chamber, since her only other option was to refuse to choose between the children, in which case, the Nazis said, they would have sent both children to the gas chamber. Sophie chose—that is true. She chose the best, she thought, of two terrible options. But she did not chose freely. Similarly, we cannot say that Lisa "freely" chose to oppress herself by staying at home with her children. Her decision—and Larry's too, for that matter—was coerced by an economic and social reality that made all of her options rotten—including the option that she picked.

Cudd's argument helps us to see, then, how a structural reality—in this case the economic reality of the wage gap—leads to the reproduction of women's oppression even if no one involved expresses any negative attitudes about the ones who are oppressed by the structure. Here is another example of the oppressive effects of the wage gap that occurs within the university employment setting. At Stanford University, for example, when both spouses work for the university, the amount of money that they will get as a family for their housing allowance is calculated in relation to the amount of the largest of their individual salaries. Because, as the wage gap tells us, the women in these cases will tend to be making less than their husbands, the housing allowance will be greater, and hence the family will be better off overall, if both spouses agree to allow more money to go toward the already higher-paid husband's salary. The policy thus encourages women to permit the wage gap between themselves and their husbands to increase, and hence to oppress themselves further. Although Stanford's policy appears outwardly gender-neutral, in effect, it further exacerbates women's oppression.

Let me give a couple of examples surrounding the issue of race that demonstrate the same point, but in relation to other social realities. Take, for example, the segregation of Blacks from Whites—who are fleeing in larger numbers to increasingly rural areas—and the fact that Blacks and minorities generally tend to be concentrated in large metropolitan areas. That is a social reality about where people live, about geography and populations. Now let's think about the effect that colleges' well-publicized preferences for geographic diversity have on their student populations in light of that geographic reality. Because Whites are more geographically dispersed and Blacks and other minorities are concentrated in clusters around large metropolitan areas, colleges' preferences for geographic diversity will disadvantage minorities, even though the policy is supposedly race-neutral. Assuming there are no race-based preferences, large numbers of minorities trying to get into Whatever College in the northeast, for example, will all compete for the spaces that are made available to applicants from New York City, and largely White applicants from the Midwest, for example, will have a better chance of getting in because of the preference for geographic diversity. Hence, the fact that minorities live in concentrated clusters will put them at a disadvantage for college entrance, given colleges' stated preferences for geographic diversity. It follows that the preferences given to applicants for geographic diversity end up reproducing systems of oppression against minorities, even though they are supposedly race-neutral.

Take, for my final example, the preferences given to the children of alumni at many selective colleges around the country. Because of past explicit practices of discrimination against minorities, most of the alumni at these colleges are White, and, given marriage patterns among the races in this country, most of their children will also be White. It follows that the preferences colleges give to children of alumni, once again, tend to disadvantage minorities, given current realities, even if no one in the admissions office has any bad attitudes towards non-Whites.

Thus, structural realities in our society lead to the continued oppression of women and minorities, even in relation to policies and circumstances that appear to be race- or gender-neutral. Larry and Lisa made their decision looking only to the criterion of family income, and colleges are making their decisions based on supposedly race-neutral standards of geographic diversity and preferences for the children of alumni. Notice further that the disadvantages experienced by women and minorities in these situations bestows advantages on men and Whites; every job the Lisas don't take, the Larrys get; and every place the minorities from New York City don't get, the White kids from several states in the Midwest get.

THE LAY OF THE LAND(MINES) IN PHILOSOPHY

The backlash against women in the profession, I want to suggest, is expressed in similarly structural ways that involve academic and philosophical traditions. In making this point I want to draw attention to three features of the backlash, two of which have appeared in the examples above. First, the oppression is subtle and complicated, since it is not the result, I am arguing, of anyone's expressed bad attitudes about women. Indeed, in the last two examples, the disadvantages resulted from explicitly race-neutral criteria, from criteria that appear to affect everyone equally, without respect to the troublesome systems of classification that our society has employed in the past (gender, race, and class, for example). Second, the disadvantages experienced by women give advantages to men. Third, because the oppression often results from what appears to be gender-neutral criteria, many of the subtle oppressions are justified by traditional, supposedly "objective" and "universal" arguments that make them even more difficult to spot. A word of caution is required here: I am not suggesting that there are *no* objective or universal arguments—I don't want to take a position on that issue here. Rather, what I am suggesting is that in many cases supposedly universal and objective arguments are trotted out in support of what really turns out to be an expression of a traditionally White male point of view. While the arguments and the reasons given often appear to be socially neutral—that is, they appear not to give preferences in relation to our society's systems of social oppression against women and minorities—on closer inspection they are not socially neutral at all.

Let me give an example from the experience which was both mine and ours, as I say. In one philosophy department I know, there is a tradition of having departmental colloquia approximately once per month at 8:00 in the evening. Attendance at these colloquia is not absolutely required, but junior faculty members are expected to give a paper at one of them every year, and there is a general understanding that you miss papers given by others at your peril. The department employed at one time three women who all had young children, and who would often complain to each other about how inconvenient the colloquia were. All three were married to men who themselves had full-time jobs, and all three families had placed their children in full-time day care during regular working hours in an attempt to meet the demands of their jobs. I suspect that all three of us women found the evening departmental obligations uncomfortable for a number of reasons. First, we often had other departmental evening demands associated with visiting speakers that could not be helped, and the colloquia added to these already existing burdens. Second, there is no doubt in my mind that we were made uncomfortable by the social fact that the absence of the mother from her children is looked upon very differently from the way the absence of the father from his children is seen—in short, we felt guilty about not spending those precious evening hours with our children. Moreover, the fact that our husbands worked made relying on them to take complete care of the children for an evening more problematic than it would have been if we had had stay-at-home dads for husbands, a condition I'll explain further below.

At one point, having heard some of these complaints, the chair was motivated to raise the possibility to department members of moving the colloquia to a time on some afternoon. There was an afternoon slot during which no classes were scheduled—a slot that was used for department meetings—and it would have been possible to hold the colloquia at that time during weeks with no department meetings. Moreover, the afternoon time would have allowed us women to attend colloquia at a time when our children were already in day care. The response to the suggestion, however, was swift and fierce. Male faculty members—including, very disturbingly, one young colleague who considers himself a feminist—argued in objective and universalized language that the evening colloquia were an important time of departmental bonding, and that anyone who did not appreciate them was not properly dedicated to the department. When one of my women colleagues came out in support of moving the time of the colloquia, many of the men in the department cast aspersions on her collegiality. Again, in making their arguments, the members used language and arguments that were supposedly objective and universalized; they talked about dedication and collegiality, and about the importance (in general) of the colloquia.

However, I would like to argue, the position on the topic taken by the male members of the department was not objective or universal at all, but reflected their social positions as men in society and in the profession. Just as the economic and geographic and historical preferences mentioned above turned out not to be socially neutral, so the preference these faculty members expressed was not socially neutral either. Take the young faculty member I mentioned above. Although his wife was a trained professional, capable of making more money than he could, she had dropped out of the job market to follow him and to raise their children. Unlike our working husbands, she was available to take complete charge of the children's care at a moment's notice—indeed, that was her specialty, just as it would be Lisa's specialty in Cudd's article. Because of their division of labor, her spouse and our colleague could expect her to take full responsibility for the children's care during evening hours without presuming to interfere in her projects or work responsibilities. We could not make the same presumptions about our working husbands. Moreover, as I suggested above, social tradition in this culture treats a father's absence from the children very differently from the way it treats a mother's absence from the children, and he would not have felt the same compulsion to be with the children in the evenings that we felt as mothers of our children. There were even physical reasons for our preference for the time change that he could not have shared. At various times my colleagues were both breast-feeding mothers who made arrangements for other forms of feeding during daytime hours, but valued their evening feeding times with their infants.

In all these ways, then, the men's preferences for the evening time—although defended with objective arguments about collegiality and dedication—actually reflected their social positions as men and fathers, rather than as women and mothers. The evening time reinforced their social positions by reasserting their wives' subordinate positions as caretakers of the children, but it violated our social positions as mothers and wives of working husbands. It also reflected their positions as fathers, whose time away from children is regarded less suspiciously than a mother's time away from her children is.

Moreover, the evening time distributed advantages and disadvantages to us based on these social roles. By reinforcing the men's social position, the evening time gave their social position a level of comfort, ease, and normality, just exactly as it made ours awkward and uncomfortable. Because the dispute was used to question the dedication and professionalism of those of us who were arguing for the afternoon time, the attempt to change the department to reflect our social position also disadvantaged us in more obvious political ways, while at the same time advantaging the young men in our department. Where our dedication and professionalism were questioned, the young men in our department who came out in support of the evening time earned bonus points in the eyes of the all-male senior members of the department, by proving their dedication to the traditionally masculine, I am arguing, standard of professionalism that the senior members held. Where we were viewed as not properly dedicated and collegial, the young men were able to win favor with the senior members of the department.

As in the cases mentioned above, in this case, too, no one expressed any negative attitudes toward women, and indeed, as I said, one of the fiercest defenders of the status quo at the time was one particular young member who considers himself a feminist. Nonetheless, the male members of the faculty fought bitterly to preserve a departmental tradition that reflected and reinforced their power and place both at home and within the department, where their point of view and their social position could continue to dominate the administrative organization of the department.

Moreover, I want to stress just how crushing and severe—how personal, really—the attack or the backlash against us women was. Again, the members' relied on supposedly objective and universalized language to cast doubt on my colleague's collegiality and her dedication to the department—indeed, to some extent, on her very "fitness" for the profession. Thus, a request for a small change in the administration of the department that would have accommodated the social position of us women was used to question the value of us women as colleagues and philosophers. The fact that the men were really defending the dominance of their social position was hidden behind language and arguments that personally devalued us. Thus, the backlash—the attack on us women—was personal, even though, as I am arguing, behind the personal attacks was a primarily political struggle. Behind the supposedly objective arguments and personal attacks, we waged a battle over the very meaning of what it means to be a dedicated, professional philosopher, and a colleague, and, most importantly, over who would control those meanings. The personal turned out to be really about politics.

I can now describe the shift in ground tactics on the part of our adversaries that I suggested characterizes the backlash. Today it is both impolitic and impolite to express negative attitudes toward women. Moreover, as I have tried to suggest, it is unnecessary to do so. Today, the battle of our adversaries involves protecting and preserving structures that are not socially neutral, but that often appear to be socially neutral, and in any case are able to reproduce themselves without the help of anyone who expresses any negative attitudes about women. The exclusion of women's (and minorities') points of view is so ingrained into the very structures of our society, as I have suggested, that it continues without any explicit help, even in cases in which the criteria used are explicitly gender- (or race-) neutral. Therefore, the backlash against women and feminists has become increasingly subtle and, paradoxically, both impersonal and personal at the same time. The backlash has become impersonal in the sense that the defenders of the status quo need not refer to their negative attitudes to defend the structures—they need only refer to the universalized and supposedly objective "standards" that already reflect and reinforce their social position. But because they can no longer attack women as a group, as they could in the "good old days" when they expressed explicit, negative attitudes about the abilities and "place" of women, they must attack us one by one. So the universalized and supposedly objective standards are trotted out and, one by one, in increasingly personal ways, it is argued that we women individually fail to meet them.

So far, the example I gave above of the way in which the backlash was felt in our story referred primarily to traditionally masculine administrative structures in a philosophy department. Other administrative techniques are used to preserve male dominance as well. In some departments, special positions are created for "spousal accommodations," which, given the structures of the profession and the ways in which they advantage men and disadvantage women, are almost always attempts to accommodate the wives of men that the departments really want. Hence, in most departments, these special positions are occupied by women, and they are accompanied by special rules that further marginalize those women. Sometimes, the special positions do not include the right to vote at department meetings, and the persons who occupy them are excluded from other administrative privileges and responsibilities. These faculty members' courses may not appear in the department's catalog, and their names may be absent from the lists of "faculty" in the department. These disadvantages are magnified into further disadvantages. At tenure-time, for example, the people in such special positions may have less-than-normal administrative service. They may also have less opportunity to receive feedback on their research, for example, when those same lists of department "faculty"—on which their names do not appear—are used to create forums in which the "faculty" members are supposed to share their work.

But the struggle is over not just the administration of philosophy, as it is in these examples, but also the content of philosophy. We women have very often brought with us new interests and critiques of the philosophical tradition that challenge views about what sorts of projects philosophy should be engaged in, and how those projects should be pursued. We also tend to forge our own alliances and networks that challenge judgments about who is a valuable philosopher. Although our male colleagues cast their arguments in objective and universalized language about what "real" philosophy is, about what "good" philosophy is, about who is a "good" philosopher, and about how we should pursue "real" philosophy, their positions on these matters, too, are often not socially neutral, just as their preference for an evening colloquium turned out not to be socially neutral either. Their often exclusive preference, for example, for arguments that are disembodied, for arguments that ignore social realities, for arguments that dwell completely in the rarefied air of the general and universal, reflects the social position of those White males who have spread out their vision and made it the dominant one, whose ignorance of the social positions of others has allowed them to be convinced that they really do represent the universal point of view, who have not had to pay attention to the social realities that limit some of our lives, and whose bodies have not been used by others to define the limits of their possibility.

And so, when a Black philosopher I know turned his attention to issues of gender and race after a distinguished career in a traditional philosophical area, and was described by his colleagues as "immature" and as having turned away from his former work in "real" philosophy, there were no negative racial attitudes being expressed. Rather, although his colleagues' definitions of what counts as real philosophy reflected and reinforced their positions as White heterosexual males, those definitions have been built in to the practice of philosophy itself. The interests the Black philosopher expressed as a result of being Black and as a result of his sexual preference were regarded as inferior and as questionable from the point of view of the profession itself, which, I am suggesting, reflects and reinforces the White male, heterosexual perspective.

Similarly, when another professor of philosophy, who himself had three children, said that a woman who has more than one child puts her career in jeopardy, he too was not expressing any bad attitudes about women. Rather, because the masculine point of view is so bound up with traditional definitions and assumptions about philosophy—so structurally embedded—his judgment was, to him, perfectly normal, reasonable and, ironically, gender-neutral. To his mind, his judgment had nothing to do with women, and everything to do with the nature of philosophy. For him, his comment follows naturally from a few assumptions about the nature of philosophy, and what he takes himself to know about people in general.

Still, his judgment nonetheless reflects the traditionally masculine, social position that is embedded in philosophy itself. He assumed, for example— perhaps correctly, even—that a woman will be more involved with her children than a man will, and he assumed that this involvement with her children will hamper her ability to engage in properly philosophical, professional activities. His assumption that what she will do in carrying out her duties as a mother will be irrelevant to philosophy, of course, reveals some things about what he takes to be the nature of philosophy. His assumption reveals, in particular, that what she will be doing when she raises her children will be irrelevant to doing real philosophy and being a good philosopher.

Why might child-rearing tasks be irrelevant to philosophy, we might ask? Perhaps he is assuming that practical activity in general is irrelevant—an assumption which reveals his social position as a White male who is not expected to do the kinds of practical activities that women (and Blacks, by the way) have traditionally been expected to do. Or perhaps he assumes that the social engagement with children is irrelevant to philosophy. But this assumption would say more about his social position and his judgments about the value of the experience of raising children than it does about philosophy. If he is assuming that child-rearing experience is irrelevant to philosophy, he is ruling it out in an a priori way, that is, without having anyone try it out first. But child-rearing experience is—a priori—irrelevant to philosophy only if his valuations and his account of real philosophy is correct. But his account of what real philosophy is presupposes that child-rearing experience is not valuable and is irrelevant. Thus, he can argue for his definitions and account of philosophy on an a priori basis only on pain of circularity: he is right about what philosophy is only if philosophy really is what he says it is, but philosophy really is what he says it is only if he is right about what philosophy is. In other words, there is no reason to accept his definition of what philosophy is, without trying things out first.

Therefore, his comment about women who have more than one child shows that his conception of the nature of philosophy is not in fact socially neutral, but reflects and reinforces the social role of Western, European-descended men and the perspective of that social role. And he presumes that a woman can be a good philosopher only if she adopts the perspective of that male social role—indeed, only if she compensates for her social role as a woman by having fewer children—so that she can spend as little time with her one child as he spent with his three children.

So we are, I submit, struggling over what "real" philosophy is, and over who is a "good" philosopher, so that behind the personal attacks on our collegiality and our worth is really a political struggle over whether the answers to those questions will continue to reflect a White male social position, or whether philosophy will finally admit of answers to those questions that reflect the social positions of other folks, of other, to use Carol Gilligan's term, voices. To echo writer and playwright Lorraine Hansberry's understanding of integration in relation to African Americans, feminists do not wish to be absorbed into "this house" of philosophy; they want to see the house rebuilt.[7] The backlash is an attempt to eliminate the threat posed by this "different voice," it is an attempt to halt the rebuilding of the house, and it is an attempt to preserve White male control over both the definition and the administration of philosophy. One of our adversaries accused us of having politicized the department, so that he could no longer speak freely and just "be himself." We, of course, had never had that luxury.

STRATEGIC AND OTHER IMPLICATIONS

If my analysis is correct, it has several implications for our thinking about the backlash and for our strategies in the face of it. On the one hand, we must acknowledge the dangerous and tragic implications of the shift in ground tactics that I have argued characterizes the backlash. We must acknowledge our institutional disadvantages. In the "good old days" when our adversaries had explicit bad attitudes about women, it was easier to dismiss people as prejudiced, and to see immediately that their judgments really had nothing to do with us personally. But today, as I have suggested, attempts to preserve the status quo are hidden behind supposedly objective arguments about what the proper standards of collegiality or professional dedication, or philosophical ability are, and these standards are wielded in personal attacks on women members of the profession—just as they were for my colleague in the story I told above. This shift in tactics leaves us doubting ourselves in ways we did not before, when the attack was openly political, when we were rejected just because we were women. As Derrick Bell puts it for the case of racism, when racism was explicit, "[w]e knew who our enemies were. They were not us. Today," he continues, "because bias is masked in unofficial practices and 'neutral' standards, we must wrestle with the question whether race or some individual failing has cost us the job, denied us the promotion, or prompted our being rejected as tenants for an apartment".[8] Therefore, I want to suggest, in this sense too we must make the personal political: we must keep in mind how to translate the personal attacks on us into political battles; we must turn our personal pain into political gain.

Moreover, because the political nature of our adversaries' positions is hidden, we bear other strategic burdens as well. Again, in their minds, *we* are the ones who, by our resistances, make things political. In the minds of our adversaries, their assumptions are natural, objective, universal. Because we bring our politics with us, they see us as women, but see themselves as just "human." Thus, for them, everything we do in front of them is political, whereas everything they do is objective, universal, and politically neutral. In their eyes, we are politicized in a way they are not.

Our politicization adds to our burden under the backlash. Because our adversaries assume that we are politicized, we have the added burden of being unable to be personal, to be "just ourselves." We share with Blacks, for example, the burden of being representatives for a whole class of people at all times. Derrick Bell argues for the case of Blacks, for instance, that Blacks face what he calls the "rules of racial standing." These are rules that Whites have imposed on the politicized Black body's statements. According to rule one, for example, when Blacks support another Black, their judgments are interpreted as merely political and are dismissed.[9] There is, I want to suggest, a similar burden applied to women that we have experienced in the profession of philosophy. When we women argued in support of a woman candidate for a position in our department, we were dismissed as "politically interested," and our opinions were given little weight, whereas the men in the department, who supposedly occupy the "neutral" position, were assumed to make objective judgments about her abilities.

Of course, the assumption that men are politically neutral is absolutely crazy, since, as we saw, men gain advantages by keeping women in subordinate positions. They gain the comfort of having their social positions reflected in the very structures of the philosophy profession, and they gain monetary and status advantages from being able to live up comfortably to the standards imposed by those structures. Hence, their preferences are just as politicized as ours, but they advance their self-interests—and those of similarly situated persons—without acknowledging that they are serving the interests of their group. As I have argued, the masculine point of view is so embedded into the definitions and administration of philosophy that our colleagues' political interests are rendered invisible to them.

Whereas rule one indicates that a Black person's perspective can be dismissed, rule three spells out an exception to this rule. According to Bell's third rule of racial standing, for example, when a Black criticizes another Black, he or she is regarded as neutral and objective, and is presumed to be correct. Bell describes the response these Blacks get as receiving "enhanced standing."[10] Again, a similar rule affects us White women as well. When one prominent feminist came and spoke at our university and unfortunately offered belittling critiques of certain other feminists, she too received "enhanced standing," and won favor with the men for being a truly "objective" person. Her arguments were also accepted as definitive proof not only that the feminist she dismissed was certainly a nut case, but that any other feminist who had found those arguments suggestive (including me) was sub-par as well. After all, they could reason to themselves, even this big-mucky-muck feminist thinks those feminists are crazy. Moreover, the belittling comments could be used to cast doubt on the whole of feminist philosophy—you see, our adversaries could think to themselves, feminism does produce crazy sub-par stuff, just as we thought, and it really is very hard to find a good feminist these days, with the exception, perhaps, of big-mucky-muck.

Again, a similar rule affects White women in the way Bell says it affects Blacks.[11] We must keep in mind constantly the political implications of our behavior by resisting, borrowing from Bell, these rules of gender standing. We must be aware, as Bell argues for Blacks, that we can never help but can only harm other women whose work we review.[12] Our laudatory comments will be given little weight and will be expected, but, as Bell remarks in a story he tells about his own experience in relation to another Black person,[13] anything we say that is critical of another woman will be regarded as instantly correct, and will be given a great deal of weight. Because of rule three, we must be very careful about what we say about each other, and how we say it, in public forums. No one is asking us to agree with each other, but we must be careful not to play into the ways in which our politicization is used to dismiss feminist work disrespectfully and out of hand, and to re-entrench men's power in the profession. I am not deceived about the burden that this self-censorship places on us as women and feminists. I cannot develop this point further here, but the chilling effect that the rules of racial- and gender-standing have on our speech is particularly troubling and burdensome in a profession such as philosophy, which relies on the dynamics of spoken and written interaction.

On the other hand, the analysis I have offered suggests that we have certain strengths as well. Coming to see how a social position can be embedded in someone's views in a way that is nearly invisible to the one who holds those views is a profoundly humbling experience, and helps to explain, I think, the greater openness and diversity that the feminist movement has been able to endorse.[14] Although the three women in the department that I mentioned in my story had different—sometimes very different—views about philosophy, we were able to forge profoundly close relationships with one another. I believe we were able to forge these relationships not just because we faced a common enemy, and not because we shared all the same experiences (which we didn't), but rather, because coming to see how one's social position may be embedded in one's views in a way that is invisible to oneself makes us epistemically humble, and willing to admit that our views may be deeply flawed, even if we don't know it. I believe this humility translates into the ability to openly support, encourage, and respect different views and approaches, in the hope that this openness will prevent the kind of self-deceived self-importance and self-assurance that we see in our adversaries.

Finally, I think that this humility has made it possible for us to begin to see the ways in which our own positions as—predominantly—White women, has shaped our views in relation to our society's other systems of oppression. This humility helps to explain, I think, how the predominantly White feminists have been able, at least to some degree, to admit of and be sensitive to the Black feminist perspective, for example,[15] and to issues of class oppression. In her article "White Privilege and Male Privilege: A Personal Account of Coming to See Correspondences through Work in Women's Studies," Peggy McIntosh discusses in a wonderfully personal and yet specific way how her awareness of men's privileges in relation to women led her to look for and become aware of Whites' privileges in relation to Blacks in America. She lists 46 advantages that she has as a White person in America, which she calls an "invisible knapsack of white privilege" because of the way in which these privileges are invisible to Whites, just as men's privileges tend to be invisible to men. The knapsack contains privileges, McIntosh says, that "I once took for granted, as neutral, normal, and universally available to everybody, just as I once thought of a male-focused curriculum as the neutral or accurate account that can speak for all."[16] Some of the privileges McIntosh lists are small, and some are clearly more weighty. Privilege 46 is: "I can choose blemish cover or bandages in 'flesh' color and have them more or less match my skin."[17] Privilege 15 says: "I did not have to educate our children to be aware of systemic racism for their own daily physical protection."[18] In all cases, as she argues, although she did not *feel* the advantages, all of the 46 great and small ways in which whiteness is assumed to be normal did in fact give her advantages, though in a way that makes the word "privilege" somewhat misleading. As she puts it, "such privilege simply *confers dominance*, gives permission to control because of one's race or sex,"[19] and she argues that these "privileges" are actually better understood to be "unearned power conferred systemically."[20]

Thus, McIntosh demonstrates the way in which an awareness of men's systemic, unearned power allowed her to accept that there were probably similar systemic advantages to being White. As she writes, "[a]fter frustration with men who would not recognize male privilege, I decided to try to work on myself at least by identifying some of the daily effects of white privilege in my life."[21] Therefore, our awareness of the subtle systems of men's advantages has opened many of us to the other systems of advantage and disadvantage that plague our society. Of course, we are not always good at this. One little-mucky-muck feminist organized a protest against her university's policy of extending health and other benefits to the partners of homosexuals but not heterosexuals. She insisted that her boyfriend should have benefits too, and claimed that the university's policy discriminated against heterosexuals. It did not seem to bother her that heterosexuals and homosexuals are not on the same legal footing, since she, of course, has the option of extending benefits to her boyfriend by marrying him, whereas a homosexual person does not have that option. Nor did it seem to bother her that the university might well have decided to "equalize" matters by canceling its policy of recognizing homosexual partners, and hence by eliminating the hard-won gains of the homosexual community. Another feminist supported a department's protest that a young, Black philosopher was being paid too much money, even though his salary had been raised in response to offers from other universities. She did not seem to notice the hypocrisy of the department's use of the principle of seniority to criticize the Black philosopher's high salary, in contrast to its generally free-market and "merit" approach to salary issues for other faculty members—not to mention its free-market, "merit" approach to its own graduate students. Still, to the degree that our positioning does succeed in stretching our awareness, it is an awareness that we can build on in working to address not only the plight of women but the plight of other disadvantaged groups in our society. If we keep our listening ears on, and if we continue to fight for the opening of philosophy to the social points of view of people from all walks of life, perhaps someday philosophy will finally begin to approach living up to its universalist billing (if such a universalism exists).

NOTES

I would like to thank Ann Cudd and another unnamed commentator (she knows who she is) for very helpful comments on and criticisms of an earlier draft of this essay. In addition, I am grateful to the American Philosophical Association's Committee on the Status of Women, which invited me to deliver a draft of this essay as part of its sponsored panel at the American Philosophical Association's Central Division Meeting in New Orleans (May 1999), and to the participants at that session. My thanks also go to the participants at the session sponsored by the Society for Analytical Feminism (American Philosophical Association Meeting, Eastern Division, December 1998), where I delivered an earlier version of this essay. Finally, I cannot overestimate the debt I owe to my unnamed sisters and one particular African American brother who shared in the battle on the front lines and helped me grow new eyes, and to those on their own fronts who supported our struggle.

1. I keep saying that the profession is currently in a backlash against women and feminists, implying a distinction between women and feminists. I do think it is important to draw a distinction, but, as I'll argue in a minute, not that important. The difference between a woman and a feminist, of course, is that a woman who happens to be a philosopher need not be committed to the project of feminism, she need not be committed to improving the plight of women as a class, which I take to be the core of the feminist commitment, and which involves, almost by definition, a

struggle for more power for women. A woman who is not a feminist, then, may well support the traditional values and hierarchies that the profession of philosophy currently endorses; she may well not in fact be a threat to the current power-structure of the profession. To be a feminist is, as I said, almost by definition to pose a challenge to the traditional philosophical structure, for a feminist is concerned with the experiences of oppression that women have had, and a feminist wishes to liberate women from that oppression. As far as I can see, liberating women from that oppression will require putting women in a position which makes that kind of oppression impossible, and, hence, will require fighting for more power for women within the relevant institutional structures. Insofar as the institutions of our culture—including the profession of philosophy—have been aimed at keeping women out of power and hence making women more oppressible, then feminism is necessarily a threat to the maintenance of that institution in its traditional form. So while a woman need not challenge the traditional values and administrative hierarchy associated with the profession of philosophy, a feminist must.

Notice that I did not say that women as a class should aim to have power over men as a class. I am not advocating (contrary to what Nietzsche, for example, thought that feminists were advocating) that we should institute a new power structure with women on top as the oppressor class, and men on the bottom as the oppressed class. What I said was that women will want to make their oppression less possible by gaining enough power within the relevant institutional structures to stop the systemic and institutional oppression of women that those institutions have traditionally supported.

I have also suggested, however, that the distinction between a woman (who happens to be a philosopher) and a feminist philosopher may not be as important as it might seem—especially for young women—because my experience suggests that there is often an attempt on the part of members of the profession to engage in a kind of preemptive strike by, for example, opposing the candidacy of a young woman whether or not she has shown any signs of being a feminist.

2. This is one way of understanding Susan Moller Okin's project in *Justice, Gender, and the Family* (New York: Basic, 1989), for example.

3. For the argument that moderates may be more dangerous to the cause of racial justice than extremists see Stephen Steinberg, "The Liberal Retreat from Race during the Post-Civil Rights Era," in *The House That Race Built*, ed. Wahneema Lubiano, (New York: Vintage, 1998), 13–47.

4. Among early feminist defenses of a structural understanding of women's oppression are, for example, Marilyn Frye's *The Politics of Reality* (Freedom, Calif.: Crossing Press, 1983) and, in legal scholarship, Catherine MacKinnon's *Feminism Unmodified: Discourses on Life and Law* (Cambridge, Mass.: Harvard University Press, 1987). More recently in critical race theory, for example, the anthology *The House That Race Built*, ed. Lubiano, is united by its contributors' commitment to the view that racism involves "the systematic operation of power at work throughout our political economy" (Lubiano's introduction, viii).

5. This is a recurring theme, for example, in bell hooks, *Yearning: Race, Gender, and Cultural Politics* (Boston: South End Press, 1990).

6. Ann Cudd, "Oppression by Choice," *Journal of Social Philosophy* 25 (special anniversary issue, 1988): 22–44. Reprinted in *Ethics in Practice: An Anthology*, ed. Hugh LaFollette (Cambridge, Mass.: Blackwell, 1997), 387–98.

7. See Robin D. G. Kelley, "Integration: What's Left?" *The Nation* (December 14, 1998): 17.

8. Derrick Bell, *Faces at the Bottom of the Well: The Permanence of Racism* (New York: Basic, 1992), 6.

9. Bell, *Faces*, 111.

10. Bell, *Faces*, 114.

11. See Bell, *Faces*, 123–24.

12. See Bell, *Faces*, 112.

13. Bell, *Faces*, 112.

14. bell hooks, for example, mentions the shift White feminists have undergone from a refusal to discuss racism to an eager willingness to discuss race and racism. While she praises this new awareness and "epistemological shift," she also cautions White feminists to be self-critical, and to continuously interrogate their own credentials in relation to their discussions of race. She also encourages White women to focus their attention on whiteness, rather than on blackness. See hooks, *Yearning*, 54–55. She again praises White feminists' sometimes insightful critiques of racism later in the book, but also criticizes White feminists for allowing racism to close their minds to Black men's contributions to the discussion of gender, and to lead them to criticize Black men's sexism more harshly than they criticize White men's sexism (hooks, *Yearning*, 65–68). Further below, the discussion of Peggy McIntosh's "White Privilege and Male Privilege: A Personal Account of Coming to See Correspondences through Work in Women's Studies," in *Race, Class, and Gender in the United States: An Integrated Study*, ed. Paula S. Rothenberg, 3rd ed. (New York: St. Martin's Press, 1992), 72–80 serves as an example of how one feminist's thinking about gender oppression led to a greater awareness of racial oppression.

15. See note six above.

16. McIntosh, "White Privilege and Male Privilege," 76.

17. McIntosh, "White Privilege and Male Privilege," 75.

18. McIntosh, "White Privilege and Male Privilege," 74.

19. McIntosh, "White Privilege and Male Privilege," 77.

20. McIntosh, "White Privilege and Male Privilege," 78.

21. McIntosh, "White Privilege and Male Privilege," 73.

BIBLIOGRAPHY

Bell, Derrick. *Faces at the Bottom of the Well: The Permanence of Racism*. New York: Basic, 1992.

Frye, Marilyn. *The Politics of Reality*. Freedom, Calif.: Crossing Press, 1983.

hooks, bell. *Yearning: Race, Gender, and Cultural Politics*. Boston: South End Press, 1990.

Kelley, Robin D. G. "Integration: What's Left?" *The Nation* (December 14, 1998): 17–19.

Lubiano, Wahneema, ed. *The House That Race Built*. New York: Vintage, 1998.

MacKinnon, Catherine. *Feminism Unmodified: Discourses on Life and Law*. Cambridge, Mass.: Harvard University Press, 1987.

McIntosh, Peggy. "White Privilege and Male Privilege: A Personal Account of Coming to See Correspondences through Work in Women's Studies." In *Race, Class, and*

Gender in the United States: An Integrated Study, ed. Paula S. Rothenberg. 3rd ed. New York: St. Martin's Press, 1992. The article has since appeared under the title "White Privilege: Unpacking the Invisible Knapsack" in the fourth edition of this volume (1998).

Okin, Susan Moller. *Justice, Gender, and the Family.* New York: Basic, 1989.

Stephen Steinberg. "The Liberal Retreat from Race during the Post-Civil Rights Era." In *The House That Race Built*, ed. Wahneema Lubiano, 13–47. New York: Vintage, 1998.

IV

STUDENT BACKLASH AGAINST FEMINISM

8

Marginalized Voices: Challenging Dominant Privilege in Higher Education

Carol J. Moeller

Since the process of experience is capable of being educative, faith in democracy is all one with faith in experience and education.

—John Dewey [1]

There is a backlash in higher education today against progressive movements. Gains of oppressed groups have been followed by fierce reactions against them. The media and other more subtle forces, I argue, fuel this backlash. Despite the perception of universities as left-wing indoctrination centers, the reality is that White supremacy, sexism, and other forms of oppression are alive and well in higher education, pervading its demographics, curriculum, pedagogies, and institutional structures. Moreover, dominant economic interests continue perniciously to shape education and media to the detriment of free and critical thinking. At best, universities have tacked on non-mainstream voices, by including such programs as Women's Studies and Africana Studies. Yet they have not fully integrated such approaches into higher education, so dominant views still appear to have the status of a *truth*. However, diversity of voices and approaches from formerly excluded groups are not just interestingly supplemental. These approaches are often corrective to dominant views, challenging their adequacy on the grounds of knowledge, not simply politics. Oppression blocks the search for truth in being bound up with mystification, processes concealing or obscuring the realities of unjust social relations. The inclusion of previously marginalized voices is essential to learning, not optional. It's crucial for knowledge, and for the realization of democracy.

These issues are not new. John Dewey, American philosopher and education theorist, exposed the same issues, showing how inequalities of power

155

and wealth weaken the nation's hopes for democracy and for genuine knowledge, given the forces of privilege and domination that tend to mystify social relations. Though Dewey was not specifically antiracist and feminist, many antiracist and feminist thinkers and activists share his insights. Further, Dewey alerts us to the epistemological challenges involved in understanding a world so shaped by power differentials. To Dewey, democracy, genuine knowledge, and social equity are inextricably linked. In the interests of learning, knowledge, social justice, and democracy, we must fight the current backlashes against social equity. Agreeing with Dewey and other contemporary thinkers, I suggest ways to change higher education in more equitable directions.

EDUCATION AMIDST THE POLITICS OF KNOWLEDGE

In this section, I describe some dimensions of the politics of knowledge. I highlight the very contested claims about the state of higher education today on the larger-than-life theme of *political correctness*. I then examine some theoretical issues of how inequalities and dominant interests can inhibit understanding of even the most concrete realities of life. I reflect critically on the context of teaching, in particular, how backlash views can interfere with free inquiry.

Political Correctness: Myths and Realities

Dewey reminds us that education and democracy are closely linked. Indeed, democracy, education, and knowledge might seem to be connected in obvious ways. In the United States, for example, education to age sixteen is by policy compulsory and free. Why? Education is defended as crucial to one's gaining the knowledge and skills to participate in the governing of society. On this ideal, education facilitates learning, develops citizenry, and enhances democracy. Contemporary debates about education may seem a bit removed from these basic ideals, and the links are not always clear between them and such topics as feminism and multiculturalism, as espoused by either their proponents or opponents. These relatively new terms and debates might seem to represent new issues, distinctively political ones, to matters of education. Some might regard these issues as disruptive, yearning for old-fashioned values of educational quality. Consider the National Association of Scholars (NAS), a conservative organization that often raises this sort of concern. The NAS claims that in recent decades standards have been eroded, the curriculum has been debased, and research has been trivialized or distorted by ideology.[2] It claims that education ought to be about truth, civilization, and the preservation of what is best of our historical and cultural legacies. To the NAS, political extremists seek to replace values of truth and quality with leftist politics, corrupting these noble dreams. The NAS, as well as the public and press following their lead, believe that "diversity," "political correctness," and other such political agenda items are replacing quality as the aim of higher education. It believes that truth is being sacrificed for politics. But is this so? Or do the backlashes against feminism, multiculturalism, and "political correctness" overstate the changes such movements as feminism have brought about?

So what is going on with these matters and education? Whose story is one to believe? Have colleges and universities been transformed into indoctrination centers for feminists, people of color, and/or gays, lesbians, bisexuals, and transgendered people? Has the disinterested pursuit of knowledge been replaced by left-wing polemics? Have affirmative action programs and "political correctness" become the primary criterion for admissions, hiring, scholarship, pedagogy, and campus life?

Despite the McCarthy-style frenzy about "political correctness," conservative correctness still holds sway. This conservative correctness of the Right is far more established, better funded, and more intransigent than the ideology of its opponents. Sexism and other intersecting oppressions still dominate the demographics, curriculum, and scholarship of academic life. While many programs such as Women's Studies and Africana Studies have survived, they are still conspicuous in their ghettoization. Their critical, corrective analyses have continued to be marginalized. At many colleges and universities, students may elect to take courses in women's history, African American literature, or feminist philosophy. Yet the bulk of the curriculum remains untouched. The average mainstream courses often remain (White, male-dominated, Eurocentric) history, (White, male, Western) literature, and (sexist Eurocentric) philosophy courses.[3] Much anecdotal, quantitative, and qualitative evidence suggests that the supposed dominance of "politically correct" universities and colleges is fiction rather than fact. However, it is not enough to say that it is a myth. We must also investigate why the general public has been so ready to believe that myth. There have been gains toward social justice in higher education, but those gains have been overshadowed by virulent backlashes against them.

The demographics of United States colleges and universities have become somewhat more egalitarian than they were in past decades. Cornel West notes that in the post–World War II era, people of color, Jews, women, poor and working-class people, and immigrants entered higher education in dramatically higher proportions than previously. Previously marginalized people, by their words, actions, and mere presence, challenged notions of the "Man of Reason" as White and wealthy. The very elites who had defined themselves and their cultures in contrast to constructions of men of color and women of all races faced them in higher numbers than before. Nor did each of these students embrace the acculturation and its related upward mobility, grateful for the opportunity to prove themselves on the elite's terms (or at least willing to seem so). Rather, many of those who made their entrée into academia found common cause with others, found their voices, and spoke out with challenges to dominant ideas.[4]

Consider that many curricular and other changes came from students' strikes and building takeovers, rather than from votes in faculty meetings. Many students demanded relevance in education. These demographic shifts and accompanying activism are partially responsible for the movements of Africana Studies, Women's Studies, Chicano Studies, Native American Studies, and Gay, Lesbian, Bisexual, Transgendered Studies. Contrast that history against that of some of the more traditional disciplines such as anthropology (though it, too, is quite new in the scheme of things). It has been argued that anthropology developed, not coincidentally, with the rise of colonialism. Ruling "the Other" requires studying "the Other."[5]

My own schooling has occurred through the development of the supposed "politically correct" assault on the academic world. I enrolled at Oberlin College in the fall of 1984. While I was there, the term "politically correct" or "p.c." came into use. Students tended to use the term not just about the content of particular views but upon the depth and sincerity with which they are held. For example, Students Organized against Racism held a forum in the spring of 1987 called "Political Correctness: Does It Keep Us from Communicating about Racism?" In such a context, our concern about "political correctness" was that fear of "saying the wrong thing" might stifle discussion. That is, some might avoid asking hard questions and grappling with issues deeply, out of fear that they might be called "racist" or "sexist" if they expressed their views. Thus, a superficial and calm near-consensus of "politically correct views" might conceal deeper misunderstandings and disagreement, inhibiting the kind of open and risky dialogue often required for learning.

In the fall of 1989 I entered a master's and doctoral program in philosophy at the University of Pittsburgh. It was there, in the more conservative climate than at Oberlin College, that I came to know the term "p.c." as a dismissal of ideas, thinkers, policies, and other items associated with movements to end racism, sexism, class oppression, heterosexism, and other forms of oppression. At Pittsburgh there was an active group of the National Organization of Scholars (an earlier incarnation of the NAS), and their affiliated wing, "Accuracy in Academia," which attacked any teachers or programs they saw as "p.c." Women's Studies, Africana Studies, and Cultural Studies were often subject to their attacks, as were teachers and classes that dealt with questions of oppression.

Yet, for this entire organized backlash against feminism and antiracism in the academic world, the general curriculum at the University of Pittsburgh was hardly left wing. The alleged "p.c." takeover was confined to the occasional teaching of texts deemed "polemical." I taught for about six years in the years of 1989–1997 and served as an undergraduate academic advisor in the College of Arts and Sciences for two years. Nowhere did I find multiculturalist and feminist values to be the norm. Rather, colleges and universities appeared to remain Eurocentric and male dominated, while "p.c." remained a term of derision hurled at anyone broaching issues of social inequalities.

The Politics of Reality

Complex dynamics can keep us from understanding the world and responding to it. Here I examine the politics of reality and the importance of critical thinking in creating better understandings of the world. I suggest that everyday life is far from transparent. Rather, our understandings tend to be mediated through dominant narratives, such as those of democracy (presumed to be capitalistic) and of citizenship (in which White male heterosexual taxpayers appear to epitomize citizenship). To know better, we must confront directly such views, developing a critical, participatory, democratic culture. This would be democracy in its fullest sense, one in which people have real power in determining the conditions of their lives.

KNOWING BETTER: IDEALS AND REALITIES

Feminist and other liberationist theorists and activists have long recognized the politics of naming reality. Oppression is often manifested and reproduced through the worldviews that make oppression appear as natural. Louise Antony makes this point: In a stratified community, where one group of people dominates others, the worldview of the dominant group can become a powerful tool for keeping those in the subordinate groups in their places. The real problem with the liberal conceptions of objectivity and neutrality begins with the fact that while they are unrealizable, it's possible for those resting comfortably in the center of a consensus to find that fact invisible. Members of the dominant group are given no reason to question their own assumptions; their worldview acquires, in their minds, the status of established fact. Their opinions are transformed into what "everybody" knows. Furthermore, these privileged individuals have the power to promote and elaborate their own worldview in public forums while excluding all others, tacitly setting limits to the range of "reasonable" opinion.[6]

Thus, dominant worldviews are disguised as universal and natural and what "everybody" knows. Iris Young describes the phenomena of "universalizing the particular," a process by which people from dominant worldviews generalize their own partial and particular perspectives to a supposedly universal perspective. Not acknowledging that their views and experiences may be far from representative of a larger society, they regard their own views as "universal" and any contrasting views as "particular" and "biased."[7]

Young argues that the very norms of impartiality are ideologically constructed so as to entrench further this sort of silencing effect. She argues that such ideas often make dominant views self-perpetuating, since they readily portray challenges to them as "biased," "crazy," or otherwise not credible. Groups are often subject to oppression in the form of cultural imperialism, a process by which a dominant, partial standard or conception of the world has been portrayed as the only legitimate standard. In such cases, oppressed groups must develop alternative accounts. They often require space to themselves for consciousness raising among group members. Such forums are crucial to developing alternative views, allowing room for some critical perspectives upon culturally imperialistic views.[8]

How do people achieve clarity about oppression, despite prevailing worldviews that inhibit such consciousness? Susan Babbitt argues that knowledge about systemic oppression is often derived through complex processes of inchoate understandings (or nonpropositional knowledge) being transformed into more articulate ideas and understandings. The structures of oppression are by no means transparent, directly announcing themselves as instances of sexism or White supremacy, for example. Rather, the very relations of oppression infect our thinking such that oppression is made to appear invisible, often by being described by prevailing thought and culture as natural, justified, or trivial. Much conceptual and activist work is required for people to recognize oppression, even to themselves. A female graduate student is often more likely to question her own abilities, in the face of subtle sexist derision, than to recognize oppression. Babbitt writes, "It would be hard to explain the fact that we know much at all about deep-rooted systemic oppression without appealing to nonpropositional understanding. For it is part of the success of ideological oppression that systemic discrimination is the behavioral norm, part of the social definition, and hence difficult to talk about, even to oneself."[9]

Babbitt argues that people are sometimes not in a position to know what is actually occurring, what their genuine interests are, and what would best serve them, until such transformation occurs as to bring about greater clarity and the envisioning of possibilities. Such is often the case with social change. Options we were not in a position to appreciate earlier now become clearly desirable. Often our previously presumed wants and interests were premised upon distorting beliefs. Once we rid ourselves of those distorting beliefs, clarity emerges. Yet, as Babbitt shows, such distorting beliefs are not simply traded in for counter-hegemonic views. They need to be developed with a society of transformation, so that new ideas are implemented and revised on the basis of their success in transforming lives for the better.

CULTURAL CONTESTATIONS

Antonio Gramsci, a political theorist, argues that social orders that serve some at the expense of others survive not by force alone but also by cultural patterns that encourage people to consent to the social order. Such social orders cultivate the habits, sensibilities, and norms that follow the interests of the status quo. Cornel West describes Gramsci's account of hegemonic and counter-hegemonic culture, applying them to the United States context.

> According to Gramsci, no state or society can be sustained by force alone. It must put forth convincing and persuasive reasons, arguments, ideologies, or propaganda for its continued existence. A state or society requires not only military protection but also principled legitimation. The legitimation takes place in the cultural and religious spheres, in those arenas where the immediacy of everyday life is felt, outlooks formed, and self-images adopted.[10]

People's everyday lives are deeply shaped by these processes of legitimation. Throughout the fabric of a given society, even the most intimate details of our lives, thoughts, and feelings can be affected by legitimating processes of hegemony which implicitly support the established social order.

Feminist movement operates in these realms of social conflict, contesting notions of tradition, education, truth, democracy, and other notions with feminist critiques. Neither the present nor the past exists as a static field. Rather, hegemonic and liberationist (counter-hegemonic) elements of culture struggle in everyday life. West remarks:

> In Gramsci's view, culture is both tradition and current practices. Tradition is understood, not as the mere remnants of the past or the lingering, inert elements in the present, but rather as active formative and transformative modalities of a society. Current practices are viewed as actualizations of particular modalities, creating new habits, sensibilities, and world views against the pressures and limits of the dominant ones. A hegemonic culture subtly and effectively encourages people to identify themselves with the habits, sensibilities, and world views supportive of the status quo and the class interests that dominate it. It is a culture successful in persuading people to 'consent' to their exploitation. A hegemonic culture survives and thrives as long as it convinces people to adopt its preferred formative modality, its favored socialization process. It begins to crumble when people start to opt for a transformative modality, a socialization process that opposes the dominant one. The latter constitutes a counter-hegemonic culture, the deeply embedded oppositional elements within a society. It is these elements the hegemonic culture seeks to contain and control.[11]

Movements for social change can become diverted by myths of meritocracy, suggesting that equal opportunity already exists. West specifically considers the notion that the United States is a meritocracy as a major part of hegemonic culture in what he calls "the prevailing Horatio Alger mystique, the widespread hopes and dreams for social upward mobility among Americans [that] nourishes the values, outlooks, and life-styles of achievement, careerism, leisurism, and consumerism that pervade American culture."[12] The fear is that efforts at collective social change can too easily shift into individualistic careerism.

In contrast, feminist and other liberationist pedagogies foster counter-hegemonic culture. West believes that, "[c]ounter-hegemonic culture represents genuine opposition to hegemonic culture; it fosters an alternative set of habits, sensibilities, and world views that cannot possibly be realized within the established order."[13]

Often oppositional elements become absorbed into dominant values through what West calls neo-hegemonic culture, which "constitutes a new phase of hegemonic culture; it postures as an oppositional force, but, in substance, is a new manifestation of people's allegiance and loyalty to the status quo."[14] As an example of neo-hegemonic culture, West cites the absorption of 1960s countercultural movements of White middle-class youth into liberal capitalist America. Oppositional visions became consumerized and diluted, and demands for radical change were moderated into mere revisions of prevailing social arrangements.[15] In the 1990s some of the progressive potential of gay/lesbian/bisexual/transgendered movements has been undermined as oppressed people have been constructed as a market niche for corporate purposes.

Moreover, many versions of feminism and multiculturalism are easily accommodated within institutional structures that remain deeply unjust. Instead of conceding to demands for social justice in education or rejecting them completely, many educational institutions have merely tagged on but not fully incorporated programs such as Women's Studies and Africana Studies. For instance, in undergraduate liberal education curricula, only courses like "Western Civilization" and "American Literature" fulfill requirements for history and literature, while "American Women's History" or "African American Literature" are considered "other."

Ideally, education might be a space of free inquiry aimed at knowledge, without succumbing to the pressures of market forces, religious directives, or government. On such a view, higher education would be a setting in which people of various backgrounds, experiences, views, and commitments pursue understanding. Diversity in inquiry would contribute to that pursuit, since it would help to challenge the dominance of any one set of perspectives and any kind of narrow-mindedness.

Yet higher education has not always embraced a diversity of perspectives, eager to correct for any previous limitations of perspective. Higher education often remains intransigent to feminist critique. Persistent oppression remains etched into higher education's structure, demographics, culture, and curricula. This structure ensures that voices from the margins get constructed as "political," "interested," and "polemical." These views are constructed as biased, against the backdrop of the mainstream, supposedly value-neutral, free intellectual inquiry, guided only by the disinterested pursuit of truth.

Nor are these patterns confined to formal education. They operate in many realms, serving to distort and disrupt our efforts to better know the world. These tendencies toward clarity and mystification occur throughout our lives, aiding learning or blocking learning, facilitating clarity or promoting mystification. Learning occurs everywhere throughout our lives, not just in formal classrooms. I argue below that changes must take place in formal education, but there ought to be parallel changes in other realms of learning, as well.

TEACHING AMIDST A BACKLASH CULTURE

Struggles between hegemonic and counter-hegemonic elements of a culture take place within classrooms, as well as in other aspects of our lives. A culture of backlash, resisting critical questions, does much to shore up hegemonic thought and sensibilities in educational settings. Consider the following glimpses into some of my own students' thinking at an eastern Pennsylvania undergraduate college, where hegemonic forces exert a palpable silencing effect upon any ideas that do not fit prevailing ideologies.

- In an introductory philosophy course, suggesting that individual behaviors can be influenced by general social views, I noted that groups that are painted as inferior or abnormal might thus seem appropriate targets. I linked this general point to hate crimes, mentioning the murder of Matthew Shepard, a gay college student in Wyoming. A male student called out, "I would have killed him too. Hey, if a guy came onto me, I'd kill him." Being a philosophy professor, I turned this moment into a teachable one, asking the student if he would kill a woman who propositioned him. He said, "No, because that's normal!" I continued to use examples and push students for reasons. The majority of the class remained highly vocal, taking only slightly less extreme positions than the student who spoke first. For example, several said they would not kill the person, merely beat the person up. One woman said, "I'd take off my shoe and beat her with it." (Meanwhile, I stood there, nervously twisting my commitment rings, wondering how many of the students knew I was gay. I was shaking nonstop for hours after class.) One brave student finally said, "Why can't you just take [a same-sex advance] as a compliment that someone finds you attractive?" "Ewww!!!" the rest of the class responded with visceral disgust.
- As I walk past a student residence near my campus office, several students sing, "If you're queer and you know it clap your hands. Clap!

Clap!" One of the students physically blocks my path, standing in my way with a threatening posture, staring me down.

• When I talk to faculty and administration about the above incidents, many of them discount them completely, suggesting that I must have misunderstood the students or that they did not mean what they were saying. They proceed to tell me that the campus is nice and friendly, that nothing like that would happen here.

• A student comments on social justice and disabilities: "If they [people with disabilities] want equal rights, why do they get those special parking places?" Other students jump in, "Yeah, if they can get to the mall, they can find their own parking places, like everybody else."

• In a feminist philosophy course, after a feminist student challenges the tendency of male students to dominate the discussions, other students responded by challenging her sanity, asking if she "had a traumatic childhood experience which made her hate men," and calling her paranoid since she "thinks sexism is everywhere." The visceral nature of these attacks is worth noting, since it had the feel of a mob attack. Several students were in tears and were visibly shaken by the end of class.

Teaching on issues of social justice, ethics, and race and gender, I have been disturbed by how much students insist upon views that are complicit with oppression. They maintain such views even in the face of much contrary evidence and without rational justification. The comments I describe above were not only problematic; they were venomously uttered.

These views were articulated not as if they were some perspectives among many. Rather, they were presented (and received by many others) as indisputable fact. When other views were referred to, they were dismissed out of hand as radically implausible, as if they were arguments for a flat earth and other debunked myths that had been so soundly refuted that no sane person would consider them.

Further, students often regard movements for social justice as fascistic, fostering antidemocratic illusions whereby people of color, "femi-Nazis,"[16] and others of their ilk would dictate what everyone could think and do. But how does critical thinking and social justice get portrayed as fascist? After all, critical thinking is intended to be radically democratic, so that each person can decide for her or himself what to believe, and casts her/his votes accordingly.

Indeed, critical thinking enables democracy, or as Chandra Talpade Mohanty argues, it is crucial to democracy. Mohanty invokes Dewey's notion that democracy has to be made and remade with each generation, since it is not merely a set of rules and procedures but a culture of critical thinking in which people think for themselves and have the power to influence the society toward their collective ideals.[17] Critical thinking is embodied in the best of feminist and antiracist pedagogies, not in knee-jerk backlashes against them that shore up the dominant ideologies. Mohanty claims that the work of this democracy-making is obscured by dominant views. She contrasts the visions of feminist pedagogies with those of the NAS, arguing that it is the former rather than the latter that enable students to gain clarity about the world and to contribute to the revitalization of democracy.[18]

Mohanty has identified a set of myths that her students, like my own, accept as fact. These beliefs seem to form the sort of "cómmon sense" that these students take for granted. They appear not to require reasons, being "obvious." Anyone challenging them appears thoroughly irrational. Regardless of texts, theories, data, and arguments that conflict with these beliefs, many students seem completely unwilling—almost unable—to question them. Otherwise intelligent students seem to have certain ideological assumptions etched so deeply into their worldviews that they reject conflicting evidence without any real consideration of them. Mohanty delineates these beliefs as follows:

a) They believe the United States is a meritocracy in which anyone can work and succeed. If anyone is not employed or does not succeed, that person is lazy. The fault lies solely with them.

b) They tend to think of freedom in a capitalistic way as the liberty to consume and to pursue their own individual interests.

c) They think of democracy as a system of formal rules and procedures. They suggest that the formal structures of procedural democracy are sufficient, that mechanisms such as voting are enough to ensure full democracy.

d) They consider the United States to be a liberal democratic nation that exemplifies freedom, leaving many individual choices up to each citizen.

e) Yet, when it comes to other nations, they believe that the United States exemplifies freedom when it intervenes in the internal affairs of other nations, including international relations. They believe that such interventions cannot be imperialistic, since the United States, as free and democratic by definition, cannot be imperialistic.[19]

Many college students today have been raised amidst heavy backlashes against feminism and antiracism, so their views are not really that surprising. These students subscribe to the ideological perspective that the United States is a meritocracy. They assert that Americans who are hardworking and talented succeed. Yet they are often nervous about their own futures, afraid of the mythic "reverse discrimination" which they believe would hold them back. They are aware of a dog-eat-dog world of economic and political uncertainties, of "down-sizing" and "managed-care" and other euphemisms;

they know well that they are among the first American generation likely to earn less than their parents in real wages. Many of my (temporarily) able-bodied, White middle-class and working-class students are terrified of losing out to specters of "minorities" who they believe have—or want—"special privileges." In their minds, structural oppression is a fiction, merely a thing of the past, a myth wielded rhetorically by "them" (those "minorities") wanting "even more special chances than they already have," which "isn't fair!" They believe that the United States is still a mythic land of opportunity in which "The cream rises to the top." Many believe that "If you get an education and work hard, you will get ahead, unless 'minorities' with 'special privileges' take all your opportunities."

I lead philosophical discussion, continually amazed at these dominant conceptions of the world, and of their proponents' resistance to critical reflection. Many have swallowed whole the United States' ideologies of merit, opportunity, and an already-level playing field. They have grown up amidst a backlash against affirmative action, against political correctness, against feminism. They recite its slogans almost in unison: "'They' want 'special rights,'" "'They' blame 'us' for all their problems," "'They' need to take responsibility for themselves," "I never oppressed anyone/owned slaves," etc.

A fundamental aim of a liberal arts education is critical thinking. However, the resistance of backlash views can pervade the learning processes such that deep critical thinking is greatly hampered. Further, the very dynamics within a classroom tend to reproduce what Mohanty,[20] following Dorothy Smith, calls, "relations of ruling," those behaviors and ideas that reinforce the subordination of oppressed groups through seemingly innocuous patterns. Social inequalities can be perpetuated in the classroom despite the best intentions of students and professors, particularly when a dominant group identity is threatened. Students will often put aside other differences for the common goal of trashing the feminists. In one of my courses, "Philosophical Issues in Race and Gender," the students seldom agreed about anything until certain baseline assumptions were challenged. Suddenly, many spoke with one voice to say what they regarded as common sense, with knee-jerk backlash responses asserting that "feminism is too extreme" or "Black people have chips on their shoulders" or "They [the "they" would shift easily from one oppressed group to another] are always making something out of nothing." Again, students spout these views frequently without critical reflection. Thoughts and feelings motivating these views remain concealed. The apparent obviousness of the claims obscures the absence of supporting reasons. The many assumptions behind them are seldom recognized or seen as problematic.

As I have suggested here, education and democracy require critical thinking. Whereas prevailing views suggest that feminism and other social movements have taken over universities, what is actually occurring is a strong backlash against these movements. In the perception that such social movements have "gone too far," oppressive elements of education have retrenched, claiming to serve the interests of knowledge and freedom. However, such backlash views, particularly in their hegemonic force, serve to diminish our abilities to think for ourselves. Instead, they enlist us in narrow visions that serve corporate interests at our own expense. But free and inclusive inquiry, with critical perspective upon backlash views, is necessary for participatory and democratic transformations of education and of our society.

FUEL FOR BACKLASH VIEWS

In this section, I consider how backlash views about social equity and justice maintain currency in the face of evidence of continued and even deepening social inequities. I suggest that the media supports such backlash views. Further, I argue that today's social inequities are sometimes subtler than in the past, such that they have a curious tendency to be simultaneously obvious and hidden. I describe some ways in which this dynamic occurs.

The "Other" Educational System: Media Influence

A major educational influence for people in the United States may not be schools but rather advertising media. Many people tend to discount the mass media, seeing it as merely entertainment, trivial, or irrelevant to life. We might think that advertising affects the thinking and lives of others but not of ourselves. Researchers suggest that the average American encounters 1800 advertising images per day.[21] In 1999 the average American spent almost 12 hours a day with some form of advertising media.[22] As the video *The Ad and the Ego* argues, the influence of corporate, underwritten media monopolizes much of the cultural space of the United States. That is the cultural space in which we might otherwise be imagining alternatives. Yet the dominance of corporate media makes present social arrangements appear as inevitable givens. Part of the media's effectiveness as propaganda and educational influence is that it is not widely regarded as having an influence, or at least not a deep one. Yet what happens when corporate interests saturate the public life of a formally democratic nation? How can its citizens be informed and freethinking when so much of our cultural landscape is thus dominated?

Consider that the bulk of United States media is owned by nine multinational conglomerates: Disney, AOL/Time Warner, News Corporation, Viacom, Seagram (Universal), Sony, Liberty (AT&T), Bertelsmann, and General Electric (NBC).[23] Media analysts McChesney and Nichols write, "It is not that the individuals who run these firms are bad people; the problem is that they do destructive things by rationally following the market cues they are given. We have a media system that is set up to serve private investors, first and foremost, not public citizens."[24] The profit motive's influence on our culture diminishes public discourse, curtailing the range of discussion and debate.

Especially in the face of the pervasive influence of the media, education should develop alternative visions, critical thinking, and free inquiry. It must serve as a pro-democratic force amidst the consumeristic, media-saturated society. However, our educational institutions are not necessarily meccas of free inquiry, uncorrupted by financial and other interests of the larger society. Educational institutions are themselves affected by corporate interests in form, content, finances, and support. In *Leasing the Ivory Tower*, Lawrence C. Soley details the increased corporate influences upon colleges and universities. "Taking their cues from conservative critics, the media have dwelled almost exclusively on a few stories about PC, and in so doing have missed the real story about academe. The real story is these investments in universities have dramatically changed the mission of higher education; they have led universities to attend to the interests of their well-heeled patrons, rather than those of students."[25]

Educational theorists have long argued that educational practices provide more than skills and content. They also reproduce social life, inculcating norms of behavior, values, beliefs, and ways of thinking about the world. Media has also been effective in portraying feminist and antiracist views in education, particularly on such issues as multiculturalism and affirmative action, as unfair, unjust, and downright anti-American. "What everybody knows" and takes for granted are ideas going against feminism and other movements for social justice, reducing critical thinking in public discourse.

Subtler Forms of Oppression: Collins on "Containment" and "Surveillance"

There are other, subtler, forms of oppression than that forced on us by the media. In *Fighting Words: Black Women and the Search for Justice*,[26] Patricia Hill Collins notes that some forms of discrimination and oppression have changed shape in recent years, making myths of meritocracy and equal opportunity seem more believable than in the days of Jim Crow. From the prior overt and officially sanctioned segregation and discrimination, patterns of White supremacy and sexism have become more covert at times. Collins uses the terms "containment" and "surveillance" to reveal these more subtle patterns. In containment, oppressed people are not excluded entirely from upper echelons. Rather, a tiny minority does make it through institutional gates to positions of higher status and authority. But this serves the dynamic of containment in two ways. First, the overwhelming numbers of oppressed people occupy positions that have not improved significantly, but the movement of the few obscures this lack of progress. Second, to achieve success often requires assimilation. Even where some have breached the higher echelons, this feat often depends upon their acculturation into the dominant order. The dominant groups and cultures thus diminish the potential critical impact of formerly excluded people.

In surveillance, oppressed people are kept under watch. Dominant group members are well socialized to be suspicious, fearful, disrespectful, and patronizing to subordinate groups. This dynamic creates tremendous pressure, internal and external, for oppressed people to achieve in situations in which they are overtly watched, judged, and accused of being unqualified. Many are told repeatedly that they are in their positions not because of merit but because of special privileges. Thus, the culture of domination continues to be reproduced.

Further, a backlash against affirmative action has resulted in bitterness and hostility toward oppressed groups. "Common sense" of the society increasingly assumes that any forms of affirmative action unfairly benefit oppressed groups at the expense of dominant groups. This point, of course, is seldom stated in such terms, since the very backlash against affirmative action often assumes that there are no such things as oppressed groups and dominant groups, since systemic oppression is presumed to be a thing of the past. Nor is the term "affirmative action," or outrage against it, applied to the treatment of military veterans or alumni legacies (descendants of an institution's alumni). My students frequently defend the practices of affirmative action for legacies. Many of my students are first-generation college students who are not likely to experience such legacy privilege, yet they defend the practice, even while acknowledging that the descendants of alumni have done nothing to earn such treatment. They do not regard affirmative action for legacies as compromising the quality of academic institutions. Yet they insist that affirmative action pertaining to race and gender necessarily compromise the quality of schools. The students' racism and sexism are betrayed by this assumed link between women, people of color, and a lack of qualifications.[27]

The myths of equal opportunity as a fait accompli keep oppression hidden. Subtler forms of oppression mutually reinforce oppression in education to maintain the status quo.

THE SPECTACLES OF OPPRESSION: OBVIOUS YET HIDDEN

Along with the media influence and the dynamics of containment and surveillance, contemporary social inequalities have a peculiar sort of visibility, which ironically can keep it obscured. Inequalities can be all around us without our understanding them. In fact, proximity can produce an opposite effect. People often seem fatigued by the sense that suffering is all around them. They do not want to be told about it. Because it is visible to them in some ways, they often resist learning and talking about the issues, being highly defended and desensitized. Many people believe that we understand the situations of youth, the underclass, victims of violence, and so on. Yet, this understanding is often limited and superficial, resulting in explanations that blame the victims of social inequities. In *Rediscovery of the Ordinary*, Ndebele discussed a similar phenomenon in predemocratic South Africa. He argues that violence and inequalities were all around, yet as spectacles rather than as three-dimensional phenomena interconnected with the rest of the goings-on of everyday life in South Africa. The effect was that horrible suffering and violence seemed both ever present and removed, with the spectacular representation of the issues making it less likely—rather than more likely—that everyday people would feel aware of what might be required for transformation.

So it is with the talk-show culture, the ultra-visibility of marginalized groups. But, seeing transgendered people, for instance, on television does not entail understanding them. Such media can contribute to the "Otherizing" of peoples, portrayed more as circus acts than as fellow human beings. Watching feminists and their opponents argue on television may increase people's sense of themselves as spectators. Once again, people are constructed as consumers and spectators rather than as comembers of a democratic republic.

In this culture, social inequalities are obvious and yet hidden, clear and yet easily explained away as failures on the part of the underclass. Critical thinking skills are necessary to enable even the most basic understanding of the society. Thus, education's role in building democracy is all the more crucial in these days of media saturation, subtle patterns of oppression, and the peculiar phenomena of oppression as spectacle.

TRANSFORMING EDUCATION AND DEMOCRACY

Revitalizing Education

So what kind of ideals and practices might improve formal education in the face of these problems, toward the revitalization of democracy? What might we dream for academia to become, particularly in and around the world of philosophy? How might such visions better serve our epistemic efforts, that is, how we know the world? Our goals do not constitute some half-baked polemical vision. Rather, they involve the old-fashioned values of education, knowledge, and democracy.

Dewey argued more than 75 years ago that democracy, education, and knowledge are linked, but not through a supposedly value-neutral inquiry of elite intellectual experts. Rather, he saw knowledge as linked inevitably to politics, inseparable from social processes of the larger society. He claimed that social inequalities and their implications have direct effects upon epistemic inquiry. He believed that the path to reliable knowledge is not to esteem value-neutral perspectives. Rather, human beings need to recognize inquiry as an inherently social practice, reflecting social patterns occurring elsewhere in society. Recognizing that no human perspective is entirely neutral, we must engage with the potential for clarity and for distortion that can arise from where we stand. Thus, rather than pretend to or attempt to occupy positions of value neutrality (an impossible hope), Dewey would rather that we engage critically with the perspectives of knowers, taking those perspectives to be inevitably socially situated. We might learn from our socially positioned situations how to examine critically these debates, practicing better epistemic methods in order to arrive at knowledge.

In so doing we can sometimes recognize general patterns of error and mitigate our tendencies toward such errors. Sometimes errors arise from social patterns that can be identified and corrected. In understanding and correcting for such systematic errors as sexist bias we can better understand the world. Like other efforts at understanding, we need to learn what is going right and what is going wrong within the very context in which we live. Not having supernatural powers of ascending to a "God's Eye View," we need to make sense of the world from within the world.

Thus, seeking improvement in education, knowledge, and the associated practices of deep democratic reflection may require a turn not to impartiality ideals but to a more realistic examination of the politics of knowledge. On this view, the NAS is wrong in claiming that academia was traditionally value-neutral and should become so again, that it was only recently being affected by politics and particularity of perspectives. Feminist and Africana Studies scholars, among others, have gone to great lengths to show the biases embedded in supposedly neutral educational systems. Many feminists and antiracists claim that corrective work is required to reveal those biases and improve methods of inquiry. They insist that this attack against "political correctness" is merely a retrenchment of those with institutional power who occlude the non-neutrality and political bias of their own views, claiming that their views and methods are value-neutral and objective. In fact, far from being value-neutral, many traditional disciplinary and educational practices have been demonstrated to have sexist, racist, and other biases that have corrupted academic inquiry. This evidence has precipitated corrective methods designed to improve the pursuit of knowledge.

Diversity and the Search for Knowledge

The genuine inclusion of oppressed peoples' voices, analyses, and knowledge is crucial to intellectual inquiry because it improves searches for knowledge. Rather than being grounded in "merely political" or sentimental gestures, such transformation is warranted for epistemic reasons, to help people know better. Satya P. Mohanty argues in *Literary Theory and the Claims of History*,[28] that "difference and individuality are not opposed to a deeper commonality, a community of purpose. Even in a world that is not fundamentally structured by (cultural) inequality, healthy pluralism is more likely than cultural homogeneity to lead to the fruitful coordination of our epistemic efforts."[29] Mohanty views cultures as fields of moral inquiry. They are experiments in living in various contexts and locations. Drawing upon many such experiments from a variety of cultures would only contribute to the inquiry. Diversity and pluralism are not external social and political values imposed onto educational practices but are key to finding knowledge. Diverse communities of inquirers tend to be more successful than homogenous ones, other things being equal.

Dewey raises some similar concerns about diversity as crucial to knowledge. He suggests that the free exchange of information and ideas is vital to knowledge. For Dewey, democracy is important not only politically and morally but also epistemologically. Like Satya Mohanty, Dewey regards societies as communities of inquiries into how to live. Dewey believes that participatory democracy is vital to understanding the world and how it might be bettered. Experts, he says, cannot settle these matters; people have to judge by their own lights what is required. They have to decide for themselves how to live, individually and collectively. Nor is this to occur by atomistic individuals pursuing their own private interests. The inquiry has to be diverse, participatory, and democratic in means as well as ends.

Identities and experience can function epistemically, in ways we may not even recognize in ourselves. Such epistemic functions often occlude oppressive patterns or relations of ruling. They thus contribute to their naturalization and apparent inevitability or givenness. Consider W. E. B. DuBois' question to Blacks, "How does it feel to be a problem?" DuBois notes that Blacks are constructed as problems, not as people. Whites, on the other hand, are constructed as people, as individuals. Whiteness carries a privilege that does not feel a need to justify itself.

Mohanty argues that multiculturalism ought to be defined in explicit terms of decolonization and transformation rather than as mere inclusion of previously marginalized voices. When considered as merely additive, not as corrective, feminist multiculturalist studies are contained, ghettoized, and minimized. Multiculturalism and feminism are sometimes emptied of substance and normative content as they get absorbed institutionally.[30] Slogans of diversity and multiculturalism can valorize difference for the sake of difference without recognizing the epistemological reasons for diverse inquiry. Diversity is important because we need to think across differences in order to better understand the world, thinking critically through mystifying views and narrow perspectives.

Marginalized voices may reflect not only differences from dominant ones but also conflicts of interests. Again, the links between power and knowledge are nothing new. Dewey addressed that theme 50 years ago. Long before the term "p.c." was coined, he acknowledged similar tensions. "If the ruling and the oppressed elements in a population, if those who wish to maintain the status quo and those concerned to make changes, had, when they became articulate, the same philosophy, one might well be skeptical of its intellectual integrity."[31] Rather than contributing to the greatest possible freedom of inquiry, education has often been hostile to non-mainstream views, thus hampering our efforts toward democracy.

Liberationist philosophies could make the most of hopes for our experiments in living to shape the world in more democratic directions. Genuinely free inquiry should enable us, individually and collectively, to understand the world and transform it for the better. The benefits of such social justice oriented philosophy are many: to the meaningfulness of our lives, to the cultivation of active citizenship in people, to the enrichment of public life, toward a more participatory democracy, and toward a greater understanding of the world and ourselves, what they are and what they might become.

Pedagogy and Privilege

So where is there space for the revitalization of democracy, for the deeper reflection as to what our nation's people truly want and need? Again, education might seem an obvious place of opportunity for free inquiry. Consider Paulo Friere's methods, in which literacy is seen as tied to critical reflection upon one's society. In Friere's initial teaching practices as described in *Pedagogy of the Oppressed*,[32] the learning groups were somewhat homogenous in having real interests that were directly opposed to dominant ideology. While there were differences among the men, women, and children in the groups, they could all be potentially united in some version of resistance to their shared oppression. Such is not always the case in overdeveloped nations, particularly the United States. Classrooms often include people of various social classes, all of whom have been influenced by hegemonic culture.

Whatever one's social position, identification with counter-hegemonic culture is far from automatic. In both short- and long-term perspectives, oppressed people may have some investment in social arrangements, however oppressive they may be in other respects. Still, what they stand to lose, especially in terms of material benefits, is often less than for dominant group members.

Indeed, part of the phenomena of privilege is that dominant group members are vehement in their defense of their own privilege, even as they deny its existence. Dominant group members claim that attention to the specifics of social location keeps them from being perceived and treated as individuals.

Members of oppressed groups are often quick to point out that they are seldom treated as individuals, but rather as embodiments of Blackness, instantiations of social myths, and so on. The point is that whiteness is coded as unmarked, un-raced neutrality, when in fact it is based upon racialized privilege. Their reference point is part of their racialized identities. The fact that they have not been forced to contend with the partiality of their perspectives is part of their privilege.

Consider Dewey's comments on privilege as cognitively distorting. Privilege tends to be invisible to those who have it. So it is in education, higher and lower. Peggy MacIntosh has described being White in the United States as carrying around an invisible knapsack of protection and authority.[33] The phenomenology of privilege is one of an absence, of not having to face indignities and barriers and obstacles faced by oppressed groups. Consider the difficulties of African Americans to catch taxicabs in big cities. Since a privileged person does not encounter a given barrier, it is unlikely that he/she will know of its existence.

Building Democracy through a Culture of Critical Thinking

What might my students' comments reflect about society and the state of democracy in the United States? They show a shallow level of analysis and political discussion found often in the United States. Clearly, our substantive democratic discussions often stop short of the sort of free inquiry that Dewey had in mind, which had citizens come together to create and recreate democratic practices continually. Dewey claims that many people act as if the "Founders" put into motion a Perpetual Motion Democracy Machine that is entirely self-sustaining.

> If I emphasize that the task can be accomplished only by inventive effort and creative activity, it is in part because the depth of our current crisis is due in considerable part to the fact that for a long period we acted as if our democracy was something that perpetuated itself automatically; as if our ancestors had succeeded in setting up a machine that solved the problem of perpetual motion in politics. We acted as if democracy were something that took place mainly at Washington and Albany or some other state capital under the impetus of what happened when men and women went to the polls once a year or so which is a somewhat extreme way of saying that we have had the habit of thinking of democracy as a kind of political mechanism that will work as long as citizens were reasonably faithful in performing political duties.[34]

Our students have not experienced much deep public political discussion. It is clear that they have encountered little challenge to their beliefs, whether at home, in the media, in school, or in their social groups. They may seldom see substantive political discussion taking place. Yet they think the Perpetual

Motion Democracy Machine will chug onward indefinitely. They see the democratic procedures as being in place. They intend to go out, make money, and do as they please.

Already in 1925, Dewey claimed that democracy and education were suffering greatly from the domination of market forces. He noted that the independent economic man was replacing a substantive notion of citizenship, that freedom was being conflated with economic activity.[35] According to Dewey,

> The assumption is or was that we are living in a free economic society in which every individual has an equal chance to exercise his initiative and his other abilities, and that the legal and political order is designed and calculated to further this equal liberty on the part of all individuals. No grosser myth ever received general currency. Economic freedom has been either non-existent or precarious for large masses of the population. Because of its absence and its tenuousness for the majority, political and cultural freedom has been sapped.[36]

Dewey claimed that deeper levels of democracy are yet to be made. That process involves experimenting in living, discovering people's genuine interests through the processes of social and political life. This process is to include everyone, not simply experts or policymakers or politicians: "The democracy that we have is an emblem of what could be. What could be is a society which develops the capabilities of all its men and women to think for themselves, to participate in the design and testing of social policies, and to judge results."[37] For Dewey, the intelligence of people and societies develops through true democratic participation. Academic inquiry must be truly inclusive and critical in order to facilitate such intelligence. Otherwise, the tendencies of the broader society to ignore oppression or explain it away become even more entrenched in formal education.

Rather than conceiving of people as independent, individualist bearers of rights only, Dewey claimed that people require active substantive involvement in building society in order even to know what they want and need. For Dewey, the citizens of our society jointly have to discover what works and what does not work, what serves the individual and collective good and what does not. These were not, nor would they ever be, closed questions. The good was to be created and discovered through political activity. Hilary Putnam remarks that, "Dewey's view is that we don't know what our interests and needs are or what we are capable of until we actually engage in politics. A corollary of this view is that there can be no final answer to the question of how we should live, and therefore we should always leave it open to further discussion and experimentation. That is precisely why we need democracy."[38] Thus, the justification for democracy is that it is a vital prerequisite to optimal epistemic inquiry. It contributes to the search for knowledge, with free flow of thought and information and the unimpeded process of offering and criticizing hypotheses.

Like progressive thinkers today, Dewey considers it vital that no class of people be excluded from this process of analysis and discovery. To Dewey, feminist and antiracist thinkers, transformation occurs not just through argument and formal procedure but also through social change. Some things may not be possible to discover until we live our way into them, transforming society in its directions and learning as we go.[39] We need to incorporate everyone's views, particularly those marginalized voices that have been stifled and dismissed. Democracy requires such full participation and inclusiveness, as does the pursuit of knowledge. A culture that welcomes inclusiveness and promotes critical thinking can build and rebuild full democratic participation and progress, with diversity being a vital resource for the development of society.

CONCLUSION

"Racism, sexism, and homophobia are learned. Therefore they can be unlearned. Better yet, why don't we just quit teaching them in the first place?" says Dr. Johnetta Cole, professor and former president of Spelman College.[40]

I have suggested that our conceptions of philosophy and education need to become more inclusive. Institutions of learning have long been "politicized." Yet this politicization has seemed invisible or normal because it has reflected the dominant views of the society. It takes broader conversations and efforts among diverse groups to reveal hidden assumptions and develop new practices, more mindful, more open to a variety of methods and perspectives. Educational institutions need to stop being assimilationist gatekeepers, permitting entrance to those who reflect the background assumptions, habits, and practices thereof. Let me be more specific. Women's Studies, Africana Studies, and other inclusivist approaches must be recognized as crucial to the entire educational enterprise. Their methods must be integrated into the curriculum. The voices of marginalized people must be received as central to human inquiry.

The epistemic practices of academic business as usual are unlikely simply to transform themselves so as to embrace social equity. On that view, the academic world would gradually become more equitable and welcoming of diversity as more voices speak up in the Conversation. I consider the actual transformative processes through Dewey's model of inquiry. On Dewey's view, education is vital to individuals and societies learning better how to flourish. He argues that great inequalities of wealth are inimical to such a process. This process has been moving along in academia and generally; it requires revitalization.

According to Chandra Mohanty and Jacqui Alexander, the liberatory potential of democratic practices must be distinguished from the ideological

constructions of democracy: "The term 'Democracy' has often been uti-
lized in the service of repressive national and international state practices.
However, the analytic and political importance of thinking about the egalitarian and emancipatory aspects of democracy at this time in history cannot be underestimated—after all, democracy does have to be made and
remade by each generation."[41] This remaking must involve a radical participatory element, since, as Alexander and Mohanty argue, "if democracy
is to be government by the people,"[42] that people must be all-inclusive
and characterized by liberatory decolonizing practices. This process entails the broadening of conversations by including participants, topics,
and methods previously excluded. Backlash gets in the way of these efforts since it inhibits learning. Institutionalization and co-optation of transformative efforts also get in the way of inquiry, since they contribute to the
narrowing of discussion. Generally, thinking that one already knows
something can provide mindless resistance to learning. The general public, our students, and ourselves, all require the revitalization of learning,
democracy, and political life in order to sort out what we need to flourish,
individually and collectively. This can be discovered only through experiments in living.

These inquiries cannot be conducted simply in an Ivory Tower. Rather, we
might take our lead from Deweyan, feminist, and multiculturalist understandings of what presently hamper our democratic lives. These would include inequalities, the failure of social arrangements to enable everyone to
cultivate her/his capacities and talents, and the scarcity of deeply democratic
discussions and decision making throughout society. This lack would include the premature narrowing of topics, methods, and visions of what has
already appeared credible to those with institutional power. As privilege distorts, so democracy can clarify. As backlash limits our inquiries, so transformative theory and practice can expand our inquiries. Such transformation is
thus epistemologically valuable, not simply morally and politically. For philosophy, academia, education, democracy, and social change, such critical
pedagogical practices enable development of education, democracy, and
knowledge. Since these are empirical matters, we shall discover through
democratic participatory experiment what contributes to human flourishing.
On these models, we can utilize the diversity of experiences and perspectives and understandings as materials from which to sort out what is best for
all. Like other forms of inquiry, the free exchange of information and hypotheses can enable learning. Rather than leaving oppressed people outside
of or begging to be admitted to traditional enclaves of power and privilege,
oppressed people can be sought out, recognized as having valuable perspectives that are crucial. Thus, diversity of views, backgrounds, and methods can be valued as vital to understanding the world and what it might become.

NOTES

I want to acknowledge Anita Superson for her generous and thoughtful editing of this essay and Koffi Maglo for providing insightful feedback on an earlier version. I appreciate Dr. Ebow Sam Quainoo, Dr. Tina Richardson, Dr. Kwame Buafo-Arthur, the Fulbright and Hays sponsors of Ghana 2000, and my friends in Ghana for giving me an experience of a vibrant democratic culture, providing a contrast to elements of U.S. culture I have described here. To the various students, colleagues, and friends who have been my allies, thank you. This essay is dedicated to the memory of Tamara Horowitz.

1. John Dewey, "Creative Democracy: The Task before Us," in *John Dewey: Political Writings*, ed. Debra Morris and Ian Shapiro, 244 (Indianapolis, Ind.: Hackett Press, 1993).

2. NAS Web Page, National Association of Scholars Publications.htm. <http://www.nas.org>.

3. See, for example, John K. Wilson, *The Myth of Political Correctness: The Conservative Attack on Higher Education* (Durham, N.C.: Duke University Press, 1995).

4. Cornel West, "The New Cultural Politics of Difference," in *Out There: Marginalization and Contemporary Cultures*, ed. Russell Ferguson, Martha Gever, Trinh T. Minh-ha, and Cornel West, 19–36 (Cambridge, Mass.: MIT Press, 1990).

5. Johnetta Cole is one person who has made that argument. Public Lecture, Oberlin College, Oberlin, Ohio, 1987.

6. Louise Antony, "Quine as Feminist," in *A Mind of One's Own*, ed. Louise Antony and Charlotte Witt, 213 (Boulder, Colo.: Westview, 1993).

7. Iris Young, *Justice and the Politics of Difference* (Princeton, N.J.: Princeton University Press, 1990), 10.

8. Young, *Justice*, 58–61, 115.

9. Susan Babbit, *Impossible Dreams* (Boulder, Colo.: Westview, 1996), 200.

10. Cornel West, *Prophesy Deliverance: An Afro-American Revolutionary Christianity* (Philadelphia, Pa.: Westminster Press, 1982), 119.

11. West, *Prophesy*, 119.

12. West, *Prophesy*, 120.

13. West, *Prophesy*, 120.

14. West, *Prophesy*, 120.

15. West, *Prophesy*, 121.

16. Note, the very term "femi-Nazi" is a brutal appropriation of social justice values and discourses.

17. John Dewey, as cited by Chandra Talpade Mohanty, Public Lecture, University of Pittsburgh, March 9, 1993.

18. Mohanty, Public Lecture.

19. Mohanty, Public Lecture.

20. Chandra Mohanty, "Cartographies of Struggles," in *Third World Women and the Politics of Feminism*, ed. Chandra Mohanty, Lourdes Torres, and Ann Russo (Bloomington: Indiana University Press, 1991).

21. Harold Boihem and Chris Emmanouilides, *The Ad and the Ego: Truth and Consequences* (Video Cassette, Parallax Pictures, San Francisco, Calif.: California Newsreel, 1996).

22. John Nichols and Robert W. McChesney, *It's the Media, Stupid* (New York: Seven Stories Press, 2000), 27.

23. Nichols and McChesney, *It's the Media*, 28.

24. Nichols and McChesney, *It's the Media*, 31.

25. Lawrence C. Soley, *Leasing the Ivory Tower: The Corporate Takeover of Academia* (Boston, Mass.: South End Press, 1995), 5.

26. Patricia Hill Collins, *Fighting Words: Black Women and the Search for Justice* (Minneapolis: University of Minnesota Press, 1998).

27. Michael Eric Dyson argues a similar point in *Race Rules: Navigating the Color Line*, (New York: Vintage, 1996). There, Dyson argues that affirmative action regarding race is often more sharply challenged than that regarding sex or other categories. Dyson argues that the historically White supremacist constructions of intelligence linger today, contributing to this presumption that people of color would be less qualified than Whites.

28. Satya Mohanty, *Literary Theory and the Claims of History: Postmodernism, Objectivity, Multicultural Politics* (Ithaca, N.Y.: Cornell University Press, 1997).

29. Mohanty, *Literary Theory and History*, 247.

30. See Chandra Mohanty's "On Race and Voice: Challenges for Liberal Education in the 1990s," *Cultural Critique* (winter 1989–90): 179–208. Mohanty shows how anti-oppression training programs have been watered down as they have become institutionalized in educational systems.

31. John Dewey, "Philosophy and University, September 15, 1926," reprinted in *The Later Works of John Dewey, 1925–1953, Vol. 2, 1925–1927,* ed. JoAnn Boydston, (Carbondale: Southern Illinois University Press, 1984).

32. Paulo Freire, *Pedagogy of the Oppressed* (New York: Continuum, 1970).

33. McIntosh, Peggy, "White Privilege and Male Privilege: A Personal Account of Coming to See Correspondences through Work in Women's Studies," in *Gender Basics: Feminist Perspectives on Women and Men,* ed. Anne Minas (Belmont, Calif.: Wadsworth, 2000), 32–38.

34. Dewey, John, "Democracy—The Task before Us," in *John Dewey: Political Writings*, 241.

35. See Dewey, *John Dewey: Political Writings*, 48, for example.

36. Dewey, *John Dewey: Political Writings*, 125.

37. Hilary Putnam, *Renewing Philosophy* (Cambridge, Mass.: Harvard University Press, 1992), 199.

38. Putnam, *Renewing Philosophy*, 189.

39. Babbitt, *Impossible Dreams*, 200.

40. Johnetta Cole, *Conversations: Straight Talk with America's Sister President* (New York: Doubleday, 1999).

41. M. Jacqui Alexander and Chandra Talpade Mohanty, "Introduction: Genealogies, Legacies, and Movements," in *Feminist Genealogies, Colonial Legacies, Democratic Futures,* ed. M. Jacqui Alexander and Chandra Talpade Mohanty, xxx (New York: Routledge, 1997).

42. Alexander and Mohanty, Introduction, xxx.

BIBLIOGRAPHY

Alexander, M. Jacqui, and Chandra Talpade Mohanty. "Introduction: Genealogies, Legacies, and Movements." In *Feminist Genealogies, Colonial Legacies, Democratic*

Futures, ed. M. Jacqui Alexander and Chandra Talpade Mohanty. New York: Routledge, 1997.

Antony, Louise. "Quine as Feminist." In *A Mind of One's Own*, ed. Louise Antony and Charlotte Witt. Boulder, Colo.: Westview, 1993.

Babbitt, Susan E. *Impossible Dreams: Rationality, Integrity, and Moral Imagination.* Boulder, Colo.: Westview, 1996.

Boihem, Harold, and Chris Emmanouilides. *The Ad and the Ego: Truth and Consequences.* Video Cassette, Parallax Pictures, San Francisco, Calif.: California Newsreel, 1996.

Cole, Johnetta. *Conversations: Straight Talk with America's Sister President.* New York: Doubleday, 1999.

Collins, Patricia Hill. *Fighting Words: Black Women and the Search for Justice.* Minneapolis: University of Minnesota Press, 1998.

Dewey, John. *John Dewey: Political Writings*, ed. Debra Morris and Ian Shapiro. Indianapolis, Ind.: Hackett Press, 1993.

———. *The Later Works of John Dewey, 1925–1953, Vol. 2, 1925–1927*, ed. JoAnn Boydston. Carbondale: Southern Illinois University Press, 1984.

Dyson, Michael Eric. *Race Rules: Navigating the Color Line.* New York: Vintage, 1996.

Freiere, Paulo. *Pedagogy of the Oppressed.* New York: Continuum, 1970.

McIntosh, Peggy. "White Privilege and Male Privilege: A Personal Account of Coming to See Correspondences through Work in Women's Studies." In *Gender Basics: Feminist Perspectives on Women and Men*, ed. Anne Minas, 32–38. Belmont, Calif.: Wadsworth, 2000.

Mohanty, Chandra. "On Race and Voice: Challenges for Liberal Education in the 1990s." *Cultural Critique* (winter 1989–90): 179–208.

———. "Cartographies of Struggles." In *Third World Women and the Politics of Feminism*, ed. Chandra Mohanty, Lourdes Torres, and Ann Russo. Bloomington: Indiana University Press, 1991.

Mohanty, Satya. *Literary Theory and the Claims of History: Postmodernism, Objectivity, Multicultural Politics.* Ithaca, N.Y.: Cornell University Press, 1997.

NAS Web Page, National Association of Scholars Publications. http://www.nas.org.

Ndebele, Njabulo S. *Rediscovery of the Ordinary: Essays in South African Literature and Culture.* Johannesburg, South Africa: COSAW, 1991.

Nichols, John, and Robert W. McChesney. *It's the Media, Stupid.* New York: Seven Stories Press, 2000.

Putnam, Hilary. *Renewing Philosophy.* Cambridge, Mass.: Harvard University Press, 1992.

Soley, Lawrence C. *Leasing the Ivory Tower: The Corporate Takeover of Academia.* Boston, Mass.: South End Press, 1995.

Wilson, John K. *The Myth of Political Correctness: The Conservative Attack on Higher Education.* Durham, N.C.: Duke University Press, 1995.

West, Cornel. *Prophesy Deliverance: An Afro-American Revolutionary Christianity.* Philadelphia, Pa.: Westminster Press, 1982.

———. "The New Cultural Politics of Difference." In *Out There: Marginalization and Contemporary Cultures*, ed. Russell Ferguson, Martha Gever, Trinh T. Minh-ha, and Cornel West, 19–36. Cambridge, Mass.: MIT Press, 1990.

Young, Iris. *Justice and the Politics of Difference.* Princeton, N.J.: Princeton University Press, 1990.

9

Transforming Resistance: Shifting the Burden of Proof in the Feminist Classroom

Alisa L. Carse and Debra A. DeBruin

INTRODUCTION

In her extraordinary book *Teaching to Transgress*, bell hooks powerfully recalls her own education.

> It was as a student in segregated black schools called Booker T. Washington and Crispus Attucks that I witnessed the transformative power of teaching, of pedagogy. In particular, those teachers who approached their work as though it was indeed a pedagogy, a science of teaching, requiring diverse strategies, approaches, explorations, experimentation, and risks, demonstrated the value—the political power—of teaching. Their work was truly education for critical consciousness. . . . For years I have relied on those earlier models of excellent teaching to guide me. Most specifically, I understood from the teachers in those segregated schools that the work of any teacher committed to the full self-realization of students was necessarily and fundamentally radical, that ideas were not neutral, that to teach in a way that liberates, that expands consciousness, that awakens, is to challenge domination at its very core.[1]

As feminist and other liberatory pedagogies recognize, promoting the full self-realization of students requires enacting a vision of teaching considerably at odds with the traditional conception of students as passive intellectual vessels into which instructors pour knowledge. Realizing the "transformative power of teaching" requires us, as teachers, to encourage students to play an active role in their education and become participants in communities of learning. It requires students to realize their unique perspectives in those communities, and to open themselves to the perspectives of others. It requires that they develop the skills with which to critically evaluate ideas

181

and perspectives, and the insight to recognize that such critical evaluation necessarily involves engaging unfamiliar ideas and perspectives with an open mind.

This ideal of transforming students is an inspiring one. But we should recognize that it cannot be achieved without struggle—indeed, *struggles* of many kinds. Perhaps this should come as no surprise, if hooks is right that "to teach in a way that liberates, that expands consciousness, that awakens, is to challenge domination at its very core"—and we believe that she is right. To list just a few such challenges: Teachers struggle with their conception of their role in such a learning environment, and their understanding of how to perform it. Students struggle with their conceptions of themselves, of others, of their broader society. They all struggle with potentially, and often actually, volatile classroom dynamics. Such challenges arise in a more obvious way when the content of the discussion is overtly "political." Yet they also surface when we attend to the dynamics of discussion about other sorts of topics as well—who speaks? Who is silent? What tones are used, what qualifiers? Whose ideas carry weight? Attending to these issues, as well as to more overtly political subject matter, impels us to confront the phenomenon of privilege. And such a confrontation is often met with resistance. We believe this resistance represents a form of backlash in the classroom, a form that is at once a testimony both to the growing authority and power of feminist and liberatory ideas and perspectives, and to the continued vulnerability of these ideas and perspectives, particularly when they come from marginalized and historically underprivileged thinkers. We shall examine this sort of backlash in the classroom, suggesting ways that it can be fruitfully countered and constructively transformed, so that all students in the classroom may become empowered.

PRIVILEGE

Privilege is a central issue in courses with feminist content, but we must attend to it in any course in which we employ feminist pedagogy. Even if privilege is not the topic of conversation, it affects the dynamics of conversation. Most generally, to be privileged is to enjoy certain advantages: benefits, opportunities, rights, immunities, or permissions not all enjoy. While privilege, so understood, may manifest itself overtly (e.g., all-male clubs, wealthy public school districts, etc.), patterns of privilege can comprise less overt forms of advantage as well.[2] We shall highlight one such subtler form of privilege as vital to our concern with pedagogy. As Margaret Little writes,

> One of the central and most familiar themes of feminist theory is that human society, to put it broadly, tends to be androcentric, or male-centered. Under an-

drocentrism, man is treated as the tacit standard for human: he is the measuring stick, the unstated point of reference, for what is paradigmatic of or normal for humans. . . . [W]hen we want to refer to humans independently of gender, it is man that is cast for the job: in language ("Man does not live by bread alone"); in examples (such as the classic illustration of syllogistic reasoning, "All men are mortal, Socrates is a man, therefore Socrates is mortal"); in pictorial representations (according to the familiar depiction of evolution—still used in current biology texts—the indeterminate primate, gradually rising to bi-pedalism, is inevitably revealed in the last frame to be a man). . . . Over time, our substantive conception of what is normal for humans has come to be filled in by what is normal for men.[3]

Male interests, male needs and vulnerabilities, male biology, and certain models of male biography have come to represent "normal and natural" interests, needs, vulnerabilities, biological conditions, and biographical trajectories of humans as such. Women's experiences, our distinctive attributes, vulnerabilities, and needs are correlatively perceived as "sex-specific deviations from that allegedly universal standard;"[4] we are inclined, as Little contends, "to anchor man as the reference point and view woman's nature as a departure from his."[5]

This form of male privilege, which frames our "tacit standards" and "unstated points of reference," has serious consequences for women. As Catharine MacKinnon has observed,

Men's physiology defines most sports, their health needs largely define insurance coverage, their socially designed biographies define workplace expectations and successful career patterns, their perspectives and concerns define quality in scholarship, their experiences and obsessions define merit, their military service defines citizenship, their presence defines family, their inability to get along with each other—their wars and rulerships—defines history, their image defines god, and their genitals define sex.[6]

We could expand MacKinnon's list to include many more examples of androcentrism.[7] Stephanie Wildman and Adrienne Davis put the general point nicely when they say, "Male privilege thus defines many vital aspects of American culture from a male point of view. The maleness of the view becomes masked as that view is generalized as the societal norm, the measure for us all."[8]

Of course, patterns of privilege are organized not only around gender but (among other things) around race, ethnicity, and sexual orientation. As with gender privilege, these other forms of privilege valorize the characteristics and experiences of some as neutral or normal, and stigmatize those of others as different or deviant. As Martha Minow explains, these invisible forms of privilege sanctify "prevailing social arrangements as natural and good. The chief effect of this is to deposit the problem of difference on the person or group of persons identified as 'different' from the unstated norm."[9] "Too often in this country," Henry Louis Gates Jr. has maintained, "we speak today as if race is something that blacks have, sexual orientation is something that gays have. Gender is something that women have. Ethnicity is something that so-called 'ethnics' have. So if you don't fall into any of those categories, then you don't have to worry about any of those things."[10] These forms of deviance from the social norm all carry serious consequences, akin to those we have already noted in the case of gender privilege. For White people—both women and men—becoming critically aware of unstated assumptions that reinforce patterns of privilege requires, among other things, becoming aware of what Joyce E. King has called "dysconsious racism." As King characterizes it, dysconsciousness is an "uncritical habit of mind (including perceptions, attitudes, assumptions, and beliefs) that justifies inequity and exploitation by accepting the existing order of things as given."[11]

It is important, then, to notice that challenging domination requires attention to ways in which gender is inextricably bound to other factors, such as economic status, ethnicity, sexual orientation, religious identity, educational level, and the like. It requires awareness of the way privileges along a multiplicity of social and economic axes can affect the advantages and disadvantages of gender.[12] Indeed, it is simply misrepresentative to talk generically about gender privilege or to address questions of gender as such.

Moreover, precisely because they frame tacit standards and unstated points of reference, the forms of privilege we have highlighted here tend often to be largely invisible, especially to those who enjoy them. The relative invisibility of privilege poses a serious problem for programs of empowerment. The full self-realization of all persons cannot be achieved in a culture that is structured by privilege that goes largely unrecognized while it defines some persons as the standard for the culture and others as "an inferior departure or deviation from . . . [that] standard."[13] Teaching aimed at "challenging domination at its very core" must therefore be teaching that acknowledges the classroom itself as a "site of inequalities," and that aims to unveil patterns of privilege, to sensitize students to the injustices these patterns constitute, and to empower students to contest those injustices.[14]

This challenge must be a multifaceted one, as a growing body of literature in feminist and other liberatory pedagogies attests. In many cases, it involves a reconstruction of the content of the curriculum. But it goes beyond the content of coursework, to implicate, among other things, models of learning, expressions of teacher authority, the role of subjective experience in academic conversation, and class dynamics. Each aspect of the challenge is apt to be met with resistance (not only by students, but often also by colleagues, though it is on student resistance that we focus in this essay). As Shoshanna Felman writes, "Teaching . . . has to deal not so much with *lack* of knowledge, as with resistances to knowledge."[15]

RESISTANCE AND THE BURDEN OF PROOF

Resistance in the feminist classroom has many familiar faces. Sometimes it takes somewhat indirect forms of avoidance—absence from class, apparent indifference, a reluctance to participate in discussion, failure to do the reading assignments, or to meet other requirements of the course. More often—and centrally, for our purposes—resistance expresses itself in more direct forms: annoyance, hostility, the stubborn refusals to take seriously provocative materials, or all-too-blithe or nonchalant dismissals of views accused to be too "radical," "ideological," or "extreme." At one level, this is no surprise. Feminist teaching seeks to be transformative, and thus to engage students in thinking about issues and ideas that are often difficult or upsetting. To the extent that feminist ideas and challenges disrupt, to the extent that they do have force, students may employ resistance as a form of backlash, an attempt to hold the disruptions of powerful ideas at bay and maintain a privileged status quo. The challenge of effective teaching in such contexts is to inspire engagement rather than disengagement, and curiosity rather than indifference and hostility; it is to equip students to cope constructively and critically with sometimes disruptive and disorienting ideas. But doing so requires that we be attuned to patterns of resistance, patterns we can then work to dismantle or redirect.

Our aim is to highlight one pattern of resistance in particular, one that encompasses many familiar faces of resistance. We will refer to this pattern as the "burden of proof" configuration of the classroom. Effective teaching crucially requires that we be sensitive in an ongoing way to the broad concern *how the burden of proof is distributed in the classroom* and that we strive to ensure its distribution is just.

Consider the following pattern of behavior, which has been repeated many times in our classrooms over the years: Certain students sit back in their seats, arms crossed, conveying the attitude "Prove it to me," while others in the class lean into the discussion, jumping through hoops to provide the proof demanded. The groups conveying the demand can vary, depending upon the particular challenge to privilege being raised at the time, and on the idiosyncratic dynamics of the particular class. (Even groups who lack relative privilege can, for complicated reasons, have a stake in resisting challenges to privilege.) But in each instance of this pattern, certain students rest easily on invisible privileges, while others toil to disrupt that repose. Often, the struggle is far less about convincing those who pose the demand than it is about much more basic things: being heard at all, being taken seriously. That one group of students should simply assume that they have the power to confer or withhold equal status to other players in a class discussion—other students, the professor, the author of reading material—is outrageous, but it is also quite banal.

Instances of the pattern can be quite glaring. For example, one of us assigned bell hooks' "Representations of Whiteness"[16] in one of our classes. In this piece, hooks writes that, for many Blacks, whiteness signals not purity, goodness, and moral elevation (as standard cultural figurations and assumptions presuppose), but moral depravity, cruelty, dirtiness, and terrorism. Hooks vividly recalls her own frightening childhood introductions to White folk, and even tells a story about expressing ideas from this paper as an adult at a "progressive" conference on Cultural Studies, where she was one of only a few racialized participants, and hearing of her views being laughed at as "ludicrous" by White women behind her back. Several White students in the class studying this paper joined in the disparagement of hooks' work, declaring her thesis about whiteness "ridiculous" and "preposterous," and dismissing the claims of the article in disbelief. They did not, at first, question their own authority, as Whites, to determine the legitimacy of hooks' claims, which were, after all, largely autobiographical claims and descriptive cultural observations and reports, an articulation of her own and others' experiences, perceptions, and feelings.[17] The handful of racialized students in the class then had to confront the burden of how—or whether—to respond, in a situation loaded with peril for them, and in which they were cast in an inferior position at the outset.

Or again, we might reflect on a related pattern we have noted in teaching material that questions the focus of the feminist movement on concerns of privileged White women.[18] Such work commonly provokes the critical response (especially from White women) that there is no need to transform the feminist movement to make it more inclusive because it is absurd to assert that the experiences or concerns of women who are not White or privileged differ in any fundamental way from those of women who are (concerns about sexual objectification and violence, the burdens of domestic and child care labor, the economic implications of divorce or single motherhood, unjust workplace structures, inadequate healthcare access are often cited). Indeed, it is often further argued, transforming the feminist movement would most likely just be divisive and hence disempowering for all women, making it harder to strive for change. In this kind of example, as in the first, the burden of proof is placed on those who would challenge the status quo. This is to be expected. But these examples are more complicated, and more problematic than that. They both involve a more insidious form of privilege: there is a presumption on the part of those leading the charge in the classroom that they bear the mantle of authority, that their perspectives are neutral and "normal," their vulnerabilities and challenges somehow generic and representative. There is at issue no correlative concern that they might have failed to "hear" the points being made in the materials, nor that these materials deserve detailed and rigorous consideration on their own merits, even from those who in the end choose to disagree.

Resistance to the perspectives of others is often especially strong if those views are expressed with anger, and not in the coolly dispassionate style more typical of academic speaking and writing. Students are often so disturbed by the expression of anger that they reject the content of an account because they object to the tone of that account. This protective use of the norm of dispassionate, disengaged academic discourse thus shields students from taking seriously, let alone acknowledging, both the appropriateness of the message and the appropriateness of the righteous anger, and so leaves background privileges unruffled.

Moreover, the presumption of authority extends to include the power to determine what shall be accepted as an appropriate sort of response to the original demand for proof. Indeed, pervasive norms of academic discourse can undergird general dismissal of the use of personal stories, firsthand accounts, anecdotes, and narratives—even those whose tone and message is neither angry nor righteous. Yet precisely because one goal of transformative teaching is the heightened awareness of unstated norms and tacit assumptions about what is normal, natural, neutral, or representative, vivid firsthand accounts and rich personal narratives can serve a crucial role in expanding students' imaginations and sensitivities to perspectives and struggles other than their own. On the flip side of this ledger, students who begin to see the value of sharing their own experiences and stories can pose resistance to theory and to any attempts to abstract from the particularity of personal narratives in addressing broad patterns or devising general analyses. Depending on the particular class dynamic, burden-of-proof dynamics can work in both directions. A class resistant to too much disruption of familiar preconceptions and assumptions may recoil from the tasks of imagination and empathy invited by stories and examples. A class resistant to theory or abstract analysis will tend to privilege concrete analyses, and to express indifference or hostility when class discussion takes a more theoretical turn. In both instances, resistance impedes understanding.

Who speaks is often as much an issue as what they say, or in what tone they speak. For instance, Ingrid Banks writes of her experience in academe,

[B]lack professors teaching black studies have to deal with our intellectual interventions in the classroom as always being personalized or politicized. When I critique white privilege or advantage, I often hear the voices of white students saying, "of course she believes all this, she's black." In addition, when I critique sexism in black communities, I see my credibility among black male students slipping because of who I am. It doesn't matter that my critiques are grounded in clear and well thought out arguments that I and others have written about. My position is always blatantly politicized in the classroom given the relationship between my race and gender and what I teach.[19]

Invisible privileges grant authoritative voices to some, while denying them to others. In a class designed to throw into question many fundamental assumptions and expectations concerning something as basic as, say, race or gender privilege, the question of authority—both of teacher authority and of speaker authority more generally—is a spiked and important one. Denying authority to a speaker is one way to refrain from open and serious engagement with her or his claims and proposals. Such denials of authority can take a variety of forms, from passively dismissive, to outright hostile. Consider, for example, the case of the teacher who was referred to as a "she-devil" who is "nuttier than a ten-cent fruitcake" in a student complaint about her undergraduate course in feminist philosophy.[20] When authority is denied the teacher, the course itself can be imperiled as a viable forum for serious inquiry and exploration.

Such resistance can go beyond dismissal of particular accounts, or tones of voice, or voices, to encompass rejection of the enterprise of a class in its entirety. Robert Bezucha's description of a senior seminar he taught on women's history illustrates this point.

> The second session rapidly degenerated into a power struggle between me and several male members of the seminar. Whenever I tried to initiate discussion they would resist my leadership by joking and chatting, and generally trying to create an atmosphere around the table to reflect their attitude that this course was irrelevant to their education. The harder I tried to be serious, the more they pulled against me.[21]

In cases such as this, the "burden-of-proof" dynamic is taken to such an extreme that discussion is closed down. The message, in effect, is that those on whom the "burden" is placed are not even contenders in a debate. The formation of resistant camps in a class—of collective dismissal or denigration of the course materials and subject matter—can deeply disrupt the classroom as a place of learning. Such power struggles challenge not only teachers but other students as well, who wish to take the course seriously but are impeded, and who must thus, also, determine whether and how to respond.

If these forms of resistance—of "lashing back"—go unchallenged, so do the underlying, unjust privileges. The ways in which race, class, educational level, gender, and other crucial factors intersect with and shape the actual forms violence and injustice take for particular individuals and groups of individuals remains obscure. The experiences and vulnerabilities of those members of the class who are already marginalized are further marginalized, their voices further silenced, their authority further repudiated—indeed, their role as equal players in the discussion further denied. Thus, patterns of exclusion and injustice are perpetuated, not addressed.

These dynamics concerning the burden of proof pose pervasive difficulties for teachers who wish to empower all of their students. The phenomenon seems most familiar in courses devoted primarily to "political" content, but can arise in any course in which a teacher explicitly attends to the structure of privileges underlying classroom interactions (e.g., who speaks with authority, who timidly, who interrupts whom, in any classroom).

TRANSFORMING RESISTANCE

How are teachers who are devoted to transformation to work with backlash of the sort we have explored? How are we to ensure that all students are empowered, that all participate as equals, that the burden of proof is shared? How do we teach in a way that facilitates open-minded learning and respectful discussion about material that is often difficult, provocative, and disorienting for students? How do we meet the challenge of managing the intense, emotionally charged discussions that often emerge as we strive to foster open communication of sensitive, controversial issues? How do we manage class discussion without controlling it? How do we challenge students, and thus put them at risk, without allowing them to become too dependent upon us—to cling to us as life rafts in a choppy sea—rather than learning to swim the waves themselves? We do not have answers to all these questions. We do, however, wish to share some general reflections on them.

There are, of course, many "tricks of the trade." One can alternate different kinds of writing formats, and different sorts of performative tasks in the presentation of ideas, including both writing assignments inviting personal reflection on issues, assigned readings, or the student's own experience, and more "formal" assignments in which students are required to articulate a position on an issue and defend it rigorously against sturdy objections, or carefully and precisely explicate and evaluate a position or argument offered in a text for the course. There are techniques for legitimating student speakers, and drawing silent students into speech—being scrupulous about "mirroring" students, attentive to issues of air space (who speaks how much for how long), and attuned to patterns of loyalty and identification within the class, patterns that can bolster and entrench resistant dynamics or tendencies of withdrawal.

One can, for example, require students systematically and regularly to shift seating arrangements or assign students to small discussion groups with alternating membership and rotating leadership. One can institute occasions for contained, around-the-circle testimonial in which each student must in turn speak, with no intervening commentary; or have students write short essays, to be read (anonymously or not) by another member of the class. Robin Dillon describes turning off the lights in her classroom and asking her students to sit on the floor as a way to break up overwrought class dynamics, and truculent periods of class discord.[22] Many of us experiment with formats and techniques.

What we wish to emphasize is the importance of what Susan Kuntz and Carey Kaplan beautifully phrase "freewheeling and inventive pedagogy."[23]

Freewheeling and inventive pedagogy is pedagogy that is responsive to particular class dynamics, and creative and experimental in its approach. We also wish to move the discussion beyond the sharing of particular teaching strategies, to offer our reflections on the fundamental character of the feminist classroom.

At the outset, we must recognize that the college or university classroom is in many ways itself a privileged arena, a "safe place" for reflective, constructive, even—at times—playful inquiry into difficult issues, including issues that deeply divide our society. A place removed from the fray of the streets, from workplace pressures, domestic demands, and relational intimacies and loyalties, the classroom can be a protected and peaceable forum for open and careful consideration of provocative and disruptive ideas.

At the same time, the classroom is not always a safe place in all respects, *nor should it be*. Teaching that strives to "expand consciousness," to "awaken" students and thereby to "challenge domination at its very core" is teaching that can put students and teachers at risk. Such teaching engages students in struggle that is sometimes uncomfortable and often unsettling, even when it is, at the same time, acknowledged to be illuminating and transformative—even, that is, when the "pay-off" is clear to students and teachers alike. Moreover, the "pay-off" is not always clear to all students, and student resistance can itself, as we have tried to convey, upset the "safety" of the class. Indeed, in extreme cases, student resistance can put an entire course in jeopardy.

At the heart of the sort of openness feminist teaching seeks to encourage is the development of a heightened consciousness of the multiplicity of unstated assumptions that structure the way we think, what we expect, and how we relate to each other. There are a number of questions we must ask if we are to aspire to heightened awareness of our unstated norms in the classroom itself. Among the most basic of them are the following: Whose perspectives are taken as normal in the classroom? Whose are seen to be different or quirky? Which perspectives does the class treat as uncontroversial, which as dubious or impenetrable? What kinds of claims are judged authoritative? Which cases are presumed to be representative or paradigmatic? Which questions and issues are deemed fair game? Which speakers are granted presumptive authority? Whose standpoints are rendered invisible or irrelevant? What should investigation and analysis within the academic discipline look and sound like?

Standing assumptions about the answers to these questions reflect the practices of inquiry and analysis, cultures of teaching and learning, and patterns in the ascription of authority that have dominated institutions of higher learning, advantaging some students while disadvantaging others—labeling their concerns, experiences, worldviews and modes of interaction deviant, rendering them invisible or irrelevant. These problems are particularly potent ones in the feminist classroom.

As with all forms of teaching, teaching as a feminist must aim to encourage students to think hard—in a disciplined, rigorous, imaginative way—about difficult ideas and questions. We must try as teachers to balance being open and warm with our students on the one hand, and being tough and exacting on the other. It is crucial to convey to students high standards of intellectual engagement and precision, to offer them ample opportunity to develop an earned sense of authority and confidence as thinkers, and to inspire students' curiosity and desire to learn. In the feminist classroom, precisely because of the challenge of student resistance, these objectives can be harder to realize than they are in other teaching contexts.

Though the transformative classroom is not, in all ways, a "safe" classroom, we must, as teachers, strive to ensure its safety in one sense at least: it must be an arena characterized by a climate of mutual respect, in which the exclusion, denigration, and dismissal of some by others is impermissible. To be sure, the positive regard at the core of mutual respect is undermined by overt and ugly forms of bigotry and hatred. But it is imperiled as well (and more often in the classroom) by more seemingly innocuous forms of "tunnel vision" that are rooted in indifference toward others or ignorance about them, in the disinclination to take others seriously, to recognize their status as authoritative speakers or contenders in the debate, or to hear their ideas openly—dispositions we are often not aware of in ourselves. In short, mutual respect is undermined by the many often "dysconscious" and unacknowledged biases and aversions that are in fact at play in our resistance to treating others as equals, or being genuinely capable of hearing what they have to say.[24] These tendencies make their way into the classroom. And they make the job of teaching hard.

There is no question that if we are to ensure that the burden of proof is shared in our classrooms, the stigma of "difference" may not be imposed consistently on some students (most likely those already marginalized in society at large), however subtly it is done. Our students, whatever else they aspire to accomplish in the class, must engage one another as equals; they must strive to support a learning culture that is characterized by lively, open, curious, fair-minded, and inclusive inquiry and debate. These may seem like lofty-sounding ideals, but they are minimal conditions of a just classroom.

Sustaining a respectful environment in the classroom—one aimed at the empowerment of all students and their participation as equals—requires sustaining an environment in which students are moved to acknowledge their own prejudices and aversions, their patterns of ignorance, naivete, indifference, and fear. This requires *trust* among the students and between the students and the teacher.

Creating an atmosphere in which such trust is warranted requires that, as teachers, we both encourage and *model* skills of open-minded inquiry, courage, humility, and fellow-feeling. We will need, as teachers, to confront our own fears about openly facing issues of gender, race, sexual orientation and the conflicts and emotions they are likely to introduce in the classroom. The classroom is a forum in which many difficult and emotionally loaded issues can legitimately and constructively arise, both through the materials studied and through class discussion. Doing this will require us to relax expectations that the classroom can remain a cool and dispassionate refuge, for these are troublesome issues, with personal ramifications, that are likely to provoke heated and emotional discussion.

We will, as well, need to become aware of those tendencies we may have that work in subtle ways to exclude and disempower students. For example, do we call on male students more often than on female students, or ask factual questions of females while inviting the males to examine, probe, explore and opinionate? Do we continue to associate intellectual talent with certain forms of "masculine" comportment (e.g., a confident and decisive verbal manner)? Do we ascribe more authority to male voices and inflections, to male gestures than to female gestures, to White Anglo-American styles than to African American or Latino styles of address and presentation? How does this, in turn, affect our orchestration of class discussion, the points to which we return, or those that receive the most attention and scrutiny? Are we less sensitive than we should be to widespread patterns of dismissal and interruption suffered in the classroom, or more tolerant than we should be of them?[25] Among other things, what are our own unstated assumptions concerning whose speech has authority, what modes of speech are authoritative, whose experiences count, and on whom the burden of proof rests?

Moreover, we will need to create and sustain cultures of learning in which students are willing to suspend judgment even while reflecting critically, to stand corrected, and to risk "incompetence" (as Maria Lugones puts it)[26]—at least enough so that real listening can go on. Trust is essential in such a culture. Such trust can be further fostered by engaging students in meta-reflections—that is, reflections about the class's own reflective processes, and the dynamics of privilege and resistance playing themselves out in these processes. "Going meta" like this can be both illuminating and facilitative of open-minded learning and mutual respect. Students are invited to see themselves as active participants in a process of learning that is dynamic, interpretive, and critically reflective rather than as passive vessels who are to sit in expectation of being filled with "neutral" information by their teachers.

This means we need to guide students in giving up the expectation that they will emerge from the course with more clarity and decisiveness on the issues than they had when they came in. We must openly address the idea that acknowledging and accepting confusion, ambiguity, and complexity can be a sign of maturity and wisdom. Disorientation and confusion can be stepping stones in a process of growth and expanded understanding. While welcoming confusion, we can, at the same time, strive for clarity about the sources of our confusion. The hope is less that students will emerge from class with clear positions on issues (though they sometimes do) than that they will emerge more aware and articulate, better able to reflect rigorously and carefully about tough issues, more able to appreciate and understand a multiplicity of perspectives on the issues addressed.

At the same time, we must confront the bugbear of unconstructive and politically disabling epistemological relativism—the view that there are individual perspectives, particular narratives, and nothing more can be said.[27] We need to equip students with skills of critical reflection that can enable them to see personal stories and particular anecdotes and cases as emblematic or revelatory of cultural patterns of inequality and exclusion. While encouraging subjective narratives, anecdotes, and personal accounts, we must also work to teach skills of critical analysis that can give thematic structure to our narratives, and extrapolate from them to the identification of patterns of injustice, exclusion, and silencing that they exemplify.

Trust can also be cultivated if we are sensitive, not just to the fact of resistance in our classrooms, but also to the *sources* of this resistance. Sometimes the source of resistance is less indifference or denigration than fear. More "privileged" students, especially those who take feminist course material seriously, are apt often to fear discovery of their own complicity in harmful cultural and social practices. They fear confronting their own privilege, and resist the painful acknowledgment of their participation in social and political practices and institutions that exclude and subordinate others. Such discovery can elicit a sense of guilt, and feelings of exposure that are embarrassing, shame-inducing, and painful, even when students regard their own participation as unconscious or naive.[28]

Furthermore, becoming aware of privilege, and coming to care about one's role in social injustices, in the suffering or denigration of others, implicates one, not only in the problem of injustice at hand, but in positive responsibility to do something about the problem—to work for change. As bell hooks writes,

> Feminist education—the feminist classroom—is and should be a place where there is a sense of struggle, where there is visible acknowledgement of the union of theory and practice, where we work together as teachers and students to overcome the estrangement and alienation that have become so much the norm in the contemporary university.[29]

This, in turn, can disrupt one's life-as-usual, opening up many painful questions about who one is and who one wants to be. Students may simply shut down open-minded inquiry, desiring to stay with what is comfortable and familiar. They may struggle to resist the sort of disruption and disorientation of their self-understanding, their relationships, and their culture or society that ensues from an expanded consciousness of privilege. Such resistance can

emerge dramatically, for example, in the face of discussions of sexual violence, pornography, eating disorders, or the reliance of career women with
children on an underclass of underpaid women to care for their children—
issues that strike a particular chord of vulnerability for many classroom populations.

As Kuntz and Kaplan suggest, disarming such resistance often requires de-
fusing concerns about blame.[30] One can convey that, just as privilege is in
part a matter of one's role in social and institutional structures and patterns
of practice, so too, the kind of awareness we are aiming to encourage is less
about "who is to blame" than about the roles one is (wittingly or unwittingly)
playing in social and institutional structures and patterns of practice that are
harmful or unjust. In addition, if students are to become open to their own
accountability in forms of injustice, it is often imperative that we ensure that
class discussion takes a constructive turn, pursuing not only descriptions and
diagnoses of problems, but also possible solutions to the problems.

Resistance to the perspectives of others (and its ugly consequences) is not
the only challenge of striving for open-minded learning. Success in this endeavor also comes with risks. As Sandra Bartky so beautifully describes in
her essay "Toward a Phenomenology of Feminist Consciousness," discussions of oppression can lead students to see their social "reality" as deceptive—many things are not what they have always seemed to be. Hence, students become unsure of what to think or how to act. This disorientation is
exacerbated by a couple of further difficulties. The transformation of the students' consciousness can create tensions in their relationships with their families, friends, and significant others, leaving the students even more unsure
of what to think or how to act. In addition, this transformation of consciousness can prompt students to see themselves as victims, or as unfairly privileged, or simply to become depressed about the injustices in their society.[31]
And there is nothing empowering about wallowing in one's depression, or
one's victimization, or the guilt associated with one's privilege. The challenge here is to help students move beyond the wallowing to what Bartky
calls a "consciousness of strength," "a joyous consciousness of one's own
power, of the possibility of unprecedented personal growth."[32] Again, it becomes crucial that class discussion take a constructive turn.

Finally, as we have by now suggested many times, a primary objective in
the feminist classroom is to sharpen students' skills of critical analysis and argument. We can do this by working with students on the examination and
assessment of positions, proposals, and arguments offered by the thinkers
we study, and by guiding them into the disciplined and lucid development
of their own positions on social, moral, and political questions. Beyond inculcating analytical skills, however, we must also try to encourage in students skills of moral imagination and empathy, a heightened attunement to
the conditions and vulnerabilities of others, and the ability to engage con-

structively and respectfully in dialogue with others whose perspectives may be fundamentally different from their own. The so-called banking model of education[33] should be rejected not only because it portrays students as passive minds into which knowledge is deposited, but also because it depicts learning as a purely intellectual exercise. The empowerment of all students demands much more than intellectual fitness. Among other things, it requires courage: the courage to risk incompetence, to face one's complicity in injustice, or to embrace the power one has conventionally been denied.

Asking teachers to emphasize the role of both intellectual and moral virtues in learning is asking a lot. Yet truly transformative teaching geared toward the empowerment of all students demands no less.

NOTES

This essay results from further reflection on two papers: "Empathy, Imagination, and Critical Independence: Can We Teach Students Virtue? (And Why We Need To)" (Carse) and "Challenges and Risks Involved in Meeting the Objectives of Feminist Pedagogy" (DeBruin), both presented at the Special Session on Feminist Pedagogy, sponsored by the Society for Analytical Feminism at the 1997 Pacific Meeting of the American Philosophical Association in Berkeley, California. Warm thanks to fellow presenters Sandra Bartky, Keith Burgess-Jackson, and Marcia Homiak, and to the audience present at the session for a lively and fruitful discussion of transformative teaching. Special thanks as well to Lynne Tirrell for her inspiration, to James Carse, Ann Cudd, and Anita Superson for their valuable feedback on earlier drafts of this essay, to Ramona Ilea for her first-rate research and editorial assistance, and to Elizabeth Chambers for her assistance with manuscript preparation.

1. bell hooks, *Teaching to Transgress: Education as the Practice of Freedom* (New York: Routledge, 1994), 50.

2. Wildman, Stephanie M., and Adrienne D. Davis, "Language and Silence: Making Systems of Privilege Visible," in *Critical Race Theory: The Cutting Edge,* ed. Richard Delgado, 573–79 (Philadelphia: Temple University Press, 1995).

3. Margaret O. Little, "Why a Feminist Approach to Bioethics?" *Kennedy Institute of Ethics Journal* 6, no. 1 (1996): 3–4.

4. Sandra L. Bem, *The Lenses of Gender* (New Haven and London: Yale University Press, 1993), 41.

5. Little, "Feminist Approach," 5.

6. Catharine A. MacKinnon, *Toward a Feminist Theory of the State* (Cambridge, Mass.: Harvard University Press, 1989), 224.

7. For helpful discussions of androcentrism and of concrete implications of this sort of gender privilege, see Bem, *Lenses*; Debra A. DeBruin, "Justice and the Inclusion of Women in Clinical Studies: An Argument for Further Reform," *Kennedy Institute of Ethics Journal* 4 (1994): 117–46; Debra A. DeBruin, "Identifying Sexual Harassment: The Reasonable Woman Standard," in *Violence against Women: Philosophical Perspectives,* ed. Stanley French, Wanda Teays, and Laura Purdy, 107–22 (Ithaca, N.Y.: Cornell University Press, 1998); Susan Estrich, *Sex and Power*

(New York: Riverhead Books, 2000); Little, "Why a Feminist"; Martha Minow, *Making All the Difference: Inclusion, Exclusion, and American Law,* (Ithaca, N.Y.: Cornell University Press, 1990); Wildman and Davis, "Language and Silence."

8. Wildman and Davis, "Language and Silence," 575

9. Minow, *Making All the Difference.*

10. Henry Louis Gates Jr.'s acceptance speech for an honorary degree bestowed by Haverford College, May 19, 1996. Text provided by the Haverford Alumni Association.

11. Joyce E. King, "Dysconscious Racism: Ideology, Identity, and the Miseducation of Teachers," *Journal of Negro Education* 60, no. 2 (1991): 133–46, esp.135.

12. For an excellent discussion of the "intersection" of gender with other factors, see Kimberle W. Crenshaw, "Beyond Racism and Misogyny: Black Feminism and 2 Live Crew," in *Words That Wound: Critical Race Theory, Assaultive Speech, and the First Amendment,* ed. Mari Matsuda, Charles Lawrence, Richard Delgado, and Kimberle W. Crenshaw, 111–32 (Boulder, Colo.: Westview, 1993).

13. Bem, *Lenses of Gender,* 46.

14. Diana L. Gustafson, "Embodied Learning: The Body as an Epistemological Site," in *Meeting the Challenge: Innovative Feminist Pedagogies in Action,* ed. Maralee Mayberry and Ellen Cronan Rose, 249 (New York: Routledge, 1999).

15. Shoshana Felman, "Psychoanalysis and Education: Teaching Terminable and Interminable," *Yale French Studies* 63 (1982): 21–44.

16. bell hooks, *Black Looks: Race and Representation* (Boston: South End Press, 1992), 177.

17. Replete, we should add, with quotes and firsthand accounts. In response to the women who dismissed her analysis of "whiteness," hooks (in *Black Looks*) writes, "Their inability to conceive that my terror . . . is a response to the legacy of white domination and the contemporary expressions of white supremacy is an indication of how little this culture really understands the profound psychological impact of white racist domination" (177).

18. See, for example, the work of Angela Davis, *Angela Davis: An Autobiography* (New York: Random House, 1974); Angela Davis, *Women, Race, and Class* (New York: Vintage, 1983); Angela Davis, *Women, Culture, and Politics* (New York: Random House, 1989); bell hooks, *Ain't I a Woman? Black Women and Feminism* (Boston: South End Press, 1981); bell hooks, *Feminist Theory: From Margin to Center* (Boston: South End Press, 1981); bell hooks, *Yearning: Race, Gender, and Cultural Politics* (Boston: South End Press, 1990); hooks, *Teaching*; hooks, *Black Looks*; Audre Lorde, *Sister Outsider* (Trumansburg, N.Y.: Crossing Press, 1984); Gloria Anzaldua, ed., *Making Face/Making Soul: Haciendo Caras* (San Francisco: Aunt Lute Foundation Books, 1990); Cherrie Moraga and Gloria Anzaldua, eds., *This Bridge Called My Back: Writings by Radical Women of Color* (New York: Kitchen Table Press, 1983); Maria Lugones, "Playfulness, 'World'-Traveling, and Loving Perception," *Hypatia* 2, no. 2 (1987): 3–19; Crenshaw, "Beyond Racism"; Mari Matsuda, "Public Response to Racist Speech: Considering the Victim's Story," in *Words That Wound: Critical Race Theory, Assaultive Speech, and the First Amendment,* ed. Mari Matsuda, Charles Lawrence, Richard Delgado, and Kimberle Williams Crenshaw, 17–51 (Boulder, Colo.: Westview Press, 1993); Mari Matsuda, *Where Is Your Body?: And Other Essays on Race, Gender, and the Law* (Boston: Beacon Press, 1996); Patricia Hill Collins, *Black Feminist Thought* (Cambridge, Mass.: Unwin and Hyman, 1990); among others.

19. Ingrid Banks, "Resistance in Two Acts: Practical and Ideological Implications," *Feminist Teacher* 12, no. 1 (1998): 32.

20. Anita Superson, "Sexism in the Classroom: The Role of Gender Stereotypes in the Evaluation of Female Faculty," *APA Newsletter on Feminism and Philosophy* 99, no. 1 (1999): 46–51. [Chapter 10]

21. Robert Bezucha, "Feminist Pedagogy as a Subversive Activity," in *Gendered Subjects: The Dynamics of Feminist Teaching*, ed. Margo Culley and Catherine Portuges, 81–95, esp. 88 (New York: Routledge and Kegan Paul, 1985).

22. In private conversation.

23. Susan Kuntz and Carey Kaplan, "Gender Studies in God's Country: Feminist Pedagogy in a Catholic College," in *Meeting the Challenge: Innovative Feminist Pedagogies in Action*, ed. Maralee Mayberry and Ellen Cronan Rose, 227–49, esp. 234 (New York and London: Routledge, 1999).

24. For a forceful discussion of forms of bias and "unconscious aversion" as subversion of justice, see Iris Marion Young, *Justice and the Politics of Difference* (Princeton, N.J.: Princeton University Press, 1990), esp. chapter 5: "The Scaling of Bodies and the Politics of Identity."

25. Roberta M. Hall and Bernice Sandler, "The Classroom Climate: A Chilly One for Women?" prepared by the Project on the Status and Education of Women of the Association of American Colleges, Washington, D.C., 1982; Alisa L. Carse, "Inclusive Pedagogy: Challenges and Strategies," *APA Newsletter on Feminism and Philosophy* 92, no. 1 (1993): 47–51.

26. Maria Lugones, "Playfulness," 3–19, esp. 16–17.

27. Sandra Bell, Marina Morrow, and Evangelina Tastsoglou, "Teaching in Environments of Resistance: Toward a Critical, Feminist, and Antiracist Pedagogy," in *Meeting the Challenge: Innovative Feminist Pedagogies in Action*, ed. Maralee Mayberry and Ellen Cronan Rose, 23–46, esp. 24 (New York: Routledge, 1999).

28. See, for example, Nyla Branscombe, "Thinking about Gender Privilege or Disadvantage: Consequences for Well-being in Women and Men," *British Journal of Social Psychology* 37 (1998): 167–84.

29. hooks, *Teaching to Transgress*, 51.

30. Kuntz and Kaplan, "Gender Studies," 236.

31. Sandra Lee Bartky, *Femininity and Domination: Studies in the Phenomenology of Oppression* (New York: Routledge, 1990), 15–18.

32. Bartky, *Femininity and Domination*, 16, 21

33. Paulo Freire, *Pedagogy of the Oppressed* (New York: Herder and Herder, 1972).

BIBLIOGRAPHY

Anzaldua, Gloria ed. *Making Face/Making Soul: Haciendo Caras*. San Francisco: Aunt Lute Foundation Books, 1990.

Banks, Ingrid. "Resistance in Two Acts: Practical and Ideological Implications." *Feminist Teacher* 12, no. 1 (1998): 29–39.

Bartky, Sandra Lee. *Femininity and Domination: Studies in the Phenomenology of Oppression*. New York: Routledge, 1990.

Bell, Sandra, Marina Morrow, and Evangelina Tastsoglou. "Teaching in Environments of Resistance: Toward a Critical, Feminist, and Antiracist Pedagogy." In *Meeting the Challenge: Innovative Feminist Pedagogies in Action*, ed. Maralee Mayberry and Ellen Cronan Rose, 23–46. New York: Routledge, 1999.

Bem, Sandra L. *The Lenses of Gender.* New Haven and London: Yale University Press, 1993.

Bezucha, Robert. "Feminist Pedagogy as a Subversive Activity." In *Gendered Subjects: The Dynamics of Feminist Teaching*, ed. Margo Culley and Catherine Portuges, 81–95. New York: Routledge and Kegan Paul, 1985.

Branscombe, Nyla. "Thinking about Gender Privilege or Disadvantage: Consequences for Well-being in Women and Men." *British Journal of Social Psychology* 37 (1998): 167–84.

Carse, Alisa L. 1993. "Inclusive Pedagogy: Challenges and Strategies." *APA Newsletter on Feminism and Philosophy* 92, no.1 (1993): 47–51.

Collins, Patricia Hill. *Black Feminist Thought.* Cambridge, Mass.: Unwin and Hyman, 1990.

Crenshaw, Kimberle W. "Beyond Racism and Misogyny: Black Feminism and 2 Live Crew." In *Words That Wound: Critical Race Theory, Assaultive Speech, and the First Amendment*, ed. Mari Matsuda, Charles Lawrence, Richard Delgado, and Kimberle Williams Crenshaw, 111–32. Boulder, Colo.: Westview, 1993.

Davis, Angela. *Angela Davis: An Autobiography.* New York: Random House, 1974.

———. *Women, Race, and Class.* New York: Vintage, 1983.

———. *Women, Culture, and Politics.* New York: Random House, 1989.

DeBruin, Debra A. "Justice and the Inclusion of Women in Clinical Studies: An Argument for Further Reform." *Kennedy Institute of Ethics Journal* 4 (1994): 117–46.

———. "Identifying Sexual Harassment: The Reasonable Woman Standard." In *Violence against Women: Philosophical Perspectives*, ed. Stanley French, Wanda Teays, and Laura Purdy, 107–22. Ithaca, N.Y.: Cornell University Press, 1998.

Estrich, Susan. *Sex and Power.* New York: Riverhead Books, 2000.

Felman, Shoshana. "Psychoanalysis and Education: Teaching Terminable and Interminable." *Yale French Studies* 63 (1982): 21–44.

Freire, Paulo. *Pedagogy of the Oppressed.* New York: Herder and Herder, 1972.

Gustafson, Diana L. "Embodied Learning: The Body as an Epistemological Site." In *Meeting the Challenge: Innovative Feminist Pedagogies in Action*, ed. Maralee Mayberry and Ellen Cronan Rose, 249–73. New York: Routledge, 1965.

Hall, Roberta M., and Bernice Sandler. "The Classroom Climate: A Chilly One for Women?" Prepared by the Project on the Status and Education of Women of the Association of American Colleges, Washington, D.C., 1982.

Hogue, Cynthia P. "Talking the Talk and Walking the Walk: Ethical Pedagogy in the Multicultural Classroom." Part 1 of 3. *Feminist Teacher* 12, no. 3 (1998): 89–106.

hooks, bell. *Teaching to Transgress: Education as the Practice of Freedom.* New York: Routledge, 1994.

———. *Ain't I a Woman? Black Women and Feminism.* Boston: South End Press, 1981.

———. *Feminist Theory: From Margin to Center.* Boston: South End Press, 1981.

———. *Yearning: Race, Gender, and Cultural Politics.* Boston: South End Press, 1990.

———. *Black Looks: Race and Representation.* Boston: South End Press, 1992.

King, Joyce E. "Dysconscious Racism: Ideology, Identity, and the Miseducation of Teachers," *Journal of Negro Education* 60, no. 2 (1991): 133–46.

Kuntz, Susan, and Kaplan, Carey. "Gender Studies in God's Country: Feminist Pedagogy in a Catholic College." In *Meeting the Challenge: Innovative Feminist Pedagogies in Action*, ed. Maralee Mayberry and Ellen Cronan Rose, 229–47. New York: Routledge, 1999.

Little, Margaret O. "Why a Feminist Approach to Bioethics?" *Kennedy Institute of Ethics Journal* 6, no. 1 (1996): 1–18.

Lorde, Audre. *Sister Outsider.* Trumansburg, N.Y.: Crossing Press, 1984.

Lugones, Maria. "Playfulness, 'World'-Traveling, and Loving Perception." *Hypatia* 2, no. 2 (1987): 3–19.

MacKinnon Catharine A. *Feminism Unmodified: Discourses on Life and Law.* Cambridge, Mass.: Harvard University Press, 1987.

———. *Toward a Feminist Theory of the State.* Cambridge, Mass.: Harvard University Press, 1989.

Matsuda, Mari. "Public Response to Racist Speech: Considering the Victim's Story." In *Words That Wound: Critical Race Theory, Assaultive Speech, and the First Amendment*, ed. Mari Matsuda, Charles Lawrence, Richard Delgado, and Kimberle Williams Crenshaw, 17–51. Boulder, Colo.: Westview, 1993.

———. *Where Is Your Body?: And Other Essays on Race, Gender, and the Law.* Boston: Beacon Press, 1996.

Mayberry, Maralee, and Ellen Cronan Rose, ed. *Meeting the Challenge: Innovative Feminist Pedagogies in Action.* New York: Routledge, 1999.

Minow, Martha. *Making All the Difference: Inclusion, Exclusion, and American Law.* Ithaca, N.Y., and London: Cornell University Press, 1990.

Moraga, Cherrie, and Gloria Anzaldua, ed. *This Bridge Called My Back: Writings by Radical Women of Color.* New York: Kitchen Table Press, 1983.

Superson, Anita. "Sexism in the Classroom: The Role of Gender Stereotypes in the Evaluation of Female Faculty." *APA Newsletter on Feminism and Philosophy* 99, no. 1 (1999): 46–51.

Wildman, Stephanie M., and Adrienne D. Davis. "Language and Silence: Making Systems of Privilege Visible." In *Critical Race Theory: The Cutting Edge*, ed. Richard Delgado, 573–79. Philadelphia: Temple University Press, 1995.

Young, Iris Marion. *Justice and the Politics of Difference.* Princeton, N.J.: Princeton University Press, 1990.

10

Sexism in the Classroom: The Role of Gender Stereotypes in the Evaluation of Female Faculty

Anita M. Superson

SOME ANECDOTES

On my first day of teaching, a male student raised his hand and asked with genuine skepticism, "Could you tell us your qualifications for teaching this class?"

When one of my best male students found out in the fourteenth week of the semester that I not only had a master's degree, but also a Ph.D., he responded, "This changes everything," suggesting that he did not believe what I had said until this point.

During a discussion about moral skepticism, an older male student interrupted me to say, "That's not the skeptic's position. I'll tell you what the skeptic's position is," and then tried to set me straight on a topic I have been researching and publishing in for some ten years. He later complained to the chairperson that I was too young to be teaching the course.

During a complex lecture on Hume's moral theory, a female graduate student asked, "Did you get these notes from a class you took in graduate school, or are you just making this up?" This incident occurred shortly after I returned the students' papers on which I had commented extensively.

A male student in an upper-division course, who repeatedly displayed confusion about the issues, sat in the back of the room and through my detailed lectures shook his head "No," suggesting that I did not know what I was talking about. When I reprimanded him for his behavior after class, he told me in no uncertain terms that I did not know how to do philosophy.

On the third day of an introductory-level class, I twice told a couple of disruptive male students to leave the room, but they did not budge. I then told them that I was not going to lecture any more until they left, but they remained in their places. Finally, I left. The students preferred to have the class miss a lecture than to acknowledge their disrespectful behavior and give me the upper hand.

On the first day of an introductory-level course, when I walked into the room two male students in the back row said out loud, "All right!," suggesting that since I was a young-looking female, the class would be a "piece of cake."

In the course of a long discussion during which I went over a male student's paper with him line by line, he sat back with his arms folded across his chest and asked, "What mood are you in when you grade these papers?"

The second time I taught an introductory feminism course, a male student not in the class wrote a highly disparaging editorial about me in the independently owned school paper. In it he claimed that "the professor just howls at the males and preaches her feminist teaching to the females in the class," and that my course was "really about hatred." He referred to me as "the She-devil in charge," and suggested that I had unfair power over the students since I controlled the grading.

In a sixteen-week health care ethics course, attended mostly by students from typically conservative fields such as premedicine, I briefly discuss the treatment of women in the health care system and conservative, moderate, and liberal positions on abortion. My teaching evaluations commonly include derogatory descriptions, such as "bitch" or "Nazifem."

Every female professor I know has relayed to me similar anecdotes. I surmise that male and female students often harbor sexist beliefs about women that are common in society at large. Women are both expected to be and believed to be more emotional than rational, passive, supportive, nonassertive, deferential, caring, and nurturing. For female professors, these traits translate into the expectations and beliefs that they are less competent than their male colleagues, are easy graders, grade according to emotion instead of reason, are more tolerant of disruptive behavior in class, give students breaks on cheating, let students control the class, are less logical and more disorganized, and so on. In contrast, men are expected to be and believed to be aggressive, more rational than emotional, knowledgeable, directive, in control, and so on. The traits that men are both expected and believed to exhibit are the same traits that characterize the stereotypical—but not necessarily ideal—professor, which is not surprising since most professors have been and still are men. Thus female, but not male, professors find themselves in conflicting roles: the role of female and the role of professor.[1] This conflict is made apparent in students' ratings of female professors in evaluations.

THE BACKLASH

The student behaviors I have relayed in the anecdotes are not merely examples of sexism. I want to argue that, both in themselves and as reflected in teaching evaluations of female instructors, they function to maintain a back-lash against women. In her well-known book *Backlash: The Undeclared War against American Women*,[2] Susan Faludi argues persuasively that 1980s America experienced a backlash against women's progress. Faludi explains backlash as an episode in which resistance to women's rights and indepen-dence is in an acute stage. Backlashes, she observes, have always been trig-gered by the perception—accurate or not—that women are making great strides. These outbreaks are backlashes because they have always arisen in reaction to women's "progress," caused not simply by a bedrock of misog-yny but by the specific efforts of contemporary women to improve their sta-tus, efforts that have been interpreted time and again by men—especially men grappling with real threats to their economic and social well-being on other fronts—as spelling their own masculine doom.[3]

A backlash, then, is an episode of intensified sexism caused by the per-ception that women are gaining power. Various behaviors occurring during a backlash attempt to set back women to the position they previously held—that is, to halt their accrual of power.

A variety of factors contribute to keeping women down in, and/or out of, the academy. One is sexism in the classroom, expressed informally in stu-dents' behavior as described in the anecdotes, as well as formally in teach-ing evaluations grounded in gender bias. Teaching evaluations often play a significant role in decisions about raises, promotion, and tenure. Insofar as they reflect gender bias, they can function to keep women out of power. In-formal sexist classroom behavior can have a similar effect, since it places an extra burden on women, causes undue stress, and makes women act in guarded ways in the classroom, all of which contribute to an unpleasant if not hostile environment. It can drive women away from the profession, or negatively affect their teaching, and hence teaching ratings.

Faludi attributes the cause of a backlash especially, if not exclusively, to men who feel threatened by women's progress. This includes hostile—usually male—students (such as those described in some of my anecdotes) who make the classroom environment threatening, and who negatively rate women—especially those who import feminist ideas into their courses—on teaching evaluations. It includes also hostile colleagues and administrators who weight heavily this and other negative information in deciding a woman's fate in academia. But while this small, albeit outspoken, minority might get the backlash going, participants in a backlash do not have to feel threatened by women's advancements; they can simply be uncomfortable with them. Both male and female students often tacitly endorse sexist stereotypes. Nor need it be the case that participants in a backlash inten-tionally aim to set back women. Once a backlash gets going, sexist practices are put into place and anyone can participate in sustaining male domination even without reflection. Most students I have described in the anecdotes fall into this class; they have no political analysis of their actions. Colleagues and administrators too commonly also lack feminist vision, though I believe that they are responsible for sustaining the backlash in a deeper way than students. The power to change the way women are evaluated in the academy rests with them, and they have a legal obligation not to discriminate against their employees with respect to their compensation, terms, conditions, or privileges of employment on the basis of sex.[4]

THE STUDIES

Interpreting studies is always controversial. Nevertheless, I believe that the studies done on teaching evaluations of female faculty are instructive. They reveal that teaching evaluations are affected in a complex way by students' expectations which, in turn, are shaped by gender biases about professor behavior. We can learn lessons from these results, which, I believe, have to do with the backlash against feminist-inspired progress.

When looked at generally, studies on teacher ratings and gender yield mixed results. One survey revealed that "laboratory" studies of student ratings of hypothetical instructors yielded no difference in the overall ratings of male and female teachers in the majority of cases, but in a few of the remaining, males were rated more highly than females. In no study did females receive higher ratings than males.[5] But in eight of twenty-eight studies conducted on actual teachers that had statistically significant differences, female instructors had slightly higher overall evaluations than did male instructors.[6]

But closer inspection is revelatory. The ratings of female instructors divide up along the lines of whether these instructors conform to gender stereotypes. More exactly, the studies can be divided into four categories, including those demonstrating that students (1) reward conformists, (2) penalize nonconformists, (3) penalize conformists, and (4) reward nonconformists. Let me speak briefly to the fourth category. In the few studies showing that students rate highly nonconforming female professors, researchers attribute these results to students' perceiving these women as exceptions.[7] Undoubtedly, women who succeed in very male-dominated disciplines have to be much better all around than their male counterparts, in which case merit subverts sexism in their ratings.[8] In each of the remaining three categories, I want to argue that a negative or a positive rating for sexist reasons contributes to the backlash against women.

Rewarding Conformists

Several studies show that students rate female instructors more highly than males because they conform to traditional female stereotypes. One four-year study revealed that 75 percent of the time male instructors received significantly higher ratings than female instructors on questions about fairness, thought stimulation, organization, nonrepetition, knowledge, and overall rating of the course, but females were rated more highly on sensitivity and student comfort.[9] Another study testing for students' perception of the "feminine" quality of warmth, found that students perceived female instructors to be warmer, more encouraging, and less authoritarian than men.[10] Female instructors' global ratings in this study were significantly higher than those of males, influenced by their ratings on willingness to assist, encouraging expression, and ability to arouse and sustain interest. A third study showed that female professors are rewarded more than males for being nurturing or supportive when it comes to grading.[11] If a male professor were to raise a student's expected grade by one point, his total score on the 100-point evaluation would rise by 3.36 points, but if a female were to do the same, her evaluation would rise considerably more—by 5.65 points.

Were ratings on "masculine" and "feminine" traits not variable along gender lines, we might conclude that students prefer and rate highly professors with both traits. But these studies do not show this. Instead, they suggest that students expect female professors to exhibit "feminine" traits, and when they perceive that they do, they rate them highly. In essence, they rate a female highly because she is a good woman, not a good professor. To reward a professor for being a good professor is to acknowledge that she or he does and should have institutional power. In contrast, to reward a female professor for conforming to gender stereotypes is to reward her for exhibiting traits that are typically inconsistent with having power and being able to use it in a meaningful way, including being subservient, nurturing, easy—in short, nonthreatening.

I want to suggest that even positively rating women for these sexist reasons contributes to the backlash. Rewarding women for being feminine effectively disciplines gender conformity, punishing women who are not conventionally feminine, and rewarding behaviors that mark inferiority and maintain male domination. For instance, being nonassertive makes a woman reticent to complain about unfair practices in the workplace, such as pregnancy leave policies. Being deferential makes a woman less likely to speak her mind in department meetings. Being nurturing makes a woman devote much of her time to "ego-feeding" which takes away time from her other work and can lead to a loss of self.[12]

Penalizing Nonconformists

Consistent with studies showing that female faculty are rewarded for conforming to gender stereotypes are studies showing that they are penalized with lower ratings for not conforming. Several studies show that to achieve the same student ratings on likeability, supportiveness, and even competence, female professors are required to be warmer and more social than their male counterparts, and engage in feminine behavior such as smiling and making eye contact.[13] Female professors are also rated more negatively than males for not being nurturing or supportive when it comes to grading. In one study, female professors were rated more harshly than males for being hard graders.[14] It seems fair to conjecture that female faculty get docked more often than males for straying from their expected gender roles, which is to be expected since they simultaneously inhabit conflicting roles of woman and professor.

Female instructors are similarly penalized for violating gender norms surrounding classroom presentation style.[15] The "feminine" style of classroom presentation allows for a lot of student input, whereas the "masculine" style of presentation consists in lecturing. In one study, the more classroom time a female instructor spent in presenting material by way of lecture, the lower were her likeability ratings, but the more time male instructors spent lecturing, the higher their likeability ratings.[16] The same study also found no evidence that students resent female instructors who use their authority in the classroom, so long as they temper this authority with interactive teaching methods. Interactive teaching can unite the conflicting roles of the female professor as "woman" and as "professor" by, for example, creating a classroom atmosphere where students are equal partners in the pursuit of knowledge. The study found that female professors who display authority in "feminine" ways—for example, by responding to student challenges with great patience, or reprimanding students in a friendly rather than embarrassing way—are not penalized on evaluations, but they are penalized if they display authority in stereotypical male ways. Male professors' likeability ratings, in contrast, are not affected by displaying authority using solely negative evaluations, and admonishing interruptions from students. Thus hostility toward women in positions of power is revealed in formal studies of teaching ratings as well as in informal anecdotal evidence.

Some studies show that faculty who teach Women's Studies courses or raise feminist issues in the context of other courses are downgraded in their evaluations. One found that for students to accept a female instructor's authority and judgment in presenting "a balanced interpretation of pertinent viewpoints," it is doubly important that she be seen as compelling, self-assured, and professional.[17] This suggests that if a female instructor brings up feminist or other politically controversial perspectives, she will be rated negatively if she has not also convinced students of her competence. Some researchers attribute feminist-influenced negative ratings to the fact that feminist issues "are more likely than many others to challenge students' personal assumptions" and hence generate anger, and to "be viewed as extraneous and not 'real,'" thereby detracting from perception of the faculty member as competent.[18]

Further evidence that a rejection of women's power is at the root of discrepancies in teaching evaluations of female and male instructors can be found in several studies demonstrating differences in the way female and male students rate instructors. These studies have mixed results, and some show no discrepancies. Others, however, show that the lowest ratings given to female instructors come from male students. One study found that male and female students rated male professors similarly, but male students frequently rated female professors the lowest on "masculine" qualities including appropriate speech, fairness, thought stimulation, and nonrepetition.[19] Another found that male students rated female professors significantly lower than males on teacher appeal and effectiveness, scholarship, organization and clarity, dynamism and enthusiasm, and overall teaching ability, the most negative ratings being given by male engineering majors, traditionally a conservative group.[20] A third study found that male students rated female social science instructors (but not male social science instructors or female women's studies instructors) lower than did female students on preparation, decisiveness, participatory decision making, and likeability.[21] A fourth found that women receive the most negative ratings when they are in nontraditional fields, especially from male students who hold conservative views about women's roles.[22]

Women are aberrations in the academy, which makes students see them as women first, professors second, all the while trying to fit them into one mold. At worst, some students do not want women in power; women should not be professors at all, they claim. At best, many students implicitly assume that women should be very different kinds of professors than men, exhibiting contradictory "feminine" and "professorial" traits. Men, on the other hand, are seen as professors and men at the same time—there is no differentiation and so no conflict between their roles. Thus men start off ahead of women in the classroom. Rating female faculty negatively for the sexist reason that they are not "feminine" contributes to the backlash because, first, it can negatively affect a woman's success in academia; second, it perpetuates the view that men are better professors than women; third, it sends the message that women should exhibit "feminine" traits, or risk punishment by students; and fourth, it may make female professors more guarded than males in the classroom, negatively affecting their self-confidence and student's perception of their competence.

Penalizing Conformists

Still other studies show that even if female instructors conform to gender stereotypes, students do not necessarily reward them, and conformity may even lead to other penalties. Female faculty spend significantly more time holding office hours and give students more personal attention than males.

Students expect this: 40 percent reported that they would not hesitate to call a female professor at home, but only 19 percent said they would call a male professor at home.[23] Yet 20 percent of the students judged their female professors to be "insufficiently available," while only 8 percent made the same judgment about their male professors.[24] Conformity, then, is expected, but for this reason is not necessarily rewarded; to be rewarded, female faculty have to be exceptional.

Furthermore, female instructors have lower ratings for conforming to gender stereotypes when the stereotypical traits obviously conflict with those students commonly associate with a good professor. One study found that the more female professors solicited students about their understanding of the material, and the more time they spent in responding to students' questions, the lower they were rated on competence, a "masculine" trait.[25] Additionally, even though a greater number of interruptions by students raised a female professor's likeability rating, it lowered her competence rating, though not significantly.[26] Another study found that students are less tolerant of what they perceive as a lack of formal "professionalism" in female professors' behavior in the classroom. Formal professionalism includes being very organized, maintaining tight control of discussion, and clearly outlining student responsibilities, versus being more laissez-faire and requiring students to assume a greater burden of responsibility.[27] Thus, female faculty are stuck in a "double bind": studies show that they are penalized both for not conforming and for conforming to gender stereotypes.

There is also a "double burden": when it comes to rating professors, students expect only female professors to exhibit both "feminine" and "masculine"/"professorial" traits. One study suggests that although male professors need to be strong in organization, explanations, and dynamism to receive favorable ratings, female professors need to be strong in these "male" areas as well as in "female" areas such as being sensitive to students' feelings, treating students with respect, and making students feel free to express their ideas.[28] Another found that "a highly structured instructional approach . . . was consistently more important for women's performance ratings than for men's,"[29] suggesting that female professors' "female" traits need to be "tempered" by "male" traits. Another study found that male students rated most highly female social science instructors (versus male social science instructors and female Women's Studies faculty) who had both the "feminine" traits of friendliness, frequent smiling, and frequent eye contact, as well as the "masculine" traits of confidence and decisiveness.[30] One set of researchers concluded, "if female instructors want to obtain higher student ratings, they must be not only highly competent with regard to factors directly related to teaching but also careful to act in accordance with traditional sex role expectations."[31]

Penalizing female faculty for these sexist reasons contributes to the backlash in ways other than stifling their success. It perpetuates the view that men are better professors than women since men are serious, while women are unprofessional. And it treats women unfairly. In a culture in which women are socialized to conform to female stereotypes as a part of male dominance, some women are likely to turn out having the relevant traits. But to penalize women for exhibiting these traits is unfair; men are in fact rewarded, or at least experience no drop in their ratings, when they conform to male stereotypes. Women do not enjoy the same freedom men have to teach in different ways, within the bounds of competence and effectiveness; in effect they are denied equal opportunity to flourish in their profession.

Suggestions

We need to acknowledge that sexism shapes the teaching evaluations of female faculty, and to act counter to this injustice. There is, unfortunately, no easy solution. Professors and administrators can try to make students aware of sexist biases, but in the short term they cannot expect to change them significantly, since their biases stem from deeply held beliefs that are generated and supported by sexist structures and practices in a patriarchal society. We should not advocate that female professors accommodate sexist expectations of their students; capitulation to sexism is hardly a feminist strategy. Furthermore, this requirement unfairly burdens them, and is otiose because the mixed results of the studies show that there is no one "right" way for female professors to behave.

One purported solution is to reconstruct radically teaching evaluations to prevent sexism from creeping in, but I am skeptical about its likely success. We might be able at least to screen for gender bias if evaluations asked students to describe their ideal professor, and then say how their own professor measured up. This would check for bias in much the same way as asking for a student's expected grade checks for bias from a student who does poorly in the class. But it does not eliminate bias. And since gender bias can be more subtle than the bias a student receiving a poor grade harbors, gender-biased evaluations do not obviously come across as hostile, and so cannot be dismissed as aberrant.

Since bias is so difficult to eliminate, and people hard to change, the solution seems to rest with how evaluations are interpreted. Many universities have tried to mitigate the effect of student biases by instituting peer reviews and/or teaching portfolios, to be used in conjunction with evaluations. Peer reviews are suspect: unless we have good reason to believe that our colleagues, most of whom are men, do not harbor the same sexist expectations about women's behavior, we can expect the biases to be duplicated.

Teaching portfolios show more promise in mitigating the effect of gender bias, though problems exist. Too often those making the relevant decisions ignore them and make judgments based solely on global ratings. They often judge a professor's ratings in comparison to her or his colleagues' ratings, but since most professors are male, the very bias portfolios aim to avoid may be replicated. Further, a female professor using a teaching portfolio to explain how sexism affected her ratings can be perceived as making excuses. Overcoming the power of negative ratings in one's file is difficult: numbers speak louder than words. No individual teacher knows exactly how sexism factors into her ratings, so she will not be able unequivocally to explain away negative ratings, and there is no quick and easy formula for compensating for discrimination.

Yet if teaching portfolios are taken seriously, these problems might be overcome. I want to put the burden on universities to stop tolerating sexism; as employers, they need to convince us that they do not discriminate against any employee with respect to her compensation, or terms, conditions, or privileges of employment, which is legally and morally required. They need to try to end, rather than sustain, the backlash. They can begin to do this in a number of ways. First, administrators, chairpersons, and members of tenure and promotion committees all need to be made aware of, and take seriously, the results of the kind of studies I have discussed. Second, universities need to select people for these positions who are sensitive to sexism, not resistant to feminism, and do not want to dismiss this evidence as trivial. Third, universities should allow female faculty the opportunity to address gender biases in their teaching statements, and weigh teaching statements more heavily than ratings themselves when a persuasive case can be made that the ratings are lower due to gender bias. Fourth, perhaps most important, universities need to require those involved in decisions about salaries, promotion, and tenure to show clearly and exactly how they have accounted for the demonstrable sexism in teaching evaluations. Failure to take even these minimal steps renders moot a university's commitment to equality of opportunity. Women's advancement to positions of power in academia does little good if they will be judged according to sexist standards when they come to occupy these positions.

NOTES

This essay was originally published in the *APA Newsletter on Feminism and Philosophy* (Philosophy Documentation Center, 1999), 46–51. I thank the anonymous referees for the *Newsletter* for their helpful comments. I thank especially Cressida Heyes for arduously reviewing several drafts of this work, and for providing numerous insightful comments that made me rethink and clarify my views on many issues.

1. See Elaine Martin, "Power and Authority in the Classroom: Sexist Stereotypes in Teaching Evaluations," *Signs: Journal of Women in Culture and Society* 9, no. 3 (1984): 482–92, esp. 486, for this view.

2. Susan Faludi, *Backlash: The Undeclared War against American Women* (New York: Crown, 1991).

3. Faludi, *Backlash*, xix.

4. Civil Rights Act of 1964, EEOC Guidelines on Discrimination Because of Sex, 29 C.F.R. Sec. 1604.11(a) (1980). The guidelines also prohibit discrimination on grounds of race, color, religion, and national origin. In this paper, I focus entirely on gender issues, although I believe that similar points can be made about race as well as the intersection between race, gender, sexual orientation, and so on. At the least, much anecdotal evidence suggests to me that racial stereotyping negatively affects student ratings of non-White instructors, and contributes to an often hostile classroom environment.

5. Kenneth A. Feldman, "College Students' Views of Male and Female College Teachers: Part 1—Evidence from the Social Laboratory and Experiments," *Research in Higher Education* 33, no. 3 (1992): 317–75, esp. 328 and 342. See also Kenneth A. Feldman, "College Students' Views of Male and Female College Teachers: Part 2—Evidence from Students' Evaluations of Their Classroom Teachers," *Research in Higher Education* 34, no. 2 (1993): 151–91.

6. Feldman, "Part 2," 153.

7. Jim Sidanius and Marie Crane, "Job Evaluation and Gender: The Case of University Faculty," *Journal of Applied Social Psychology* 19, no. 2 (1989): 174–97. See also Sheila Kishler Bennett, "Student Perceptions of and Expectations for Male and Female Instructors: Evidence Relating to the Question of Gender Bias in Teaching Evaluation," *Journal of Educational Psychology* 74, no. 2 (1982): 170–79, esp. 175.

8. The connection between being exceptional and having high ratings is not a necessary one. A former dean of the University of Kentucky informed me that across the college, female faculty, many of whom undoubtedly are exceptional, consistently had lower global ratings on their teaching evaluations than males. My point is that high ratings can be attributed to merit. Also, rating highly women who are perceived to be exceptions is consistent with believing that women as a group are not as good as men. Thus we cannot infer from high ratings of exceptional women that sexism has disappeared, and the backlash ended.

9. Susan A. Basow, "Student Evaluations of College Professors: When Gender Matters," *Journal of Educational Psychology* 87, no. 4 (1995): 1–10.

10. Bennett, "Student Perceptions," esp. 174–75.

11. Laura I. Langbein, "The Validity of Student Evaluations of Teaching," *PS: Political Science and Politics* 27, no. 3 (1994): 545–52.

12. The idea of "ego-feeding" comes from Sandra Bartky. See her "Feeding Egos and Tending Wounds: Deference and Disaffection in Women's Emotional Labor," in *Femininity and Domination: Studies in the Phenomenology of Oppression*, ed. Sandra Lee Bartky, 99–119 (New York: Routledge, 1990).

13. Diane Kierstead, Patti D'Agostino, and Heidi Dill, "Sex Role Stereotyping of College Professors: Bias in Students' Ratings of Instructors," *Journal of Educational Psychology* 80, no. 3 (1988): 342–44. See also Martin, "Power and Authority."

14. The study showed that if a student's expected grade is an "A," a female professor will be rated, on a 100-point scale, 2.5 points lower than a male professor. If the student's expected grade is a "C," a male professor would have a rating of 88.08, but a female professor, 81.06, over seven points lower. See Langbein, "The Validity of Evaluations."

15. Anne Statham, Laurel Richardson, and Judith A. Cook, *Gender and University Teaching: A Negotiated Difference* (Albany, N.Y.: SUNY Press, 1991).

16. See Statham, Richardson, and Cook, *Gender and University Teaching*, 11, 17, 66, 76, 77, 117, and 120. But the sexism is asymmetrical, due to both the results of the studies, and the reasons for professors' ratings. The studies to which I refer show that women are penalized for both conforming and not conforming to female stereotypes, ratings which, I am arguing, are grounded in sexism. In contrast, men are either rewarded, or at least not penalized, for both conforming to male stereotypes, and for exhibiting both "masculine" and "feminine" traits, which is to be expected since both are acceptable or good ways for a professor to be, but only when the professor is male. The most telling study, however, would test student responses to male professors who exhibited only "feminine" traits. A negative rating of these professors would likely be attributed to the sexist reason that they are too much like women.

17. Bennett, "Student Perceptions," 176.

18. Bernice Resnick Sandler, Lisa A. Silverberg, and Roberta M. Hall, *The Chilly Classroom Climate: A Guide to Improve the Education of Women* (National Association for Women in Education, 1996), part 4, 57–63, esp. 61.

19. Basow, "Student Evaluations," 6–7.

20. Susan A. Basow and Nancy T. Silberg, "Student Evaluations of College Professors: Are Female and Male Professors Rated Differently?" *Journal of Educational Psychology* 79, no. 3 (1987): 308–14, esp. 310, 311.

21. Martin, "Power and Authority," 485, 491.

22. Basow, "Student Evaluations," 9.

23. Bennett, "Student Perceptions," 176.

24. Bennett, "Student Perceptions," 177. Basow and Silberg, "Student Evaluations," confirmed Bennett's results. They found that both male and female students rated female professors lower than male professors on availability to and contact with students.

25. Statham, Richardson, and Cook, *Gender and University Teaching*, 117.

26. Statham, Richardson, and Cook, *Gender and University Teaching*, 119.

27. Bennett, "Student Perceptions," 173–74.

28. Basow, "Student Evaluations," 8.

29. Bennett, "Student Perceptions," 176.

30. Martin, "Power and Authority," 491.

31. Kierstead, D'Agostino, and Dill, "Sex Role Stereotyping," 344.

BIBLIOGRAPHY

Bartky, Sandra. "Feeding Egos and Tending Wounds: Deference and Disaffection in Women's Emotional Labor." In *Femininity and Domination: Studies in the Phenomenology of Oppression*, ed. Sandra Lee Bartky, 99–119. New York: Routledge, 1990.

Basow, Susan A. "Student Evaluations of College Professors: When Gender Matters." *Journal of Educational Psychology* 87, no. 4 (1995): 1–10.

Basow, Susan A., and Nancy T. Silberg. "Student Evaluations of College Professors: Are Female and Male Professors Rated Differently?" *Journal of Educational Psychology* 79, no. 3 (1987): 308–14.

Bennett, Sheila Kishler. "Student Perceptions of and Expectations for Male and Female Instructors: Evidence Relating to the Question of Gender Bias in Teaching Evaluation." *Journal of Educational Psychology* 74, no. 2 (1982): 170–79.

Civil Rights Act of 1964, EEOC Guidelines on Discrimination Because of Sex, 29 C.F.R. Sec. 1604.11(a) (1980).

Faludi, Susan. *Backlash: The Undeclared War against American Women.* New York: Crown, 1991.

Feldman, Kenneth A. "College Students' Views of Male and Female College Teachers: Part 1— Evidence from the Social Laboratory and Experiments." *Research in Higher Education* 33, no. 3 (1992): 317–75.

———. "College Students' Views of Male and Female College Teachers: Part 2— Evidence from Students' Evaluations of Their Classroom Teachers." *Research in Higher Education* 34, no. 2 (1993): 151–91.

Kierstead, Diane, Patti D'Agostino, and Heidi Dill. "Sex Role Stereotyping of College Professors: Bias in Students' Ratings of Instructors." *Journal of Educational Psychology* 80, no. 3 (1988): 342–44.

Langbein, Laura I. "The Validity of Student Evaluations of Teaching." *PS: Political Science and Politics* 27, no. 3 (1994): 545–52.

Martin, Elaine. "Power and Authority in the Classroom: Sexist Stereotypes in Teaching Evaluations." *Signs: Journal of Women in Culture and Society* 9, no. 3 (1984): 482–92.

Sandler, Bernice Resnick, Lisa A. Silverberg, and Roberta M. Hall. *The Chilly Classroom Climate: A Guide to Improve the Education of Women.* National Association for Women in Education, part 4 (1996): 57–63.

Sidanius, Jim, and Marie Crane. "Job Evaluation and Gender: The Case of University Faculty." *Journal of Applied Social Psychology* 19, no. 2 (1989): 174–97.

Statham, Anne, Laurel Richardson, and Judith A. Cook. *Gender and University Teaching: A Negotiated Difference.* Albany, N.Y.: SUNY Press, 1991.

V

WHERE PROGRESS?

11

When Sexual Harassment Is Protected Speech: Facing the Forces of Backlash in Academe

Ann E. Cudd

A campus is a terrible place to correct people's thinking.

—California State Sen. Bill Leonard, R (Upland)[1]

INTRODUCTION

Freedom of expression and the right to equal opportunity often conflict. There may be no place where the conflict is more immediate and more wrenching than in our colleges and universities. In this chapter I discuss the conflict of interests in freedom of expression and freedom from gender discrimination. The feminist struggle to secure legal recognition of sexual harassment as a form of gender discrimination is one of the ongoing battlefields of backlash. This battle rages especially over what is called hostile environment sexual harassment. While those opposed to feminism have largely accepted the idea that quid pro quo sexual harassment is wrong, they do not agree that environments hostile to women are an illegitimate form of discrimination. Some refuse to see any form of sexual harassment as gender discrimination; they see all sexual harassment claims as a kind of inappropriate prudery or as paternalism toward women.[2] Some see them as a coercive outcome of "political correctness."[3] They argue that the threat of hostile environment sexual harassment lawsuits censors speech and chills the educational climate. Thus those opposed to feminism have attempted to take the high moral ground by claiming that hostile environment sexual harassment charges violate rights to free speech on the part of men. I want to argue that, properly understood, hostile environment sexual harassment is a real form of gender discrimination that hinders women from competing on a level playing field with men, and that the appeal to free speech to protect hostile harassers is a form of backlash against feminism.

The broad aim of the hostile environment sexual harassment law as applied to colleges and universities, to rid the campus of gender discrimination, fails in the face of the current judicial interpretation of the constitutional protection of free speech, however. If it is to be consistent with that interpretation, the law must allow much of what causes hostile environments for women to go unrestricted, and so fail to meet the constitutionally supported goals of equal opportunity and freedom from discrimination. Under the proper understanding of the First Amendment, I shall argue, hostile environment sexual harassment law would come somewhat closer to achieving the goals of both the First and Fourteenth Amendments by fostering the speech of oppressed classes as well as those in the dominant majority, and by helping to overcome the legacy of inequality and discrimination against women that still affects them today. In light of this conflict between current First Amendment doctrine and equality, I argue that colleges and universities have a special responsibility to support the expression of those who would end discrimination and to criticize and remove support from those who would continue it.

SEXUAL HARASSMENT LAW

In the midst of a persuasive and increasingly militant Civil Rights movement, the U.S. Congress passed the Civil Rights Act of 1964. Title VII of this act prohibits employers from discriminating by race, color, sex, religion, or national origin and established the Equal Employment Opportunity Commission (EEOC) to formulate policies for governmental enforcement of Title VII. Title IX of the Elementary/Secondary Education Act of 1972 similarly prohibits educational institutions receiving federal funding from discriminating, and this law is overseen by the Office of Civil Rights of the Department of Education.[4] Colleges and universities have been slow to develop sexual harassment policies.[5]

The EEOC recognized sexual harassment as one of the main forms of gender discrimination in employment. EEOC policy describes sexual harassment that employers may be found liable for in the courts. The policy describes two kinds of sexual harassment: "quid pro quo" and "hostile environment." An employer commits an act of sexual harassment if he or she makes "unwelcome sexual advances, requests for sexual favors, and other verbal or physical conduct of a sexual nature constitute sexual harassment when the submission to such conduct is made either explicitly or implicitly a term or condition of an individual's employment." Quid pro quo sexual harassment occurs when "submission to or rejection of such conduct by an individual is used as the basis for employment or educational decisions affecting the individual," while hostile environment sexual harassment occurs when "such conduct has the purpose or effect of unreasonably interfering with an individual's work or educational performance or creating an intimidating, hostile, or offensive environment for working or learning."[6] As courts have interpreted the law, a showing of sexual harassment of either form must pass the "disparate treatment" test, that is, a plaintiff must show that she or he is being treated differently in employment because of her or his race, color, sex, religion, national origin, disability, or veteran status.

While quid pro quo sexual harassment has rarely been challenged, legal scholars and laypersons challenge hostile environment sexual harassment law on the ground that it contradicts freedom of speech as outlined in the First Amendment of the Constitution and interpreted by current First Amendment doctrine.[7] Scholars argue that the Supreme Court showed some support for hostile environment law in *Meritor Savings Bank v. Vinson*,[8] a case that upheld the successful lawsuit of Michele Vinson, a teller-trainee at the Meritor Savings Bank in Virginia. She complained that her supervisor made her work environment intolerable through such actions as repeated demands for sex (that she felt compelled to comply with several times), forced intercourse, and fondling her in public. In its decision the Court said that hostile environment sexual harassment must be "sufficiently severe or pervasive to alter the conditions of [the victim's] employment and create an abusive working environment."[9] Because the behavior included as violent an action as rape, this case does not decide when speech alone would be actionable hostile environment sexual harassment.[10] One important case decided in Federal District Court, *Robinson v. Jacksonville Shipyards, Inc.*[11] (hereafter "*Jacksonville Shipyards*") turned on expression alone. In *Jacksonville Shipyards*, Lois Robinson, one of only a few female welders in the shipyards, successfully sued on grounds that her fellow workers created a hostile environment through their display of pinups, sexual innuendo and jokes, and various sexual and demeaning remarks and gestures toward her. Thus employers and educational institutions have sought to meet the implied stricter standard by prohibiting not only quid pro quo sexual harassment speech, but also *speech that creates a hostile environment.* In 1998 the Supreme Court handed down a similar decision in *Faragher v. City of Boca Raton.* Writing for the (7-2) majority, Justice Souter wrote, quoting Faragher's brief, the "power to supervise—[which may be] to hire and fire, to set work schedules and pay rates—does not disappear . . . when he chooses to harass through insults and offensive gestures rather than directly with threats of firing or promises of promotion."[12] But this is not settled law, nor, to judge from the kinds of discussions I hear in the hallways about it, are people at all clear about what constitutes sexual harassment. Thus the question arises: What is hostile environment sexual harassment, and does it place restrictions on speech that conflict with the First Amendment protections of free speech? Further issues arise in educational contexts: How does Title IX protection differ from Title VII regulation of the workplace? How are the different relations between and among faculty, students, and nonfaculty employees of a university regulated by Title IX with respect to hostile environment sexual harassment?

My own interest in these questions stems from a personal experience of attempting, together with a group of faculty, staff, and students, to implement the sexual harassment policy of the college at which I taught, and subsequently being sued by those who were accused of sexual harassment for violating their First Amendment rights to free expression. This chapter will attempt to sort out the issues of free speech, sexual harassment, and First Amendment protections on college and university campuses, using our experience as an illustrative case study.

CASE STUDY: ALPHA TAU OMEGA V. OCCIDENTAL COLLEGE

In early November 1992, the ATO fraternity of Occidental College published an internal newsletter that mysteriously leaked to the college at large. The newsletter included an invitation to the brothers to a party, urging them to bring their friends, whom the newsletter referred to as "buddies and slutties." It also included a violent, misogynistic poem that depicted in a humorous tone a woman being violently raped. When the newsletter became public, a group of faculty, staff, and students called "Advocates Working against Sexual Harassment" (hereafter, "the Advocates") decided to file a formal complaint of sexual harassment against the fraternity for this and a series of similar incidents over the previous few years. While some of these incidents had been "investigated" by the Greek Review Board—an internal policing body made up solely of fraternity and sorority members and administrators of the college—the perpetrators had never been punished with more than a stern letter, and these had clearly been ineffective in stopping the behavior. Though the Advocates thought that the newsletter itself was degrading and potentially threatening, the college sexual harassment policy would not allow for this one incident to constitute harassment. Since we alleged "hostile environment" and not "quid pro quo" sexual harassment, we needed to establish a pattern of such behavior to constitute harassment. The Advocates also cited several other incidents in our complaint: a similar newsletter from the previous year, an incident of indecent exposure by several members of the fraternity on campus, an incident in which one woman was followed and threatened and ultimately had the vehicle that she used for her on-campus

job defaced by misogynistic graffiti. While some of the Advocates had sec-
ondhand knowledge of fraternity members having committed rapes in the
fraternity house, none of the victims were willing to come forward, and so
these charges could not be included in the complaint. The Advocates felt that
the pattern of incidents outlined in the charges against the fraternity evidenced a prolonged climate of hostility and disrespect for all women on
campus. We felt that it was our duty as Advocates to take action.

Upon hearing of the complaint, the fraternity brothers staged one of their
semi-annual "runs" that consist of some of the brothers and their friends from
the football team marching over to a sorority house in a drunken state, chanting misogynistic songs similar to the one in the newsletter, and exposing
themselves in front of the house, then returning to their fraternity house. The
fraternity "scribe" who had written the first newsletter then published the
same poem in another newsletter that also listed the names of the student advocates and other well-known feminist students, describing the complaint as
a "witch hunt." This newsletter was (again under mysterious circumstances)
left on tables in the college library, addressed: "Attention ATOs and whoever
else finds this letter." The Advocates then included these incidents in our list
of charges in an attempt to bolster evidence for the pattern of behavior required by the sexual harassment policy.

The complaint against the fraternity differed from other sexual harassment
complaints that had been heard at the college in several ways. First, both the
complainants and the accused were groups of persons. Past complaints had
always pitted one individual against another. Second, the complainants had
not all themselves witnessed most of the incidents named in the complaint.
They were charging that the fact that there was a pattern of harassment and
intimidation of women on the campus harassed them as well by creating a
hostile environment on campus for all women. Third, the complainants
charged the fraternity as a whole, even though some of the individual members were not present for any of the incidents, and only passively received
the newsletters. Fourth, all of the accused (the fraternity members) were students, but some of the complainants were students and some were faculty
members. None of these factors appeared to preclude a complaint under the
policy, however. Thus there was a great deal of uncertainty on the part of all
parties about what would result from a hearing.

At Occidental College, the sexual harassment policy in place during the
1992–93 school year provided for an associate dean to be the investigating
officer in such complaints. The investigating officer would interview both
sides in the dispute and decide when and how to bring the complaint to a
hearing. The dean of the college was to be the adjudicating officer should a
formal hearing be held. By the time the complaint was filed and both sides
were interviewed, there was only a week left before final exams for the fall
term, so the associate dean decided to wait until students returned in January

to hold the hearing. Unknown to her and the Advocates, a new law would become effective on January 1, 1993, in California that would affect the complaint. This law (SB 1115) revised chapter six of the California Education Code, to decree that students at public and private (except religious) colleges and universities in California would have the same rights to free speech that would apply to someone, say, on a street corner. The law states in summary, "It is the intent of the Legislature that a student shall have the same right to exercise his or her right to free speech on campus as he or she enjoys when off campus."[13] This meant that colleges and universities could no longer regulate speech on grounds that they are a "limited public forum" in which speech may be restricted more by content.[14] The statute specifically excepted sexually harassing speech, or speech that was otherwise allowed to be restricted by the U.S. Constitution. The legislative history of this bill showed that it had been sponsored by the conservative minority in the California house, and that it was aimed at curtailing speech codes and "political correctness" on campuses, but it had won unanimous approval by the legislature. The code provided for both injunctive relief and attorney's fees; if the plaintiffs won not only would the college or university have to drop all attempts to punish the behavior, but it would have to pay their legal fees as well, whatever those turned out to be.

John Howard, a lawyer and founder of the conservative think tank, Center for the Study of Popular Culture, whose aim is to stamp out "political correctness" on college campuses, contacted the ATO fraternity and offered to represent them on contingency in a lawsuit against the college and the Advocates for violating their rights to free speech and for defamation. A group of the ATO members ultimately became the plaintiffs in a suit against the four professors among the Advocates, the college, the president and trustees of the college, and one student. The charges amounted to accusing the defendants of violation of free speech[15] and defamation, and sought both injunctive relief and attorney's fees.

The lawsuit presented some practical as well as moral difficulties for a small liberal arts college with a tightly strained budget. The sexual harassment policy was relatively new, but was carefully constructed and seemed fair and right in line with the college's nationally recognized emphasis on diversity and equal opportunity. Yet, if the president and the other defendants were to go to trial to defend their sexual harassment policy, they would open the college, and potentially the individual professors as well, to great legal expenses that they could not possibly recoup. While the law provides attorney's fees for the plaintiffs should they win, it does not provide that for the defendants should they win the case. A countersuit was not a feasible option; given the existence of the statute and the fact that it had not yet been tested, there was little chance for the defendants successfully to argue that the suit was a mere nuisance suit, even if that were the true intent of the plaintiffs.

And given that civil trials such as these were taking approximately five years to come to an overburdened court docket, it seemed that the college would be in for a protracted and thus expensive battle. While feminist legal scholars who were contacted by the Advocates believed that we had a good case, the college's own conservative legal firm advised them that we could easily lose. Hence, the college decided to settle the case out of court, and the professors and student defendant reluctantly agreed.[16]

This case raises several important issues for colleges and universities who are trying in good faith to erase the effects of historical discrimination against minorities and women. First, should they attempt to carve out a notion of speech that could be prohibited or sanctioned? That is, are there reasonable constitutional grounds on which it can be argued that racist or sexist speech, however narrowly defined, can be limited? If so, what is the properly narrow definition of the limitable speech and what are the grounds on which the limits are justified? If there are not grounds legally to prohibit some forms of discriminatory speech, how ought colleges and universities to respond to it? In order to answer these questions we need to get clear on sexual harassment and on the constitutional guarantee of freedom of expression.

THE NATURE OF SEXUAL HARASSMENT

To understand the nature of sexual harassment as a form of gender discrimination it is necessary first to understand the nature of oppression, especially the oppression of women. Oppression is a socially located, institutionally manufactured system of harms against a group of persons whose group status is identifiable independently of the harm they suffer.[17] It is socially located in the sense that the conditions for oppression exist within particular societies; oppression of any particular group is not necessary or universal, and the group features of the oppressed in one society may be similar in all other respects to oppressors in another. By saying that it is an "institutionally manufactured system of harms," I mean that oppression consists of a large number of smaller harms that come about through small and large inequalities in the legal, social, and linguistic norms of the society. Oppression, to borrow Marilyn Frye's perspicuous metaphor, is a cage for the oppressed, where each of the bars on the cage is some obstacle to social, political, or moral equality that by itself would constitute only a minor barrier, but altogether the bars create an inescapable cage. The oppressive harms need not disqualify the oppressed groups from citizenship, but they must significantly lower the life prospects of the dominant groups in the society. Finally, oppression is a group phenomenon, where the group identity constitutes a significant portion of the self-identity of most of its members, and that identity is independent of the harms they suffer as a group. Women are such an oppressed group in our (and nearly every, if not absolutely every) society. They suffer from harms great and small in comparison to otherwise equally situated men, such as unequal pay for equal work, denigration of their traditional work, unequal and greater share of the total work of society, more menial, tedious work, sexual objectification, sexual violence, unequal political and corporate power, and unequal access to military and police power.

Women have fought long and hard to force society to recognize the severity and pervasiveness of gender discrimination, but it is still difficult to get many people to take it seriously. The legislative history of Title VII reveals that it is a mere stroke of irony that impelled "sex" to be included among its protected classes.[18] Sexual harassment is often the subject of tittering and jokes among people who like to think that the problem is that women can't take a joke or have delicate sensibilities and thus cannot fit into the normal work environment that includes a "normal, healthy sexual banter." Women's entering the workplace in large numbers has in many men's eyes ruined it for them. It has chilled and impersonalized the climate of the workplace, making work a far less socially fulfilling experience for them. Similar remarks are heard about the classroom. Chester Finn laments that before the advent of "political correctness," "the campus was a sanctuary in which knowledge and truth might be pursued—and imparted—with impunity, no matter how unpopular, distasteful, or politically heterodox the process might sometimes be."[19] He goes on to assert that academics have enjoyed "almost untrammeled freedom of thought and expression for three and a half centuries."[20] But, of course, these were centuries during which Jews, Blacks, and women (among others) were prohibited from even attending universities.

Women do not, as a class, complain about sexual banter because it is "off color" or rude, they complain because it both reveals and reinforces the position of women as the subservient sex, as the sexual objects of men. They complain because it is difficult to believe that one's colleagues, professor, or supervisor is taking one seriously as a fellow worker or student when they discuss women as "cunts," "bitches," "whores," or simply sexual conquests, or when their fellow workers' or professor's preferred office decorating scheme portrays women as sexual objects for use by men. Then even if the colleague, professor, or supervisor *is* otherwise treating her fairly, a woman in this position is burdened with (well-founded) anxiety and feelings of inferiority that are neither fair nor conducive to optimal work.

Sexual harassment only contingently involves sex at all. This may sound paradoxical, but consider this argument: Sexual harassment involves three basic kinds of wrongs. These wrongs only contingently involve sex; they can be accomplished by other means as well. Thus the wrong of sexual harassment, and so what constitutes it as a category of behavior, only contingently involves sex. The three wrongs are coercion, harassment, and domination. In quid pro quo sexual harassment, the perpetrator coerces (or attempts to coerce) the victim into having sex.[21] Coercion is rarely involved, though, in hostile environment sexual harassment. The perpetrator commits the wrong of harassment when the behavior would constitute simply legal harassment per se,[22] but uses sexual propositions, sexual innuendo, jokes, catcalls, and the like. The perpetrator commits the wrong of domination when he sends one of two messages: that he is superior by virtue of his sex since she is essentially a sex object for men (the sexual message), or that she is not welcome in his workplace or campus department because of her sex (the hostility message).[23] To "send a message" the perpetrator need not intend that the message be just as it is interpreted, but it must be a reasonable interpretation of the behavior, in light of the full social context of the behavior. Since oppression is an institutionally located phenomenon, messages can be sent to oppressed groups through words and actions that have conventional, stereotypical meanings of hostility and contempt. Furthermore, because it is group based, these messages are sent to all the members of the group, not just the one at whom the message is explicitly directed. Thus, when someone commits the domination wrong of sexual harassment it harms all women. This group harm is what makes the domination wrong of sexual harassment, unlike the other two wrongs, sui generis.[24] Sometimes all three wrongs are present, sometimes only one or two. This accounts for the fact that it is possible, though rare, for a woman to sexually harass a man: the woman commits the wrong of harassment by means of talk or other expressions of sex.[25] A woman cannot easily send the message of domination to a man since her actions rarely could send the message that he is a mere sex object or that he is not welcome.[26] Attempts to send such messages are more likely to backfire. It is also clear that men of certain minorities could be dominated as well as harassed by means of sex because cultural stereotypes about their sexual nature support such messages.

The domination harm of hostile environment sexual harassment is particularly closely related to the backlash against feminism. Feminism is a progressive social movement whose goal is to end the subordination of women. For those who are antifeminist, who wish to turn back the clock on progress, the restrictions on hostile environment sexual harassment are anathema. Of course, it would not be rhetorically successful to say that one is in favor of hostile environment sexual harassment. To even admit that there is such a thing would be tantamount to giving up the high moral ground to feminists. So backlash must take the form of opposing the claim that there is any such harm as hostile environment sexual harassment, or of opposing restrictions on hostile environment sexual harassment by claiming that to do so sacrifices something of even greater social value. In the present case the fraternity members and their lawyers chose to pursue the latter tactic.

In the ATO case, the newsletters and other behaviors of the fraternity sent the sexual message and the hostility message, and in the case of the one student who was confronted, followed, and whose vehicle was defaced, perhaps simple harassment was also committed. But the most pervasive and harmful effect of their behavior was the domination wrong. The Advocates held that the fraternity members were intimidating, denigrating, and degrading all women by their speech and actions. They were sending both the sexual and hostility messages. This analysis implies that (male) students were dominating (female) faculty. I think a good case can be made that domination was going on: the fraternity was sending the message that women are sexual objects and inferior to men, so this applies to all women, regardless of their status in the college. Because the claim that women are inferior to men and sexual objects of men is still made and believed in many quarters in society, this is a conveyable message. Furthermore, fraternities are well connected and known to be quite powerful on college campuses, and this is true at Occidental College as well.[27]

Because it is about domination and harassment, sexual harassment is not a kind of "mere offense" like witnessing someone doing something obscene or scatological in nature. Rather it is what Joel Feinberg terms "profound offense," much like racial epithets are. Profound offenses are not mere nuisances that are harmful only when one is forced to witness them; they "would continue to rankle even when unwitnessed, and they would thus be offensive even when they are not strictly speaking nuisances at all."[28] Unlike mere nuisances, profound offenses are "deep, profound, shattering, serious," they offend our minds not merely our senses or lower sensibilities, and they are experienced as impersonal at least in part.[29] By "impersonal" he means that profound offenses outrage the victim even if he or she does not witness them because they are "a shocking affront to his or her deepest moral sensibilities."[30] However, using the notion of social group from my analysis of oppression a deeper understanding of "impersonal" can be developed. Profound offenses denigrate or degrade the group with which one self-identifies (or to which one is assigned by others), and thus harm every member of that group. If sexual harassment were about sex, if it were about women's squeamishness to "normal, healthy, sexual banter," then it would be right to classify sexual harassment as mere offense. In those cases in which the wrong of sexual harassment is domination, in which the message sent by the behavior is hostility and contempt for all women, sexual harassment is a profound offense.

Gender discrimination harms women in ways very similar to the harms of racial discrimination. Mari Matsuda argues that racist speech is approximately in the middle of a continuum of kinds of racial discrimination.[31] Among the harms for the direct victims she lists "fear in the gut to rapid pulse rate and difficulty in breathing, nightmares, post-traumatic stress disorder, hypertension, psychosis, and suicide."[32] Victims are restricted in their personal freedom. Nontargeted groups then tend to distance themselves, making it more difficult "to achieve a sense of common humanity" among members of different racial groups. Racism forces "well-meaning dominant-group members to use kid-glove care in dealing with outsiders."[33] No matter how we resist it, she argues, it implants a racist message in all people's minds by forcing us to categorize by race and to make at least an initial judgment using a racial stereotype. Even the most well-meaning antiracists of all races find themselves waging an inner struggle against invasive stereotypes. Likewise, gender discrimination exists in a variety of forms, ranging from less serious forms such as stereotypes to violence and rape. Sexual harassment also comes in many forms; hostile environment sexual harassment that sends the domination message is the one that I claim is the most like racist speech. It makes women afraid for their jobs and sometimes their safety and even their lives, it perpetuates dangerous and harmful stereotypes, and it sends the messages of hostility, inferiority, and degradation. As racist speech pits persons of different races against each other, sexual harassment pits men against women, making it more difficult for them to achieve a sense of common humanity within or between other social groups. Many race theory scholars note that racist speech denigrates the humanity of racial minorities by picking out their race as the fundamentally important moral fact about them. Sexual harassment picks out women's sexual nature, specifically their nature as the objects of men's desires, as the salient fact about them in contexts in which their skill, their intelligence, and their ability to do the job ought to be the only relevant issues.[34] In these ways, racism and sexism are impersonal, and so profound offenses.

Feinberg notes that religious persons are profoundly offended by sacrilege and nationalistic persons by flag-burnings in the same way that Nazi marchers in Skokie profoundly offend the Jewish residents, or cross-burnings profoundly offend African Americans, because the "profoundly offended states of mind in the two kinds of example may *feel* very much alike."[35] Reliance on the subjective affective state of the victim to determine whether an offense is profound is problematic. I would agree with those who think that speech that might be termed "sacrilege" is doubly protected by the Constitution, and the recent Supreme Court ruling in *Texas v. Johnson*,[36] which I would also agree with, clearly protects burning the flag as a means of political expression. In order to argue that, unlike sacrilege and flag-burning, hostile environment sexual harassment through expression alone may be restricted, it must be clearly distinguished from the former cases. The sacrilege and flag-burning cases show that it is simply wrong-headed to look only at the way that an individual victim of profound offense feels because of the offense. Such a subjective criterion is too arbitrary, too connected to individuals' personal histories, to make reasonable law, since the law must give fair notice of what is prohibited. The ground of the distinction lies in the objective fact of oppression. Only those groups who are oppressed can suffer from the harm of domination I explored above. This is because it is possible to send the message to only one of them that they are unwelcome, unequal, and worthy of contempt because of their group membership. In order not to be tempted to conflate profound offense with mere offense, or even with cases of sacrilege or disrespect to the national flag, in discussing the domination form of hostile environment sexual harassment, I prefer to call it "gender discrimination," suggesting a profound rather than mere offense.

While sexual harassment law focuses on the harms done to individuals by individuals, this does not adequately address the harm that is done generally by gender discrimination. Anita Superson has suggested that we define sexual harassment objectively, without reference to the attitudes of either direct recipients or perpetrators. She argues that the determining factor is "whether the behavior is an instance of a practice that expresses and perpetuates the attitude that the victim and members of her sex are inferior because of their sex."[37] This definition captures the idea that what is wrong with sexual harassment is that it is gender discrimination. Since a charge of sexual harassment would not be based on a feeling or an intention, it clearly distinguishes sexual harassment from mere offense. Further, the wrong of sexual harassment is relativized to a social, historical context in which it is possible to "express and perpetuate the attitude" that one sex is inferior. Since it is not now possible to send that message with respect to men, for example, this sort of wrong could not be done to men. If it becomes impossible to send that message about women, then sexual harassment will be obsolete with respect to women as well. Also, the objective definition allows us to distinguish this sort of profound offense from religious sacrilege or flag-burning. Superson's objective definition of sexual harassment would classify the ATO case as hostile environment sexual harassment. There would be no problem about the perpetrators or victims being groups. The only issue is whether the behavior is part of a practice that expresses and perpetuates the attitude that women are inferior because of their sex. The repeated nature of the events and the fact that they emanated from a fraternity, a group exclusively constituted by men for the purpose of maintaining sexual segregation and social power for their sex, shows that the behavior is a practice. The misogyny and the degradation of the terms used to refer to women express the attitudes that women are the inferior sex. While men are their "buddies," (i.e., their friends), women are their "slutties," (i.e., their degraded sexual objects).

While the objective definition returns sexual harassment properly to its roots in discrimination law, it poses two First Amendment difficulties. Suppose the behavior in question is the following statement in a classroom or faculty meeting: "women on average have lower spatial and mathematical abilities, and thus should not be accorded affirmative action in hiring in departments of mathematics, natural science, and engineering." While this statement is surely based on tenuous research and questionable inferential reasoning, it is a paradigm example of protected speech that would "express and perpetuate the attitude that the victim and members of her sex are inferior because of their sex." While clearly harmful, it is the sort of speech that needs to be heard and that people need to be allowed to make because it has such important implications for academic freedom, and for social policy formation and willing compliance with it. Thus Superson's definition is too broad to be consistent with the goals of the First Amendment.

There is also a legal difficulty with recognizing the domination harm of sexual harassment that I have described. Domination, under my description, is quite similar to what has been called "group defamation." In *Beauharnais v. Illinois*,[38] the Supreme Court upheld a law that prohibited some forms of group defamation, but a later case, namely *Times v. Sullivan*,[39] narrowed the definition of actionable defamation in a way that legal scholars agree has effectively overturned *Beauharnais*, and disallows action against group defamation.

Nonetheless I want to argue that the objective definition offers a legitimate interpretation of a sexually harassing hostile environment. It best captures the spirit of Title VII of the Civil Rights Act and Title IX of the Elementary/Secondary Education Act as they apply to "sex" (read: gender). For non-expressive conduct (such as the indecent exposure aspect of the ATO behavior) the objective definition would be consistent with the Constitution.[40] With expression, though, the definition needs to be narrowed. To see how much narrowing needs to be done we need to turn to the Constitution and First Amendment doctrine.

PROTECTED SPEECH AND EQUAL PROTECTION

Among other freedoms it grants, the First Amendment prohibits governmental interference with freedom of expression. It states: "Congress shall make no law . . . abridging the freedom of speech." The interpretation of the First Amendment in scholarship and case law, known as "First Amendment doctrine," extends and clarifies these few words. First Amendment doctrine is broader than a literal reading; neither Congress *nor any state* may violate these freedoms and speech includes *other forms of expression*. It is also narrower in allowing certain kinds of restrictions on speech: commercial speech may be limited to protect consumers from fraud and false advertising and to protect firms from unfair competition, private citizens can successfully sue for libel, the state may punish treasonous statements, states and localities may outlaw expression that disturbs the peace (i.e., "fighting words") provided that it does so in a content-neutral way, or they may place "time, place, and manner" restrictions on speech.

There are two ways to justify rights: as intrinsically valuable or as instrumentally valuable for some social or political purpose. First Amendment scholars have justified broad free speech rights both ways. Since most would grant at least some of the above restrictions on free speech in civil society, even if they are considered intrinsically valuable, they do not trump *all* other individual rights and social goals. Thus, we need to specify the balancing procedure for free speech. Further, it seems clear that we should not treat all speech equally; the balancing procedure needs to classify speech by its value and the value of the opposing interest. First Amendment doctrine accords political speech, speech that is intended to express and taken as expressing a view on a political or social policy matter, the highest value. The best defense of free speech, in my view, lies in its instrumental values, as seen from the perspective of a social contractarian moral theory, (though I believe that nothing turns on how, precisely, the value of free speech is justified). The ability to express one's views makes it more likely that a social agreement can be forged that all will accept, while being prohibited from expressing them would surely lead to some believing that their view has not been taken into account. In a democracy it is necessary at least that everyone feels that she can express her political views, and so could come to have a following for her view if only she is persuasive enough. Speech criticizing existing government policies gets very high instrumental value on these grounds. Additionally, there are the Millian arguments for free speech on the grounds that the only access to the truth is through airing and winnowing diverse ideas in free and open debate. Thus, the freedom of political expression is instrumentally very important as a means to political stability and to truth. Furthermore, freedom of expression allows persons to alter their government when it fails to embody the will of the people; states that have lost the consent of the governed are just the states most liable to restrict political expression. One might also argue that one's personhood itself is at stake in political expression, since if one may not express her deeply held political view she is denied the respect accorded to equal members of the contract. I take political expression to be a basic moral value, and therefore rightly a part of the First Amendment of the Constitution. However, these arguments do not show that political speech must be free at all times and places with respect to all content; the state may place reasonable restrictions on the time, place, or manner of the expression if these restrictions genuinely do not eliminate one's ability to express one's views. For example, one need not have the right to break into my bedroom in order to express one's political view. On the other hand, it would be too much restriction not to allow one to air one's views in some manner in the same town that I live, no matter how offensive I and my neighbors find the speech. Localities must allow even abhorrent political speech some of the time.

The arguments that show that political expression is a fundamental moral right also show that the state ought to respect the principle of content-neutrality with respect to the restrictions that it does place on political speech. If the state does not respect content-neutrality, then it burdens some political views more than others, and this could rob some persons of the right to air their views in public, sacrificing any of the instrumental values of political speech. Therefore, the time, place, and manner restrictions that may be placed on speech must apply to all speech; pro-choice and pro-life activists alike must be required to file for a permit to march through the streets.

The Court traditionally has taken political speech to be fundamental, and therefore applies strict judicial scrutiny to laws that restrict it. This means that any law that places blanket restrictions on political expression must be justified by a compelling state interest, and the only such interest that has withstood strict scrutiny is the interest in preventing "immediate, irreversible, and serious harm to the nation."[41] It is beyond the scope of this essay to justify this degree of severity in the judicial review of laws that restrict freedom of expression, but I think that it is justifiable in light of our political traditions. One apparent blanket restriction of expression has been to outlaw the use of "fighting words," i.e., words that tend to cause an immediate breach of the peace.[42] The fighting words doctrine is content-neutral, however, in that *any* such words, whether coming from the political right, left, center, or from religious or antireligious sentiments would be so restricted. An important recent test of the principle of content-neutrality was *R.A.V. v. St. Paul*, in which a local law in St. Paul, Minnesota, prohibiting certain kinds of hate expression was struck down. The complainant in the case had been convicted by the St. Paul ordinance for burning a cross on the lawn of an African American family. The ordinance outlawed hate expression and specified burning crosses on someone's lawn as an example of hate expression, because of its historical message of hatred, inferiority, and its historically credible threat of violence. Justice Scalia, writing for the majority, argued that the state has no legitimate interest in judging a political message by its content. He stated that "the only interest distinctively served" by the St. Paul ordinance "is that of displaying the city council's special hostility towards the particular biases thus singled out."[43] Since this is not a compelling state interest, the majority reasoned that it was not enough to warrant restriction of expression. *R.A.V.* shows that current First Amendment doctrine will not allow content-based restrictions on speech.

Justice Scalia's reasoning seems wrong to me on two counts: (1) the kind of political expression that a cross-burning represents is of lower value than civilly intended and delivered speech acts; (2) there is a much stronger state interest in restricting hate messages like cross-burnings that is specifically endorsed by the Constitution. I shall return to these points shortly as the argument develops.

Justice Scalia is right about some things in his decision: the Constitution will not allow a racist message to be censored purely on the ground of the propositional content of the message. The First Amendment has never considered a whole category of speech, *because of its content*, to be unacceptable because it is false or immoral and I don't see First Amendment doctrine changing in this regard. Some have argued that it *should*, that we have a moral obligation to change it.[44] But it would be extremely difficult to draw the line between the kind of racist speech that is morally wrong and clearly false, and that which is either arguable or which we would want persons to be able to argue about. Kingsley Browne[45] makes this argument persuasively: if we want persons to be able to argue that, say, "race does not correlate in any regular way with intelligence, nor would there be any moral significance if it did," then we have to allow persons to state the negation of that sentence. Clearly that is an important claim to be able to make in social policy debates. Therefore, we have to allow persons to say, at least in a calm and civil manner, false and morally objectionable racist things. Wrongness in itself cannot be justification for ruling out speech. The case for outlawing racist speech will have to rest on the harmfulness of the manner of the speech, not its falsehood. The harm must be weighed against any value the speech can be said to have. However, the value of the expression may be limited by the manner in which it is delivered.

Charles Lawrence argues that restrictions on the use of racial epithets in face-to-face encounters should be allowed by a properly conceived First Amendment doctrine for two reasons.[46] First he points out the great harm that racist epithets cause: they are like slaps in the face to the victim, provoking rage, not thought or reasoned argument. The First Amendment is not intended to protect batterers. However, this is not a strong argument against protecting a form of speech, since, as Feinberg points out, religious persons might feel similarly slapped by seriously sacrilegious speech. As I argued earlier, the subjective feelings on the part of the hearers cannot be the test of what speech is protected and what is not. Lawrence's second argument is more persuasive: allowing racial insults thwarts the instrumental purpose of fostering more speech and thus more political debate. Racial epithets are preemptive, in that the victim often is so stunned that they cannot respond, or doing so is precluded by their subordinated status. Andrew Altman makes an interesting observation about racial epithets that may help us to explain why they differ from ordinary political speech with equivalent propositional content, and how a response for a victim of racism or sexism could be "precluded by their subordinated status." One uses epithets partly for their perlocutionary effect in the hearer, but mainly for the purpose of what Altman terms "treating someone as a moral subordinate," which issues from their *illocutionary force*.[47] While perlocutionary acts are doings in linguistic form, illocutionary force comes from linguistic meaning. As perlocutionary acts are conventional acts that are not necessarily related to the propositional content of the words through which they are performed, the illocutionary force of a word or phrase is a conventionally constructed meaning that is not equivalent to the literal propositional content of the phrase. The illocutionary force of a racist or sexist epithet is conventionally created subordination, unlike the naturally subordinating force of genocide or enslavement. Altman argues that moral subordination, not the dissemination of ideas, is the principal purpose of racial epithets and slurs. But the same cannot be said of civilly presented hate speech, or insults that do not attack the identifying feature of an oppressed class. When someone makes the claim that "you are contemptible for being a homosexual," she is not *in making the claim* treating you as a moral subordinate, though her claim would indicate that she would like to do so. If she calls you a "fag" she is treating you through her word as a moral subordinate. If an insult attacks an individual for some feature that is unrelated to any oppressed group identity, there is no conventional meaning in that insult that issues from stereotypes or other aspects of oppression. If someone says, "you are a slob," she is indicating contempt for your appearance, but not treating you as a moral subordinate because, conventionally, slobs are not moral subordinates.

To treat as a moral subordinate is to deny someone the possibility of entering into a debate about her status. This observation confirms Lawrence's view that racial epithets are not constitutionally valuable political speech. Racial epithets tend to preclude political speech by the hearers of them, and thus instrumental value of racial epithets is very low; a "discussion" that begins with a White man calling a Black man a "nigger" will not lead to a civil discussion of the merits of racial segregation as a social policy. To engage in political debate one must treat the others in the debate as moral equals. The moral status of women and minorities is not open to debate. One can argue what equality means, and how best to manage differences, but to treat them as moral subordinates is not to engage in political debate. This means that face-to-face racial epithets should not be considered to be in the same category as political speech. Since the point of an epithet is to degrade or suggest unworthiness of moral standing, the only valuable use would be disquotational, for example, in the statement of an ordinance or policy that prohibits the use of them, or in a class discussing race issues. Now we can see how Scalia is wrong on the first point: cross-burnings, like racial epithets, are to be accorded less instrumental and intrinsic value than ordinary political speech, even though it is true that they convey a message, because they are conventional ways to treat Blacks as moral subordinates.

There are some gender slurs that treat women similarly as moral subordinates. (The words I listed earlier, for example.) These words tend to suggest that women are to be equated with their sexual anatomy, or that their role and function in life is be the sexual servants of men. Lawrence and Altman provide us with a justification for a limited hostile environment sexual harassment restriction on speech. However, many cases of hostile environment sexual harassment, including the ATO case, do not involve these words. But if, like cross-burnings, the behavior is conventionally loaded with oppressive illocutionary force so that it amounts to treating women as moral subordinates, then even if it is expression, it should be proscribed.

Since the First Amendment right to free speech is not absolute, one might ask if there are other constitutionally guaranteed rights or additional values represented in the Constitution that conflict with some forms of free speech. Richard Delgado, Charles Lawrence, and others have presented arguments in favor of restrictions on free speech from this constitutional perspective. Delgado expands the list of constitutional interests that might support restrictions on racist speech.[48] He argues that the Constitution stands firmly against the denigration of humanity and privacy inherent in racist speech, since it is inconsistent with such constitutional principles as universal suffrage, prohibition of cruel and unusual punishment, protection against unreasonable search, and abolition of slavery. These values are endorsed in the Constitution, but are they inconsistent with all racist speech? Racist speech is cruel, but not punishable by the government. Nor can it be plausibly construed as unreasonable search nor even a reinstitution of slavery. Finally, racist speech could only be truly inconsistent with universal suffrage if it were to be successful in getting legislation passed that denied racial minorities suffrage. But that means that the legislation, not the speech that supports it, is unconstitutional. While racist speech harms persons by degrading them and suggesting that they may be the subjects of these violations of constitutional rights, the speech itself does not violate those rights. Still, Delgado succeeds in showing that the Constitution endorses the goals of ensuring equality, and of ending the legacy of racial discrimination.

Lawrence focuses on the "equal protection" clause of the Fourteenth Amendment, and the subsequent use made of it in *Brown v. Board of Education of Topeka*. In his view, *Brown* already commits us to some regulation of speech. It articulates a principle that is central to understanding the equal protection clause: that the meaning of racial segregation is to create a superior and an inferior caste. "*Brown* held that segregated schools were unconstitutional primarily because of the *message* segregation conveys,"[49] so Lawrence argues that there is precedent for regulating content of racist speech. One argument against this reading of *Brown* is that it confuses conduct and speech. *Brown* strikes down laws that segregate, and that means not that no one may propose or discuss such a law, but that the state may not enforce it. Another objection is that it precludes the government, not private individuals, from segregating by race. The Civil Rights Act of 1964 proscribes some racist speech, e.g., the signs saying "Coloreds" and "Whites," of private individuals. The forms of precluded speech fall under the categories commercial or government speech, however, not political speech. Lawrence's point is that what is harmful about these forms of racist speech, the reason that they are outlawed by the Civil Rights Act, is that they send the message of inferiority and degradation. Thus, he argues, the Act outlaws *the messages* themselves, and they are clearly political messages.

Do these arguments give us justification to outlaw *any* forms of racist or sexist political speech? I think not. However, I do think that these considerations justify a different reading of the First Amendment. Under current First Amendment doctrine, no kinds of messages can be singled out as especially unworthy. Nothing could be more clearly a message of degradation and inferiority than the burning cross in the *R.A.V.* case, yet the ordinance that outlawed it was struck down because it was not content-neutral. I have argued that Scalia's reasoning in that case is flawed by his failure to consider how the message is delivered. We can now see how his reasoning is flawed in the second way, namely, by his false claim that the state has no particular interest in prohibiting the message of cross-burnings other than an arbitrary whim of the local government. As Delgado and Lawrence remind us, fighting discrimination and insuring equal protection of the law are constitutionally sanctioned interests.

I suggest the following balancing procedure for weighing free speech concerns against equal protection concerns. We must consider first whether the expressive conduct conveys a political message; if not, then it may be restricted for important state interests. If it does convey a political message, then before we call for strict judicial scrutiny we need to ask if it does so in the manner of racial epithets, i.e., in a way that stifles further expression by treating someone as a moral subordinate. If it is that sort of conventionally loaded speech-precluding speech, then less than strict scrutiny is called for. Still, the state may only preclude it if there is a strong state interest in doing so. In the case of expressions that conventionally treat persons as moral subordinates, the strong constitutional interest in equal protection overwhelms the small instrumental or intrinsic value of such expression. In the case of sacrilegious messages or flag-burnings, there are strong constitutional interests in *allowing expression* of these messages. The First Amendment requires that the state take no interest in religious matters, including antireligious messages. And one of the most important instrumental purposes of speech is for criticizing the government, which is just the intended message of flag-burning. Thus *Texas v. Johnson* and *R.A.V. v. St. Paul* need not stand or fall together.

To summarize this section: the First Amendment protects all private political speech from blanket suppression, unless it is deemed to cause immediate, irreversible, and serious harm to the nation. These protections are justified by the high instrumental and intrinsic value of political speech. However, some restrictions on the time, place, and manner of the expression are allowable, provided that they are content-neutral restrictions and that they do not amount to blanket restrictions on any political view. Furthermore, fighting words may be restricted, again subject to the proviso that the law is content-neutral. Finally, I have argued that the narrow category of racial and gender epithets, and expressive conduct that has the same illocutionary effect of treating persons as moral subordinates, ought to fall outside First Amendment protections, though that exclusion is not now consistent with First Amendment doctrine, as is clear from Justice Scalia's opinion in *R.A.V. v. St. Paul.*

Under current First Amendment doctrine, then, the ATO case would have resulted in a loss for the Advocates, as the college's conservative law firm advised. Given the balancing procedure I have argued for, though, the Advocates would have had a better case. The newsletters included a gender slur, which would fall outside of protected expression, but also a misogynistic poem. This raises the possibility that there is a conceivable artistic value in the poem that would override the state's interest in prohibiting expression. Whichever way the courts would decide this, however, the other events in the complaint would not fall under First Amendment protections because they are either like racial epithets (in the case of the misogynistic graffiti) or like cross-burnings (in the case of the chanting, self-exposing men at the sorority house).

CONCLUSION

There remains one further point to consider in favor of using hostile environment sexual harassment law to reduce gender discrimination on campuses. Colleges and universities are special environments for several reasons. First, they are places where speech and other forms of expression, including political speech, is routinely judged, graded, excluded, and encouraged according to its content. That is, as Cass Sunstein argues, their whole purpose.[50] Academic life subjects the speech of both faculty and students to constant review and discipline. Schools regularly penalize bad speech with dismissal or disapproval. If they did not they would not be doing their jobs; there would be no academic standards. Furthermore, if professors lost their right to control speech in the classroom, classes could become chaotic jumbles of non sequiturs and disruptive emotional outpourings. Clearly this sort of control must count as a reasonable time, place, and manner restriction. Teachers must have the right to disallow irrelevant speech and disapprove of badly argued speech, and they must have the leeway to make judgments on this matter. Contrary to California State Congressman Bill Leonard's view (the epigraph to this article), campuses are great places for correcting people's thinking, and that's why people support them.

This need to control speech for the sake of orderly classes does not extend beyond the classroom or faculty office, however. What about extracurricular behavior, as in the case of the ATO's? The second reason to regard colleges and universities as special cases is because they nurture our young people and reach them at a formative stage in moral development. Therefore, they have a special responsibility to encourage the fundamental liberal values of equality and freedom from discrimination. Schools have the opportunity to instill values and shape the development of society. However, there are competing values at issue: freedom of speech vs. equality. Clearly colleges and universities (at least state-supported ones) ought not to sponsor racism and sexism, but just as clearly they ought not to stand for thwarting political speech. The special responsibility argument upholds the value of speech as much as that of equality, especially given the traditional argument for academic freedom. But colleges and universities ought to recognize an even greater special responsibility because women and minorities were excluded from even de jure equal opportunity in the academy for so long, further exacerbating social and political inequality. The argument suggests not that colleges and universities should thwart speech, but that they enforce equality and support speech that promotes it.

Third, college and university campuses are also often the homes of the young people who attend them. Not only are they places where people discuss serious social and political matters, but also where they eat, play, study, make friends, and recreate. No one who lives there can easily escape the campus either to avoid a hostile environment or to propound one's political views. This suggests that the campus can require a high degree of civility in expression, but again that it cannot thwart political expression.

Colleges and universities have a special ability and therefore special responsibility to help eradicate sexual and racial discrimination, and to erase the effects of these on their victims. This makes them prime battlegrounds for the forces of progress and backlash. Where recognition of hostile environment sexual harassment is a clear example of progress, the ATO case, with its alliance of conservative legislators, legal think tanks, and fraternity brothers is a clear example of backlash. The stakes are high, and the two sides are calling in reinforcements. Progressive colleges and universities cannot win this on the legal battlefield at present. However, though current First Amendment doctrine prohibits colleges from punishing much dangerous and harmful racist and sexist speech, colleges and universities have vast resources for supporting speech. When the ATO case was beginning to look like a loss to the Advocates, and a victory for the forces of backlash, the college was asked for support in fighting against sexism through funds for speakers and rape crisis services, more female security officers, women's self-defense courses, and a reappraisal of the role of fraternities in the college. Most of all what was wanted was a clear statement of disapproval from the administration.

For example, they could cancel classes for a day and support a teach-in on racism and sexism. One of the most important steps that progressive colleges and universities could take would be to remove all support for fraternities permanently. They have shown by their history of misogyny and bigotry that they are not an institution to be supported by equality-seeking social institutions.[51] There is, in short, much that colleges and universities could do to stop supporting sexism and racism and to begin supporting the speech of those who seek equality without violating students' legal or moral rights.

NOTES

An earlier version of this essay appeared in *The Kansas Journal of Law & Public Policy* 4, no. 1 (fall 1994): 69–81. I would like to thank Julie Maybee, Russ Shafer-Landau, Cynthia Willett, and the University of Kansas Department of Philosophy for comments given on this essay at a departmental colloquium. I also thank the audience of a presentation of this work at the Feminist Ethics and Social Policy Conference in Pittsburgh, November 1993, and especially Debra DeBruin for helpful remarks. Finally I owe a great intellectual and personal debt to my fellow members of the "Oxy Four," but most especially Marcia Homiak.

1. Quoted by Linda Seebach, "Putting Teeth in the First Amendment," *Daily News* (Glendale, Calif.), 21 January 1993, 19.

2. Mane Hajdin holds the former view in "Why the Fight against Sexual Harassment Is Misguided," in *Sexual Harassment Issues and Answers*, ed. Linda LeMoncheck and James P. Sterba, 77–81 (New York: Oxford University Press, 2001). Katie Roiphe holds the latter view in "Reckless Eyeballing: Sexual Harassment on Campus," in *Sexual Harassment Issues and Answers*, ed. Linda LeMoncheck and James P. Sterba, 249–60 (New York: Oxford University Press, 2001).

3. Richard Bernstein holds this view in "Guilty if Charged," in *Sexual Harassment Issues and Answers*, ed. Linda LeMoncheck and James P. Sterba, 187–94 (New York: Oxford University Press, 2001).

4. Elsa Kircher Cole, *Sexual Harassment on Campus: A Legal Compendium*, 2nd ed. (Washington, D.C.: National Association of College and University Attorneys, 1990).

5. Much has been done in the years since this essay was originally written (1994). See Leslie Pickering Francis, *Sexual Harassment as an Ethical Issue in Academic Life* (Lanham, Md.: Rowman & Littlefield, 2001).

6. Barbara T. Lindemann and Kenneth D. Sulzer, "Sexual Harassment: Definitions and Legal Issues for Faculty Advocates," unpublished document presented at Occidental College, October 1992.

7. Catharine MacKinnon, in *Only Words* (Cambridge, Mass.: Harvard University Press, 1993), points out that these free speech objections to sexual harassment only arose recently, see pp. 49–55. A recent article that makes this objection quite explicitly is Kingsley R. Browne, "Title VII as Censorship: Hostile-Environment Harassment and the First Amendment," *Ohio State Law Journal* 52 (1991): 481–550.

8. For this claim see, e.g., Cass R. Sunstein, "Liberalism, Speech Codes, and Related Problems," *Academe* 79 (July–August 1993): 14–25; Anita M. Superson, "A Feminist

Definition of Sexual Harassment," *Journal of Social Philosophy* 24, no. 1 (spring 1993): 46–64; Browne, "Title VII as Censorship."

9. *Meritor Sav. Bank, FSB v. Vinson*, 477 U.S. 57 (1986).

10. Browne, "Title VII as Censorship," has pointed out that there is little constitutional difference between a case of pure speech and one in which speech is a part of the alleged offense. The question in either case is whether speech of this sort may be restricted. If not, then speech cannot form even a part of the case.

11. *Robinson v. Jacksonville Shipyards, Inc.*, 760 F.Supp., 1486 (M.D.Fla. 1991).

12. *Faragher v. City of Boca Raton*, U.S. (1998), reproduced in part in *Sexual Harassment Issues and Answers*, ed. Linda LeMoncheck and James P. Sterba, 376–82 (New York: Oxford University Press, 2001).

13. Act of Sept. 30, 1992, 1363, (codified as amended in sec. 66301 Cal. Educ. Code).

14. There is a real question whether this law would withstand constitutional challenge because it appears to violate the property rights of private colleges and universities. For the purposes of my interest, I shall assume that the law would be upheld.

15. The new California law in effect made a *statutory* right to free speech for students; it would not make sense to say that one individual (or group of individuals) violated the constitutional right of free speech of another, since the Constitution requires that "Congress shall make no law . . ."

16. A similar case occurred at about the same time regarding a newspaper column in the California State University at Northridge newspaper. The column was derogatory toward gays and lesbians. The university was forced by financial considerations to back down there as well. It is also possible that other states or the U.S. Congress could pass similar laws; a bill similar to Chapter 1363 was introduced at the federal level during the 102d Congress by Rep. Henry J. Hyde (R-Ill.), called the *Collegiate Speech Protection Act of 1991*, though it never made it out of committee. I owe the reference to this bill to a memo written by Albert Rodriguez and Wayne Flick of Latham & Watkins, attorneys at law, January 18, 1993.

17. For a fuller development of mine and similar ideas of oppression, see Ann E. Cudd, "Enforced Pregnancy, Rape, and the Image of Woman," *Philosophical Studies* 60 (1990): 47–59; Marilyn Frye, "Oppression," in *The Politics of Reality* (Trumansburg, N.Y.: Crossing Press, 1983); and Marilyn Friedman and Larry May, "Harming Women as a Group," *Social Theory and Practice* 2 (1985): 208–34.

18. Congressman Howard Smith of Virginia only proposed including sex as a ploy to defeat the entire Civil Rights Act, reasoning that surely it would be ridiculous to think that women ought to be granted any more civil rights, and that it might therefore cause some congressmen to vote against the entire act. See Deborah L. Rhode, *Justice and Gender* (Cambridge, Mass.: Harvard University Press, 1989), 57.

19. Chester E. Finn, "The Campus: An Island of Repression in a Sea of Freedom," in *Today's Moral Issues*, ed. Daniel Bonevac, 110 (Mountain View, Calif.: Mayfield, 1992).

20. Finn, "The Campus," 111.

21. Because quid pro quo sexual harassment is not my subject I shall ignore for my purposes arguments suggesting that it is really a fair trade rather than a form of coercion. See Michael Bayles, "Coercive Offers and Public Benefits," *The Personalist*

60, (spring 1974): 139–44 for this argument, and Nancy Tuana, "Sexual Harassment: Offers and Coercion," *Journal of Social Philosophy* 19, (summer 1988): 30–42, or John C. Hughes and Larry May, "Sexual Harassment," *Social Theory and Practice* 6 (fall 1980): 249–80, for responses.

22. Browne notes that the "conventional definition of 'harassment' . . . generally connotes a pattern of conduct aimed at a particular person and intended to annoy." Browne, "Title VII as Censorship," 486.

23. The terms "sexual message" and "hostility message" are Kingsley Browne's; see Browne, "Title VII as Censorship," 491.

24. This point responds to an objection first raised to me by Richard Cole, that sexual harassment law is redundant with other laws that protect persons from defamation, coercion, and harassment. My response is that there is a completely new harm in some forms of sexual harassment, namely, the domination harm.

25. In a recent case in California, Sabino Gutierrez, a man, successfully sued Maria Martinez, his female supervisor, for repeated unwelcome sexual propositions. *New York Times*, 21 May 1993, A15.

26. Perhaps in woman-dominated professions it would be possible to send the message to men that they are not welcome. This is also difficult to do, though, since men have normally been accorded more status than women in these professions. Consider the examples of the male principal of the elementary school, the male head librarian, the male head chef or waiter in the finer restaurants. Furthermore, being welcome in a woman-dominated profession is a dubious honor for many men.

27. In the same year as the complaint, faculty-initiated discussion of discontinuing college support of fraternities and sororities was immediately stonewalled by the director of annual giving, who argued that fraternity alumni donate indispensable funds to the college. If anything, the fraternity men had more power than the faculty advocates, at least in setting policy about the fraternities.

28. Joel Feinberg, *Offense to Others* (New York: Oxford University Press, 1985), 51.

29. Feinberg, *Offense,* 58–59.

30. Feinberg, *Offense,* 59.

31. Mari J. Matsuda, "Public Response to Racist Speech: Considering the Victim's Story," in *Words That Wound,* ed. Mari J. Matsuda, Charles R. Lawrence III, Richard Delgado, Kimberle Williams Crenshaw, 1–52 (Boulder, Colo.: Westview Press, 1993).

32. Matsuda, "Public Response," 24.

33. Matsuda, "Public Response," 25.

34. Richard Delgado, "Words That Wound: A Tort Action for Racial Insults, Epithets, and Name Calling," in *Words That Wound,* ed. Mari J. Matsuda, Charles R. Lawrence III, Richard Delgado, Kimberle Williams Crenshaw, 89–110 (Boulder, Colo.: Westview Press, 1993) may disagree with my claim that sexual harassment is as profoundly harmful as racist speech, when he appears to endorse the *Second Restatement of Torts* when it gives as an example of a "mere insult" the statement: "You are a God damned woman and a God damned liar." To distinguish racist speech from mere insult he claims that "racial insults are different qualitatively because they conjure up the entire history of racial discrimination in this country" (100). I agree with his criterion for profound harm that there be an entire history of severe discrimina-

tion against a group. The history of discrimination against women is also severe and longstanding.

35. Feinberg, *Offense*, 53.

36. *Texas v. Johnson*, 491 U.S. 397 (1989).

37. Superson, "A Feminist Definition of Sexual Harassment," 58.

38. *Beauharnais v. Illinois*, 343 U.S. 250 (1952).

39. *New York Times v. Sullivan*, 376 U.S. 254, 270.

40. Although the indecent exposure incident sends a message, and thus would appear to be a form of expression, I am using the term in the more restricted legal sense here. That is, the sense in which the Constitution together with liberal principles of civility would allow such conduct to be constrained despite its potential message-sending character.

41. Jeffrie Murphy and Jules Coleman, *Philosophy of Law* (Boulder, Colo.: Westview Press, 1990), ch. 2.

42. *Chaplinsky v. New Hampshire*, 315 U.S. 568 (1942).

43. Justice Scalia, quoted in Linda Greenhouse, "The Court's 2 Visions of Free Speech," *New York Times*, 24 June 1992, A13. See also *R.A.V. v. St. Paul*, 1992 U.S. Lexis 3863 (22 June 1992).

44. Matsuda, "Public Response," 35.

45. Browne, "Title VII as Censorship."

46. Charles R. Lawrence III, "If He Hollers Let Him Go: Regulating Racist Speech on Campus," in *Words That Wound*, ed. Mari J. Matsuda, Charles R. Lawrence III, Richard Delgado, Kimberle Williams Crenshaw, 53–88 (Boulder, Colo.: Westview, 1993).

47. Andrew Altman, "Liberalism and Campus Hate Speech: A Philosophical Examination," *Ethics* 103 (January 1993): 302–17.

48. Delgado, "Words."

49. Lawrence, "Regulating Speech," 59.

50. Sunstein, "Liberalism."

51. There seems at last to be some recognition of this and some attempts to eliminate fraternities and sororities. See Eric Hoover, "New Scrutiny for Powerful Greek Systems," *Chronicle of Higher Education*, 8 June 2001, A35.

BIBLIOGRAPHY

Altman, Andrew. "Liberalism and Campus Hate Speech: A Philosophical Examination." *Ethics* 103 (January 1993): 302–17.

Bernstein, Richard. "Guilty if Charged." In *Sexual Harassment Issues and Answers*, ed. Linda LeMoncheck and James P. Sterba, 187–94. New York: Oxford University Press, 2001.

Bayles, Michael. "Coercive Offers and Public Benefits." *The Personalist* 60 (spring 1974): 139–44.

Browne, Kingsley R. "Title VII as Censorship: Hostile-Environment Harassment and the First Amendment." *Ohio State Law Journal* 52 (1991): 481–550.

Cole, Elsa Kircher. *Sexual Harassment on Campus: A Legal Compendium*. 2nd ed. Washington, D.C.: National Association of College and University Attorneys, 1990.

Francis, Leslie Pickering. *Sexual Harassment as an Ethical Issue in Academic Life.* Lanham, Md.: Rowman & Littlefield, 2001.

Cudd, Ann E. "Enforced Pregnancy, Rape, and the Image of Woman." *Philosophical Studies* 60 (1990): 47–59.

Delgado, Richard. "Words That Wound: A Tort Action for Racial Insults, Epithets, and Name Calling." In *Words That Wound,* ed. Mari J. Matsuda, Charles R. Lawrence III, Richard Delgado, and Kimberle Williams Crenshaw, 89–110. Boulder, Colo.: Westview, 1993.

Feinberg, Joel. *Offense to Others.* New York: Oxford University Press, 1985.

Finn, Chester E. "The Campus: An Island of Repression in a Sea of Freedom." In *Today's Moral Issues,* ed. Daniel Bonevac, 110–14. Mountain View, Calif.: Mayfield, 1992.

Friedman, Marilyn, and Larry May. "Harming Women as a Group." *Social Theory and Practice* 2 (1985): 208–34.

Frye, Marilyn. *The Politics of Reality.* Trumansburg, N.Y.: Crossing Press, 1983.

Hajdin, Mane. "Why the Fight against Sexual Harassment Is Misguided." In *Sexual Harassment Issues and Answers,* ed. Linda LeMoncheck and James P. Sterba, 77–81. New York: Oxford University Press, 2001.

Hoover, Eric. "New Scrutiny for Powerful Greek Systems." *Chronicle of Higher Education* 8 June 2001, A35.

Hughes, John C., and Larry May. "Sexual Harassment." *Social Theory and Practice* 6 (fall 1980): 249–80.

Lawrence III, Charles R. "If He Hollers Let Him Go: Regulating Racist Speech on Campus." In *Words That Wound,* ed. Mari J. Matsuda, Charles R. Lawrence III, Richard Delgado, Kimberle Williams Crenshaw, 53–88. Boulder, Colo.: Westview, 1993.

LeMoncheck, Linda, and James P. Sterba, eds. *Sexual Harassment Issues and Answers.* New York: Oxford University Press, 2001.

Lindemann, Barbara T., and Kenneth D. Sulzer. "Sexual Harassment: Definitions and Legal Issues for Faculty Advocates." Unpublished document presented at Occidental College, October 1992.

MacKinnon, Catharine. *Only Words.* Cambridge, Mass.: Harvard University Press, 1993.

Matsuda, Mari J. "Public Response to Racist Speech: Considering the Victim's Story." In *Words That Wound,* ed. Mari J. Matsuda, Charles R. Lawrence III, Richard Delgado, Kimberle Williams Crenshaw, 17–51. Boulder, Colo.: Westview, 1993.

Murphy, Jeffrie, and Jules Coleman. *Philosophy of Law.* Boulder, Colo.: Westview, 1990.

Rhode, Deborah L. *Justice and Gender.* Cambridge, Mass.: Harvard Univ. Press, 1989.

Roiphe, Katie. "Reckless Eyeballing: Sexual Harassment on Campus." In *Sexual Harassment Issues and Answers,* ed. Linda LeMoncheck and James P. Sterba, 249–60. New York: Oxford University Press, 2001.

Seebach, Linda. "Putting Teeth in the First Amendment." *Daily News* (Glendale, Calif.), 21 January 1993, 19.

Sunstein, Cass R. "Liberalism, Speech Codes, and Related Problems." *Academe* 79 (July–August 1993): 14–25.

Superson, Anita M. "A Feminist Definition of Sexual Harassment." *Journal of Social Philosophy* 24, no.1 (spring 1993).
Tuana, Nancy. "Sexual Harassment: Offers and Coercion." *Journal of Social Philosophy* 19, (summer 1988): 30–42.

12

Women in Philosophy: A Forty-Year Perspective on Academic Backlash

Linda A. Bell

Issues facing women have certainly changed since I entered graduate school in the early 1960s. Framing what I see as the differences between then and now is the fact that there didn't seem to be any sort of women's movement at that time. Granted, as we now realize, appearances of that time were often quite deceptive. The culture was overhung with an extremely opaque ideological façade woven from dominant myths about the society, particularly about gender, race, economics, and militarism, a façade waiting to be torn asunder and to have its falsity revealed by the Civil Rights, Antiwar, and Women's movements. Nevertheless, the myths were so prevalent and the pressures to accept the dominant vision so strong that many of us would have greeted a term like "women's movement" as an oxymoron.

As I began thinking about the ways things have changed, my sense of the time led me to see the sexism I experienced earlier as quite different from more recent instances. I found myself agreeing with Susan Faludi when, in *Backlash: The Undeclared War against American Women*, she characterizes backlash as "an attempt to retract the handful of small and hard-won victories that the feminist movement did manage to win for women," that it involves "episodes of resurgence" of "fear and loathing of feminism." I and probably most of those tormenting me were not aware of victories that women had achieved. After all, I had never seen a philosophy professor who was a woman; nor had I seen, much less taken classes with, many female professors in other areas. Though many high school teachers had been women, their employment was by then seen as acceptable, along with that of nurses and secretaries, not as any sort of controversial advance.

Thus, I simply assumed that what I encountered in graduate school was sexism rather than backlash: in other words, that it was what Faludi would

see as part of the "bedrock of misogyny," the "hostility to female independence [that] has always been with us." Such "fear and loathing of feminism,"
she notes, "is a sort of perpetual viral condition in our culture" and not in the
"acute stage" of backlash. Outbreaks of backlash, she says,

> have always arisen in reaction to women's "progress," caused not simply by a
> bedrock of misogyny but by the specific efforts of contemporary women to im-
> prove their status, efforts that have been interpreted time and again by men—
> especially men grappling with real threats to their economic and social well-
> being on other fronts—as spelling their own masculine doom.[1]

As I think more about this, I realize my assumption may have been
somewhat naive and that those who harassed me and tried to drive me out
of philosophy may have had a considerably better sense of history than I
had; but I suspect not. Some women being allowed the vote wasn't too
threatening to men by that time since women—those who were allowed to
vote—did not seem to be using the vote to improve their own status, voting rather in ways that paralleled "their" men's votes; and other women
weren't allowed to vote at all since Jim Crow had not yet been overthrown
in the South. I doubt, too, that many of the men who challenged me had
the slightest fear that I and the trickle of other women enrolled in graduate
programs in philosophy and other bastions of maleness might be the beginning of a wave that could ultimately threaten not just their masculinist
assumptions but also their prerogatives, particularly their entitlement to
professional positions. Most of them, on the contrary, were probably so
thoroughly steeped in the cultural teachings of the 1940s and 1950s that I
and the few other women they saw breaking with tradition no doubt just
seemed oddities, more abnormalities than threats, especially if most of us
could be driven, by whatever measures were necessary, from the areas reserved for men.

So I think I'm right to see my early experiences of misogyny in philosophy
generally as being of a different sort from later ones, even though I recognize that some of the perpetrators might have seen my very presence in graduate school (along with that of the one other woman in my year of admission) as a "takeover" by women. After all, Audre Lorde is pointing to an
extraordinarily common tendency when she discusses the way oppression
"ascribes false power to difference": "To the racist, Black people are so powerful that the presence of one can contaminate a whole lineage; to the heterosexist, lesbians are so powerful that the presence of one can contaminate
the whole sex."[2] If those in power tend to see "others" as dominant when, in
fact, only one or two of their number have managed to make it into an area,
then I suppose that any and all gains by such "others," no matter how few in
number, how isolated, and how sporadic, may seem extremely significant.
Their exaggerated sense of those "gains" could lead perpetrators to regard

their ensuing heterosexist or racist or sexist reactions in the way Faludi does those she characterizes as backlash.

Since many if not all such reactions would then be reactions to *perceived* progress by the group in question, this would, of course, obliterate or render very problematic a distinction like Faludi's between backlash and "American society's long-standing resistance to women's rights."[3] Still, when I think of the laid-back smugness of most of the earlier responses to me and contrast that to the greater shrillness and tenacity of many of the later ones, I cannot help but think Faludi is correct in separating backlash from other forms of sexist (and by extension heterosexist and racist) behavior. The smugness in the former suggests that I wasn't seen as much of a threat.

Instead of concentrating on my memories of such subjective features, though, I propose simply to present the reactions I experienced earlier and to compare them to later ones, bringing to view elements of contrast that I hope will illuminate some objective differences, increase the general understanding of the history of sexism and misogyny in academe, and ultimately throw much-needed light on the current backlash in the academic sphere. I shall focus on three areas of change. The first is that of blatant sexism and racism. The second is the area of admissions and hiring, including affirmative action, its implementation, and disputes about it. And the third concerns advice given to women entering the field of philosophy. In the first area, I see considerable change, most of it positive, though with some unfortunate and problematic effects. In the second, I acknowledge some improvement in admission and hiring patterns but a growing nastiness in the rhetoric. In the third—that of advice—unfortunately, I still see many of the same problems but recast in terms that are more insidious than similar advice I was given early in my career.

In terms of blatant sexism, let me share a few of my early encounters, beginning with some of the earliest.

By the time I left Chicago in 1968 with an M.A. from Northwestern University, a degree that was very nearly terminal in more senses than one, I had taught for three years around Chicago and had already seen at least one of my applications dismissed because of my gender. When I applied to teach in an adult extension program at the University of Chicago, the interviewer had mused quite openly about his concern that a woman wouldn't be able to "handle" the adults in the classes. I tried to keep his intentional though generic insult from stinging by picturing those obstreperous adults standing on chairs and scampering about the room like the energetic grammar school children whom he wouldn't have thought twice about entrusting to women. He only stopped his musing, rather abruptly, when I quietly responded that I thought denying women employment on such grounds was no longer legal, wishing that I had a cord protruding from my bag to suggest that I might be taping his remarks. I doubt, though, that the implied threat would have caused him anything more than momentary discomfort since the Civil Rights Act's inclusion of women was not yet taken seriously and actually suing on the basis of such discrimination was still not even the stuff of dreams for most of us. This incident occurred, I believe, in 1967 or early 1968.

By that point, I was quite battered from my experience at Northwestern University where I had been mercilessly taunted by male graduate students from the time I arrived in 1963 until I was unceremoniously dumped in 1966. Initially, they admonished me that no women had made any significant contributions to philosophy, denying with a straight face the non sequiturs implicit in their scoffing at my mention of Simone de Beauvoir and in their concluding that *I* had no business being in graduate school. Then they upped the ante by solemnly observing that women didn't belong in *most* important jobs since, for example, no one would take seriously the direst of news so long as it was delivered in a female voice. They knew the scoffing and needling disturbed me and probably realized as well that their glib and usually invalid dismissals of my best counterattacks and counterexamples upset me even more by effectively dismissing me as a philosopher and even as a rational creature. To some extent, they were enacting their societal position as the dominant, a role that entitled them to ignore me, to dismiss my arguments without paying much attention, and to play with me in ways they would not have allowed themselves to deal with someone to whom they thought they owed respect.[4] But they went beyond such enactment, probably because they couldn't resist the opportunity to bully. They wanted me to know not only that I was usurping a place in graduate school and in philosophy but also that I was so ill-suited for it that they felt no obligation whatsoever to pay the least attention to my pathetic little arguments, the only ones, they were certain, that I would be capable of constructing.

Even more painful was the harassment by the professor who pronounced with such a sneer the "Mrs." he insisted on using for me when he called the class roll. He knew very well what he was doing when later he announced so pompously to me and a number of male students that fellowships were "wasted" on women who would only, after all, marry, get pregnant, and drop out of school. It was obvious that he wasn't *just* propounding another bogus domino theory but was actively trying to discourage me in my intellectual pursuits.

The professor's torment of me may actually have been an instance of backlash, especially given the rumors that his salary was less than his philosopher wife was making at a neighboring university. Also suggestive of resentment of women's successes was the derisive mocking of an earlier student on which he launched one day in class. His seemingly unprovoked tirade suggested that he might still have been seething over his inability to derail her from completing the Ph.D. in his department. Unlike more recent perpetrators of backlash, though, this professor knew he could engage in such behavior with complete impunity, that he need not worry about possible repercussions. Even if he saw and resented women making some inroads onto turf he considered male, he could afford a certain smugness, knowing that more than tenure protected him from any direct threat.

As I began this essay, my suspicion was that younger women in philosophy today haven't run into anything quite so blatant as the above examples in the way of sexism, harassment, and undisguised and unadorned expressions of misogyny. If that were true, I would be delighted. Unfortunately, what I have heard as I presented—formally and informally—earlier versions of these remarks to largely female audiences indicates that the change in this regard has not been quite as extensive as I had previously believed. Quite a few much younger women have assured me that they have been subjected to remarks and treatment on par with the examples I have offered. Thus, with evidence of women's progress visible almost everywhere in our society, I am forced to admit that current instances of backlash in academe are not necessarily any more subtle or insidious than the earlier expressions of misogyny I encountered. I realize, too, that I should not be surprised by this since many feminists have called attention to the fact that many attacks on women have become louder, more vicious, and even more violent as women have advanced and as women and feminist concerns have received increasing recognition.

Sometimes, though, backlash has moved in a different direction. The sort of which I was thinking concerns the aftermath of some very positive changes and reflects the wisdom of recognizing that change usually comes at a cost, especially when less than wholehearted. In these cases, expressions of misogyny are softened and even disguised to look like its opposite, perhaps out of fear that someone would otherwise object, perhaps out of a more insidious determination to use whatever new ammunition is made available as the result of the despised changes.

As I think back over most of the early harassment I faced, I see *as advantage* the fact that issues in most of those early battles were clear and unambiguous. None of my attackers made, or felt any need to make, an attempt to disguise his misogyny or even bad arguments. As a woman, I simply was not deserving of the respect that would have required honesty or seriousness. There were, as far as I could see, no elements of backlash in the students' challenges. These were frontal attacks pure and simple: misogyny expressed straightforwardly by those who not only believed in their inherent superiority to all women but also knew that their right to bully and torment those supposedly inferior to themselves was thoroughly supported by the laws and social structures surrounding them.

Today, even those most viciously opposed to the admission or hiring of women and minority men are often sufficiently attuned to the times that they cast a mantle of tolerance, egalitarianism, and even antiracism and antisexism over their activities and most especially over their objections to candidates for teaching positions. Though their activities and objections may ultimately keep those deemed undesirable out of their institutions no more than did the more forthright expressions earlier, other effects of their camouflage and subtlety are likely to be quite different, placing victims in the difficult position of having to sort through assurances of tolerance and even enthusiasm about diversity designed to create a sense that anyone who suspects sexism must be paranoid. It was obvious in those early battles that my actual performance was not being challenged. It wasn't even noted. It was simply *assumed*, given my gender, that I had no ability *worth noting*. The clarity of this fact was especially important to my survival once I got beyond resonating like a tuning fork to any and all challenges (after all, I could see my shortcomings; and I, too, had been indoctrinated with the belief that individuals of my gender were ultimately suited only to be men's helpers, not their professors).

Moving on to the second area, I can attest to changes in admission and hiring policies, particularly since some were so important in my own career. Once the law began to be seen as acknowledging women's right to a modicum of fair treatment in the public sphere, if not in the so-called private one, I felt the effect of this change in a positive way though I saw a backlash set in rather quickly. The inclusion of women in civil rights legislation, along with a growing threat of court challenges, slowly resulted in some perceived pressure to hire women and minority men, if only as window dressing, so that the institutions and businesses could point to those employees and say, in effect, "Some of my best employees—well, maybe not the best, but some of my employees, at any rate—are [fill in the blank]." Much of the affirmative action I have seen has been of this sort, the result of a fear of litigation or of a slight embarrassment that the organizations, institutions, or businesses *might* be perceived as less than fair.

However less than honorable its motivation, this reaction helped some of us get positions in academe. In my case, it was a mixed blessing since it turned out that the department chair simply saw my hiring as a way to increase the size of the department and had no intention of keeping me (even though he did admit to someone that I was "pretty good for a woman"). I think he was so accustomed to White male prerogatives that he believed this slight nod by the university to "others" could be turned around quite easily. Still, I was hired; and while I had to fight for tenure against his and the department's non-recommendations, I won and endured, admittedly with a great deal of help from prominent and very generous philosophers and from wonderful friends. Later, I was even promoted to professor with the endorsement of the department and a different chair. By that point, I suspect, even those who would have liked to rid themselves of me thought there was little they could do even if they wished to prevent my promotion. After all, the college was now, as a matter of course, using outside evaluations of the published work of each and every candidate for promotion and tenure; and I had already won once in that venue by seeking such evaluations on my own from highly respected individuals who wrote generous evaluations even though most knew nothing of me besides the request I made and the papers I sent them.

While that fight was extraordinarily difficult, nevertheless being hired *was* a benefit, something many who engage in backlash refuse to recognize. Although the workload was heavy and severely restricted the amount of reading and writing that I could do, still it gave me the opportunity to live, at least *some* of the time, the life of the mind that I so desired. It gave me a chance to work with students, to encourage them in their frequently difficult efforts to think for themselves, and to help those who needed a boost to get over the hurdles, beyond racist and sexist mistreatment, and through the bureaucratic red tape encountered so commonly by unconventional students. Particularly important to me was the fact that even the battles I fought, regardless of how painful, exhausting, and time-consuming many of them were, disclosed and developed hitherto unacknowledged abilities as I learned to argue on my feet and not just on paper.

While academe as a whole opened its doors a bit and particular areas within it even made huge strides toward greater openness and inclusiveness, others changed little and quickly fell back into old, comfortable, racist and sexist hiring patterns. The later hirings, though, became part of the backlash, accompanied as they were with affirmative action rhetoric. Today, affirmative action mandates continue to require good faith efforts to reach beyond the groups hired in the past, but, from my experience, little more. I have seen women and minority men with superb qualifications culled out of searches, some quite recent ones, owing to the vocal and mean-spirited opposition of a few colleagues. The latter respond to my accusations of racism and sexism with protestations of great indignation at being so misunderstood and even falsely accused, assuring me that they are indeed open, even anxious, to hire a woman or a minority man—if *only* one who was good enough would present herself or himself since, as they have actually and quite earnestly said, all they really want is to hire "the best man for the job." Then they lead the charge to hire yet another White man.

In fact, they leave these confrontations satisfied that I am the one with an agenda, not they, and priding themselves on their high standards while referring to me as having none. On the other hand, I leave angry and amazed at the often incredible ways that those allegedly much prized standards shift from candidate to candidate and from search to search. After all, I've seen a male candidate touted as an excellent choice for a position in continental European philosophy because, given that he works in that area as well as in analytic philosophy, he will be able to "bridge" those areas and thus be a colleague for all the philosophers in the department whereas a woman doing feminist research was scowlingly dismissed as not "sufficiently Continental" because she was working with both analytic and Continental thinkers. This "fact" was somberly supported by the claim that her footnotes citing analytic thinkers outnumbered those with Continental references, a counting that apparently wasn't deemed necessary in the case of the man.

Now affirmative action is either under fire or judged illegal in many institutions throughout the country. This part of the backlash, both inside and outside of academe, has been quite successful, in part because of gains made by women of all groups and by minority men and in part because of the equal opportunity façade cast over institutions and businesses by the creation and supposed enforcement of rules and regulations that seem fairer and more inclusive. The gains have been quite real for the individuals hired, though often little more than tokenism and window dressing. The equal opportunity façade is also misleading as, for example, institutions like my own regularly claim on letterheads and all official publications to be an "equal opportunity/affirmative action employer," suggesting this as accomplished fact rather than as assertion of aspiration. In addition, some actually present themselves as more diverse than they are by using unrepresentative photographs in the literature they make available.

While much of the façade is merely rhetorical, perhaps such flourishes have helped to create the illusion that the underlying reality is now fair, that the United States is a color-blind society. Perhaps Ronald Reagan's constant repetition of this claim while he was president helped, too. Maybe some actually thought he was wearing Dorothy's ruby slippers and clicking the heels together as he uttered the refrain. None of this, singly or together, accounts for the widespread assumption that fairness prevails, but perhaps the situation doesn't need an explanation. After all, the phenomenon is such a common one as dominant groups react to even the slightest loss of power as a major catastrophe and are all too ready to believe that those who profit do so unjustly.

Still, I find myself wondering how much of the academic opposition to affirmative action is encouraged by duplicitous hiring committees or individuals who, while they don't actually hire women and minority men, often make such a show of doing so that one would think that no White men need apply. How often, I wonder, have interviewers actually told less than stellar White male candidates that the departments were "under a mandate" to hire "a woman or a Black" (the dichotomy in which the debate is frequently cast)? And what, I continue to wonder, happened to that alleged mandate when the actual job offers were made? Was "a woman or a Black" hired? I suspect not since I've heard too many of these claims and haven't seen the large numbers of women and minority men in the profession necessary for such "mandates" to have been carried out.[5]

One of the most vicious aspects of the present anti-affirmative action debate, probably the most difficult from which to defend oneself, is the supposedly earnest concern for the happiness of those "truly talented and meritorious" individuals whose misfortune it is to belong to the groups targeted by affirmative action. Opponents of affirmative action wail about the pathetic situation of those women and minority men who, because of affirmative action, supposedly will never know whether they were hired because of their ability.

The disingenuousness of this argument nearly overwhelms me when I think of all the sons of alumni, politicians, and other prominent or wealthy parents, even of all the White men of my generation and of earlier ones, who never, as far as I can tell, lost a moment to anxiety over whether their ability entitled them to *their* positions. Moreover, even though they couldn't help but see that women and minority men were not being treated fairly and were themselves participating in some of that treatment, it would be quite a stretch for me to imagine that *any* of the White men at Northwestern worried about whether they could compete successfully if minorities and White women were treated more fairly. Most probably lacked sufficient self-consciousness to experience such anxiety.

That lack of self-consciousness in the privileged, enviable as I may have thought it at various times in my life, is encouraged and supported by our system of oppression and is an important part of what has enabled it to survive for so long. Ours is, after all, a system in which the privileged see themselves not as gendered and raced or even as privileged, but rather as the norm, and are often highly offended if anyone else calls attention to their sex or race in ways that would invoke "invidious" comparisons of themselves and those "others" who are clearly gendered and/or raced. An exception to this was a young White man I encountered somewhat later, who observed that his family connections guaranteed him a position at a particular college in his home state when he completed his degree. While this admission, made with no apologies, did not endear him to fellow graduate students, he nevertheless gave no indication of suffering unduly from self-doubt, only seeming relieved and grateful to have a job awaiting him in spite of the tight job market in philosophy. While he was one of the least arrogant and nicest of the many privileged men I had known, he was the only one I had ever heard acknowledge his privilege in any way.

Nor do opponents of affirmative action grant for a moment that without some pressure felt by those in positions to admit and to hire, previous patterns would very likely have continued unabated, with the result that most or all of the individuals whose happiness is supposedly of such great concern would never have had a chance to study medicine, philosophy, or whatever, in the virtually or entirely all-White and all-male medical and graduate schools. Presumably, self-doubt is far, far worse than not having an opportunity to do what we most want to do with our lives! I can only conclude that the tears shed by the purveyors of this argument are not real ones, but rather a very effective way to divert attention from the system of White male privilege.

That this is a diversionary technique is what makes it such a successful backlash strategy. By separating those who are "truly deserving" from those who supposedly are getting something they don't deserve as a result of affirmative action, these challengers present themselves as genuinely caring individuals at the same time that they appeal and probably even add to the widespread resentment against those perceived to be getting something for nothing. In doing so, these individuals present what is at best a fiction, namely, that those without adequate credentials are profiting from affirmative action, but one that has the consequence of hiding a system that all along has been granting White men, sometimes very mediocre ones, benefits that they didn't deserve, just because they were White and male.

Besides camouflaging this reality, the concern about the deserving who presumably will never know whether they were hired or admitted for their merit blissfully ignores the fairly obvious fact that *all* those hired are unlikely to know whether they were hired for their ability or for some extraneous reason that might mortify them if only they knew. The argument, in fact, *presumes* that all others are hired for reasons of greater merit. Unfortunately, this just isn't the way the world works; and I suspect the arguers know it as well as I do. Many White men are hired because of their gender and race or because, as Derrick Bell has observed,[6] those hiring simply feel more comfortable with them, a consideration that indicates how much class may influence hiring. Others are hired not so much for their stellar credentials but rather far more because of their perceived political leanings, particularly in terms of those battles currently being played out in the hiring departments or institutions. Still others may be hired just because they are sufficiently bland and inoffensive that those hiring can settle on them. The purveyors of backlash seem not to value truth overly much.

Finally, I want to say something about the advice that young women are being given today. Some of it seems no different from advice given earlier. Though I may deeply appreciate the motive behind much of the advice (namely, getting more women tenured), I find myself uncomfortable whenever I see anyone—but especially someone like "Ms. Mentor" (aka Emily Toth)—cautioning young women in academe to "conform," to "make nice," generally not to rock the boat until they are tenured.[7] I, too, was given this advice when I began to challenge a set of statutes crafted by what was then a very heavy-handed and backward administration at Georgia State University. Not only did I not have tenure when I fought the administration over particularly unacceptable aspects of this document, but I am convinced that I would *not* have been tenured had I sat back quietly and participated in the desired faculty rubber-stamping of what was proposed. The chairman[8] who offered me the advice had no intention of tenuring me, no matter what I did, later admitting that he wanted my position to be a "revolving door" so that "fresh blood" would always be in the process of circulating through a department that he feared would otherwise become "overtenured" (the mixed metaphors were his, not mine).

His rationale about fresh blood made me very conscious of his and others' eyeteeth but revealed quite clearly the falsity of the advice I had been offered "for my own good." That advice had been far more in his interest than mine since being able to control the faculty was generally seen by the higher administration as a, if not *the*, mark of a good chairman. It was not my good that was at stake for him but rather his own or at best the good of the department (as he saw it), it being far more in my interest to be known around the campus as a somewhat outspoken—even "abrasive"—woman. Had I been the wallflower I was advised to be, the dean would have been quick to second the nearly unanimous recommendations against my tenure and promotion he received from my department. Because I was known as a protester and because I sought and received outside evaluations of my work by some very prominent philosophers, the dean *did* think twice, perhaps fearing I would not leave quietly; and I won the fight.

When I was given the advice, it was duplicitous and designed to undermine the effects of affirmative action; and it seems no better now. When Ms. Mentor gives it in the context of waiting until being tenured to try to change what's wrong with the institution, it perversely appeals to women's desire to be "good girls," to be recognized for their accomplishments without having to call attention to them, and to believe that basic fairness can be counted on in academic institutions. Thus, however inadvertently, the advice plays a role in the backlash. Far better to observe that both rocking the boat and not rocking it can be dangerous for women and then to discuss strategies for negotiating some of the pitfalls on both sides.

Other advice being offered to women in philosophy may be just as problematic. When I was discussing this paper with a younger friend, she began fuming about the admonitions against having children to which she had been subjected far more recently. Apparently much of this advice was offered to her at one of the meetings of the Society for Phenomenology and Existential Philosophy. As she fumed, I thought once again of my experience at Northwestern where I recognized so quickly and so clearly that pregnancy would undermine any chance I might have for a philosophical career, slight though that chance might have been given the fact that the very *possibility* of pregnancy seemed sufficient to many to indicate that I couldn't be serious about philosophy. I fumed with her, angry that women are still being told that they can't be philosophers *and* mothers, particularly angry that now the advice is phrased more insidiously, in terms not of the demandingness of philosophy nor even of nature having foreordained women to be men's helpmates, but rather of the needs and happiness of children and families, considerations that seem to have little salience either in the larger society or in the smaller philosophical one beyond their use in making women feel guilty for their independence and professional commitments.

This is the sort of strategy my mother might have used after all else failed to convince me not to do something, so it seems appropriate to view it as a backlash maneuver. Besides, it's been effectively used as backlash before, to prevent women from asking for and then from using the vote and to get them out of the factories and back into the home after the last war. Once again, though, the repackaged misogyny of backlash makes the position of young women in academe even more difficult than the one I was in as I experienced such nasty frontal attacks. After my fume, however, I rejoiced that my younger friend is tenured *and* is raising with her partner two seemingly well-adjusted children.

While that covers the three areas on which I have chosen to focus my remarks, I need to conclude by giving voice to the sadness I felt as I was thinking about and writing this analysis. I have fought many battles in academe, and I have lived long enough to see *some* significant changes, including, at my institution, the hiring of women and minority men, the formation of African American Studies and Women's Studies departments, more genuine faculty governance, and a far less adversarial stance between the institution and untenured faculty, with deans now recognizing new faculty as an investment that is lost when faculty are not retained because improperly mentored. My sadness comes from my recognition that my own discipline seems one of the most recalcitrant to change. I'll never understand why philosophy, the proud discipline of Socrates and the examined life, attracts such a large number of mean-spirited individuals who are so reluctant to examine their own prejudices, so fearful of change, and so determined to narrow the province of philosophy to a point where it cannot touch their own or their students' lives. Having found in philosophy a way to free myself from the narrowness, racial bigotry, and sexism of the segregated, Jim Crow South in which I grew up, I have always been baffled by colleagues who find nothing liberating in philosophy, who try so hard to prevent others from doing so, and who in fact create understandings of philosophy itself that involve a narrowness almost as stifling as that against which I rebelled in my society.

Maybe that aspect of academe, too, will change someday, but meanwhile those professors eagerly fight for narrowness and exclusivity, grasping excitedly onto any studies that support their sense that women and minority men have gotten more than enough and eagerly joining the backlash by becoming members of groups that oppose multiculturalism and a diversification of the academic "canon." One recently cited a study supposedly indicating that women in philosophy today actually find jobs more easily than do men, self-righteously glaring at the rest of us as he asked if we wanted to be part of such "clear injustice." Unfortunately, it will never occur to him either to think that if women are being hired more readily it just might be because they are in fact better than their male competition. Neither will he ever worry about the injustice of his department's past behavior, so blatantly reflected by the fact that only one search in that department's entire history has ever led to the hiring of a woman, an outcome that owed a great deal to the pressure placed on it by a newly hired chair. Misogyny, alas, is alive and well in academe, steadfastly working to prevent changes in the social, political, and economic environment that would make things fairer, cleverly adapting through backlash maneuvers to those it is unable to prevent by using them against further change.

NOTES

An earlier version of this work was presented in 1999 as part of a generational panel on women in the profession, sponsored by the Committee on the Status of Women in SPEP (the Society for Phenomenology and Existential Philosophy). Since I was clearly representing previous generations of women philosophers, I began by giving my credentials as such. They included my arriving at Northwestern University in the fall of 1963, just after John Wild left, supposedly having single-handedly rejected me the previous year. I was told that he feared my becoming, with my mathematics major, a female analyst (a creature sufficient to strike fear in the heart of a Continental philosopher). This was, I believe, a year or so before SPEP was founded. In fact, I think I went to its first meeting in Evanston. The essay itself owes a great deal to my writers' group, Charlene Ball, Valerie Fennell, Elizabeth Knowlton, and Libby Ware.

1. Susan Faludi, *Backlash: The Undeclared War against American Women* (New York: Crown, 1991), xviii-xix.

2. Audre Lorde, "Scratching the Surface," in *Sister Outsider: Essays and Speeches* (Trumansburg, N.Y.: Crossing Press, 1984), 51.

3. Faludi, *Backlash*, xviii.

4. Peggy McIntosh, "White Privilege: Unpacking the Invisible Knapsack," *Creation Spirituality* (January/February 1992): 33–35, 53, suggests that part of racial privilege is an entitlement to ignore the language and culture of people of color, very like the aspect of gender privilege that allows men to ignore the complaints of women. More recently, Iris Marion Young, "Five Faces of Oppression," in *Justice and the Politics of Difference* (Princeton, N.J.: Princeton University Press, 1990), 57, connects this privileged ignoring with respect. As she says, "To treat people with respect is to be prepared to listen to what they have to say or to do what they request because they have some authority, expertise, or influence."

5. Comparative statistics to support or rebut my suspicion are probably nonexistent since what I really want to know is how many men and how many women seeking positions in philosophy did not find any and how many in both groups were people of color. It would help, although it would not answer my question, to know the comparative numbers of new Ph.D.s as well as of new hirings each year for the last 10 or 15 years, particularly if the latter were separated into tenure-track positions and others, including part-time. The statistics I did find in American Philosophical

Association (APA) Online ("Philosophy as a Profession: Data on the Profession, Selected Demographic Information on Philosophy Ph.D.'s," 1995) dealt only with the year 1995. They indicated a not-very-rosy picture in terms of philosophy Ph.D.s: a far higher percentage of women were employed part-time (19.2 percent compared to 4.6 percent for men), in a field where of the 8300 Ph.D.s at that time, 82.6 percent were male and 17.4 percent female, and 5900 were academically employed.

6. Derrick Bell, "A Law Professor's Protest," in *Faces at the Bottom of the Well: The Permanence of Racism* (New York: Basic, 1992), 127–46.

7. Emily Toth, *Ms. Mentor's Impeccable Advice for Women in Academia* (Philadelphia: University of Pennsylvania Press, 1997), 160–66, 171.

8. I use this term advisedly since this was a time when chairs were always referred to as "chairmen" and the few women in this position seemed to accept the designation, some even to relish their linguistic anointment as one of the boys. Were I more consistent, I would probably continue to use the term in many cases so that language would not camouflage continuing sexist realities. This tendency to camouflage has, I fear, made it seem that things have changed more than they have when the reality in many cases is that only the language used to depict the reality has changed, another change that has been enlisted in the support of academic backlash.

BIBLIOGRAPHY

Bell, Derrick. "A Law Professor's Protest." In *Faces at the Bottom of the Well: The Permanence of Racism*. New York: Basic, 1992.

Faludi, Susan. *Backlash: The Undeclared War against American Women*. New York: Crown, 1991.

Lorde, Audre. "Scratching the Surface." In *Sister Outsider*. Trumansburg, N.Y.: Crossing Press, 1984, 45–52.

McIntosh, Peggy. "White Privilege: Unpacking the Invisible Knapsack." *Creation Spirituality* (January/February 1992): 33–35, 53.

Toth, Emily. *Ms. Mentor's Impeccable Advice for Women in Academia*. Philadelphia: University of Pennsylvania Press, 1997.

Young, Iris Marion. "Five Faces of Oppression." In *Justice and the Politics of Difference*. Princeton, N.J.: Princeton University Press, 1990.

Index

248; internalization of, 90, 169, 173, 250; personal, 141; in philosophy, ix, 13, 90–91; responsibility for ending, 210; and sexual harassment, 217–18, 225, 237; socialization, 166; from students, xix-xxii, 50–52, 165, 182, 189; systematic nature of, 10, 11–12, 20, 81, 90, 135, 138–41. *See also* bullyism; burden of proof; disadvantage; discrimination; double standard; equality; Faludi, Susan; feminist epistemology; feminist legal theory; free speech; harm; hostility; ideology; male socialization; marginalization; misogyny; neutrality; oppression; politicize; power; privilege; progress; resistance; sexism; sexual harassment; stereotype
Banks, Ingrid, 187
Bartky, Sandra, 194
Bell, Derrick, 145, 254
Bezucha, Robert, 188
Blackburn, Simon, 21
Blair, Anita, 79, 80
blaming the victim, 97, 101–2, 104, 110, 170
Blanchard, W. H., 99
Bleier, Ruth, 29
Bordo, Susan, 29
Brandom, Robert, 50
breast-feeding, 120, 140
Brison, Susan, 107, 108
Brown v. Board of Education of Topeka, 231
Browne, Kingsley, 25, 27, 71
bullyism: directed at feminist philosophy, 31–34; directed at women, 248, 249. *See also* backlash, forms of
burden of proof, in classroom, 185, 186, 187, 188, 189, 191

capitalism, 8, 9, 124, 159, 162, 165, 175, 176
Center for the Study of Popular Culture, 222
Citadel, 94, 98, 100

Civil Rights Act of 1964, 218, 234, 235, 248
classroom dynamics, 182, 184, 186–88
Clinton, William Jefferson, 77
collegiality, 140–145
Collins, Patricia Hill, 168
Conley, Frances, 109
consciousness, transformation of, 194. *See also* critical thinking; democracy; education
containment, 168–69
critical race theory, 134, 135
critical thinking, 166, 168, 170, 182, 193, 194. *See also* education
Cudd, Ann, 136–37, 140
cultural imperialism, 160, 183

Daplan, Corey, 189, 194
Davidson, Donald, 21
Davis, Adrienne, 183
de Beauvoir, Simone, 248
Delgado, Richard, 108, 234, 235
democracy: and critical thinking, 165, 174; and education, 156; and free speech, 230; and inclusion, 175, 177; and knowledge, 172, 175; students' view of, 165
Devlin, Patrick, 22
Dewey, John, 155, 156, 164, 170–71, 172, 174, 175, 176
dignity, 6, 7, 8, 13, 105, 106, 108. *See also* respect
Dillon, Robin, 189
disadvantage, 24, 26, 28, 104, of professional women, 141, 142–43; systematic, 20, 138–39. *See also* discrimination; harm; oppression
discrimination: and career advancement, 122, 130; freedom from, 217, 218, 235–36, 237; gender, 102, 218, 223; and group harm, 109–11; racial, 80, 138, 226; responsibility to eliminate, 111, 237; systematic, 93, 102–4; and wages, 81. *See also* backlash; disadvantage; harm

About the Contributors

Linda A. Bell is professor of philosophy and director of the Women's Studies Institute at Georgia State University in Atlanta, Georgia. In addition to feminist theory, she teaches, writes, and publishes in the areas of existentialism, ethics, and Continental philosophy. Her publications include: an anthology of philosophers' statements about women, *Visions of Women*; a development of an ethics from the writings of Jean-Paul Sartre, *Sartre's Ethics of Authenticity*; and an existentialist feminist ethics, *Rethinking Ethics in the Midst of Violence: A Feminist Approach to Freedom*. She coedited *Overcoming Racism and Sexism* with David Blumenfeld. Presently developing a collection of essays dealing with various aspects of her own experience and the role this experience plays and ought to play in her philosophizing, she is happiest when she is able to muddle up and render ambiguous an issue or distinction generally regarded as clear, settled, and beyond dispute.

Keith Burgess-Jackson, J.D., Ph.D., is associate professor of philosophy at the University of Texas at Arlington. His work has appeared in such periodicals as the *Canadian Journal of Philosophy*, *The Southern Journal of Philosophy*, *The Canadian Journal of Law and Jurisprudence*, *Public Affairs Quarterly*, *Metaphilosophy*, *Journal of Medical Humanities*, *Philosophy and Rhetoric*, *Criminal Justice Ethics*, *Journal of Social Philosophy*, *The Journal of Ethics*, *Social Theory and Practice*, *Sophia*, and *Hypatia*, as well as in other legal and historical publications. He is the author of *Rape: A Philosophical Investigation*, and the editor of *A Most Detestable Crime: New Philosophical Essays on Rape*. He is coauthor with Irving M. Copi of *Informal Logic*. His current project is a book entitled *Deontological Egoism*.

Alisa L. Carse, Ph.D., is associate professor of philosophy at Georgetown University and a Teaching Affiliate of the Kennedy Institute of Ethics. Her teaching and research are centered in moral theory, social and political philosophy, moral psychology, and feminist theory. Her current research is focused in a "quartet" of related papers exploring cultural, moral, and political subordination and its antidotes.

Martha Chamallas is professor of law at the University of Pittsburgh. She has written extensively on the topics of sexual harassment, wage discrimination, gender and race bias in personal injury law, and feminist legal theory. Her most recent articles have been published by the *Southern California Law Review*, the *University of Pennsylvania Law Review*, and the *University of Chicago Law Review*.

Ann E. Cudd is professor of philosophy and women's studies and director of women's studies at the University of Kansas. Her main areas of research are social and political philosophy, rational choice theory, and feminist theory. She is currently writing a book on oppression.

Debra A. DeBruin, Ph.D., is assistant professor at the Center for Bioethics and the Department of Medicine at the University of Minnesota Medical School. She recently completed a Greenwall Postdoctoral Fellowship in Bioethics and Health Policy at Johns Hopkins and Georgetown Universities. She has served as a health policy fellow in the Democratic office of the Health, Education, Labor and Pensions Committee of the United States Senate and has also worked as a consultant to the National Academy of Science's Institute of Medicine and the National Bioethics Advisory Commission. Her areas of interest include feminist ethics, the ethics of research involving human participants, and public health policy.

Julie E. Maybee is assistant professor of philosophy at Lehman College, in the City University of New York. She specializes in nineteenth-century Continental philosophy, African philosophy, and philosophy of race. She has published in journals such as *Man and World, African Philosophy*, and *International Journal of Applied Philosophy*. She is currently writing a book on Hegel's logic.

Carol J. Moeller is assistant professor of philosophy at Moravian College. She received her Ph.D. and certificates in both cultural studies and women's studies at the University of Pittsburgh. She is presently a Greenwall Fellow in Bioethics and Health Policy at Johns Hopkins University and Georgetown University.

Anita M. Superson is associate professor of philosophy at the University of Kentucky. Her areas of interest are moral skepticism and feminism. Her work is published in journals such as *Dialogue: Canadian Philosophical Review, Journal of Value Inquiry, Journal of Social Philosophy, The Southern Journal of Philosophy,* and *Social Theory and Practice.*

Mark Owen Webb is assistant professor of philosophy at Texas Tech University, where he works in philosophy of religion and epistemology. He is particularly interested in the epistemology of testimony, and what it shows about general epistemic principles.

Cynthia Willett is associate professor of philosophy at Emory University. She is the author of *Soul of Justice, Maternal Ethics and Other Slave Moralities,* and the editor of *Theorizing Multiculturalism.* She is currently working on education and comedy.